Unruly Equality

The publisher gratefully acknowledges the generous support of the Valerie Barth and Peter Booth Wiley Endowment Fund in History of the University of California Press Foundation.

Unruly Equality

U.S. ANARCHISM IN
THE TWENTIETH CENTURY

Andrew Cornell

UNIVERSITY OF CALIFORNIA PRESS

University of California Press, one of the most distinguished university presses in the United States, enriches lives around the world by advancing scholarship in the humanities, social sciences, and natural sciences. Its activities are supported by the UC Press Foundation and by philanthropic contributions from individuals and institutions. For more information, visit www.ucpress.edu.

University of California Press
Oakland, California

Library of Congress Cataloging-in-Publication Data

Cornell, Andrew, 1977– author.
Unruly equality : U.S. anarchism in the twentieth century / Andrew Cornell.
    pages   cm
    Includes bibliographical references and index.
    ISBN 978-0-520-28673-3 (cloth : alk. paper)
    ISBN 978-0-520-28675-7 (pbk. : alk. paper)
    ISBN 978-0-520-96184-5 (ebook)
    1. Anarchism–United States—History—20th century.   I. Title.
II. Title: U.S. anarchism in the twentieth century.
    HX843.C667   2016
    335'.8309730904—dc23
                                                    2015022451

24   23   22   21   20   19   18   17   16
10   9   8   7   6   5   4   3   2   1

For Ellie

I am undertaking something which may turn out to be a résumé of the English speaking anarchist movement in America and I am appalled at the little I know about it after my twenty years of association with anarchists both here and abroad.

W. S. VAN VALKENBURGH
Letter to Agnes Inglis, 1932

From the start, anarchism was an open political philosophy, always transforming itself in theory and practice.... Yet when people are introduced to anarchism today, that openness, combined with a cultural propensity to forget the past, can make it seem a recent invention—without an elastic tradition, filled with debates, lessons, and experiments to build on.

CINDY MILSTEIN
Anarchism and Its Aspirations, 2010

Librarians have an "academic" sense, and can't bear to throw anything away! Even things they don't approve of. They acquire a historic sense. At the time a hand-bill may be very "bad!" But the following day it becomes "historic."

AGNES INGLIS
Letter to Highlander Folk School, 1944

To keep on repeating the same attempts without an intelligent appraisal of all the numerous failures in the past is not to uphold the right to experiment, but to insist upon one's right to escape the hard facts of social struggle into the world of wishful belief. We grant such a right to the weak, the infirm, to the tired radical, to the escapists. But we do deny such a right to the revolutionary whose main weapon is an unflagging will and an unblunted sense of reality.

Vanguard: A Libertarian Communist Journal, 1934

CONTENTS

TABLES AND FIGURES

TABLES

FIGURES

ACKNOWLEDGMENTS

This book has been a long time in the making, and I am grateful to many people who have helped me along the way. The first time that I can recall contemplating anarchism was as a thirteen-year-old skateboarding proto-punk attempting to decipher the lyrics to the Dead Kennedys' album *Bedtime for Democracy*. I was fortunate to take part in the politicized punk, hardcore, and riot grrl music scenes of 1990s, which provided me with an ethical compass and taught me much about feminism, antiracism, imperialism, and queer liberation. Anarchism was always part of the mix in these overlapping communities of writers, activists, and musicians, but even as a teenager I sensed the relationship between punk and anarchism to be a complex one. As I began to study anarchism more assiduously, I found that the histories of anarchism available to me generally concluded in the 1920s, after Emma Goldman was deported from the United States. Yet I knew of, and counted myself part of, a contemporary international anarchist-punk movement that was symbolized, for me, by the British band and political collective Crass. For years, I searched for a book that would tell the history of anarchism in a way that helped me connect the dots between Emma Goldman and Crass. Eventually I realized that no one had written such a book, and that, in line with a core tenet of punk, I should do it myself. I therefore owe an enormous debt of gratitude to all the hardcore kids and zine writers who set me on this path. I particularly want to recognize the Basement Children crew, in Chicago, and the residents of 425 Davis Street, in Kalamazoo, who opened many important vistas for me.

I first conceptualized this book project when, in the months after the 1999 Battle of Seattle, it became clear that neither journalists nor academics understood the roots of contemporary anarchism. At that moment, it seemed that a historical explanation of the goals, tactics, and organizational forms of what were being called the "new anarchists" would help cement the emerging coalition of global-justice activists and, thereby, contribute to far-reaching social change. I, of course, had no clue how massive a project I was undertaking, how long it would take to come to fruition, and how many things would change in the meantime. I would not have attended those life-changing demonstrations in Seattle had I not been involved with Students Organizing for Labor and Economic Equality as an undergraduate at the University of Michigan. Nor would I have known about the resources available for reconstructing the history of twentieth-century anarchism had Julie Herrada not befriended me and nurtured my love of archives during the years I held a work-study position at the University of Michigan's Labadie Collection. I am touched that Julie has encouraged me in this project and served as a sounding board for my ideas for nearly twenty years.

The book began as a dissertation in the Program in American Studies at New York University. My stellar dissertation committee—Andrew Ross, Lisa Duggan, Nikhil Pal Singh, Stephen Duncombe, and Randy Martin— not only taught me crucial concepts and the craft of research but also modeled the art of remaining engaged scholar activists. Randy Martin was one of the friendliest and most humbly brilliant people I have known, and he will be greatly missed. Neil Brenner, Jennifer Morgan, and Madala Hillaire also improved my time at NYU markedly.

Among the many brilliant students I collaborated with and learned from at NYU are several that I especially want to thank: André Carrington, Miles Grier, Dawn Peterson, Miabi Chatterji, Emily Thuma, Rich Blint, Zach Schwartz-Weinstein, Johana Londoño, Steve Fletcher, Stuart Schrader, Christy Thornton, Marisol Lebrón, Jenny Kelly, Vivek Bald, Elizabeth Mesok, Zenia Kish, and Michael Palm. It was a privilege to work with the Graduate Student Organizing Committee, Grad/Undergrad Solidarity, and the *Left Turn* magazine collective during my years in New York. Jessica Harbaugh provided invaluable levity, insight, and emotional support over the long years during which I was crafting the dissertation and the book proposal. I will be forever grateful to Francis Feeley for bringing me to the Université Stendhal, welcoming me into his home, and engaging with my ideas. I also am appreciative of the Williams College American Studies Program, especially Mérida Rúa, Robin Keller, and Dorothy Wang, for their friendly collegiality during the year I spent as a visiting professor in Williamstown.

This book would not have been completed nearly so soon had it not been for the generous resources provided to me by the Mellon Foundation and Haverford College. I am incredibly appreciative of Craig Borowiak for organizing a faculty seminar, "The Anarchist Tradition, Revisited," and inviting me to participate as a Mellon postdoctoral fellow. Laura McGrane, Emily Cronin, Kerry Nelson, and James Weissinger of the John B. Hurford '64 Center for the Arts and the Humanities, and Margaret Schaus of the Magill Library, were as friendly as they were helpful during my two years at Haverford. I tried out some of the ideas that appear in the book during two semesters of my courses Anarchisms: Old and New, and Social Justice Traditions: 1960s to Occupy Wall Street. I thank all the students in those classes for their feedback and insights. I have particularly benefited from extended conversations with Kate Aronoff, Eva Wu Collier, Dillon Chestnut, Joel Rice, and Julia Tannenbaum. I am also grateful to the participants and audience of the March 2015 "Anarchism, Decolonization, and Radical Democracy" symposium at Haverford.

My study of anarchism has benefited significantly from conversations and collaborations with members of the Institute for Anarchist Studies and the North American Anarchist Studies Network, especially Cindy Milstein, Paul and Lara Messersmith-Glavin, Joshua Stephens, Maia Ramnath, Kenyon Zimmer, Jesse Cohn, Dana Ward, Dana Williams, Andrew Hoyt, and Nathan Jun. The ideas in the book have been most influenced by conversations that have played out over many years with a number of individuals who have become dear friends and intellectual collaborators: Josh MacPhee, Harjit Singh Gill, Chris Dixon, and Dan Berger. I particularly thank Chris and Dan for commenting on portions of the manuscript.

In 2011, I published *Oppose and Propose! Lessons from Movement for a New Society* (AK Press). That book grew out of research at first intended for this book, and I have continued to build on the conceptual framework I began developing there. I thank everyone who helped that project materialize, because that book and the positive responses to it that I've received have helped me persevere to finish this much larger project. I thank Molly McClure for the guidance she provided me as I was completing *Oppose and Propose!* and apologize for unintentionally overlooking her help in the acknowledgements.

I thank the archivists at the Labadie Collection, Tamiment Library, Beinecke Library, and Swarthmore College Peace Collection for their assistance over the years, and each of the individuals I interviewed for the book, including those, such as Ken Knabb, whose comments do not appear directly in the text. I appreciate the advice and patience of Niels Hooper, Bradley DePew, and Kate Hoffman at the University of California Press, and the copyediting of freelancer Bonita Hurd. The thoughtful feedback that Barbara Epstein, Ruth Kinna, Andrej Grubacic, and Rebecca Hill provided about an earlier draft of the book was enormously helpful during the revision process. I have many additional friends to thank for fun times, enlightening conversations, and endless encouragement: Tom Thompson, Jen Angel, Jamie McCallum, Charles Weigl, Laura Portwood-Stacer, Kevin van Meter, Shon MackFessel, Matt Dineen, Alex Knight, Matt Meyer and Meg Starr, Dana Barnett, Willow Sharkey, Dara Greenwald, Chris Crass, Jon Strange, Adam Kuthe, Ana Kogan-Goldstein, Chris Taballerio, Rich Miles, Adie Fontenot, Dusty Morris, Hadley Moore, Andrea Koch, Melissa and Rodolfo Palma, Sara and Stacey Falls, Emily and Mark Griffioen, Kate Wilson, Emmalee Conner, SO O'Brien, Sarah McAbee, and Kevin Mooney.

Throughout this long, exhausting process, Pete Cornell, Jo Wiley, and Kerstin Cornell have been extraordinarily supportive, patient, and loving family members. I'm eternally grateful to them and am excited to welcome Tim McKernan into our lives.

Ellie Shenker spent countless hours copyediting the manuscript and preparing the index for this book, so in a sense it is her book also. I am humbled and deeply grateful for the love, support, and dedication she has given me, not only in completing this book, but in all things. It is hard to find the words to express what sharing the last three years with Ellie has meant to me. I count myself among the most fortunate people in the world knowing that I have the privilege of spending my life with her.

Introduction

Unruly Equality examines the anarchist movement in the United States during the years bookended by the First World War and the war in Vietnam. However, in writing it I was motivated by questions regarding anarchism and the broader political Left of the early twenty-first century. Anarchism has experienced a remarkable resurgence during the past two decades as antiauthoritarian principles and strategies have seeped into social and political movements around the globe.

In the United States, anarchist organizers have played key roles in economic justice campaigns—from the infamous 1999 Battle of Seattle to the 2011–2012 Occupy movement, which impelled Americans in hundreds of cities and towns to publicly challenge the power and privilege of banks and corporations.[1] U.S. anarchists have augured an upswing in radical environmental activism, worked to check the growth of mass incarceration, challenged U.S. militarism, and expanded radical feminist, queer, and trans liberation movements.[2] Scholar-activist Chris Dixon, moreover, describes a broader North American "anti-authoritarian current" in which principles, strategies, and forms of organization that anarchists have promoted for over a century dovetail with those developed by women of color feminists, by prison abolitionists, Zapatistas, and others seeking to articulate a radical politics attuned to the ways power now functions.[3]

If anything, anarchist ideas have proven even more influential in Europe, Latin America, and other parts of the world. Since the 1990s, anarchist and autonomist networks have anchored European alterglobalization struggles, climate camps, and campaigns for "real democracy." In Greece, militant anticapitalists routinely oppose austerity policies, police brutality, and neofascist thugs in the streets.[4] While often eschewing the term *anarchism* itself, radical movements in Argentina, Brazil, Mexico, and elsewhere have turned toward self-managed workplaces, neighborhood assemblies, and autonomous mutual aid projects that accord closely with anarchist principles. Indeed, the Latin American Left as a whole continues to experiment with means of resolving the dialectical opposition between "top-down" state socialist and "bottom-up" anarchist strategies.[5] Meanwhile, Japanese anarchists are leading revitalized antinuclear campaigns in the wake of the Fukushima Daiichi nuclear disaster, and anarchists promoted visionary alternatives throughout Hong Kong's Occupy Central encampments.[6] Anarchist black blocs appeared in Egypt's Tahrir Square during Arab Spring demonstrations, and in 2014 the world watched as Kurdish militias fought off advancing Islamic State fighters while working to institute a nonstatist and feminist "democratic confederalism" heavily indebted to the anarchist tradition.[7]

Anarchism is by no means the only ideological framework prompting individuals' radical activism today. However, its presence is so substantial, domestically and globally, that conversations about how to grow movements for social justice that ignore it will prove incomplete and distorted. Anarchists have demonstrated their ability to call large protest movements into being and to craft counterinstitutions that work to alleviate social problems on a small scale. Yet scholars, journalists, and activists from other political tendencies have sharply criticized a variety of anarchist practices—from anarchists' insistence on consensus decision-making to their valorization of property destruction—as harmful to movement building over the long run. Anarchism appeals to some social groups (often those who are relatively privileged) more than to others and remains loosely organized and rife with internal dissension. Though anarchists articulate a wide-ranging critique of unjust power relations, their capacity to create stable mass-movements capable of developing winning strategies—to say nothing of the coherency of the alternative systems anarchists propose—remains to be seen.

Anarchism needs to be discussed. Yet activists, scholars, and journalists often find it difficult to do so in a deeply informed, conceptually clear fashion. Its growing visibility notwithstanding, anarchism remains to many a profoundly confusing political ideology. The very terms *anarchy, anarchism,* and *anarchist* are so overcoded with meanings and burdened by associations that people frequently talk past one another, or resort to awkward attempts at humor, even when attempting to discuss them in good faith. Misunderstanding is compounded by the fact that significantly less has been written about the history of anarchism, especially after World War I, than about other radical traditions that inform present-day grassroots organizing. This often leads anarchists to assert timeless articles of faith and critics to respond with glib generalizations, leading to intermovement acrimony and frustration. It is vital, then, for those seeking social transformation to reassess the history of anarchist movements and the intellectual frameworks motivating anarchists to undertake activism. This book is one contribution to that project. Unlike any other study, it explores and explains the evolution of anarchism in the United States between the years 1916 and 1972. This may at first appear to be an odd time span on which to focus, but it is impossible to comprehend and evaluate recent anarchist practices without understanding the ways the movement evolved in this earlier period. It was during the middle part of the twentieth century that the priorities, tactics, and base of supporters that define contemporary anarchism first came into focus.

CONTEMPORARY ANARCHISM AND HISTORIOGRAPHY

The purpose of *Unruly Equality* is to intervene in two scholarly conversations simultaneously. For a decade, a variety of academics and movement participants have articulated the key characteristics of contemporary anarchist and para-anarchist movements, but they have not adequately explained how continuities and divergences within the anarchist tradition have shaped these practices.[8] Meanwhile, historians of the broader American Left routinely ignore or undervalue the influence of anarchism during the twentieth century, producing a skewed view of contemporary movement dynamics. To cite just one example, Michael Kazin's *American Dreamers: How the Left Changed a Nation,* published just months before Wall Street was "occupied" in 2011, offered no explanation for the renewed interest in anarchism, dismissing it as a naive, youthful aberration in two short paragraphs.[9] What is missing from both of these fields of inquiry is the history of anarchism in the twentieth century. Given this absence, even champions of the new movements admit to being flummoxed about their origins. In 2008 the radical pacifist and labor lawyer Staughton Lynd celebrated the fact that we are witnessing a "revival of libertarian socialist thinking all over the world."[10] Even so, he acknowledged that "how those currents of thought and idealism survived or reached the United States from abroad is a story yet to be told. . . . I, for one, perceive the emergence of a new movement as a great mystery for which we who went before can only be deeply grateful."[11] That story is precisely what this book seeks to recover.

Part of the "great mystery" is that while twenty-first-century anarchists retain many features characteristic of earlier iterations (strident anticapitalist beliefs, nonparty organizational forms, a style of rhetoric that implies contempt for the targets of their criticism), there are other ways in which they look, think, and act quite differently than their predecessors. Indeed, Israeli political theorist Uri Gordon suggests,

> Contemporary anarchism is only in small part a direct continuation of the nineteenth- and early twentieth-century anarchist movements, which had effectively been wiped off the political scene by the end of the Second World War. Instead, the roots of today's anarchist networks can be found in the processes of intersection and fusion among radical social movements since the 1960s.[12]

Cindy Milstein, an anarchist organizer in the United States, agrees:

> At the dawn . . . of the twenty-first century, a renewed anarchism was now definitively far beyond its initial classic period of "no gods, no masters." It subscribed to a fully nonhierarchical sensibility, an array of anti-oppression principles, and the notion of pre-figurative politics. . . . This contemporary anarchism stressed a do-it-ourselves culture and mutual aid, radical ecology, collectively run spaces and projects, more explicitly queer, feminist, and people of color organizing, and various types of self-governance (often an affinity group-spokescouncil version, and frequently linked to consensus).[13]

The political scientist Joel Olson, active in the Love and Rage Revolutionary Anarchist Federation during the 1990s, recently noted that within contemporary anarchism the locus of criticism has shifted from class oppression to social hierarchy more generally. "This analysis of hierarchy," he says, "has broadened contemporary anarchism into a critique of all forms of oppression, including capitalism, the state, and organized religion but also patriarchy, heterosexism, anthropocentrism, racism, and more."[14] Like the idea of "intersectionality" that arose from the feminism of women of color at roughly the same time, the concepts of "hierarchy" and "social domination" have helped anarchists to analyze the ways in which vectors of power reinforce one another and to surpass reductionist theories that foreground one form of domination as a lynchpin, the removal of which will topple the other forms automatically. Olson also recorded shifts in the strategies emphasized by contemporary anarchists:

Organizing working-class movements, which was so central to the Wobblies and other anarchist or anarchistic organizations of the late nineteenth and early twentieth centuries, has given way today to creating "autonomous zones" like infoshops, art spaces, affinity groups, and collectives on the one hand, and glorifying large-scale protests, riots, and sabotage on the other.[15]

While this overlooks the current of "class-struggle anarchists" engaged in workplace organizing in some parts of North America, Olson captures much of the zeitgeist of contemporary anarchist activity. Laura Portwood-Stacer, a participant-observer of the milieu, demonstrates that anarchism functions today as both a social movement and a youth subculture; in many parts of the country it is difficult to disentangle these aspects.[16]

The themes and terminology these writers invoke, representative of the literature on contemporary anarchism, help explain the periodization, the conceptual categories, and the research questions that frame this book. As the quotations noted earlier indicate, it has become commonplace to distinguish a period of classical anarchism (roughly, the 1860s to 1940) from a period of contemporary anarchism that was inaugurated in the late 1960s, became more prominent and globally coordinated in the 1990s, and continues into the present. Some historians date the decline of the classical anarchist movement, especially that of the United States, even earlier—to the period of repression surrounding World War I.[17] Bracketing these two periods suggests that the anarchist movement was nonexistent, or at least dormant, for a period of thirty to fifty years in the middle of the twentieth century. Some scholars have suggested that, viewed across this time span, changes in the movement's base of support, issues of concern, and strategies of change are so pronounced that it is analytically helpful to acknowledge that a paradigm shift occurred in anarchist politics in or about 1968.[18]

This rough-and-ready chronology presents an intriguing set of questions. How did anarchism transform from a class-focused movement based in poor immigrant communities before World War I to one that, in the last decades of the century, focused on feminism, environmentalism, and cultural alienation while appealing primarily (but not solely) to native-born, white-middle-class youth? What accounts for the changes in the strategies and tactics favored by anarchists? At what point did the subcultural aspects of anarchism emerge? And what significance should one attribute to these transformations?

As I began to study the traces left behind by anarchists, I was surprised to find a clear line of continuity rather than any defined break in the history of

U.S. anarchism. While it is undeniable that anarchist ideas and practices evolved significantly over the course of the twentieth century, in the pages that follow I take issue with the accepted timeline and the claim that anarchism changed as suddenly as is implied by the concept of a paradigm shift—at least in the United States, the geopolitical area to which I limit this inquiry. In fact, so many developments relevant to understanding anarchism today took place during the supposed interregnum—the period between 1920 and the late 1960s, when no movement is thought to have existed—that I have chosen to confine this study to precisely that period.

In contrast to conventional wisdom, I demonstrate that although the U.S. anarchist community was small (a few thousand members at most) during the mid-twentieth century, it was intellectually dynamic, broadly networked, and subtly influential. Changes in movement culture and political analysis that scholars and activists have attributed to the final decades of the twentieth century are, in actuality, traceable as far back as the early 1940s. The story told here, then, suggests a cross-fade of emphases within anarchist culture, more than it indicates a period of dead airtime between fundamentally discordant tracks. Twentieth-century U.S. anarchism is characterized by both continuity and change. It is continuous in that we can clearly trace each generation of thinkers and activists mentoring the next, passing the values of anarchism along like a baton in a relay race. Moreover, certain questions and practices (how means shape ends, the merits of violence and nonviolence, the centrality of anarchist periodicals) recur so consistently that they appear to define the anarchist project as a whole. Yet anarchism has never been singular, and during the mid-twentieth century it underwent a complex process of combination, mutation, and evolution, wherein anarchist ideas were braided together with schools of thought emanating from psychology, pacifism, feminism, and many other sources.

To track the many ways in which anarchism has ramified during the half century under consideration, I find it useful to distinguish six aspects of social anarchist praxis.[19] These include conceptualizations and critiques of power, theories of human nature, visions of a better society, strategies to achieve those visions, forms of movement organization needed to carry out such strategies, and understandings of what sorts of people will constitute the movement's base of participants.[20] Owing to their antiauthoritarian commitments, anarchists have never asserted or enforced orthodoxies or unified party lines. Anarchism is therefore complex and diverse at any given time, and it appears especially so when examined across a span of decades.

Nevertheless, there are common and recognizable variants within each of these six categories of anarchist praxis. Equally important, we can denote beliefs and practices that conceptually contradict anarchist values and have therefore historically been excluded from anarchist repertoires of contention. We might see these as limit points that can help us define the range of ideas and practices deemed acceptable to anarchists and definitive of anarchism. For example, anarchists have disagreed about whether humans are naturally altruistic or have conflicted impulses, and about whether human nature is entirely socially constructed; no social anarchist theory, however, is grounded in a belief that humans are essentially selfish. Such a belief would contradict the theory of mutual aid, which undergirds anarchist assertions about the superfluous nature of government. The following table schematizes the conceptual positions evident in this book (as well as in contemporary intermovement anarchist debates). While many of these approaches were present in classical anarchism, some emerged over the course of the twentieth century. I hope that distinguishing the components of anarchist politics in this way will help elucidate the causes of divisions between different groups of historic and contemporary anarchists, which often appear maddeningly obscure. This may help radical theorists to critique problematic assumptions within anarchist thinking without dismissing the stronger points.

As marginalized as anarchism has always been, no intellectual or political movement exists in a vacuum. If, as I have argued, we cannot understand U.S. anarchism without noting the influence of other movements and intellectual traditions upon it, then we should also expect the recovery of this history of anarchism to shed new light on broader cultural, political, and theoretical phenomena. With this in mind, I have organized the narrative around two basic questions: What influence did changes in social structure, social and political theory, and other social movements have on anarchists? In turn, what influence did anarchists have on each of these aspects of life?

DEFINING SOCIAL ANARCHISM

Unruly Equality is concerned with a particular conception and type of anarchism: the self-conscious, international political movement opposed to most forms of coercive authority and in favor of social and economic equality for all people. Since *anarchism* has always been a contested term, a brief consideration of the word's connotations will help clarify the scope of this book.

COMPONENTS OF SOCIAL ANARCHIST POLITICS

	Human Nature	Theory of Power	Vision of New Society	Strategy	Organization	Demographic Base
Acceptable	Altruistic	Capital/state/church	Pastoral	Insurrection	Informal	Peasants and wage laborers
	Conflicted impulses	Authority	Industrial	Mass organizing	Conspiratorial	All oppressed people
	Socially constructed	Social domination	Primitivist	Prefiguration	Horizontal	Humanity
			Plural	Cultural transformation	Voluntary accountable hierarchy	Alienated youth
Unacceptable	Essentially selfish	Economistic	More stratified	Electoral, dictatorship	Authoritarian	Solely privileged people

Since the eighteenth century, at least, the word *anarchy* has signified a condition of chaos, disorder, and personal vulnerability owing to the absence of a center of power capable of enforcing rules; it is still frequently used in this way today. In 1840, however, a French radical named Pierre-Joseph Proudhon reclaimed the term *anarchy* in a fashion similar to the ways in which the word *queer* and certain racial slurs have, in recent decades, been adopted and given positive connotations by the groups of people they were meant to denigrate. Proudhon argued that under conditions of profound economic inequality, such as those that reigned in industrializing Europe, the primary role of political states was to legitimate and defend the wealth of a minority. It was this joint exercise of economic and military power that *actually* made the poor vulnerable (to hunger, disease, beatings) and ensured society would remain chaotically ridden with conflict.[21] He had faith that people could live harmoniously if state coercion and the lopsided distribution of resources was done away with, famously declaring, "Liberty is not the daughter but the mother of order." For Proudhon, then, to be an *anarchist* was to fight the enforcement of misery upon common people, and he therefore wore the term as a badge of honor. Other European socialists soon elaborated upon this conceptualization, and by the 1860s anarchism had emerged as a political ideology and a specific tendency within the broader labor and radical movements of Europe. By the end of the century, such ideas had spread around the world.

Although Proudhon's linguistic reclamation may have been conceptually brilliant, the meaning he gave to the term never fully displaced its earlier connotations. As a result, for more than 150 years, anarchists have felt compelled to begin their speeches and writings with a clarification of what they mean by *anarchy*. Authority figures tasked with quashing the movement have exploited the commonsense understanding of anarchy as chaos in depicting the intentions of anarchist organizers. The fact that many anarchists adopted assassination and terroristic bombings as a common tactic in the closing decades of the nineteenth century made this work of misinformation easier.[22] Anarchists of this sort exalted the temporary chaos caused by acts of violence against authority figures because they believed such acts would lead to a more ordered and egalitarian society, *not* because they desired chaos or suffering as an end goal.

These conflicting definitions go some way toward explaining the confusion the word *anarchism* still generates. But since the 1970s, *anarchy* and *anarchism* have taken on additional associations that further muddle the picture. In the 1970s, the influential punk band the Sex Pistols released their first single, "Anarchy in the UK," and proceeded to shock and outrage, but also captivate, radio and television audiences in a manner that purveyors of youth-culture products soon found ways to capitalize upon. The Sex Pistols' connections to anarchists were thirdhand, but in the 1980s some of the punk bands that came in their wake (Crass, Conflict, Chumbawamba) made important contributions to existing anarchist movements and progressive campaigns, such as the 1984 miners' strike in England.[23] Yet an undefined "anarchy" and the circle-A symbol popularized by punk bands quickly became go-to tropes within the music and fashion industries to symbolize teen angst, the desire to cut loose, and a shallow nonconformity. Owing to this association, anarchism is often tagged as an ill-considered, youthful rebelliousness, rather than as a sophisticated theoretical tradition and international social movement.[24]

Punk was not the only outgrowth of the 1970s that has added complexity to the term *anarchism*. In a seemingly ironic twist to global politics, anarchists have emerged as among the boldest and most persistent opponents of neoliberalism, the political ideology inaugurated, at least symbolically, by Ronald Reagan's declaration that "government is not the solution—government is the problem!" Reagan and his allies, such as the United Kingdom's Margaret Thatcher, were not, of course, opposed to all government, but rather to the forms of state regulation of business, finance, and trade that had been implemented during the twentieth century, and which had become increasingly intolerable to major economic players as conditions changed in the 1970s.[25] By the late 1990s, neoliberalism had become the hegemonic policy-making framework for centrist and conservative parties around the world, prompting resistance by many groups (including anarchists) who found their well-being endangered by the stripping away of protections and the growing economic inequality that ensued.

From the outset, neoliberal ideology was developed and promoted by a tight-knit circle of intellectuals who helped define the modern libertarian movement. The word *libertarian* has been historically contested alongside the term *anarchism*. As we will see in the chapters that follow, anticapitalist anarchists adopted *libertarian* as a moniker following World War I (partly in an attempt to avoid associations with violence), and a variety of egalitarian political thinkers, such as Noam Chomsky, have identified as "libertarian socialists" since World War II. Commonsense associations with the term began to change in the 1960s, however, when thinkers such as Murray

Rothbard and Ayn Rand began widely promoting a minimal-government, hypercapitalist, and individualist ideology they called *libertarianism*. Although most contemporary promarket libertarians accept the need for a minimal state to protect private property rights, a few extreme advocates have labeled themselves *anarchist capitalists*.[26] Well-funded by wealthy donors, libertarians continue pressuring centrist and center-right governments to extend and deepen the neoliberal transformation of the modern state. Partnering with other sectors of the right, they have exerted a powerful intellectual and financial influence on the populist Tea Party movement that emerged in the wake of the 2008 financial crisis.[27] This has led to a situation in which a government-shrinking center is besieged by "free market" forces on the Right who seek to abolish public social provisions, and on the Left by anarchists (often acting in uneasy alliance with social democrats) who furiously criticize the state's defense of corporate power and imperialist war-making.

These varied meanings of *anarchism* often congeal in strange ways. In August 2014 the *New York Times Magazine* featured a cover story about the appeal of libertarian senator Rand Paul among young Republican voters. The illustrator mimicked a flier for the legendary punk band Minor Threat and snuck a hand-drawn circle-A symbol into the magazine's masthead.[28] A year earlier, when Tea Party–affiliated Republicans forced a federal government shutdown, Senate Majority Leader Harry Reid denounced members of the caucus as "anarchists" who needed to "get a life."[29] Reid explained, "When I was in school, I studied government and I learned about the anarchists. Now, they were different than the Tea Party because they were violent. . . . [Tea Party members are] not doing physically destructive things to buildings and people, directly, but they are doing everything they can to throw a monkey wrench into every form of government."[30] In these instances, all of the term's connotations were at play: anarchism as any antigovernmental politics, anarchism as violence, anarchism as nineteenth-century anachronism, anarchism as juvenile behavior and punk rock.

With the ideological waters so muddied in 2013, the *Washington Post* took the unusual step of publishing an op-ed by a left-wing academic, titled "The Tea Party Is Giving Anarchism a Bad Name." In it, Heather Gautney clarified that "real anarchist communities operate according to radically democratic principles. They theorize, and even organize, with egalitarian political and social visions in mind." Gautney acknowledged the contradictory predicament of contemporary anarchism by noting, "Despite their anti-authoritarianism, some of today's anarchists concede that states can serve socially important functions like ensuring sound infrastructure, basic consumer protections and comprehensive social welfare (though they believe such services are better executed with decentralized communities)."[31] Understanding this ambivalence requires an account of the ways anarchists interpreted and reacted to the expansion of governmental functions, especially social democratic initiatives, during the twentieth century—an account I provide in the chapters that follow.

On the other hand, this book does not trace the growth of neoliberal and right-wing libertarian thinking in any detail, since these movements are motivated by social aims fundamentally divergent from those of the social anarchists at the center of this study. As noted, classical anarchists opposed governments because they understood their essential purposes to be upholding economic inequality and war making. Such anarchists believed that sociable impulses would lead humans to develop cooperative, egalitarian economies in the absence of state authority. In contrast, the neoliberal ideology that came to dominate global political and economic life at the end of the twentieth century seeks to eliminate precisely those government functions that were implemented in the mid-twentieth century to moderate economic inequality. These conservative critics view humans as naturally competitive, and believe that removing government restraints on the market will lead to free and just, but naturally *unequal,* societies of individuals.

While libertarians and neoliberals promote individual liberty as the supreme political value, it is a mistake to assume that unlimited individual freedom is the foundational principle of social anarchism. Instead, as Chiara Bottici has recently argued, anarchists believe in "the freedom of equals."[32] In other words, anarchists insist that a meaningful or substantive experience of freedom is possible only under conditions of economic and political equality, which, in their view, can be achieved only through ongoing practices of solidarity prompted by care for the well-being of others.

Of course, intentions are one thing and outcomes another. At times anarchists' theorizations of the functions and motivations of government have foreclosed opportunities to redistribute resources, especially after the growth of liberal welfare-state programs, and at times put them in strange company, such as when some decried federal enforcement of civil rights legislation in the American South. Moreover, right-wing libertarians do claim as precursors a coterie of nineteenth-century American intellectuals, known as "individualist anarchists," that also influenced early-twentieth-century social anarchism to an extent. Throughout the book, therefore, I point to uncomfortable moments of resonance between radical and conservative forms of antistatist politics, motivated by the belief that they are especially rich sites for evaluating the coherency of anarchist political philosophy and movement strategy.

Nevertheless, it was to emphasize the egalitarianism at the heart of anarchist ethics—the factor most clearly distinguishing anarchism from neoliberalism—that I chose *Unruly Equality* as a title for this study. Since the movement was initiated in the 1860s, anarchists have defied laws, orders, and social conventions, asserting themselves impertinently in the eyes of authorities; they have been loud, defiant, and uncontrollable—in a word, unruly. They have done so in pursuit of greater economic, social, and political equality for all human beings, making them *unruly egalitarians*. But in a different sense, unruled equality might be posited as the political ideal, the end goal, and the sociological hypothesis of the movement. Anarchists believe that political rule is constituted not solely to protect and enhance the life of humans but also to enforce inequality for the benefit of a minority at the expense of many others. Following from this, anarchists suggest that a more egalitarian society will require less ruliness—that is, less coercive power—a condition they embrace. Perhaps the most interesting aspects of twentieth-century anarchism, from the standpoint of political theory, are the ways participants have refined their conceptualization of that anticipated social order from one of *unrule* to one of *self-rule,* along with the ways their strategic thinking has evolved in light of new understandings of power and the practical successes and failings of other social movements also seeking greater freedom and equality. These mutually constitutive transformations are parsed out in detail in the eight chapters that constitute this book.

CHAPTERS AND ARGUMENT

Although there is no clear "break" in the history of U.S. anarchism, the era of World War II can be seen as something of a tipping point, when new theoretical frameworks, strategies, and constituents came to the foreground. Accordingly, *Unruly Equality* is divided into two sections composed of four chapters each. The first section traces the disintegration of the traditional anarchist movement from its zenith in the second decade of the twentieth century to its nadir at the outbreak of the Second World War. The second section examines the ways in which ideas and commitments that anarchists adopted in the 1940s, 1950s, and 1960s fundamentally shaped not only their own movement but also those of the New Left.

The book's first chapter portrays U.S. anarchism at the height of its influence in the decade before the First World War. In it, I summarize the core beliefs and strategies animating the international anarchist movement, noting the different emphases of Russian-, Yiddish-, Italian-, Spanish-, and English-speaking anarchist organizations active in the United States. Despite significant repression, the movement grew substantially in these years owing to its affiliation with the Industrial Workers of the World and through coalitions that anarchists built with middle-class progressives, based on their growing interest in free speech rights, feminism, modern art, and progressive methods of education.

Chapter 2 describes the ways anarchists resisted the United States' entrance into World War I and supported the early stages of the Russian Revolution, as well as the intense repression visited upon them in response. I consider the relationships between the antiradical Red Scare, which peaked with the violent Palmer Raids of 1919, and the Red Summer that same year, in which African American communities were violently attacked. Both can be seen as part of a larger project of class decomposition that reconfigured the racial, ethnic, and political characteristics of the U.S. working class. These changes, I suggest, debilitated the U.S. anarchist movement in the interwar years as much as the jailing and deportation of many of its key organizers.

The third chapter examines the ways anarchists attempted to reestablish and "Americanize" their movement while attending to new threats posed by fascists and communists during the 1920s. Focused on supporting imprisoned comrades at home and abroad, and finding the Industrial Workers of the World in tatters, they stumbled in search of a new labor strategy. While Jewish anarchists worked to establish rural anarchist communities and "free schools," Italians went to war with bricks and bats to stem support for fascism in Italian American neighborhoods.

Chapter 4 analyzes the ways anarchists responded to the Great Depression and the New Deal, the Spanish Civil War, and the looming specter of a second world war. Defined insurrectionist and syndicalist currents reemerged and sparred with one another in these years, yet both denounced New Deal labor reforms and social provisions as a plot to defang working-class power. Meanwhile, Jewish anarchists organized a short-lived agricultural kibbutz in Michigan, and the Catholic Worker Movement established a tradition of anarchist service to the poor. Divorced from the labor movement and internally divided over how to defeat fascism, the last vestiges of the traditional anarchist movement disintegrated in 1939.

The second part of *Unruly Equality* focuses on a new cohort of anarchists who congealed around the principles of radical pacifism, the transformative power of avant-garde literature, and a dedication to modeling, in their own lives, the new world they were seeking to create. Chapter 5 focuses on the links anarchists forged with radical pacifists in the early 1940s. Writing in new publications, college-educated anarchists drew on recent strands of psychology and anthropology to challenge traditional anarchist precepts, including the imminence of revolution and the centrality of economic oppression. Anarchist draft resisters collaborated with Gandhian pacifists to resist the racial segregation of federal prisons, influencing each other's beliefs in the process. Upon their release, they forged a politics of revolutionary nonviolence by establishing intentional communities, publications, and organizations opposed to white supremacy, poverty, and the arms race.

Chapter 6 examines the ways anarchists overlapped with circles of bohemian poets and actors in San Francisco and New York who shared their intense alienation from Cold War culture and traditional forms of Left politics. To the old anarchism of Kropotkin and Bakunin, they added elements of Zen Buddhism, sexual libertinism, and a dedication to the natural world. Rather than organizing protest campaigns, the artists focused on changing their own consciousness, establishing new forms of community based on their values, and creating beauty in a world that appeared bent on destruction. The institutions that midcentury anarchists created—from City Lights Bookstore to Pacifica Radio and the Six Gallery—would foster the growth of the Beat Generation and the broader counterculture that followed in its wake.

Chapter 7 analyzes anarchist engagements with black freedom struggles in the United States and with wars of national liberation across the globe. Through *Liberation* magazine, the War Resisters League, and other means, anarchists contributed direct action tactics and antistatist strategies to the Black Freedom Movement. In turn, the Student Nonviolent Coordinating Committee and other organizations challenged anarchists' residual focus on class antagonisms and pushed anarchists to reconsider how revolution might come about. Anarchists disagreed about how to relate to the national liberation struggles taking place in Asia and Africa, and their conflicting views regarding the character of revolutionary Cuba left them divided as the new movements of the 1960s began to erupt.

Chapter 8 weaves together the threads generated throughout the book, to indicate the multifaceted ways in which anarchists shaped the cultural and political movements known collectively as the New Left. Supportive of the concept of participatory democracy, libertarian socialists tried to lead Students for a Democratic Society in an anarchist direction but were outmaneuvered by other factions. Meanwhile, anarchist beatniks synthesized European avant-garde and ultraleft traditions with the urban insurrectional activity of African Americans to infuse 1960s counterculture organizations, such as the Diggers and White Panthers, with an eclectic doctrine of antiauthoritarian politics. Throughout the period, radical pacifists with anarchist commitments helped build antidraft organizations such as the Resistance, and women's and gay liberation groups put aspects of the anarchist tradition to their own uses.

As the 1970s dawned, the anarchist movement looked much more like it does today than it did before World War I: its members were predominantly young and middle class and were enamored of critical theory; and increasingly they were turning toward the politics of feminism and ecology. Then, as now, anarchists devoted considerable energy to living out their beliefs in daily life and expressing their politics through consumption choices, sartorial cues, and countercultural artistic practices. The book's conclusion summarizes the transformations marking U.S. anarchism between the second decade of the twentieth century and the early 1970s, and the epilogue schematically outlines how these trends have played out in the four decades since that time.

Although the primary purpose of *Unruly Equality* is to enhance understanding of the U.S. anarchist movement itself, the history told here also uniquely illuminates broader concerns and historical narratives. Anarchism is an insight generating lens through which to examine features of American social structure, such as the limits placed on national belonging and the rise of the national-security state. In particular, anarchism and the treatment of anarchists is important to the history of race and racism in the United States, just as antiracist struggles are central to the history of U.S. anarchism. For example, I demonstrate that early-twentieth-century nativists used "anarchism" as a racializing epithet to challenge the rights of eastern and southern European immigrants to claim the privileges of national belonging and whiteness, which helped build support for the sweeping immigration reforms of 1924. Anarchism must also be recognized as a vital force that nourished and linked successive generations of the American avant-garde in literature, theater, and the visual arts, long before anarchists and punk rockers formed a partnership in the late 1970s.

Most significant, perhaps, treating anarchism as more than an also-ran in the history of the American Left forces us to reconsider received wisdom about the nature and provenance of the movements of the 1960s. Sociologists writing in the 1970s claimed that anarchism was given a new lease on life by the New Left and the global movements of 1968. In actuality (with apologies to Proudhon), the New Left was as much the daughter as it was the mother of a twentieth-century form of anarchism. U.S. anarchists spent the 1940s and 1950s developing sexual and environmental politics, while the idea of simply "living the revolution" rather than directly confronting state and corporate power, central to the counterculture and the early 1970s back-to-the-land movement, owes a fundamental debt to anarchism. *Unruly Equality,* then, provides new insights into the transformation of the economic Left into the cultural Left—a shift affecting liberals and the base of the Democratic Party as much as the radical fringe.

During the years under consideration, anarchists developed a greater appreciation than their ideological predecessors for the practice of democracy as an ideal, while continuing to fiercely criticize the political activity that passes for democracy in conventional American politics. Going forward, I suspect that it would be useful to consider mid-twentieth-century anarchism as a line of egalitarian politics that was amplified, modified, and refracted as it passed through the prism of that crucial 1960s conceptual invention, participatory democracy. Since that time, it has inspired considerable experimentation in the practical exercise of egalitarian forms of democratic politics (under the auspices of the feminist, antinuclear, environmental, and alter-globalization movements), while theorists have pursued similar goals under the banners of post-Marxism, post-structuralism, women of color feminism, and decolonial politics.

I hope, then, that by connecting some dots in radical history and theory, *Unruly Equality* will prove valuable to the construction of a vital new radical democratic politics that incorporates the best elements of the anarchist tradition with those of the socialist, feminist, antiracist, anti-imperialist, and queer-liberationist traditions. Anarchism has long overlapped and drawn sustenance from each of these movements. Such cross-pollination was evident in 1916, the historical high point of U.S. anarchism. A clear reckoning of the movement in that moment is crucial for understanding all that unfolded afterward.

PART I

The Decline of Classical Anarchism

ONE

Anarchist Apogee, 1916

In the United States, the social anarchist movement reached a historical apogee in the years just before the First World War, measured by newspaper circulation figures, scope of public activities, and intellectual perspicacity. In 1916, anarchists could be found leading strikes of midwestern miners, distributing illegal birth-control information to poor women, teaching avant-garde art techniques to factory workers, and threatening to incinerate the homes of the upper class if they continued to resist demands to share their wealth and decision-making power. The ameliorative reforms championed by settlement house workers and progressive politicians in these years did not go nearly far enough, in their eyes. Accordingly, anarchists seized on a widely felt need for change and attempted to push it in a revolutionary direction. They were so feared, such a presence in the culture, that well-heeled parents turned the most notorious among them, Emma Goldman, into a bogeyman to discipline their children: "Go to bed, or Red Emma is going to get you!"

It would be misleading to speak of anarchists as succeeding in these years, since anarchism was then, as always, a marginal political current. Because they eschewed formal organizations that maintained membership rosters, it is difficult to accurately gauge how many people counted themselves as anarchists at a given moment. However, newspaper circulation records and lecture receipts suggest there were between fifty thousand and a hundred thousand adherents in 1915—a tiny but vociferous and daring portion of the country's 100 million residents.[1] Nevertheless, it is fair to discuss the *relative* success of the movement during the second decade of the twentieth century, owing to the fact that it was growing in numbers, establishing coalitions with new allies, and shaping public discourse more than it ever had before or has since. The gains anarchists made during the Progressive Era are attributable to a set of favorable social trends and to what the movement made of these conditions.

Anarchism provided participants with a broad worldview that helped them make sense of their daily lives. Despite these shared beliefs, early-twentieth-century anarchists disagreed on matters of strategy and which issues to prioritize. In the years before the First World War, three strategic tendencies—insurrectionary, syndicalist, and bohemian anarchism—distinguished themselves and sometimes clashed with one another. Language and ethnic differences also cleaved the movement in complicated patterns. Mapping the movement in such a way helps explain the various ways anarchists reacted to the crisis surrounding the First World War, as well as the complex trajectories in which their ideas, strategies, and organizational forms evolved over the decades that followed.

A TIME OF TENSION

Progressive Era anarchists saw themselves as partisans in a war with employers, government officials ensconced in the bosses' pockets, and ministers who sanctified inequality while shaming those seeking a bit of pleasure in their lives and bodies. This war was at times bloody and at other times more muted. It was expressed daily as a struggle of wills over work practices and pay rates that frequently spilled out into lopsided armed conflict: police, Pinkertons, militias, and vigilantes suppressing strikes by force of arms, with an occasional guerilla riposte targeting elite property or persons. Beneath the violence lay an incessant battle of words and images. While the mainstream press mastered the art of depicting anarchists as animalistic and mentally unsound, anarchists contributed greatly to the enduring image of the monopoly capitalist as a hog in coattails, belly so large as to render his legs virtually useless. Demographics help explain the extent of this enmity.

Since its inception in the 1880s, the U.S. anarchist movement had been primarily composed of European immigrants. In the early twentieth century, anarchists remained more likely to speak and write Yiddish, Italian, Russian, or Spanish, rather than English, as a primary language. These radicals constituted a subset of the approximately 20 million people—mostly from southern and eastern Europe but also from Asia and Mexico—who had migrated to the United States since 1880.[2] Nudged out of their home countries by religious violence and conflicts rooted in the growth pangs of bourgeois society, many were drawn to North America by recruiters who sought low-wage laborers to build the cities and staff the factories that had sprung up after the Civil War.[3] By the turn of the twentieth century, the gross domestic product of the United States had outstripped those of Germany, France, and the United Kingdom *combined,* but this newfound wealth was in no way evenly distributed.[4] A new class fraction of industrial and banking elites joined the older merchant and planter families that had long dominated national politics. Although many immigrants were shifting from near-feudal conditions to urban industrial settings, class disparities remained glaring. As a teenager, Lucy Robins Lang was easily converted to anarchism by coworkers in a garment factory after she migrated with her family from a Russian shtetl to a grim basement in a Chicago ghetto.[5]

The upper class was, in reality, buffered socially by professionals and a growing stratum of English-speakers delegated clerical and managerial responsibilities as companies shifted manual tasks to foreign-born newcomers.[6] However, such distinctions could easily slip from view in what was often experienced as a Manichean world of employers and employees. Immigrants with skills in mining and logging went to work in rudimentary camps where the superintendent's home was set off from the workers' shacks like officers' quarters from army barracks. Laborers died routinely in preventable industrial accidents that plagued mines and factories alike. While the spread of tenements, child labor, and smoke-blackened skies convinced many in the middle class of the need for new regulations and forms of assistance, others sought more transformative solutions. At least one survivor of the notorious 1911 Triangle Shirtwaist Company factory fire, Mary Abrams, became a revolutionary anarchist.[7] For Abrams and others like her, the possibility of improving one's life by voting seemed laughable.

Many immigrant shop hands came from countries in which working people had not yet gained the vote. In the United States, they encountered a baffling array of suffrage laws. Owning property was not required in order to cast a ballot, but men had to first become citizens. Chinese immigrants were barred from citizenship on racial grounds and, therefore, prevented from voting. Native Americans, overwhelmingly confined to isolated reservations, would not gain full citizenship rights until 1924. Black men were supposedly entitled to vote, but were largely prevented from doing so in the southern states, where nine out of ten of them lived. Women not otherwise disqualified could vote only in certain elections in a few western states.[8] This miasma of disqualifications created a situation in which the majority of the people living in the United States were ineligible to vote for representatives, much less seek office themselves. Nevertheless, the disenfranchised were inventing new ways of exercising power.

W. E. B. DuBois, Ida B. Wells, and their allies launched the National Association for the Advancement of Colored People in 1909 with the aim of leveraging educational programs and litigation to win respect, voting rights, and access to jobs for African Americans. Meanwhile, independent black-owned newspapers, such as the *Pittsburgh Courier* and the *Chicago Defender,* encouraged African Americans to move north, where they could organize more openly.[9] Campaigns to expand the rights of women were simultaneously on the rise, with Margaret Sanger opening the country's first birth-control clinic in 1916 and suffragists building the organizational clout needed to win passage of the Nineteenth Amendment by the end of the decade.[10]

In the same years, wage laborers fought stridently to improve pay and job conditions. Trade union membership nearly quadrupled, to approximately 3 million between 1900 and 1917, and worker militancy increased as employers responded to strikes with violence.[11] The majority joined moderate craft-specific unions grouped under the American Federation of Labor, but after 1905 the anticapitalist Industrial Workers of the World expanded rapidly, aided by anarchists and other radicals.[12] In Lawrence, Massachusetts, upward of twenty thousand textile workers struck in 1912, holding out against freezing temperatures and billy-club-wielding police to win most of their demands. The following year, thousands of silk workers in Paterson, New Jersey, struck for six months despite nearly two thousand arrests. Farther west the response to labor organizing was even more draconian. The Colorado National Guard infamously killed eleven children and nine adults when it set fire to an encampment of striking miners in 1914.[13]

The poor also organized politically. The Socialist Party united midwestern farmers with immigrant factory hands and urbane intellectuals, publishing more than three hundred newspapers and capturing 6 percent of the vote in the presidential election of 1912. Socialists sought to eventually replace capitalism by organizing trade unions and electing party candidates to office.[14] Although anarchists disagreed with strategies focused on winning voting rights, the diverse struggles to downwardly redistribute power, wealth, and dignity that began to coalesce in these years created a climate in which anarchists were able to gain greater traction and to branch out from the constituencies and issues on which they had focused since the early 1880s.

The anticapitalist anarchist movement had arisen in the United States alongside the growth of wage labor and mass migration from Europe. Its first generation consisted of exiled German socialists, such as Johann Most and August Spies, and their acolytes, who began calling for armed insurrection after losing faith in electoral strategies. By 1886, Chicago anarchists had built a militant labor federation of some fifty thousand manual workers, while anarchist newspapers, beer halls, and singing societies proliferated in New York and other cities. *Anarchism* became a household term—of opprobrium—in May of that year, when six anarchist firebrands were convicted of conspiracy after a bomb killed policemen sent to disperse a labor rally in Chicago's Haymarket district.[15] The movement waxed and waned over the next two decades as sympathizers attracted to the anarchists' "beautiful ideal" were repeatedly driven away by police crackdowns or their own misgivings about political violence.

The movement's fortunes began to change in the early twentieth century, as national politics shifted leftward and a new generation of talented anarchist organizers, such as Saul Yanovsky, Carlo Tresca, and Ricardo Flores Magón, came to the fore. By the second decade of the twentieth century, anarchists lived in coastal and midwestern industrial cities, inland mining towns, and the occasional rural commune, such as the Home Colony on the Puget Sound.[16] Most worked for wages in garment or cigar factories, mines or lumber camps, or as unwaged homemakers, attending meetings after putting in ten hours on the job.[17] Those living in cities resided in working-class neighborhoods, usually amid people who shared their primary language and country of origin. Despite anarchists' notoriety as advocates of "free love," historian Jennifer Guglielmo notes, "the anarchist movement was centered on families."[18] Most anarchists lived as monogamous couples raising children together, although many chose not to legally marry, rejecting the idea that either a church or government should regulate their emotional bonds. Families often kept bachelors as boarders, and some anarchists experimented with collective living in apartments or row houses.[19]

Although anarchists rejected loyalty to political states, ties of language and culture influenced the political tasks they prioritized. They balanced the need to organize their own ethnic communities with the desire to collaborate with other nearby anarchists, all the while remaining attentive to developments overseas—sending funds, writing articles, and demonstrating support for comrades abroad.[20]

Rather than joining a unified political party, anarchists belonged to a series of overlapping organizations linked by a broader cultural milieu. When

Morris Greenshner immigrated to New York in 1909, his cousin took him to a meeting of the Workmen's Circle, a self-help organization that paid out sick benefits and doubled as a social club. There he met a friend who encouraged him to join the Anarchist Red Cross, an organization that sent money and letters of support to anarchists imprisoned in Russia. After finding a job, Greenshner joined the anarchist Union of Russian Workers. Movement work often led to romance as well. Greenshner later recalled, "I met my wife Becky in 1910 at a May First Demonstration. Becky and I attended anarchist meetings and lectures." The couple also socialized at fund-raising balls and organized a "literary anarchist group" that sold European periodicals and sent the proceeds back across the Atlantic.[21] The Greenshners's story, and schedule, was typical for anarchist militants of their day.

In this networked political and social milieu, newspapers and journals served as de facto political centers—means of grouping anarchists by language and strategic orientation. Publishers of periodicals routinely sponsored lecture series and distributed books and pamphlets by mail. Typically, editors were revered figures who wrote much of the copy and doubled as powerful orators. When conflicts emerged, anarchists lined up according to which newspaper's editorial line they supported. In this way, publishers such as Luigi Galleani, Pedro Esteve, Alexander Berkman, and others became unofficial leaders and spokespeople of the movement.[22] Whether delivered in print, in speeches, or through theatrical productions, anarchist theory explained why the world contained so much misery and confidently assured those who would listen that it was possible for humans to live much freer, more enjoyable lives.

FUNDAMENTALS OF THE ANARCHIST WORLDVIEW

Between 1900 and 1916, U.S. anarchists continued to derive the fundamentals of their worldview from writings produced in the second half of the previous century by European anarchist militant-intellectuals such as Pierre-Joseph Proudhon, Mikhail Bakunin, Peter Kropotkin, Élisée Reclus, and Errico Malatesta.[23] These thinkers launched their inquiry into the world from the perspective of propertyless peasants and wage laborers living under conditions of scarcity during the tumult of the industrial revolution in Europe. Anarchists built on the insights of the radical republican and utopian socialist movements to insist upon broader and deeper application of the principles of the French Revolution: liberty, equality, and fraternity (the latter often articulated in the more encompassing term *solidarity*).[24] Anarchists stridently opposed capitalism, political states, and religion because they saw these institutions as inimical to the rights of all people to well-being, free expression, and the full realization of their potential.

Anarchist economic analysis adopted the critique of property relations and the labor theory of value expounded by Karl Marx. From this perspective, a small minority of people monopolized ownership of factories and fertile land, thereby coercing the majority to work for them. Paying wages lower than the total value of the commodities workers produced, the owners became rich off of others' toil. This is what led the first self-identified anarchist, Proudhon, to proclaim, "Property is theft!"[25] Appropriation of surplus value was the original and constantly reiterated injustice that structured life and fueled the rage burning within social anarchists. "Many are the lies that pass for truths," explained the Russian American anarchist Alexander Berkman in 1916. "But the greatest and most pernicious of them all is the cunning insistence on 'harmony between capital and labor.' It is the 'harmony' of inevitable, eternal discord, the symphony of master and slave, the love of the jackal for its prey."[26]

Anarchists recognized deep-seated connections between the power of the owners of productive property, church officials, and government authorities. Religion was odious to them because it preached doctrines of original sin that depicted humans as inherently dangerous to themselves and others, necessitating their submission to supernatural authority. "God being truth, justice, goodness, beauty, power and life," thundered Bakunin, "man is falsehood, iniquity, evil, ugliness, impotence, and death. God being master, man is the slave."[27] The hierarchy of God>clergy>laymen normalized hierarchical relations in other aspects of life, while religious authorities counseled respect for the existing social order. "The Church with its hoary superstitions is one of the great factors that keep the workers in obedience and submission," maintained Berkman. "Throughout history the priest—of all denominations— has always sided with King and Master. He has kept the eyes of the people riveted upon 'heavenly things' while the exploiters were despoiling them of their earthly possessions."[28]

Anarchists saw not only the church but also the governments of their day as tools wielded by the owning class—likewise, the major political parties, newspapers, and public schools.[29] They argued that parliamentary governments, even those granting universal suffrage, differed little in intention or outcome from monarchies or other authoritarian systems. Anarchists criticized political states in three main ways. First, they believed all existing states were organized to defend class privilege, which was unjustified and harmful to working people. Second, they argued that imposing laws on people, for purposes of domination or not, constituted a suffocating and unjustifiable violation of human liberty. This tenet led the anarchists to reject, a priori, the legitimacy of any form of potential socialist state as well as the use of electoral strategies to create change. Emma Goldman, for example, criticized the movement for women's suffrage by rhetorically asking, "Is it not the most brutal imposition for one set of people to make laws that another set is coerced by force to obey? Yet woman clamors for that 'golden opportunity' that has wrought so much misery in the world, and robbed man of his integrity and self-reliance."[30] Finally, anarchists argued that, without fail, power corrupted those who held positions of authority. Such corruption inevitably led officials to prioritize the expansion of institutional power and their personal privileges over all other concerns.[31]

Liberal theorists too, of course, warned of the defects of parliamentary systems and acknowledged that sovereign states impede the absolute liberty of citizens, leading some to declare government a "necessary evil." The classical anarchist theorists differed from liberals precisely in their belief that government was not only unjust but also *unnecessary*.[32] Social anarchists based this faith on their view of human nature and their interpretation of recent social trends. Pushing back against social Darwinist ideas that saw life as an unrelenting battle between classes and races, Kropotkin sought to prove that "mutual aid" among members of the same species was as important as competition in the struggle to survive in nature—and thus concern for others was equally a part of the human condition.[33]

Drawing on Enlightenment thought and on the nineteenth century's scientific optimism, anarchists insisted that humans were perfecting their use of reason and thereby discovering "laws of nature" that ordered the physical environment. Similarly, natural laws could harmoniously order human society if they were widely known. Anarchists believed that people would increasingly come to practice "moral self-government" in accordance with these laws, removing the need for external authority.[34] To detractors who saw this as dangerously naive, the anarchists argued that social context significantly shaped human behavior. The inequitable social order in which they currently lived exacerbated humans' antisocial tendencies, but an egalitarian society would reduce such impulses to a minimum. In their view, humans were not solely and essentially altruistic, but had unrealized potential for kindness and cooperation that was held in check by a social system that needlessly created false scarcity and violent conflict.[35] Anarchists pointed to the growth of institutions such as libraries, scientific societies, and social clubs as indicators that humans were increasingly organizing themselves, voluntarily, to accomplish their goals.[36]

In place of sovereign states, the anarchists agreed, workers should collectively self-manage their economic enterprises. From Proudhon forward, anarchists touted the benefits of a "federal" structure, in which workplaces or small communities would agree on how to run their affairs and then contract agreements with similar workgroups and communities further afield to accomplish tasks requiring more people or resources not locally available, always reserving a right to secede and go it on their own. Contrary to popular assumptions, then, anarchist theorists believed organizations to be necessary. However, they asserted that *voluntary* organizations were sufficient and suggested that responsibilities should be dispersed, rotated, or otherwise made accountable to the whole, as a means of minimizing the corrupting power of authority.[37]

As early as the 1870s, they sought to practice these principles in their own organizations. Referring to the International Workingmen's Association—which he was struggling, against Karl Marx, to lead—Bakunin wrote, "How can we expect an egalitarian and free society to emerge from an authoritarian organization? Impossible. The International, as the embryo of the human society of the future, is required in the here and now to faithfully mirror our principles of freedom and federation and shun any principle leaning towards authority and dictatorship."[38]

Anarchists touted the benefits of free agreement, but said little about how disagreement would be managed. Since they saw repression as government's overriding task, most viewed democratic deliberation as unnecessary. Imagining a postrevolutionary society, the German American anarchist Max Baginski asserted, "From the governing mania the foundation will be withdrawn; for those strata in society will be lacking which theretofore had grown rich and fat by monopolizing the earth and its production. They alone needed legislatures to make laws against the disinherited."[39] Moreover, nineteenth-century anarchists paid little attention to international relations beyond calling for the dissolution of borders. Though they denounced imperialism, they did not offer a systematic account of the ways in which power functioned at scales greater than the nation-state, nor did they indicate how an anarchist society might defend itself against external attack.[40] As we will see, anarchist analysis of sexual and racial oppression remained skeletal until the early twentieth century.

Given these goals and these views on human nature, what was to be done? The anarchists' strategic thinking was informed by the restiveness of the poor in Europe and Russia during the nineteenth century, and by the modes of revolutionary action common to the French Revolution of 1789, the revolutions of 1848, and the Paris Commune of 1871. Each of these momentous events was characterized by a semispontaneous insurrection in which poor people used weapons to disrupt daily life in cities and to attack police and institutions of authority.[41] Anarchists also found inspiration in the late-nineteenth-century Russian nihilists and populists who, operating under conditions of extreme repression, organized conspiratorial cells that assiduously plotted to assassinate the czar and his officials, with hopes that such attacks would inspire, or "trigger," peasant uprisings.

When mass uprisings did occur, they frequently caught radicals off guard, but nevertheless buoyed their hopes and structured the ways they anticipated change would occur.[42] Anarchists analogized revolutions to weather patterns, which were hard to forecast with any precision. Yet because they believed inequality was increasing and workers were steadily becoming aware of alternatives, they firmly held that revolution would break out soon—within a few years. When it did, they were sure, life would change quickly and dramatically. This instilled a strategic and temporal imagination that implicitly divided anarchists' lives into three periods—before, during, and after the revolution—and provided a sense of real hope that, despite current sorrows, things would soon be better. Expressive of this faith, Lucy Robins Lang titled her autobiography *Tomorrow Is Beautiful*.

It was the responsibility of anarchists, then, to speed along the process of the poor becoming conscious and overcoming their fears. When the time came they would, according to the plan, steer the course of the revolutionary upheaval around pitfalls that had mired previous upsurges. Despite this focus on confrontation, many anarchists continued to see a role for the types of cooperative enterprises and intentional communities promoted by utopian socialists in the first half of the nineteenth century. This reflected the abiding influence of Proudhon, who hoped the creation of parallel institutions, such as a Bank of the People, could offset workers' dependence on capitalist institutions, draining the latter of their power. Anarchists believed that cooperatives and "colonies" could prove to fellow workers that, in contemporary parlance, "another world is possible." Given these models, early-twentieth-century U.S. anarchists generally agreed that they should practice mutual aid in their personal lives while working to convince their

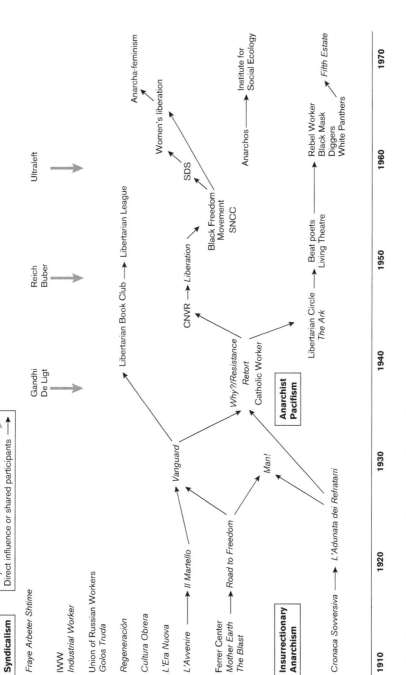

Timeline of key developments in twentieth-century U.S. anarchism.

fellow workers of the merits of a revolutionary strategy and preparing them to act.

CLASS-STRUGGLE STRATEGIES

Since the time of the Haymarket Affair, anarchists in the United States (and elsewhere) had struggled to hone a strategy that moved sufficient numbers of working people to both develop oppositional consciousness and act to fundamentally restructure their lives. During the 1880s and 1890s, many had placed hope in "propaganda of the deed," a strategy in which small, informal groups of anarchists sought to assassinate heads of state and other "class enemies." They believed that such attacks would demonstrate the vulnerability of authority figures and inspire mass insurrections by resentful but previously intimidated workers.[43] By the end of the century, however, it was becoming apparent that propaganda of the deed prompted intense, sweeping repression of anarchists, exposed the movement to agent provocateurs, and alienated working people more often than it inspired them.[44]

In the early 1900s some European anarchists abandoned the insurrectionary strategy and returned to building revolutionary trade unions, or syndicates, as Bakunin had done in the 1870s, with hopes of developing stronger ties to working-class communities. These anarcho-syndicalists encouraged workers to fight for concessions in the short term while building the capacity to stage a general strike that would topple capitalism and parliamentary government later on. The unions themselves, practicing forms of power-sharing and accountable leadership, would serve as the foundation for the "self-management" of industry and society in general.

After 1905, groups of anarchists active in the United States pursued insurrectionary and syndicalist strategies simultaneously. During the same years, a bohemian anarchism that emphasized cultural transformation also emerged. These three orientations called for different organizational forms and strategies, creating tensions and disagreements in a movement already partitioned by language and culture.

Anarcho-Syndicalism

In the United States, the shift toward anarcho-syndicalism gained steam with the founding of the Industrial Workers of the World (IWW) in 1905.

The IWW dedicated itself to organizing working people into "one big union" and called for the use of direct action—strikes and workplace sabotage—rather than the electoral strategies promoted by the Socialist Party.[45] The founders expressed the fundamentals of revolutionary unionism in the preamble to the IWW's constitution:

> It is the historic mission of the working class to do away with capitalism. The army of production must be organized, not only for the everyday struggle with capitalists, but also to carry on production when capitalism shall have been overthrown. By organizing industrially we are forming the structure of the new society within the shell of the old.[46]

This might be thought of as a prefigurative organizing practice. As Bakunin had demanded of the International Workingmen's Association (also known as the First International), the IWW's founders believed their organization should function according to the egalitarian and participatory principles that they demanded in the wider world. They intended not only to avoid hypocrisy but also to provide a venue for previously ignored and disenfranchised people to begin *practicing* freedom—implicitly acknowledging that running one's own affairs might require more than simple intuition.

As Salvatore Salerno has argued, "The nature of the influence of anarchist principles and tactics on the industrial union movement was complex and ubiquitous."[47] Native-born and immigrant anarchists participated in the union's founding convention. Some, such as Al Klemensic and Lucy Parsons, explicitly linked the new organization's strategy to the independent, militant unionism practiced by the Chicago anarchists before the Haymarket Affair.[48] However, anarchist "Wobblies" (as members of the IWW were known) shared the organization with members of the Socialist Party, Marxists who would later become leading communists, and labor organizers with less precise ideological pedigrees.

The growth of the IWW significantly enhanced the U.S. anarchist movement's ability to recruit new participants and influence the course of labor struggles. Anarchists had long criticized the American Federation of Labor (AFL) for its leaders' reformist goals, timidity, and exclusions. In 1906, Max Baginski wrote, "Condemned to pasture in the lean meadows of capitalistic economy, trade unionism drags on a miserable existence, satisfied with the crumbs that fall from the heavily laden tables of their lordly masters. . . . The American Federation of Labor is lobbying in Washington, begging for legal protection, and in return venal Justice sends Winchester rifles and drunken militiamen into the disturbed labor districts."[49] With no viable alternative in sight, anarchists had long encouraged workers to take action on their own. The IWW changed that by providing more concrete guidance and resources, such as traveling organizers and strike funds (meager as these often were). Unlike affiliates of the AFL, the IWW organized workers across divisions of race, nationality, gender, and skill and encouraged collaboration with workers in other countries.[50] Although they remained critical of the nonanarchist participants, many influential anarchists encouraged their followers to join the One Big Union. For this reason, recognizing the successes and setbacks of the IWW is necessary in order to comprehend the fate of the anarchist movement in the early twentieth century.

The IWW is best known for its use of workplace sabotage, frequent work stoppages, and advocacy of the general strike tactic, but Wobblies also developed a vibrant cultural movement.[51] Wobbly songs (most notably "Solidarity Forever") became anthems of the U.S. labor movement, but members also produced plays, poetry, and political cartoons that lambasted the wealthy.[52] Wobblies engaged in a series of "free speech fights" throughout the American West between 1908 and 1918 that reverberated in broader struggles to expand freedom of expression.[53] The IWW's promotion of a brash working-class counterculture gelled with the oppositional cultures and communities that German and Italian radical immigrants had cultivated for more than twenty-five years. This helps explain why many circles of syndicalist-minded anarchists were apt to join the IWW shortly after its formation.[54]

In March 1906, anarchists of Paterson, New Jersey, affiliated with the IWW and placed the union's logo on the masthead of their newspaper, *La Questione Sociale* (The social question). This collaboration led the IWW to launch twenty-four strikes in Paterson that year alone, preparing the ground for the momentous garment worker's strike of 1913. After *La Questione Sociale* was suppressed by the federal government in 1908, it was revived under the name *L'Era Nuova* (The new era) and served as a leading voice for union-oriented Italian anarchists, reaching a circulation of approximately three thousand copies per issue—a third of them read by supporters in the Paterson area.[55]

Carlo Tresca, the most influential organizer of Italian laborers in the United States, declared himself an anarcho-syndicalist in 1914.[56] Born to a landowning family in central Italy, Tresca became a socialist agitator and fled the country at the age of twenty-five to avoid imprisonment. Debonair and genial, Tresca worked closely with the IWW on some of its most decisive strikes, such as the 1912 Lawrence textile strike and the 1916 Mesabi Range strike. His newspaper, *L'Avvenire* (The future), complemented *L'Era Nuova* as a prominent mouthpiece for revolutionary unionism among Italians, reaching a circulation of approximately four thousand copies per issue before World War I.[57]

Anarchists from Russia, too, embraced syndicalism in the early twentieth century. After the abortive 1905 revolution against czarism, a wave of exiles settled in North America and established the Union of Russian Workers of the United States and Canada.[58] By 1912 the union had pronounced itself an anarcho-syndicalist organization; in its eleven years of existence, it grew to an estimated four thousand to ten thousand members organized into approximately fifty local chapters. It published a monthly newspaper, *Golos Truda* (The voice of labor), and established social and educational centers such as the Russian People's House in New York City.[59] Like the Italian syndicalists, the Union of Russian Workers developed close ties with the IWW, and leading figures such as Vladimir "Bill" Shatoff sought to recruit workers into both organizations.

While some Russian Jews affiliated with the Union of Russian Workers, others gravitated to Yiddish-speaking circles that read the weekly newspaper *Fraye Arbeter Shtime* (The free voice of labor).[60] The paper was edited by Saul Yanovsky, a hardworking but tactless orator who had organized Jewish anarchists in London before taking on responsibilities with the *Fraye Arbeter Shtime*. After professed anarchist Leon Czolgosz assassinated President McKinley in 1901, Yanovsky convinced the majority of Jewish American anarchists to reject propaganda of the deed in favor of nonviolent trade union, educational, and cooperative activity. A willingness to participate in unions affiliated with the AFL also distinguished Jewish anarchists from those of other nationalities.[61] Although criticized as insufficiently confrontational by other anarchists, this strategy proved attractive to large numbers of Yiddish-speaking immigrants; New York City alone was home to at least ten Jewish anarchist groups, and the *Fraye Arbeter Shtime* reached a circulation of more than twenty thousand copies *per week* in the decade before the First World War.[62]

The second decade of the twentieth century also witnessed the rise of Spanish-speaking anarchist communities in the United States. In the northeast, immigrants from Spain often socialized with the more numerous Italian anarchist communities. Pedro Esteve, an organizer hailing from Barcelona, married an Italian immigrant, Maria Roda, and recruited Spanish- and Italian-speaking dockworkers for the IWW while editing the monthly

Cultura Obrera (Workers' culture).[63] Esteve also tried to build a movement among Cuban cigar workers in Ybor City, Florida, but was run out of town by conservative vigilantes.

Efforts on the East Coast were greatly overshadowed by the initiatives of Spanish-speaking anarchists in northern Mexico and the American Southwest. There, anarchism grew out of the broader movement seeking to replace the dictatorship of Porfirio Díaz with a liberal democracy. To escape prosecution, leading liberal agitators, including Enrique and Ricardo Flores Magón, took refuge in the United States after 1904. The Magóns were born to modest means, but Ricardo completed law school before launching the newspaper *Regeneración* (Regeneration).

After the Magóns and other members of the Partido Liberal Mexicano established ties with radicals and labor organizers in the United States, their politics moved swiftly to the left. The organization built support for massive strikes in the copper mining industry and planned a series of abortive insurrections along the Texas border, earning the conspirators time in American prisons. Yet by 1910, *Regeneración* was read on both sides of the border by upward of thirty thousand farm laborers, miners, and other poor Mexicans, and it openly advocated anarchist politics and called for international working-class revolution.

When the Mexican Revolution broke out in November, the exiles and their allies launched a military expedition to occupy the cities of Mexicali, Tecate, and Tijuana, with the intent of establishing anarchist communes based on Kropotkin's vision. Routed by troops of the new republican government, the Magón brothers continued publishing *Regeneración* from Los Angeles, nurturing an anarchist movement among ethnic Mexicans in both countries.[64] Anarchists in other parts of the United States avidly followed the crisis in Mexico as it simultaneously put syndicalist and insurrectionary strategies to the test.

Insurrectionary Anarchism

Although interest in building revolutionary unions spread quickly after the IWW was established, anarcho-syndicalism did not completely displace the insurrectionary strategy that relied heavily on propaganda of the deed. In the early twentieth century, insurrectionary anarchism was promoted most eloquently and stridently in the United States by Luigi Galleani, an Italian militant in his fifties who had spent much of his adult life in exile or prison.

Cronaca Sovversiva (Subversive chronicle), the newspaper Galleani published from Barre, Vermont, reached a circulation of approximately five thousand, and small groups of Italian insurrectionists established themselves in dozens of cities and mining towns throughout the Northeast, the Midwest, and California.[65]

Galleani spurned the strategy of helping workers win immediate improvements in their lives, claiming such reforms would be short-lived and would only stabilize the system. In a major statement of his politics, Galleani wrote, "Since the anarchists value reforms for what they are—the ballast the bourgeoisie throws overboard to lighten its old boat in the hope of saving the sad cargo of its privileges from sinking in the revolutionary storm—they have no particular interest in them except to discredit their dangerous mirage, for they are sure that social reforms will come anyway, faster, more often and more radically, as attacks against the existing social institutions become more forceful and violent."[66] This thinking led him to encourage anarchists to engage in propaganda of the deed, retributive violence against authority figures, and acts of banditry and individual expropriation until accumulated resentment had pushed the broader population to insurrection.

As Vincenzo Ferrero, one of his associates, explained, "Galleani was not an individualist but was opposed to formal organization. He was for spontaneous cooperation and spontaneous action."[67] Galleani felt that anarchist federations and labor unions that delegated specific powers and responsibilities to members would suffer from the same corrupting tendencies as states. He had also witnessed the ways in which formal, public organizations had attracted police infiltration and repression in Italy.[68] Moreover, while syndicalists saw their unions as embryonic institutions of the new society, Galleani asserted that revolutionaries could not and *should* not predict the form that postrevolutionary social structures would take until after the event itself. He firmly believed that ordinary people would intuitively know how to live equitably and peacefully once the corrupting institutions of the state and capitalism had been dismantled.

For these reasons, *Cronaca Sovversiva* readers were often labeled "antiorganizational" anarchists. Nevertheless, they formed tight-knit communities of self-selecting individuals who worked closely with one another over long stretches of time, communities that proved nearly impossible for police and government agents to infiltrate.[69] Within these communities, Galleani was treated with such reverence, and proved such a domineering presence, that *Cronaca Sovversiva* readers were frequently called "Galleanists" in spite of the anarchist antipathy for designating leaders. In these ways, the Italian insur-rectionaries experienced both the benefits and the consequences of the small-group model: increased internal security on the one hand, and challenges associated with isolation and unofficial leadership on the other.

In short, both anarcho-syndicalists and insurrectionary anarchists focused on overturning class oppression, but they held opposing views on matters of strategy and organization.[70] Furthermore, while insurrectionists advocated proactive violence against class enemies, syndicalists typically extolled the use of violence only in situations of self-defense (although most acknowledged they would need to defend the anticipated general strike with arms). Differences between the two tendencies at times erupted into inter-necine fighting. Galleani and his comrades were rebuked by the IWW when they offered to lead agitation in the Italian community during the 1912 Lawrence textile strike. The choice of Carlo Tresca to lead a campaign to free Wobblies jailed during that conflict spiraled into a long-running polemic, during which Galleani declared, "We will no longer travel on the same path: no longer can you be an anarchist!"[71] At other times, especially when anar-chists faced prosecution, differences were downplayed within the movement, with the intent of maintaining as much unity as possible. Outside the move-ment, the important distinctions between syndicalist and insurrectionary tendencies were largely lost on the public and ignored by security agencies that viewed anarchism as an amorphous, inscrutable threat.

BOHEMIAN ANARCHISM: NEW ALLIES AND EMPHASES

The movement's most effective English-speaking agitators, Emma Goldman and Alexander Berkman, embraced radical unionism after 1905 but never fully repudiated the forms of political violence by which they'd earned their reputations. Russian Jews who had migrated to the United States in the 1880s, Goldman and Berkman both improved their English skills during spells in prison. Goldman became the country's most provocative and tireless anarchist orator during the fourteen years, from 1893 to 1906, that Berkman was incarcerated for the attempted assassination of strikebreaking steel mag-nate Henry Clay Frick.[72] Released from prison in 1906, Berkman gave pow-erful voice, in English, to an anarchism that shared its focus with the Yiddish-, Italian-, Russian-, and Spanish-speaking sectors of the movement, finally making some headway with native-born manual laborers. In 1916 he launched the searing monthly newspaper *The Blast* in San Francisco. However, the growth of anarchism among English speakers owed as much to the innovative appeals Goldman made to wealthier Americans as it did to a redoubling of efforts among tradesmen.

For the first quarter-century of its existence, the U.S. anarchist movement, like its counterparts abroad, had focused on fomenting a revolution to secure economic well-being for workers. Yet anarchists throughout the world found much to admire in the strands of modernist thought and art that shook up intellectual life at the turn of the century. Goldman—an international traveler and voracious reader—digested Nietzsche, Freud, German sexological studies, and realist drama. Each of these thinkers and literatures exposed ways in which social conventions and outmoded ideas restricted the lives of social groups such as women and homosexuals; each called for new modes of inquiry and expanded personal freedoms. Goldman's greatest intellectual contribution was her synthesis of ideas from these fields with traditional anarchist ideology. Her towering reputation owes to her success at building new coalitions of political actors while simultaneously articulating intellectual frameworks. Together, these efforts led U.S. anarchism into unexplored territory. In a piecemeal, exploratory fashion, a third strategic orientation emerged in the U.S. anarchist movement in the fifteen years preceding the First World War. I refer to it as a bohemian anarchism owing to the attention participants placed on sexuality and artistic expression, and to its tendency to attract intellectually inclined, middle-class radicals.[73]

When she was not on the lecture circuit, Goldman lived in Lower Manhattan, near Greenwich Village, which was fast becoming a magnet for creative and free-thinking young people. The premium they placed on communicating personal visions over achieving commercial success, along with their penchant for bucking sexual and sartorial conventions, greatly appealed to her. Goldman founded the journal *Mother Earth* in 1906, explaining that her editorial decisions would "aim for unity between revolutionary effort and artistic expression."[74] Although the journal never achieved the literary standards set by contemporary publications such as *The Masses,* it gave the anarchists a "little magazine" of their own and established Goldman and her collaborators as players in the bohemian intellectual and artistic milieu that bloomed in these years.[75]

The circle of anarchists that produced *Mother Earth* lauded *expression* in many guises: the voicing of unpopular ideas in print and in public oration; the open declaration of carnal desires by women and homosexuals; the right of women to create lives outside of marriage and the home if they so desired; responsiveness to interests communicated by children in the schoolroom and the home; and the expression of emotions and submerged perspectives in the visual arts and drama.

Defending Free Speech

Goldman first developed relationships with progressive reformers through her work to defend freedom of speech and press for radicals. After a professed anarchist assassinated President McKinley in 1901, federal and state governments prohibited anarchists from entering the country and set long jail sentences for anyone advocating the forcible overthrow of the government. These measures compounded the Comstock laws, dating back to 1873, which allowed postal officials to suppress the circulation of "obscene" materials, including information on birth control and sexuality. Goldman became a spokesperson and fund-raiser for the Free Speech League, an organization formed by lawyers and journalists in 1902 to advocate civil liberties and provide council to those arrested for violating speech codes.[76]

Members of the IWW were jailed or assaulted so routinely that the union was forced to organize a series of "free speech fights" between 1907 and 1914 simply to defend the right to openly criticize capitalism. Goldman, herself, was arrested upward of *forty* times for attempting to speak publicly. In response, the group of anarchists who helped publish *Mother Earth* tirelessly organized chapters of the Free Speech League, which appealed to wealthy progressives who believed in upholding basic civil rights.[77] After gaining their admiration, Goldman drew well-positioned allies into other anarchist causes, tapping them frequently for funds and the influence their names could bring to a cause.[78] Anarchists' work to promote civil liberties, therefore, opened space in the public sphere that they needed in order to launch more radical initiatives, while it also built ties to new social groups and enlarged movement coffers.

Exploding Norms of Gender and Sexuality

Goldman also made middle-class allies through her promotion of women's rights. After attending a birth control conference in Paris, Goldman called for the right of women to practice "family limitation." Following her lead, anarchists provided logistical support for Margaret Sanger, the country's most prominent advocate of birth control—printing her pamphlets, for instance, when professional shops refused to do so out of fear of prosecution.[79] Goldman also studied research on homosexuality and became an outspoken defender of same-sex love, lecturing on the topic as early as 1899. Like a variety of other social and individualist anarchists, Goldman believed "the sex organs ... are the property of the individual possessing them, and that the individual and no other must be the sole authority and Judge of his or her acts."[80] Sexual freedom clearly fell within the purview of the anarchists' politics, given their defense of a liberty to act that was limited only by respect for the equal liberty of others. For this reason, the anarchist communities of New York and a number of other locales provided sanctuary and acceptance for gay men and lesbians in a time of near universal hostility toward them.[81]

Though Goldman was respected by many, her iconoclastic gender and sexual politics strained her relations with many feminist contemporaries. As an anarchist communist she categorically rejected the suffragist argument that obtaining the right to vote would lead to the liberation of women. Although her own experiences taught her that economic independence was necessary for women to control their own lives, she was clear that securing the right to perform wage labor in a capitalist work environment was a half measure at best.[82]

Goldman was sometimes accused of promoting individualistic strategies of emancipation. She wrote, for example, that a woman's "development, her freedom, her independence, must come from and through herself." A woman could bring these about by "refusing the right to anyone over her body" and "by freeing herself from the fear of public opinion and public condemnation."[83] Yet, to Goldman, these practices of personal self-definition and assertiveness were only one aspect of the struggle. As Kathy Ferguson has argued, Goldman promoted an analysis of sexual politics that later theorists would describe as "biopolitical."[84] She understood that political elites and business owners each had a stake in regulating the number of children born into a society's various racial groups and social classes. "The defenders of authority," she declared, "dread the advent of a free motherhood, lest it will rob them of their prey. Who would fight wars? Who would create wealth?"[85] To Goldman's mind, the moralistic language of the church worked to obfuscate the fact that social and legal pressures placed these population-level interests above the personal concerns of individuals, encroaching on the way women and men related to their sexual urges and made use of their bodies.

Class and sexual-gender oppression were thus intimately linked in Goldman's theory.

Nevertheless, Goldman was routinely criticized by male anarchists who focused narrowly on class struggle and paid little mind to the nature of their personal relations with women. Despite routine calls for gender equality after the revolution, social anarchists devoted little attention, before the turn of the century, to systematically analyzing patriarchy as a form of power that structured society and their own lives. Even among those living as unmarried couples or sharing apartments with comrades, cleaning and cooking responsibilities generally fell to women.[86] Goldman was not alone in her efforts to change this.[87]

Beginning in 1896, female anarcho-syndicalists established a network of "gruppi femminili di propaganda" in the cities and mining towns where Italian radicals lived.[88] The groups, ranging in size from a few to a few dozen members, were composed of working women, who often tried to incorporate their daughters into their activities. Participants, such as Maria Roda, Ernestina Cravello, and Maria Barbieri, contributed frequently to the anarchist press and produced plays that challenged Catholic morality. The group in Spring Valley, Illinois, argued in the pages of *L'Aurora:* "For the emancipation of women, together with those struggles that must occur in order to attain the rights that all of oppressed humanity demand[,] . . . a woman must struggle with great zeal to emancipate herself from the tyranny and prejudice of men, and from those who foolishly consider women inferior, and often treat her like a slave."[89]

Most participants worked in factories while also performing the bulk of the unpaid reproductive labor, such as cooking and cleaning, required to raise a family. For these women, feminist activism had to challenge the economic system as well as deprecating treatment by men. Most operated at a distance from wealthier feminists, because they saw those women as complicit in the oppression of women of the working classes.[90] In 1905 Maria Barbieri wrote, "We have become human machines who stay locked in the immense industrial prisons where we lose our strength, our health and youth. . . . [And] we don't shake with rage before the pompous and contemptuous lady, who because of us wears a silk skirt from our humble labor?"[91] Goldman associated with these Italian working-class feminists, and their perspectives likely shaped her criticisms of suffrage-centered feminism. Yet, as a self-supporting editor and organizer now fluent in English, Goldman found it easier to transcend these class divisions.

After 1910, Goldman began consciously tailoring some of her lectures to appeal to middle-class audiences. She spoke frequently on the political morals of modern drama, explaining to skeptical comrades that while workers are moved to radical politics by injustices in their own lives, drama served as an important means of helping more privileged intellectuals understand social conditions and reconsider their "relation to the people, to the social unrest permeating the atmosphere." In *Mother Earth,* Goldman argued that artists and professionals were, at base, "intellectual proletarians" who had the ability to make important contributions to the social struggle if they choose to do so. "It is therefore through the co-operation of the intellectual proletarians, who try to find expression, and the revolutionary proletarians who seek to remold life," she wrote, "that we in America will establish a real unity and by means of it wage a successful war against present society."[92] During these years it became common for Goldman to deliver a speech in Yiddish one night and another in English the following evening. Drawing on figures published in *Mother Earth,* Peter Glassgold gives a sense of her reach:

> 1910: 120 lectures in 37 cities in 25 states, before a total of 40,000 people, selling 10,000 pieces of literature, distributing 5,000 free, netting over $5,300 in sales, magazine subscriptions, and paid admissions. 1911: 150 lectures in 50 cities in 18 states, before audiences of up to 1,500 people, a total of 50,000 to 60,000 at the tour's end. 1915: 321 lectures. By her own accounting, Goldman spoke before 50,000 to 75,000 people a year.[93]

Denouncing Racial Violence While Being Racialized

While Goldman served as an important bridge between feminist initiatives and the tradition of immigrant anarchism, her political work was not as far reaching in the struggle to combat white supremacy. Like other anarchists of the prewar period, Goldman regularly denounced lynchings of African Americans and noted the "racial hatred" directed against other groups, such as Chinese immigrants. Yet as Kathy Ferguson has argued, "Goldman usually mentioned race only in passing, to illustrate yet another example of the exploitation of the masses, not as a unique vector of power with its own logic and history."[94] Ferguson suggests that Goldman made sense of racism in the United States primarily by comparing it to the anti-Semitic treatment of Jews in Europe and Russia. From this perspective, racism appeared as another undesirable outgrowth of "Christian civilization" and a convenient means of keeping working people estranged from one another. During the Progressive

Era, Goldman tended to describe African Americans as unfortunate victims rather than as the oppressed but potentially powerful collective agents she believed laborers and women to be. The campaigns for broader political rights and governmental protections pursued by many black citizens, often under the auspices of the church, seem to have struck her as insufficiently revolutionary.[95]

Other sectors of the movement proved more attuned to the centrality of race to the country's development. Italian anarcho-syndicalists articulated strident antiracist and anticolonial critiques. A 1909 article in *L'Era Nuova* argued, "The discovery of America marks the beginning of a period of destruction, which lasts even today for the shame of humanity. The white race continues its systematic destruction of the races of color. When it cannot succeed with violence, it adopts corruption, hunger, alcohol, opium, syphilis, tuberculosis—all weapons as good as guns and cannons." The article acknowledged the centrality of racial oppression to the structure of U.S. American society and hinted at the transformative potential of black freedom struggles: "We believe that within a short time what they call the Negro Problem will give more trouble to the United States, more than they have already had from any other serious issue, even bigger than the Civil War."[96]

Spanish-speaking anarchists, too, regularly addressed racism. Given that their primary U.S. readership consisted of a racialized national minority that had steadily been dispossessed of its land since the end of the Mexican-American War, it is not surprising that the Magón brothers regularly denounced the racist treatment of Mexican Americans. Placing the 1910 lynching of a Mexican man in the context of structural racism, Ricardo Flores Magón cleverly highlighted the constructed character of the idea of savagery. "Mexicans are not admitted to hotels, restaurants, and other public establishments in Texas," he asserted. "How many men of our race have died because a white-skinned savage decided to prove his ability with firearms by shooting at us?—and without having any dispute with us!"[97] Beyond anarchists' written analyses, their most concrete contributions to combating structural racism may have lain in their work of building interracial unions that opposed exclusionary hiring practices and racist wage differentials.

Even those anarchists who denounced structural and personal violence against indigenous peoples and peoples of African and Mexican descent appear unaware of the ways they were implicated in the larger racial system that structured all aspects of life in the United States. Following the massive influx of poor immigrants—first from Ireland, and later from southern and eastern Europe—U.S. citizens established a complex racial system in which recent arrivals held an intermediary position between native-born whites and peoples of color, wherein they were expected to prove their fitness for social inclusion through self-comportment, their treatment of other racial groups, and the beliefs they espoused.[98] As Jewish, Russian, and Italian immigrants, the majority of anarchists in the United States were considered part of these "inbetween people."[99] *As anarchists,* they had an inadvertent but significant role in the establishment of such a racial category in the first place. The antiauthoritarian ideas, political violence, and sexual nonconformism practiced by anarchists became grist for nativists and conservative journalists, who represented the new immigrants, as a whole, as unfit for U.S. citizenship. Such representational practices functioned as part of a larger process of racialization in which inegalitarian social structures and demeaning cultural depictions of social groups developed in a mutually reinforcing manner.[100]

The view of anarchists as European immigrants with a congenital proclivity to violence became a common trope during the Red Scare that followed the Haymarket Affair of 1886, in which a bomb killed police officers attempting to disperse an anarchist rally.[101] Newspaper editors and cartoonists routinely depicted anarchists as animals, infectious pests, and as tools of the devil.[102] When graced with a human form, anarchists were nearly always drawn with dark skin, scraggly beards, a hunched posture, and bulging eyes.[103] While such imagery implied insanity, it also keyed to the era's stock racist depictions of African Americans.[104] Thomas Nast, a cartoonist famous for drawing Irish immigrants as simian-like, helped hone this caricature through his illustrations of the anarchist Johann Most. Nast visually cemented the connection when he created a cover for *Puck* magazine that pictured anarchism as a snake with an ape-like human head.[105] As Kenyon Zimmer has shown, the influential criminologist Cesare Lombroso lent such associations a patina of scientific truth when he "diagnosed the anarchist as a specific 'criminal type' characterized by mental and physical abnormalities, all rooted in biological 'atavism' and therefore heritable."[106]

Publishers revived these racist representations after Leon Czolgosz assassinated President McKinley in 1901, but with a twist.[107] After Czolgosz claimed he was inspired by Goldman's lectures, journalists insisted she had been the mastermind behind the crime. Newspapers alternately depicted her as a devil and a seductress, owing to her notoriety as proponent of "free love."[108] This should not be surprising, as sexual practices have historically formed a primary means by which "white" people have evaluated the civilizational standing of others. Time and again, sexual and familial practices have been deemed dangerous when departing from white middle-class Christian norms, thereby justifying the differential treatment of people of other "races." Given the ways racism structured life in the United States, therefore, anarchists' nonnormative sexual practices, like their embrace of political violence, had repercussions that extended far beyond their own movement.

In the wake of anarchist attacks, the incidence of a threat originating within a group (poor southern and eastern European immigrants) was generalized to an intrinsic quality of the whole, leading to what William Preston Jr. describes as "a fateful and erroneous identification of alien and radical" that would endure for decades.[109] As John Higham wrote over fifty years ago, "The anti-radical tradition remained a major nativist attitude, picturing the foreigner as steeped in anarchism or at least as an incendiary menace to that orderly freedom which Americans alone could supposedly preserve."[110] In this sense, *anarchist* functioned as a racializing term during the nineteenth and early twentieth centuries, when the racial status of European immigrants was uncertain.[111]

Developing Modern Education

In the early decades of the twentieth century, U.S. anarchists pursued educational work with greater élan than they had previously, by speaking eloquently in English, linking anarchism to a wider variety of issues, and creating new institutional platforms for the work of consciousness-raising and the transmission of values. Notably, mainstays of the *Mother Earth* circle, such as Harry Kelly and Leonard Abbott, bolstered anarchist educational and cultural efforts by establishing the Francisco Ferrer Center in 1911. Named after an anarchist educator executed by the Spanish government, the center hosted evening and weekend classes for adults and a day school for the children of radical workers.[112] Ferrer maintained that schools established by church and state officials reproduced class relations and authoritarian values. Yet "modern schools" that supported children's own curiosities and promoted libertarian and cooperative values could help bring a new society into being.[113]

The Ferrer Center served as a meeting ground in which the city's many anarchists groups interacted with one another and the broader Left. On Friday nights, multiethnic crowds of manual laborers and intellectuals packed in to hear talks delivered by famous figures such the lawyer Clarence

Darrow and the muckraking journalist Lincoln Steffens.[114] "Among subjects threshed out," Harry Kelly recalled, "were economics, politics, sex, psychology, psychoanalysis, literature, art, drama, the Single Tax, Socialism, Guild Socialism, Anarchism, and Syndicalism."[115] This burst of activity was paid for, in the main, by wealthy benefactors Goldman had cultivated in her free-speech fights, such as Alden Freeman, an heir to Standard Oil money who, as a gay man, appreciated her lectures on sexuality.[116]

Promoting Artistic Modernism

The Ferrer Center also helped establish artistic modernism in the United States. In Europe, modernist painters such as Pablo Picasso, Camille Pissarro, and Kees van Dongen had established ties to anarchists in the 1890s. The artists incorporated anarchist critiques of wealth inequality, despoliation of nature, and colonialism into paintings intended for bourgeois galleries and into satirical cartoons published in anarchist newspapers.[117] After the turn of the century, like their counterparts abroad, a growing coterie of American artists worked to break the power art academies held in arbitrating what subject matter and which formal techniques qualified a work as fine art.[118] Anarchists supported these efforts, establishing partnerships that would shape the future of their movement as they did so.

Among the leading opponents of academic art in the United States was Robert Henri, a painter inspired by the illustrators of Émile Pouget's scandalous French anarcho-syndicalist journal, *Le Père Peinard*.[119] After befriending Goldman, Henri launched an art seminar at the Ferrer Center in 1911, covering the walls with examples of the new styles and attracting students such as George Bellows, Rockwell Kent, and Man Ray, all of whom later gained recognition as canonical American modernists. Max Weber, a Ferrer Center artist and early proponent of futurist and cubist techniques, encouraged his fellow students at the center to "take time off from the life-[drawing] class," and "go out among the people who toil in the mills and shops, go to scenes of bridge construction, foundries, excavation" to capture the zeitgeist of the times.[120]

Welcomed by anarchists at the Ferrer Center, Greenwich Village bohemians reciprocated by inviting anarchists to literary salons and by lending financial and moral support to workers fighting to unionize. Most famously, Village artists staged the *Paterson Pageant,* a play in which striking silk workers from Paterson, New Jersey, dramatized their struggle before a capacity crowd in Madison Square Garden. Anarchist writers such as Hutchins Hapgood repaid the favor, showering praise on the city's modern artists. While other critics panned the Armory Show of 1913, now credited with introducing European postimpressionism to American audiences, Hapgood defended it as "vital" and compared it to the IWW's attempts to overthrow "old forms and traditions."[121] Similar collaborations between artists and anarchists also bloomed in Chicago and rural "artists colonies," such as Provincetown, Massachusetts.[122]

In this way *anarchism* became a byword for fearless, innovative expression, and artists saw anarchists as allies and a source of inspiration, even if they rarely adopted anarchist ideas *tout court*.[123] As a result, some anarchists began to view avant-garde cultural expression and innovative forms of education as strategies for inculcating libertarian and egalitarian values that might supplement, if not entirely supplant, older models of change. In 1916, though, these cultural strategies were only emergent tendencies in the broader anarchist movement. Promotion of sexual, artistic, and educational freedom was just beginning to elbow in on the issue of economic injustice and the strategies of syndicalism and insurrection.

A crisis that occurred in 1914 suggests the challenges of integrating these forms of struggle. That summer, while painters daubed canvases and school-children played games on the first floor of the Ferrer Center, Berkman and a half dozen associates met in the center's basement to plot an attack on the suburban mansion of John D. Rockefeller, whom they held responsible for the April massacre of striking miners in Ludlow, Colorado. However, on the Fourth of July, three anarchists and a bystander died when the bomb that the three were preparing in a nearby apartment house accidentally exploded.[124]

The response to this incident indicated the depth of class antagonism during this period. Some twenty thousand people attended a memorial rally in Union Square to honor those who lost their lives. From the dais, Berkman and others boldly endorsed the type of political violence their expired comrades had intended to carry out. Clearly, anarchism proved attractive to a significant swath of society, and, in the face of the brutal repression of unionists, thousands of people saw retributive political violence as acceptable, perhaps even necessary.

Yet despite the facade of unity at the memorial, Harry Kelly and others who ran the Ferrer Center were growing weary of armed attacks and recognized that it was unwise to hold elementary school classes a few feet above a room used to plan acts of terrorism. In response, Kelly hatched a plan to move the school to a more serene environment outside the city. To pay for the school, anarchists would collectively buy a piece of farmland and carve it into residential plots, leaving a few acres for the school at the center. As we will see in chapter 3, this dream came to fruition in the spring of 1915 with the creation of the Stelton Colony near present-day New Brunswick, New Jersey.[125]

STRATEGY AND THEORIES OF POWER

Although immediate danger was averted by moving the Modern School out of the city, the underlying tensions in the anarchist movement were not so easy to solve. As early as 1908, Kelly voiced a broadly shared concern that the English-speaking sector was growing detached from the foreign-language sectors and becoming "a movement for individual self-expression rather than collective revolution." He worried that "instead of participating in the trade unions, organizing the unemployed, or indulging in soap box oratory, we rent comfortable halls and charge ten cents admission."[126]

Kelly was hardly alone in his class-centric thinking; his perspective was dominant among anarchists and was a defining feature of the pre–World War II "old left" more broadly. The anarchist Kate Wolfson recalled that in the second decade of the twentieth century, she and her sister "went to Emma Goldman's lectures on drama and birth control, which we regarded as secondary issues. We were fiery young militants and more concerned with economic and labor issues, and we resented her dwelling on such things as theater."[127] This was not entirely fair criticism, since many anarchists managed to support workers' struggles *and* reach out to wealthier audiences in this period. Perhaps a deeper problem was that the new emphases chaffed against a variety of assumptions at the heart of anarchist social theory.

Berkman, for instance, regularly published news and analysis about Goldman and Sanger's birth control efforts in *The Blast*. Yet he felt the need to frame and delimit agitation around gender inequality for readers. In a short article criticizing the suffrage movement, he wrote, "It is not woman, as a sex, that is the victim of existing conditions. It is only the *working* woman—exactly as the working man."[128] Reproductive freedom, he implied, was a worthy cause only insofar as it aided working-class women and provided leverage in the class struggle. But by focusing on realms of expressive freedom, Goldman and her collaborators not only discovered new middle- and upper-class constituencies for the movement but also added novel layers of complexity to anarchists' notions of how power operates, what freedom entails, and what forms of action are most suited to bringing about change.

Without abandoning class issues, Goldman and the Italian anarchist feminists had begun to craft an analysis that suggested male domination functioned in unique ways and emanated from individuals and institutions additional to the sources of class domination. Implicit in such a view was the idea that anarchists would need to develop new strategies and tactics to address these forms of oppression if they were truly committed to their core values of liberty, equality, and solidarity. Put differently, twenty-first-century U.S. anarchists would criticize Kelly for propounding a "class reductionist" rather than an "intersectional" analysis that understood domination to occur simultaneously on a variety of axes—namely, those of class, race, gender, and sexuality—in ways that reinforced one another.

Kelly's question about whether social change demanded the concerted effort of "masses" of people acting in unison, or whether it could be affected through the piecemeal efforts of individuals and small groups, also relates to this issue. Implicit in his advocacy of the former position lay an understanding of the conditions of freedom and unfreedom based in class relations under capitalism. Since it was nearly impossible for propertyless workers to support themselves outside of a capitalist economy, structural transformation was seen as the only realistic way to achieve economic freedom. Taking class conflict as the implicit model for all freedom struggles, however, ignored the possibility that efforts seeking other dimensions of liberty, such as gender equality, might offer rebels greater room for maneuvering within the current system.

In a broader sense, Goldman's advocacy of gender and sexual freedom aligned with her circle's support for libertarian pedagogies and artistic modernism. We might interpret each of these campaigns as efforts to resist what, following the French theorist Michel Foucault, are now often referred to as disciplinary modes of power. Anarchists challenged the right of clergy, doctors, lawyers, and politicians to define which physical acts and romantic attachments were recognized as moral, healthy, and legal (and thereby, *normal*) and which ones were to be shunned, shamed, and punished as *abnormal*.[129] Likewise, the defense of modernist styles of art challenged the authority of art academies to pronounce realistic representation and bourgeois subject matter to be the only acceptable—and therefore economically viable—measures of achievement.

Following the 1913 Armory Show, reviewers routinely described modernist painting and sculpture as "perverse" and "degenerate" art—precisely the same medicalizing and moralizing discourse applied to homosexuals and anarchists themselves.[130] Such uses of expert knowledge to classify, distinguish, and privilege certain people and practices over others constituted a different, somewhat more subtle, technique for exerting power than the techniques anarchists had tended to discuss—namely, that of policemen bringing wooden truncheons to bear on the skulls of striking workers. By beginning to explore the ways social domination is reproduced psychologically and in the realm of implicit and explicit cultural norms, then, this sector of the movement was broadening, rather than narrowing, the struggle against oppressive forms of coercive authority.

Anarchists had traditionally seen power as something exercised by people outside of the anarchist community. The turn to matters of gender and sexuality, however, led some to reconsider their relations with their parents, spouses, and comrades. The Italian American anarcha-feminist Titì, for example, asserted in 1906 that "the axiom of domination begins at birth when a girl learns her place in life." Such thinking led Camillo Di Sciullo to remark to his comrades: "Don't you know that the first campaign to do is that of the family? Build a little anarchist world within your family and you will be able to see how it strengthens, how it becomes easier to launch other campaigns!"[131] The idea that anarchists would need to alter their own behavior, and that the movement should function as a model of the future anarchist society, became increasingly prominent as the century wore on. Such ideas, when followed to their logical conclusion, contributed new cracks in the foundational belief that a fast-approaching revolution would usher in a realm of freedom in near-millennial fashion.

Though shortsighted in some ways, Kelly's critique did presciently warn against the tendency, which grew later in the century, for some purported anarchists to simply live their own lives in as free a fashion as their social status allowed (as "bohemians," "dropouts," or "punks") without investing themselves in struggles to create lasting structural transformations that would increase security and life options for the least well off. He thereby acknowledged the challenges of establishing a coalition of political actors who inhabit different social positions through use of a few broad watchwords, such as *freedom*.[132]

In summary, the first fifteen years of the twentieth century represented a period of great dynamism for the anarchist movement in the United States. It reached a numerical zenith in these years, owing significantly to the organizing vehicle provided by the IWW. Drawing on new intellectual resources, anarchists also began to broaden their understanding of power and their critique of existing society. The demographic composition of the movement began to change accordingly, as middle class and wealthy individuals became involved. Anarchists also added cultural transformation, or "culture war," to their strategic repertoires, which had previously been limited to syndicalism and insurrectionism. Whereas nineteenth-century anarchists had developed noncommercial folk countercultures within their ethnic communities (and in their native languages), early-twentieth-century anarchists began to engage in the realm of high culture. Their intellectual collaborations with artists who explicitly arrayed themselves against bourgeois values set the stage for the succession of revolutionary avant-garde cultural movements that shaped the twentieth-century Left in fundamental ways. In retrospect, however, the new directions U.S. anarchists began exploring appear to constitute something of a false start.

The diversity of language groups, class backgrounds, issues, and strategies at play in the Progressive Era presented significant obstacles to movement coherency and unity of action. More immediately, the outbreak of the First World War provided an opportunity for the anarchists' many opponents to engage in an all-out effort to crush them. Losing some of its most innovative thinkers to exile, and facing a series of domestic and international crises, the anarchist movement retreated from its prewar engagements with gender, sexuality, and art. These would not become vital to anarchist politics again until the mid-1940s.

TWO

The Red and Black Scare,
1917–1924

When Mollie Steimer and Ella Antolini joined the anarchist movement in 1916, it was fast growing, intellectually dynamic, and ingrained in the daily lives of their friends, family, and neighbors. In social background, Steimer and Antolini were fairly typical recruits. Both had immigrated to the United States with their families in 1913—Steimer from Russia and Antolini from Italy. Mollie, a bright-eyed fifteen-year-old, whose dark hair fell in tight ringlets, immediately went to work as a sewing machine operator in a New York City dress factory to help her family pay rent. Ella, petite and outgoing, was afforded a year of elementary school before she, too, was compelled to take a factory position, in New Britain, Connecticut, at age fourteen.[1] Although the girls had little formal schooling, they spent their formative years immersed in politicized immigrant communities that placed a high value on self-education.

Ella's brother, Alberto, subscribed to *Cronaca Sovversiva,* the Italian-language anarchist newspaper published in Vermont by Luigi Galleani. Alberto's friends—including August "Gugu" Segata, whom Ella married in 1916—were members of the Gruppo I Liberi, one node in a network of Italian insurrectionary groups that extended throughout the Northeast and into the Midwest.[2] Ella immersed herself in the activities of this community, acting in the radical plays produced by anarchist *filodrammatica* groups.

Steimer, meanwhile, discovered that many of the young women who drove New York City's garment industry were avid readers of radical social theory. The labor historian Melech Epstein recounts that in the second decade of the twentieth century it was common to see young women queuing up at factory time-clocks with tomes by Karl Marx and Peter Kropotkin tucked under their arms.[3] It was while reading the latter's book, *The Conquest of Bread,* that Steimer first encountered the vision of a world in which workers were their own bosses that went by the name "anarchism."[4] Soon she found her way to social events organized by the Union of Russian Workers and lectures at the Ferrer Center in Harlem. The ideals she learned in these venues spoke to her deeply.

For all the community, purpose, and education the movement offered workers like Steimer and Antolini, 1916 was a particularly dangerous year to become an anarchist. The decision to plunge into anarchist politics would soon cost each young woman dearly. The United States' entrance into the Great War provided authorities with an urgency and an opportunity to curb the mushrooming influence of various movements seeking the redistribution of power and wealth. Anarchists, who were becoming more sophisticated organizers and public speakers while still refusing to eschew political violence, became prime targets of a multipronged counterinsurgency operation that began in 1917 and lasted for five years.

Most U.S.-based anarchists fiercely opposed the brutal conflict known today as the First World War. Early on, anarchists predicted that conscription and other war-related hardships would prompt working-class uprisings within the warring states. Dread of mass casualties, then, was counterbalanced by anticipation of revolutionary insurgency. "Behind the catastrophe," wrote Ricardo Flores Magón, "Liberty smiles."[5] Such hopes were greatly magnified by the outbreak of the Russian Revolution in 1917, leading some anarchists, including Steimer and Antolini, to go all out when choosing how to respond, tactically, to conscription, press censorship, and police repression of their activities.

Yet the anarchists misjudged the balance of forces. As American soldiers departed for the trenches, a growing nativist and antiradical fury arose alongside a legal net that authorities wove to constrain and excise anarchist, socialist, and syndicalist war resistance. "Throughout the country," historian Paul Avrich recounts, "anarchist clubhouses were raided, men and women beaten, equipment smashed, libraries and files seized and destroyed."[6] Anarchists, more than any other group, resisted such attacks. Some struggled to circulate their ideas in print, no matter how difficult and what the consequences. Others responded with violence of their own, leading to an escalating cycle of repression and reprisal. By 1921, however, the tide of reaction had rolled back many of the advances made by radicals in earlier years. Although the movement itself survived, the momentum anarchists had built over the previous decade did not.

The story of this conflict, often designated the Red Scare of 1917–1921, has been told many times, and in more detail than space allows for here.[7] My primary concern is to compare the different avenues taken by ethnically and strategically distinguished subgroups of anarchists during these years and to demonstrate the ways in which political and social developments tied to the war shaped postwar anarchist practices. It is clear, as many scholars have argued, that the destruction of vital institutions and resources, alongside the imprisonment and deportation of key organizers, starkly diminished the movement's capacity. Placing the Red Scare in a broader frame, however, exposes the ways in which the conflicts of this period also led to changes at the levels of state formation and social structure, which in turn shaped the postwar fortunes of U.S. anarchism as significantly as warrantless arrests and the destruction of mailing lists.

Specifically, I suggest that antiradicalism, paired with wartime economic contingencies, opened the door to an overhaul in immigration policy that fundamentally revamped the ethnic and racial character of the U.S. working class. This cut off the most significant source of prewar recruits to the anarchist movement: southern and eastern Europeans. In other words, there would be far fewer Mollie Steimers and Ella Antolinis in the 1920s and 1930s. These altered conditions also promoted the growth of a new constituency of urban industrial workers, whom anarchists were not prepared to organize: African Americans. This meant that the conservative offensive during and immediately following the First World War grew into an effort not only to repress radicals but also to decompose the working class as a whole.[8]

ANARCHISTS AND WORLD WAR I

Conventional histories claim that the Great War, which engulfed Europe between 1914 and 1918, was the fault of an anarchist—one Gavrilo Princip, who assassinated the archduke of Austria, Franz Ferdinand. In fact, Princip was a Yugoslav nationalist, not an anarchist, and deep-seated national rivalries, economic competition, and republican longings structured the simmering conflicts that erupted into mechanized war, eventually claiming the lives of over 9 million people. Fighting raged in Europe for more than two years before American military forces intervened. When Austria declared war on Serbia in July 1914, U.S. anarchists, employers, and government officials were preoccupied with Progressive Era domestic conflicts. The National Guard had massacred the Ludlow, Colorado, miners in April, and the bomb intended for John D. Rockefeller, as retribution, detonated on July 4, killing the New York anarchists who had built it. As class tensions roiled, intellectuals continued to debate the artistic revolution presaged by the previous year's Armory Show and medical professionals challenged laws restricting the distribution of birth control information.

Yet involvement in the war, in one fashion or another, was unavoidable. President Wilson touted his noninterventionist stance while campaigning for reelection in 1916, but he simultaneously initiated a nationwide campaign of "preparedness," including armament manufacture and military drilling. A revitalized patriotism built on racial animus became the order of the day, as journalists and politicians demanded "100 percent Americanism" from citizens and resident aliens alike. Most members of the international anarchist movement, meanwhile, denounced the metastasizing conflict—Russia, Germany, Britain, Belgium, and France, had piled on by August—as the clearest example yet of the dangers posed by the values undergirding bourgeois life: greed, domination, nationalism, and militarism.

In May 1915, luminaries of the international movement, including Emma Goldman, Alexander Berkman, Bill Shatoff, and others based in the United States, issued a manifesto on the war. Though disgusted by the "butchery," they were not surprised. The statement argued that "armed conflict, restricted or widespread, colonial or European, is the natural consequence" of a society built on class oppression. Moreover, "none of the belligerents [was] entitled to invoke the name of civilization or to declare itself in a state of legitimate defense," since all had pursued "a ceaseless increase in the budgets of death" and were either masters of far-flung colonial empires or brutally repressive of their own people.[9]

Anarchists claimed that the war only served to benefit the rich, and they linked conscription to other means by which elites denied the autonomy of working people. Writing in Berkman's newspaper, *The Blast,* in early 1916, Reb Rainey applauded Margaret Sanger's recent fight to decriminalize birth control information and tied women's right to control reproduction to the antiwar effort: "Too long has woman moistened the world with blood gifts wrung from her unwilling frame.... She has received, sustained, brought forth endlessly, for what? For 'the new crop,' as Bismarck called the new edition of infant soldiers-to-be, after the Franco-Prussian war. And this because the printed words, 'prevention of contraception' have been labeled unspeakably vile by the very ones who trade on the workability of the process." The

July 1916 cover of *The Blast* featured a political cartoon composed of a cannon labeled "Preparedness" aimed at a crowd of workers carrying picket signs inscribed with the demand "The full product of our labor." Elimination of the radical labor movement was "the real purpose of preparedness."[10]

Yet the war also gave succor to many anarchists. Shortly after the fighting began, Ricardo Flores Magón wrote in *Regeneración:* "Let us hope that governments and the bourgeoisie will be weakened by this stupid war, and that this will facilitate our triumph. The good should flee this war and prepare themselves for the one to come: the class war." By September 1915, Magón was certain that the burdens of war would provoke the confrontations anarchists had long urged. "The great battles in the trenches will end on the barricade and with the mutinies of the rebelling people, and the national flags will fall, giving place to the red banner of all the disinherited of the world," he assured readers. Luigi Galleani agreed, passionately declaring in one stump speech after another that anarchists were, according to one motto, "Against the war, against the peace, for the revolution!"[11]

While Goldman, Magón, and Galleani spoke for most anarchists, opposition to the war was not unanimous. Peter Kropotkin shocked the international movement by endorsing the Allies' military campaign shortly after the fighting began. The doyen of anarcho-communism felt that Germany's militarism and authoritarian national culture posed serious threats to liberties won throughout other parts of Europe, and therefore he urged anarchists to help defeat it. He found support from a number of influential antistatists throughout Europe, including Jean Grave and James Guillaume.[12] After some equivocation, the New York–based Yiddish weekly *Fraye Arbeter Shtime,* too, adopted Kropotkin's position. In doing so it became the only major anarchist periodical in the United States to support the war, earning considerable enmity from other factions in the process.[13]

Unlike in Europe, where the social democratic parties famously abandoned their antimilitarist, internationalist stance, the major organizations of the U.S. Left, including the Socialist Party and the Industrial Workers of the World (IWW), remained outspokenly opposed to the war alongside the majority of the anarchists. They were also joined by a contingent of pacifists who criticized the war and pledged not to fight. Many pacifists were members of historic peace churches—such as the Quakers, Mennonites, and Brethren—while others were feminists who linked war with masculine personality traits.[14]

The Left's call for a class solidarity that cut across national allegiances was anathema to the patriotic sentiment that swelled when the United States entered the war. Opinion leaders took opposition to the war seriously, worrying that it could impede the process of raising an army and producing war matériel. They also feared domestic sabotage with intent to aid the enemy, after calculating that more than 4.6 million people living in the United States had been born in the countries constituting the Central Powers.[15] Yet the war also presented opportunities for business owners to challenge the growing militancy of labor unions and for other conservative groupings to further their agendas. Since the United States' productive capacity was harnessed to the needs of the military during the war, factory and mine owners argued that strikes threatened national security and therefore justified the intervention of federal authorities, military personnel, private guards, and citizens groups to defeat them. Churches and anti-vice organizations relished the opportunity to silence radicals who had made a game of flouting moral codes, while opponents of women's suffrage jumped at the chance to link feminist demands with threats to national security.[16] Some native-born workers, likewise, used the politically polarized environment to limit the numbers of racialized working people—both from the South and from southern Europe—moving into their neighborhoods and places of employment.

The Wilson administration, in collaboration with these powerful constituencies, seized on the determined antiwar stand of the Left to reign in a whole series of efforts to make social and political life more egalitarian. The president warned citizens of "the passions and intrigues of certain active groups and combinations of men amongst us who were born under foreign flags" and who "injected the poison of disloyalty into our most critical affairs, [and] laid violent hands upon many of our industries."[17] Together, this coalition of interests enacted a complex—though not always coordinated—campaign of class decomposition that severely undercut the power of the organized Left and enabled a reorganization of the country's class structure and racial order. The process began with one of the most extraordinary assaults on freedom of expression in the nation's history.

THE ESPIONAGE AND SEDITION ACTS AND THE IMMIGRATION ACT OF 1917

Events moved quickly during the first months of 1917. In March, strikes and demonstrations provoked by wartime suffering in Russia cascaded into a revolutionary situation in which Czar Nicholas II abdicated and a provisional liberal government was established. The uprising fulfilled the anarchists' prophecies of wartime revolution; they were also elated to learn that Russian workers had established workplace and citywide soviets (decision-making councils) that shared the self-managing ethos of anarcho-syndicalism. On April 6, the United States entered the war on the side of the Allies after intercepting a German telegram encouraging Mexico to join the Central Powers and reclaim its former territory in the southwestern United States. Congress passed new conscription legislation in May requiring men in their twenties to register, whether or not they were citizens.[18] Anarchists in New York immediately organized a series of mass meetings to protest the draft, and Emma Goldman hashed out a platform for a new organization, the No Conscription League. A May 18 rally drew upward of eight thousand participants and crackled with tension. At a second event in June, police dragged off draft-age men who could not prove they had registered—an early instance of the "slacker raids" that became commonplace across the country.[19]

On June 15, 1917, President Wilson signed the Espionage Act, which delineated punishments for foreign spies and prohibited organized resistance to the war. The act made it a crime to promote the victory of enemies, to "cause or attempt to cause insubordination, disloyalty, mutiny, refusal of duty, in the military," or to obstruct military recruiting and the draft.[20] Violations could be punished by a ten-thousand-dollar fine and twenty years' imprisonment. The Espionage Act also delegated to the postmaster general the power to ban from the mail any issue of a publication found to violate the act's provisions and to permanently revoke a publication's second-class mail status. Revocation often made the fulfillment of subscriptions prohibitively expensive.[21]

A great deal of repressive legislation followed. The Trading with the Enemy Act required periodicals to submit, at their own expense, English translations of all materials published in a foreign language or lose mailing privileges. Over the next two years, at least twenty state governments adopted "criminal syndicalist" laws that banned organizations that advocated sabotage or other "unlawful methods" to accomplish "industrial or political reform."[22] When a liberal Montana judge interpreted the Espionage Act narrowly, allowing for some antiwar speech, Congress passed an amendment countermanding the ruling and broadening the act's authority. Whereas the Espionage Act punished activity that actually impeded the work of the army, this new Sedition Act made it a crime to "utter, print, write or publish any disloyal, profane, scurrilous, or abusive language about the form of government of the United States . . . [or] encourage resistance to the United States."[23]

A government apparatus expanding at all levels gave these new laws teeth. The Department of Justice, headed by Attorney General A. Mitchell Palmer, enforced the Espionage Act. Palmer delegated responsibility to the recently formed Bureau of Investigation (a precursor to the FBI), where many responsibilities fell to an ambitious young agent, J. Edgar Hoover.[24] State legislatures launched their own investigations—the Lusk Committee of New York being perhaps the most notorious—while municipal police departments created or expanded "red squads" and other special investigation units.[25] Officials wasted little time deploying these new legal mechanisms against anarchists, the IWW, and other left-wing organizations.

The same day the Espionage Act took effect, police arrested Emma Goldman and Alexander Berkman. They charged the pair with violation of the Selective Service Act, which had become law in May, and which, the anarchists were happy to learn, carried a maximum two-year jail sentence, instead of the Espionage Act's twenty.[26] Berkman's agitational newspaper *The Blast* ceased publication immediately, while the staff of *Mother Earth* managed to publish one more issue before the journal was permanently banned from the mail.[27] Berkman and Goldman were quickly found guilty and shipped to federal penitentiaries in Atlanta and Kansas, respectively.

In April, federal agents had suppressed *L'Era Nuova,* the Italian language anarcho-syndicalist newspaper based in Paterson, New Jersey. On June 17, they raided the Lynn, Massachusetts, offices of the Italian insurrectionary journal *Cronaca Sovversiva,* arresting its editor, Luigi Galleani, and printer, Giovanni Eramo, for counseling readers to dodge the draft. The newspaper's publisher, Carlo Valdinoci, was also indicted, but investigators were unable to locate him. *Cronaca Sovversiva* was, thereafter, prohibited by the U.S. Postal Service, though militants continued to distribute it by motorcycle.[28] Galleani, had, indeed, urged readers to refuse to register. On his advice, approximately sixty Italian anarchists traveled clandestinely to northern Mexico, where they made preparations to return to Italy. The group believed the Russian Revolution would soon spread to other countries, and they were eager to join the struggle in their country of birth when the moment came.

The Spanish-language *Regeneración* lost its mail privileges in 1917 but survived until March 1918, when Magón published a manifesto calling for "anarchists of the entire world and workers in general" to prepare for revolution. He was indicted under the Espionage Act and slapped with the maximum twenty-year sentence.[29] With its editor shipped off to Leavenworth State Penitentiary, the main organ of Mexican American anarchism ceased publication.

The emphasis placed on the suppression of anarchist periodicals by federal authorities provides insight into aspects of the movement's structure. Newspapers were among the easiest targets for federal officials because they typically published an address and the names of editors and contributors. Before the Red Scare period, it was uncommon for contributors to conceal their identities with noms de plume. The informal nature of the anarchist movement complicated efforts to charge activists who kept lower profiles. With no central party apparatus, membership rosters did not exist; one could not be a "card-carrying anarchist." However, subscription lists seized in raids on newspaper offices helped authorities track radicals throughout the country. After the raids began, editors went to great lengths to conceal such lists, not only to protect their subscribers from arrest but also as a means of reestablishing contact after the repression had subsided. For these reasons, periodicals were arguably the most vital institutions of the early-twentieth-century anarchist movement, but also the most vulnerable because they were so visible. The fact that each was edited independently ensured a breadth of opinion, rather than a party line, in less repressive periods. But it also made much more difficult a coordinated response designed to ensure movement continuity in a period of crisis, such as that of 1917.

That a few anarchist periodicals survived the Espionage and Sedition Acts owed more to individual maneuvering, internal disagreement, and historical chance than to a unified movement strategy. Although Carlo Tresca's syndicalist newspaper, *L'Avvenire,* was not raided, it was deemed unmailable by the postmaster so frequently that Tresca found it financially impossible to continue publishing after August 1917. Instead of directly challenging the suppression of *L'Avvenire,* however, he quietly purchased and began editing an anticlerical newspaper, *Il Martello* (The hammer). Tresca avoided publishing any essays directly critical of the war effort while the fighting continued, but made his position known through antimilitarist graphics that slid by the censors.[30] As a result, the paper was not suppressed and was well-placed to serve the anarcho-syndicalist movement in the 1920s.

The *Fraye Arbeter Shtime,* on the other hand, was not legally repressed, since it supported the war effort and complied with government regulations. Nevertheless, a mob invaded the paper's office and smashed equipment. This did little to mitigate the hostility directed at the paper by other anarchists, who saw the publishers' position as a breach of principles and solidarity with the rest of the movement. *Golos Truda,* the newspaper of the anarcho-syndicalist Union of Russian Workers (URW), avoided government suppression in a different way. After the February revolution toppled the czar, leading members of the URW, including Bill Shatoff and *Golos Truda* editor V. M. Eikhenbaum (known as Voline), returned to Russia. They brought their printing press with them and reestablished the newspaper in Petrograd with the intent of organizing anarchists to topple the liberal government headed by Alexander Kerensky.[31]

Anarchists were by no means the only radicals pursued in 1917. The IWW, a mass organization with approximately a hundred thousand members, was an easy target for authorities. On September 5, 1917, Bureau of Investigation agents simultaneously raided and seized files from sixty-four IWW halls across the country. They handed down federal indictments for 166 union leaders soon afterward.[32] As historian Ted Morgan notes, "This was the first Justice Department experiment in a massive, multicity raid, designed to cripple an organization by subjecting its leaders to costly and protracted court proceedings."[33] In April, nearly one hundred IWW members were convicted of interfering with the war effort and handed ten- to twenty-year prison terms. The raids and other acts of wartime persecution had a devastating impact on the union, as intended.[34] Federal authorities also severely disrupted the activities of the Socialist Party. Chairman Eugene Debs was sentenced to ten years in prison for delivering an antiwar speech in Ohio in 1918. In total, nearly fifteen hundred people stood trial for violating the wartime acts; two-thirds of them were convicted.[35] Thousands of others learned they were not entitled to a trial.

From the beginning, the Justice Department used the Espionage and Sedition Acts in tandem with new immigration legislation. The Immigration Act of 1917 intensified earlier antiradical provisions. Immigrants found to support anarchism could thereafter be deported at any time, regardless of how long they had lived in the country. Those discovered to have concealed anarchist sympathies when they were awarded citizenship could be stripped of that status. In 1918, the policy was further amended to exclude supporters of the Russian Bolsheviks from the country and to make mere association with a person or organization that advocated the forcible overthrow of the U.S. government a deportable offense.[36] Under the revised legislation, therefore, officials did not need to prove suspected radicals had committed a specific crime, only that they subscribed to certain beliefs or associated with other radicals. Since violation of immigration statutes was not considered a crime, the accused were not entitled to legal protections or required to stand trial. This encouraged the Justice Department to deport thousands of immigrant radicals without the costly procedure of trying them. Between 1917 and 1920, then, the Justice Department used the Sedition and Immigration Acts in tandem, easily sweeping suspects into custody under the auspices of the former and quickly dispensing with their cases via the latter.[37]

The 1917 Immigration Act presented other, less immediate, challenges to the anarchist movement, as well. Immigration had peaked in the decade before the war, with nearly 10 million individuals—the majority from southern and eastern Europe—entering the country between 1905 and 1914. Nativists and many labor unionists called on Congress to adopt policies, such as literacy tests, to limit these numbers, but "manufacturing interests ... intent on having abundant supplies of unskilled workers on hand," repeatedly quashed such bills.[38] The war, however, dramatically recast immigration patterns. Chaos in Europe cut off the flow of new immigrants, and tens of thousands of sojourners were called home to fight. "During fiscal 1916," Roger Daniels calculates, "the total number of immigrants dropped below 300,000, fewer than half of them from Europe. Since more than 125,000 had left the country during the year, net immigration was just over 150,000." At the same time, anti-German sentiment and the growing Red Scare—in which radicals, German spies, and immigrants were frequently conflated—altered the political calculus. In 1917, Congress overrode a presidential veto, adding the long sought-after literacy test to the immigration reforms described earlier.[39]

As a result of these various factors, the number of available shop hands plummeted at the moment when American manufacturers were gearing up to produce ships, guns, and other implements of war. With highly lucrative government contracts on the line, employers' long-standing policy against hiring African Americans for factory positions dissolved with surprising alacrity. Recruiters fanned out across the American South, as they had across Europe in previous decades, and African Americans soon began making their way to the industrial cities of the Northeast and Midwest by the thousands. U.S. anarchists had long relied, for new recruits, on European immigrant communities and had long neglected to organize with or among African Americans. While the specifically antiradical planks of the 1917 Immigration Act posed the most immediate threat to the movement, the literacy test presaged deeper shifts in immigration policy that threatened to deprive the movement not only of its outspoken leaders but also of its demographic base. In 1917, however, anarchists had more immediate threats to consider.

Beyond its own legal apparatus, the government was assisted by dozens of "vigilance" committees made up of citizens eager to support the war effort by policing the home front. After President Wilson and other political leaders publicly urged citizens to form "home guards" against German spies and seditious radicals, hundreds of thousands of men and women launched new organizations, such as the American Defense Society, the National Security League, and the American Protective League, or they revived existing groups, such as the Ku Klux Klan, that had long used extralegal means to augment official state regulation of the social order.[40] The American Protective League, the largest of the wartime vigilance groups, counted 250,000 members and operated under the explicit authority of local police departments and the Justice Department.[41] Though purportedly formed to root out war dissidents, vigilance groups often worked directly at the behest of business owners seeking to eliminate unions in their facilities and towns. In July 1917, for example, deputized members of the Citizen's Protective League and the Workmen's Loyalty League of Cochise County, Arizona, rounded up twelve hundred striking IWW and AFL miners and their families, herded them into boxcars, and shipped them to the Mexican desert as a means of breaking up a two-week-old strike.[42] The ACLU counted at least fifty acts of mob violence against radicals in 1919. Patriotic groups attacked May Day parades in cities across the country, beating participants with their own pickets and flagpoles.[43]

FRAYHAYT AND THE *ANARCHIST SOVIET BULLETIN*

Anarchists correctly perceived these related threats as an all-out attempt to crush their movement and defeat their social agenda. Many believed the forces arrayed against them were too powerful to oppose and, therefore, chose to keep their heads down. Yet events elsewhere in the world encouraged others to keep fighting. In October 1917, thousands of Russian anarchists, eager to replace the provisional parliamentary government with power based in directly democratic soviets, participated in a second revolution, led by the Bolshevik Party.[44] The success of this second Russian revolution, which claimed to have placed the working class in control of country, stood in thrilling contrast to the chaos and repression shaping the lives of anarchists in the United States. Anarchists had fiercely criticized Karl Marx and his followers as authoritarians for more than fifty years. Yet the precise nature of the October revolution was difficult to discern, and the pronouncements of Bolshevik leader Vladimir Lenin had leaned in an antistatist direction since the fall of the czar.[45]

With one after another of the movement's publications suppressed under the Espionage Act, and with its most skilled organizers imprisoned for sedition, the most committed of the movement's younger cadre felt the need to take action themselves. In their eyes, the Russian Revolution proved that the period remained ripe for fundamental social transformation—*if* working people were brave and prepared enough to take the necessary steps. With labor organizing all but impossible amid the crisis, and no time for works of art and literature to transform consciousness, anarchists went back to strategic basics: propaganda of the word and propaganda of the deed with the intention of inciting spontaneous, armed insurrection. Of course, most Americans did not share the anarchists' enthusiasm. Events in Russia only heightened antiradicalism in the United States, especially after that country withdrew from the war in March 1918.

In 1917 the young seamstress Mollie Steimer, with only a year of movement experience under her belt, teamed up with a handful of other young Jewish anarchists to continue the movement's work on a "strictly underground" basis.[46] The group covertly edited and distributed a Yiddish language newspaper, first titled *Der Shturm* (The storm), and later called *Frayhayt* (Freedom). The Frayhayt Group, as it came to be known, included Mary Abrams, a survivor of the infamous Triangle Shirtwaist factory fire, and her husband, Jacob, who was an elected leader of a New York local of the Bookbinder's Union. Steimer, the Abramses, and three others shared an apartment in East Harlem, a short walk from a rented room where they secretly installed a small hand-powered printing press, and near the former Ferrer Center, which had succumbed, like many other movement institutions, to repression. Though the group members chose to print in Yiddish—perhaps because of their greater ease with the language, perhaps as a counterpoint to the *Fraye Arbeter Shtime*'s prowar position—they adorned the paper's masthead with Henry David Thoreau's famous proto-anarchist claim, "That government is best that governs not at all."[47]

Mollie Steimer and her comrades continued their activities undetected until August 1918, when the U.S. landed troops in Russia to support counterrevolutionary forces and destabilize the new government. Imagining the macabre fate their extended families and other working people would suffer if counterrevolutionary forces prevailed, the group printed thousands of leaflets in English and Yiddish calling for a general strike to oppose U.S. intervention. Although they deposited many leaflets in mail slots, they also threw handfuls of the fliers off the roofs of buildings near the garment factories of the Lower East Side. This romantic flourish cost the group dearly.

Men who caught copies of the leaflets as they fluttered to the ground outside a factory on Houston Street immediately alerted the police. When officers searched the building, an employee named Hyman Rosansky had copies of the leaflet in his jacket pocket. Threatened by the police, he copped to having thrown the fliers, and turned informant to reduce his charges. Overnight, police captured and interrogated Frayhayt Group members Mollie Steimer, Jacob Abrams, Jacob Schwartz, Hyman Lachowsky, and Samuel Lipman.[48] When Lachowsky refused to cooperate, he was beaten so severely that the other detainees later testified seeing him "'lying with his head on the desk,' his eyes black and blue, 'all beaten up, with some of his hair on the floor.'"[49] In October the six arrested comrades stood trial for violating the Sedition Act. Jacob Schwartz was unable to appear before the court, having died of injuries sustained during his own interrogation. The remaining men were sentenced to twenty years each and Steimer to fifteen—solely for circulating a flier calling for a strike. The ruling outraged prominent liberal jurists and journalists, who rallied to defend the anarchists' right to expression, as they had in the days of the Free Speech League. The defendants were released on bail pending an appeal to the Supreme Court shortly before the armistice was signed, ending the war in Europe, in November 1918.[50]

The end of official hostilities, while surely a relief, did not satisfy the anarchists' criteria for a just and peaceful world. The fact that hundreds of thousands were thrown out of work in the postwar reconversion process attested to this fact. Similar hardships prompted workers in Germany, Hungary, and elsewhere in Europe to strike and take to the streets, in attempts to apply the Bolshevik's winning strategy in their own countries. Meanwhile, the ceasefire in Europe seemed to have little effect on the prosecution of radicals in the United States. Despite the bloody suppression of *Frayhayt,* anarchists continued to prioritize the circulation of their ideas, believing resolutely in the power of the written word to move others to action.

While out on bail, Steimer helped launch a new clandestine periodical, the *Anarchist Soviet Bulletin.* Steimer worked with about six others, including former *Mother Earth* mainstay Hippolyte Havel, to compose the English-language paper, which the Union of Russian Workers distributed "in the principal cities."[51] Primary editorial responsibilities fell to Marcus Graham, a young firebrand who would become an important, but polarizing, figure in the movement for the next two decades. Graham had emigrated with his orthodox Jewish family from Romania to Philadelphia at age fourteen. He discovered anarchism in the pages of the *Fraye Arbeter Shtime* and was mentored by Joseph Cohen, a stalwart of Philadelphia's Yiddish anarchist movement. Graham fled to Canada with the outbreak of the war but slipped back over the border and made his way to Manhattan in early 1919.[52]

A one-page broadsheet which first appeared in April of that year, the *Anarchist Soviet Bulletin* was a desperate effort to goad the working people of America into insurrection. The name clearly indicated where its editors' sympathies and expectations lay. The *Bulletin's* first issue responded to the widespread economic dislocations that followed the armistice and painted the administration's war rhetoric as hypocritical. "If [Germany] invading Belgium was a crime," asked the editors, "then what is our union with the world's reactionary forces to destroy the Russian revolution to be called?" But a careful analysis of the postwar conjuncture was not the paper's intent. "We are out to urge ACTION!" the anonymous editors declared. After sketching a system of self-managed workplaces, they beseeched readers to "organize Anarchist Commune Soviets and organize them SECRETLY, as soon as our numbers grow large enough, making us so strong as to assert ourselves in the OPEN, we will DO it—by beginning to take over the FACTORIES, MINES, and FARMS of America."[53] The *Bulletin* then proceeded on pure bluster, reporting the formation of worker soviets in a half dozen cities. Graham, Steimer, and the others seem to have reckoned that the illusion of a revolutionary upsurge already in progress would spur readers to take steps of their own.[54]

While Graham and Steimer's hopes for American soldiers and laborers to spontaneously form a federation of soviets appear naive in retrospect, it was not unreasonable of them to encourage mass working-class upheaval during the spring of 1919. That year, the United States experienced one of the largest strike waves in its history. In January, 35,000 Seattle shipyard workers struck over wages and hours. When management refused to budge, the Central Labor Council—heavily seeded with IWW militants—organized a 60,000-person-strong general strike.[55] The eventual defeat of the general strike did not eliminate workers' willingness to challenge economic conditions. Robert K. Murray notes that, nationwide, "in March there were 175 strikes, in April, 248; May,

338; June, 303; July, 360; and August, 373." During the summer of 1919, approximately 164,000 walked picket lines in New York City alone.[56] In September, Boston policemen struck for the right to unionize, opening the door to rioting and looting among the city's poor. The same month, a nationwide strike of more than 365,000 workers, led by future Communist Party chairman William Z. Foster, shut down the steel industry. Six weeks later, the miners went out.[57] Amid this outpouring of worker solidarity and militancy, authorities feared radicals emboldened by the Russian Revolution would attempt a similar feat at home. The authors of the *Anarchist Soviet Bulletin* were only too happy to encourage such a development.

Another form of social conflict rocked the country during the summer of 1919 as well. The movement of thousands of African Americans into the war industries, in the face of deep-seated racism, produced conflicts in cities throughout the Northeast. During the summer of 1919, white mobs violently sacked recently formed African American neighborhoods in Chicago; Washington, D.C.; Baltimore; and other cities, leaving a trail of death, injury, and burnt-out homes in their wake. Flames and blood became so common that African American newspapers dubbed it the "Red Summer."[58] As the summer wore on, black citizens organized to resist these incursions and began defending their lives and property with force. Alarmed officials and media commentators linked such acts of self-defense to the strike wave and to anarchist resistance to the war. The Army Military Intelligence Division reported that the "IWW and other radical organizations, both white and black, have played their part in inciting the negroes to the recent outbreaks in Chicago and Washington."[59] Such claims of affiliation cut both ways, associating two racialized and feared social groups with one another, conflating the (sometimes violent) acts of resistance each felt compelled to take in defense of their rights, and legitimating the legal campaign and violence arrayed against them. The racial anxiety undergirding the period's concurrent crises was often expressed explicitly. In response to threats posed by "unwise and radical Negro leaders and Bolshevists," Mississippi senator Byron Harrison called on Congress to arm the vigilante "home guards" to help "law-abiding white people" protect themselves.[60] Yet elites played the divide both ways, recruiting tens of thousands of African American and Mexican American workers to serve as replacements for striking factory workers. Having faced exclusion from many AFL unions and hostility in the neighborhoods, many (but not all) workers of color declined to practice class solidarity unilaterally.[61]

For these and other reasons, the strikes and riots of 1919 failed to coalesce into a seizure of the means of production and only deepened the authorities' desire to clamp down on radicalism. Shortly after the first issue of the *Anarchist Soviet Bulletin* was published, Marcus Graham was arrested and held on Ellis Island after police found copies of the *Bulletin* in his suitcase. Detained for a month, he was released while the government compiled evidence to deport him. He was then rearrested, beaten during a daylong interrogation, and returned to Ellis Island for another six months. The young editor was eventually released because officials could not prove his country of origin and he refused to provide the information himself.[62] Over the same period, Mollie Steimer was placed under continuous surveillance and arrested on *eight* separate occasions. In April 1920, while jailed in New York on disorderly conduct charges, she learned that the Supreme Court had upheld the Sedition Act sentence, and she was transferred to the Jefferson Penitentiary, in Saint Louis, to begin her fifteen-year sentence.[63]

THE AMERICAN ANARCHIST FIGHTERS

In April 1919, the same month that the *Anarchist Soviet Bulletin* made its debut, Italian insurrectionary anarchists who were grouped around *Cronaca Sovversiva* escalated a campaign they had begun two years earlier, of violent resistance and retaliation to the war, antiradical repression, and deportations. In September 1917, followers of Luigi Galleani interrupted an outdoor "loyalty rally" organized by a pastor in an Italian neighborhood of Milwaukee, Wisconsin. When anarchists ran onto the stage and attempted to tear down an American flag, police opened fire, killing two and wounding another. One of the men shot by the police returned fire with a pistol, injuring two officers. Police arrested eleven anarchists at the scene and beat additional members of the group when they raided its club the next day.[64] As they had done while confronting the Frayhayt Group, which had been found leafleting, authorities reacted to the Italians' nonviolent symbolic action—their attempt to remove an American flag—with deadly force.

In response, some of the Galleanisti who had fled to Mexico the previous spring returned to the United States and planted a pipe bomb in the church of the pastor who organized the loyalty rally. Police discovered the bomb and brought it to their station, where it exploded, killing ten officers and a bystander. In November, a judge sentenced each of the eleven Milwaukee anarchists (who were in jail when the pipe bomb exploded) to twenty-five years in prison. Upon hearing this news, the insurrectionaries who had planted the pipe bomb determined that more reprisals were in order. Carlo Valdinoci, former manager of *Cronaca Sovversiva,* called upon nineteen-year-old Ella Antolini to do her part for the movement. During the first month of 1918, the young seamstress traveled west to help Valdinoci transport dynamite inconspicuously from Ohio to Chicago. On the last leg of her journey, a train porter found Antolini suspicious, searched her bag, and discovered the dynamite alongside a loaded pistol. Interrogated in Chicago, Antolini remained mum. She was sentenced to eighteen months in prison for possession and transportation of dynamite, and landed in the same penitentiary as Emma Goldman and the socialist orator Kate Richards O'Hare, both of whom doted upon her like a daughter.[65] Later that year Steimer would be sentenced to 180 months for circulating literature. This sentencing discrepancy can be attributed, primarily, to the fact that police could not definitely prove Antolini was an anarchist at the time of her trial.

Despite her intentions, investigators discovered clues in Antolini's prison correspondence that helped them track her coconspirators. Federal agents raided the *Cronaca Sovversiva* offices a second time and discovered a mailing list containing the addresses of three thousand subscribers. The Bureau of Investigation wasted little time in raiding the homes and clubs of subscribers throughout the country, turning hundreds of Italian immigrants over to the Bureau of Labor to initiate deportation proceedings. The ultramilitants spent the better part of a year preparing their next move. In February 1919, they distributed leaflets throughout New England, signed "the American Anarchists," that announced, "Deportation will not stop the storm from reaching these shores. The storm is within and very soon will leap and crash and annihilate you in blood and fire. You have shown no pity to us! We will do likewise. And deport us! *We will dynamite you!*"[66] True to their word, the Galleanisti prepared thirty mail bombs timed to explode on May Day 1919. They mailed the bombs to leading industrialists, such as Nelson Rockefeller, as well as to politicians, lawyers, and judges involved in strikebreaking or deporting radicals. The housekeeper of a senator from Georgia lost her hands when one of the bombs exploded, but the majority of the packages were intercepted at the post office, where they had been held up for insufficient postage.[67] News reports led many to see the botched conspiracy as the harbinger of imminent revolution, inducing a wave of panic across the country.

Then, on June 2, bombs exploded almost simultaneously at the homes of judges and political officials in seven cities across the northeastern United States. Again, none of the explosives reached their intended targets. When Antolini's friend Carlo Valdinoci attempted to place a bomb under the home of Attorney General A. Mitchell Palmer, he tripped, detonating the device as he fell on it. Mitchell's home was damaged but he and his family survived the blast. Valdinoci was not so lucky—police called to the scene immediately began collecting limbs and sections of his scalp that they discovered dangling from nearby trees to use as evidence in their investigation. At other bomb sites, police found leaflets similar in style and content to those discovered in February, this time signed "the Anarchist Fighters."

On June 19, 1919, Luigi Galleani; *Cronaca Sovversiva*'s bookkeeper, Raffaele Schiavina; and eight of their associates were rearrested as alien anarchists in violation of the Immigration Act. Five days later they were deported to Italy, before detectives had compiled enough evidence to consider questioning them regarding the explosions.[68] Though its perpetrators were never prosecuted, the Galleanisti "bomb plot," occurring amid the 1919 strike wave and the Red Summer, provided the rationale for Attorney General Palmer to order the government's most extensive campaign of arrests, prosecutions, and deportations of radicals to date.

THE PALMER RAIDS AND RESISTANCE ON ELLIS ISLAND

By November 1919 the Bureau of Investigation had determined that the May 1 and June 2 bombs plots had been orchestrated by anarchists, at least some of them of Italian heritage, but it still lacked evidence to finger specific individuals. With the strike wave, the bomb scare, and the summer riots coalescing into a sensation of insecurity, calls for a full-scale assault on dissidents and agitators reached a fever pitch. Attorney General Palmer began preparing for a massive, nationwide roundup of radicals, beginning with the Union of Russian Workers.[69] As an avowedly anarcho-syndicalist labor union composed of Russian immigrants, the URW seemed to mark the exact political location where the anarchist bombers, Wobbly general-strike organizers, and Russian Bolsheviks intersected. Justice Department agents remained indifferent to the fact that the URW fell squarely in the mass-organizing, rather than the insurrectionary, camp of anarchists. Nor did they care that many of the union's most prominent members had returned to

Russia where, by 1919, they were vigorously agitating against Lenin's centralization of political power while trying to avoid capture by the secret police.[70]

On November 7, agents raided the Russian People's House in New York City looking for members of the URW, which maintained offices there. Agents attacked students and teachers attending night classes, beating some with wood torn from the building's banister and tossing them down staircases. They hauled approximately two hundred individuals to Department of Justice offices, where they interrogated them about membership in the union. Agents simultaneously raided URW halls in Detroit, Baltimore, and nine other cities throughout the country, detaining more than a thousand individuals.[71] In justifying this massive roundup of immigrant radicals, Attorney General Palmer not only invoked the need for security, but also tapped into racial fears and concerns about the breakdown of family and sexual norms. In *Forum* magazine he claimed that revolution was "licking at the altars of the churches, leaping into the belfry of the school bell, *crawling into the sacred corners of American homes, seeking to replace marriage vows with libertine laws,* burning up the foundations of society."[72]

The federal raids prompted local agencies to carry out their own warrantless arrests of foreign-born radicals. On November 8, under directions from the Lusk Committee, "700 police raided seventy-three radical centers, arrested more than 500 individuals, and seized tons of literature."[73] Captured anarchists from New York were held on Ellis Island. Soon after Berkman and Goldman completed their sentences for violating the Selective Service Act, they were charged with violations of the Immigration Act and moved to Ellis Island.

The mass arrests did not break the will of anarchists to resist, however. A Lusk Committee agent responsible for spying on a group of Brooklyn anarchists intercepted packages of radical periodicals illegally mailed to detainees on the island.[74] Unable to receive material from outside, some detainees attempted to create a handwritten anarchist newspaper, the *Ellis Island Anarchist Weekly,* inside the holding cells of the detention center. The paper provides a window onto the activities of the political detainees:

> Thinking they can imprison or kill ideas, by imprisoning, killing, deporting, or wounding individuals expounding those ideals, the authorities of Ellis Island have separated all comrades from the other detained persons on the island. The reason: because we used to have meetings and discussions spreading and learning [*sic*] the other prisoners, the ideas we have learned and are being detained for.[75]

The *Ellis Island Anarchist Weekly*, 1919, a handwritten newspaper intended for circulation among anarchists detained on Ellis Island during the Red Scare of the World War I era. Courtesy of Miscellaneous Manuscripts, Labadie Collection, University of Michigan Library (Special Collections Library).

Nor did the detainees' loved ones quietly accept their arrest and likely deportation. Aided by radical attorney Harry Weinberger, families demanded visitation rights and lodged appeals for wives and children to be transported back to Russia with their incarcerated relatives. Despite these efforts, immigration officials refused to even provide notice regarding the date of departure. On Saturday, December 20, groups of workers arrested on November 7 in Cleveland, Pittsburgh, Buffalo, Hartford, and other cities were transported by train to New York and ferried to Ellis Island. At dawn the following morning, guards marched 249 detainees onto an old army transport ship, the *Buford,* which promptly departed for Russia.[76] Most were URW members, but approximately 40 anarchists with other movement credentials, such as Goldman and Berkman, were placed aboard. They shared the ship's tight quarters with crew members and 250 soldiers sent to guard against any attempted seaborne uprising. Mollie Steimer, Samuel Lipman, and Jacob Abrams remained imprisoned on shore when the *Buford* departed Ellis Island. Lipman's lover, Ethel Bernstein, however, shared a cabin with Goldman and the only other female deportee, Dora Lipkin.

The *Buford* was already miles at sea when news of its departure broke in the daily newspapers. The following morning, nearly 150 enraged and heartbroken family members and comrades, mostly women, assembled at the lower Manhattan ferry to Ellis Island, demanding to know if their loved ones had been placed aboard the transport ship. When officials refused to disclose which captives had been deported or to allow anyone to visit those remaining, the women launched a minor riot. A twenty-four-year-old Russian named Clara Brooks stepped forward, proclaimed herself an anarchist, and shouted, "Down with this dirty, rotten government! They have taken my husband, and are taking the husbands, fathers, and brothers of us all!"[77] The crowd then surged toward the dock. Brooks and another woman punched out the glass of the gatekeepers' booth and others began throwing "a volley of stones and other missiles" at the ferry office.[78] Determined to reach the island, the crowd snapped a guard railing and ran for a boat. The first policeman to arrive on the scene was surrounded and beaten by the crowd. Only a "detail of coast guards with fixed bayonets" was able to drive back and contain the bloc of outraged anarchists.[79] Brooks was arrested and jailed for two days on disorderly conduct charges. The *New York Times* learned that her husband, Abe, was indeed aboard the *Buford.* A member of the URW, he had been arrested in Washington Square Park for "circulating anarchist literature which protested against the presence of American troops in Russia"—likely the Frayhayt Group leaflet that had landed Mollie Steimer and the others in jail.[80]

Less than a week after the *Buford* sailed, Attorney General Palmer launched a second set of raids, this time targeting the membership of two newly formed communist parties. Aimed at eliminating the groups, which had broken from the Socialist Party at Lenin's urging, the January raids directly affected far

Senya Fleshin, Mollie Steimer, and (reclining) Samuel Lipman in Leningrad, 1922. Steimer and Lipman were deported to Russia after being convicted of violating the Espionage and Sedition Acts. Courtesy of the Pacific Street Films Photographs Collection, Tamiment Library/Robert F. Wagner Labor Archives, New York University.

fewer anarchists than those carried out in November. Nevertheless, those anarchists still at liberty recognized that they remained under heavy surveillance. Officials claimed that the *Buford* would soon be followed by other "arks" carrying foreign-born radicals out of the country. Indeed, a total of 3,068 people were deported during the 1919 fiscal year, followed by 2,762 in 1920 and an additional 4,514 during 1921.[81] During the three years constituting the height of the Red Scare, then, more than 10,000 immigrants were deported, most of them for their radical beliefs and their determination to express them. On November 23, 1921, Mollie Steimer and her Frayhayt Group comrades Samuel Lipman, Jacob Abrams, and Mary Abrams joined the forced exodus on a ship bound for Russia. After more than a year of fund-raising and legal maneuvering, their attorney had convinced the government to commute their long prison sentences to immediate and permanent exile.[82]

The Galleanisti bomb campaign of May and June 1919 prompted intense investigation. Relying on undercover infiltrators, the Bureau of Investigation tracked down the people who printed the leaflet found at the scenes of the June 2, 1919, bombings. They arrested printshop employees and insurrectionary anarchists Roberto Elia and Andrea Salsedo in February 1920, secretly detaining them in Manhattan for two months. During a brutal interrogation, Salsedo confessed to his role in the conspiracy and implicated many of his comrades. At the end of March, Salsedo smuggled a letter to a comrade in Boston, Bartolomeo Vanzetti, describing the conditions of his detention but not admitting he had provided information.

On May 3, while Vanzetti gathered money for the men's defense, Salsedo plunged to his death from the fourteenth-floor window of his makeshift jail cell in the New York offices of the Justice Department. Although evidence later showed that Salsedo almost certainly jumped, Boston anarchists accused the government agents of murdering him. The next day's headlines exposed the illegal detention, throwing the investigation into disarray. Two days later Elia was transferred to Ellis Island and deported to Italy.[83]

Upon learning of the confessions, Vanzetti, his friend Nicola Sacco, and two other members of Boston's Grupo Autonomo, Mario Buda and Ricardo Orcianni, shifted into high gear. Save for Orcianni, each of these men had spent the summer of 1917 in Mexico with other *Cronaca Sovversiva* subscribers, and Buda, if not also the others, had helped organize the Milwaukee actions that landed Ella Antolini in prison. On the night of May 5, 1920, the men attempted to retrieve Buda's car from a repair shop in order to transport incriminating literature—and, most likely, explosives—to a secure hiding place. However, Buda was under investigation for a series of recent robberies, and the garage owner alerted local police. After the anarchists split up for the evening, officers snared Sacco and Vanzetti as they made their way home. The anarchists lied about their itinerary and reasons for carrying pistols. Eventually, both were charged with participating in stickups during which men had robbed and killed payroll guards in South Braintree, Massachusetts.[84] Vanzetti was quickly convicted on a robbery charge in a trial that relied heavily on racializing stereotypes of Italians and Red Scare antiradicalism.

Through interviews with aging Italian anarchists in the 1970s and 1980s, historian Paul Avrich learned that after being informed of the arrests of his comrades, Buda hid out in New Hampshire for two months. When Sacco and

Vanzetti were indicted for murder, Buda traveled to New York City and purchased a horse, a carriage, and a large cache of dynamite. On September 16 he parked the carriage on Wall Street, outside the U.S. Treasury Building and the offices of J. P. Morgan. Buda walked away from the cart shortly before it exploded, killing thirty-eight people. He soon sailed for Italy, never to be apprehended for his role in any of the bombings.[85] Beginning in 1920, then, the Italian anarchists of the Galleani school had the difficult task of organizing a campaign to exonerate and free their imprisoned comrades Sacco and Vanzetti while avoiding implicating any additional participants in the string of bombings they had carried out since 1915.[86]

If the Wall Street bombing is construed as the anarchists' final move in their deadly face-off with federal authorities, the government's coup de grâce was less spectacular but much more damaging to the movement over the long term. It took the form of thoroughgoing revisions to the nation's immigration policies.

IMMIGRATION REFORM AND THE END OF THE RED SCARE

The Red Scare that had begun in 1917 finally began to wane in the spring of 1920. A combination of factors contributed to the changed national mood. In January, state representatives from New York found they had overreached the limits of extrademocratic tolerance when they voted to disbar five fellow assemblymen elected on the Socialist Party ticket, charging them with disloyalty and providing comfort to the enemy owing to their opposition to the war. Harsh criticism from the mainstream press and liberal politicians mounted quickly. Even to many supporters of the roundups of radicals, the exclusion of elected officials charged with no crime seemed to set a dangerous precedent. During the same months, the postwar industrial reconversion progressed, leading to improved economic conditions and a corresponding decline in strike activity. Also important, by 1920 the attempted postwar communist revolutions in eastern Europe had been defeated, lessening concerns that the Bolshevik revolution would spread to North America. Still, in September 1921, more than four years after the Espionage Act was approved and nearly two years since the Palmer Raids had commenced, American anarchists remained in an extremely precarious position. Writing anonymously in *Free Society*—the new name given to the *Anarchist Soviet Bulletin*—Marcus Graham observed, "As long as the time for open revolutionary agitation and action in defiance of the State has not arrived, we shall continue conspiratively [*sic*].[87]

Yet as the arrests of radicals tapered off and Wilson's successor, Warren Harding, called for the repeal of the Sedition Act and other wartime measures, immigration regulation only intensified. In 1921, Congress introduced a temporary "national origins" quota system that severely limited the number of eastern and southern Europeans allowed into the country. Debate over the measure took place in 1920, during the height of the Red Scare. The Johnson-Reed Immigration Act of 1924 reduced the quotas and made the system permanent.[88] Immigration fell to approximately three hundred thousand individuals per year for the rest of the 1920s, a third of the prewar average. Of those now admitted, most were British, Canadian, Mexican, or German subjects. The new regulations reduced yearly immigration from Italy more than 90 percent.[89] Roger Daniels notes, "The general debate on immigration law in 1924 was never a question of whether immigration should be restricted further, but rather, how severely . . . and which kinds of immigrants should be allowed to enter."[90]

The consensus, in 1924, that immigration should be severely restricted, is striking given that employer organizations had vehemently opposed and successfully defeated restrictive legislation before the war. A decade of immigrant radicalism, combined with the specter of the Russian Revolution, seems to have altered employers' calculus in choosing labor pools. The war made the previously unimaginable a necessity. "With the main sources of immigrant labor suddenly shut off," David Roediger has argued, "capital turned to the recruitment of workers racialized as nonwhite, not 'in-between.'"[91] Clearly, by 1924, manufacturers felt secure enough staffing their facilities with workers of color, especially African Americans, to allow the flow of impoverished Europeans to be tamped off. The attacks on black communities during the Red Summer of 1919 warned these arrivistes that interfering with white prerogatives—whether those of the boss or of their coworkers—would come at a serious price.

The break in European immigration had a wide-ranging effect on the cultures of the preexisting immigrant communities as well. Mae Ngai suggests, "The cutoff of European immigration created conditions for the second generation of those immigrants who had come to the United States from the 1890s to World War I to more readily assimilate into American Society. The loosening of these ethnic groups' ties to their homelands facilitated that process."[92] Ironically, the geographically selective restriction of immigration, achieved through explicitly racialized argumentation, led in two decades' time to the incorporation of already arrived European "ethnics" into the privileges of whiteness, including a higher standard of living. Such assimilation demanded—and incentivized—a declining commitment to radical politics within immigrant communities between the world wars. Reorienting itself to address this fundamentally recomposed class of workers would prove one the most difficult challenges—and there were many—faced by a postwar anarchist movement decimated by five years of repression.

THREE

A Movement of Defense,
of Emergency, 1920–1929

When the *Buford* chugged away from Ellis Island on December 24, 1919, twenty-three-year-old anarchist Rose Pesotta was both incensed and dismayed. The deportations represented an enormous setback to the movement that had shaped her life in New York. More immediately, her lover, Theodore Kushnarev, was aboard—forcefully returned to the couple's native Russia alongside Pesotta's role model, Emma Goldman. While the repression of the Red Scare years cowed many anarchists into curtailing their activities, it led Pesotta to redouble her efforts. In this, she was atypical. On the whole, U.S. anarchists carried out their work dutifully, but with a fair measure of disappointment and foreboding, during the 1920s. This is not surprising, given the variety and scope of the challenges they faced.

The movement had lost many of its sharpest intellects and ablest organizers in a few short years—Emma Goldman, Alexander Berkman, and Luigi Galleani to exile; Ricardo Flores Magón to death while he was in custody; Bill Shatoff and Voline to the irresistible call of the Russian Revolution. Those anarchists who remained, and remained active, struggled to adjust to a world transformed by the social dislocations of war, the suppression of radical unionism, and the explosive growth of mass production and marketing that characterized the new decade. Other changes occurred simultaneously. Women won the right to vote in 1920 and, throughout the decade, stretched conventions surrounding work, dress, and deportment. Immigration from Europe was curtailed mid-decade, while the internal migration of African Americans to cities led to complex reconfigurations of urban space, understandings of race, and employment patterns. While navigating these cultural and structural developments, anarchists faced serious threats posed by the rise of fascism and authoritarian communism—in Europe and closer to home.

Histories of U.S. anarchism often discuss the 1920s as a period in which an irreversible process of decline, set in motion by the Red Scare, slowly played itself out. Evidence does suggest that the movement was strategically disoriented, and that it experienced a period of intellectual stagnation. Upon learning of plans to launch an English-language newspaper in 1924, Emma Goldman wrote from abroad, "Heaven knows it is necessary after so many years of silence. I confess the fact that nothing was being done in America since our deportation has been harder to bear than many other things that made life so difficult the last seven years."[1] Yet this was an overstatement, reflecting Goldman's own emphasis on agitation in English.

Although they made less of a public impact, anarchists engaged in a surprising array of initiatives over the course of the 1920s. With the Industrial Workers of the World in shambles, labor-oriented anarchists shifted their focus. Some struggled to radicalize mainstream garment unions. However, concern for Russian radicals imprisoned by the Bolsheviks eventually led these anarchists to collaborate with union moderates to prevent communists from taking control of the unions. During these years, Italian anarchists launched a mass defense campaign for their imprisoned comrades, Sacco and Vanzetti, and went to war with bricks and bats to stem support for fascism in Italian American neighborhoods across the country. Others established co-operatively financed rural colonies that provided "liberatory" schools for children and greater comfort for adults, but which distanced them from struggles in the cities. By mid-decade, immigrant anarchists recognized the necessity of English-language outlets for their ideas, given the changing composition of the labor force. Accordingly, they established "international groups," which hosted English-language forums and published the monthly newspaper the *Road to Freedom*.

All told, anarchists were torn between the strategic need to "Americanize" their movement and a sense of responsibility to assist in struggles taking place abroad that were specific to ethnic communities in the United States. For an anarchist like Rose Pesotta, who took part in nearly all these efforts, the 1920s constituted a hectic period in which the stakes were high. When we shift the frame to examine the history of U.S. anarchism *beginning* in the World War I period, rather than *ending* in it, the 1920s and 1930s appear as a difficult time in which anarchists suffered considerable setbacks but carried on, rather than an era in which the movement's complete dissolution was a foregone conclusion.

Between 1905 and 1917, the U.S. anarchist movement contributed to and benefited from the growth of the Industrial Workers of the World (IWW). However, the IWW never recovered the level of membership and stature it had boasted before the war, a circumstance that placed the anarchists' ties to labor struggles and new working-class recruits in jeopardy. The raids against, and the trials and imprisonment of, IWW leaders during and shortly after the war took an enormous toll in the form of disrupted organizing campaigns, legal expenses, loss of reputation, and the demoralization of activists handed long sentences. With wartime fears abating, the Harding administration began in 1923 to offer commutation to many Wobblies who had been detained since the Palmer Raids. However, their imprisonment had exacerbated preexisting divisions within the union, which were further compounded by political developments on the outside.

Since at least 1912, Wobblies had debated the extent to which strategic decision-making and resources should be centralized in the organization. While Wobblies generally desired for their union to be more democratic than those of the AFL, many believed the general executive board should decide which campaigns to prioritize and other matters, while the decidedly anarcho-syndicalist members insisted that local groups of workers retain the right to engage employers when and how they saw fit.[2] The growth of the communist movement added another dimension to the conflict between "centralizers" and "decentralizers" in the IWW. Many former Wobblies, such as steel organizer William Z. Foster, joined the American Communist Party after it was formed in 1919. Seeking to bring the IWW membership and infrastructure under communist leadership, the leaders of the new party encouraged the general executive board to affiliate with the Moscow-based Red International of Labor Unions, or Profintern, which sought to coordinate the activities of communist labor organizations around the world. Already aware of the Bolshevik repression of the noncommunist Left in Russia, anarchist and syndicalist Wobblies strenuously resisted this move.

Disputes raged in IWW publications throughout the early 1920s, and members even organized themselves into bat-wielding gangs to thwart communist takeovers of local union halls. The tensions came to a head during the annual convention of 1924. After nearly a month of parliamentary maneuvering, shouted threats, and fistfights, two factions, one based in the Northwest and another in Chicago, claimed the IWW mantle. Subsequently, the Profintern shifted its focus to "boring from within" AFL unions and abandoned attempts to subsume the IWW. Remaining independent from the Communist Party proved a Pyrrhic victory, however. Membership continued to decline, from a prewar high of at least a hundred thousand to less than ten thousand in 1928. As the broader labor movement ebbed over the course of the decade, the IWW launched few organizing drives and focused instead on educational efforts, such as circulating its newspaper. The number of IWW unions actually exerting power in workplaces dwindled into the single digits.[3]

In the 1920s, the IWW became more clearly aligned with anarchism and has remained so since that time. Yet this ideological consolidation was achieved through attrition, rather than conversion, of the union's other factions. Although true believers continued to rent storefront "union halls" in New York, Chicago, and a few other cities, after 1924 the IWW was no longer able to build mass radical unions and, through them, bring large numbers of U.S. wageworkers into the anarchist movement.

Jewish anarchists operating within the AFL's garment unions responded to challenges similar to those faced by anarchist Wobblies, but they made different choices. The decision by the editors of the *Fraye Arbeter Shtime* (The free voice of labor, FAS), the weekly Yiddish-language anarchist newspaper, to support the Allies during the First World War led to complex outcomes in the postwar period. Yiddish-speaking anarchists came out of the war institutionally stronger than other sectors but politically more moderate. In 1919, longtime editor Saul Yanovsky left the FAS to edit the internal weekly newspaper of the International Ladies' Garment Workers' Union (ILGWU), which was printed in Yiddish, Italian, and English.[4] With Yanovsky's departure occurring on the heels of the Red Scare and the voluntary return of many readers to Russia, the future of the FAS was imperiled. In response, Jewish anarchists convened in October 1921 to launch the new Jewish Anarchist Federation, which would be tasked with maintaining the newspaper and coordinating other activities. New York City remained the center of Jewish anarchism in the 1920s, but groups also existed in cities such as Chicago, San Francisco, and Los Angeles.[5] The assembled activists appointed Joseph Cohen as the new editor of the FAS. Cohen had organized Philadelphia's Radical Library and helped steer New York's Ferrer Center before moving to the Stelton Colony (the anarchist intentional community in New Jersey) with his wife. The group also took the opportunity to distinguish their vision of anarchism from insurrectionist perspectives and popular representations in wide circulation at the time. They explained,

We are revolutionists but not terrorists. We work to bring near the complete reconstruction of the social order. We fight every attempt to interpret our theory as an encouragement to deeds of violence and expropriation. Expropriation when practiced by individuals or small groups is one of the most harmful deeds to the revolutionary movement. The expropriation of the natural social wealth will be carried out by the organized organizations, in the interests of the entire society.[6]

The statement affirmed the group's long-standing strategic orientation toward mass organizing, especially through labor unions. It also functioned as one of the few public rebukes of the bomb campaign carried out by Italian insurrectionary anarchists over the previous two years. Despite the new federation's clear strategic differences with the bombers, the statement was carefully worded to avoid implicating specific groups or individuals and to maintain deniability concerning whether anarchists were involved with any explosions they had not directly claimed. The desire to shield fellow radicals from the law made it difficult and divisive for the movement to rigorously debate the consequences—and the strategic implications—of actions taken independently by different sectors during the period of crisis. Instead, the different groups carried on as they saw fit.

As in earlier years, a set of institutions with overlapping memberships knit together the lives of Jewish anarchists. Audrey Goodfriend, who would make important contributions to the movement in the 1940s, recalled,

My parents were Jewish anarchists, so I was introduced to the *Fraye Arbeter Shtime* at a very young age and participated in the fund-raising affairs. They had picnics in the summertime and an annual three-day bazaar, with actors and singers at Irving Place. My father was secretary of a Workmen's Circle anarchist branch, which was called the Ferrer Branch. Then, when [Rudolf] Rocker died, it became the Ferrer-Rocker Branch. My father was also a member of the Modern School Association. They always had a convention around Memorial Day, and we would go out to Stelton. And my father was a member of the Jewish Anarchist Federation. My friend Sally Genn's father used to sell the FAS in the streets. My other friend Lilly's father was also part of the branch, and they were all very involved in the garment workers union—the ILGWU.[7]

Beginning in 1924, many anarchist families, including the Goodfriends, moved from Manhattan to co-operative apartment complexes built by Jewish unionists and radicals in the south Bronx.[8] The co-ops were intended to provide more space, fresh air, and communal resources than the tenements of the Lower East Side had to offer. In addition to their many other activities, the Goodfriends participated in the informal "Am-Shol Group," which consisted of anarchists living in the Amalgamated Co-ops and the Shalom Aleichem Houses.

The rich life born of this institutional matrix had attracted Rose Pesotta to anarchism in the years before the war. Born in 1896, Pesotta immigrated from Derazhnya, Russia, to New York in 1913, the same year as Mollie Steimer and Ella Antolini. While Pesotta was still an adolescent, her older sister had introduced her to clandestine revolutionary circles in Russia, where she read Bakunin and Alexander Herzen and was inspired by female revolutionists such as Vera Figner.[9] Like Steimer, Pesotta began sewing shirtwaists upon her arrival in the United States. She soon joined Local 25, the ILGWU's largest, with over twenty thousand members. Local 25 was home to dozens of radical women who worked to give unionism a "soul" by hosting classes in English, politics, and art, and by organizing summer excursions and other activities outside the workplace.[10] They hoped that labor unions might begin to fulfill many of the social functions that churches and synagogues had provided to earlier generations. In addition to participating in union activities, Pesotta sat in on classes and lectures at the Ferrer Center and the Stelton Colony in New Jersey. She also participated in the mass anticonscription rally organized by Goldman and Berkman at Madison Square Garden in May 1914.[11]

During the trying years of the Red Scare, Pesotta focused her energies on union work. Anarchists and socialists had founded the garment unions in the 1890s; and they remained active in the second decade of the twentieth century, when the ILGWU and the Amalgamated Garment Workers grew rapidly through massive, aggressive strikes. The 1920 constitution of the ILGWU declared it a democratic socialist organization dedicated to the abolition of capitalism.[12] Yet as the union grew in size and influence during the second decade of the twentieth century, its leaders backed away from revolutionary rhetoric. As the union's official historian, Benjamin Stolberg, acknowledged, "Many of the officials—managers, business agents, organizers, secretaries of this or that—were old-timers who had gradually degenerated into smug routineers."[13] The October 1917 revolution in Russia, however, buoyed the spirits of anticapitalists throughout the world, infusing them with a sense that sweeping changes were, in fact, possible if a core of militants acted boldly to overcome organizational ossification.

In 1919 Pesotta joined a Shop Delegate League inspired by the Russian soviets and by the shop delegate movement of England. The British movement sought to restructure labor unions in order to combat bureaucracy and ensure greater member control.[14] This appealed to the young ILGWU radicals who

Rose Pesotta, secretary of the Road to Freedom Group, member of the Anarchist Red Cross, and, later, vice president of the International Ladies' Garment Workers' Union (date unknown). Courtesy of the Pacific Street Films Photographs Collection, Tamiment Library/Robert F. Wagner Labor Archives, New York University.

linked a postwar employment slump and deteriorating work conditions with the conservative tendencies of the union's top officers. The dissidents promoted a system in which each factory would appoint representatives to city-wide councils with decision-making powers, as a means of giving more sway to those spoiling to confront the bosses head-on. This was an initiative that many anarchists could get behind. Before the war, Jewish anarchists were often criticized for organizing within "reformist" AFL unions rather than within the revolutionary IWW. However, wartime raids and criminal-syndicalism laws had enfeebled the IWW, while the shop delegate movement aimed to put more bite into the trade unions. As historian Melech Epstein notes, "The broad aims of the shop delegate system brought together socialists, anarchists, syndicalists, communists, and other dissidents."[15] Pesotta was elected to the executive board of her local in 1920 as a representative of this coalition reform effort.[16] Although it represented an exciting opportunity, the position placed Pesotta in the middle of an unfolding transnational conflict between anarchists and the nascent communist movement.

Relations between Russian anarchists and Bolsheviks oscillated between expectant collaboration and violent hostility for four years after the czar was defeated in 1917, making it difficult for anarchists in the United States to know how to relate to communists. After the February revolution, Russian anarchists helped industrial workers establish "workers' councils," or soviets, in the major cities—a process Lenin endorsed in his April Theses—and participated in the Bolshevik-led insurrection that toppled the provisional government in October. However, when the Bolsheviks took control over local soviets and trade unions in the fall of 1917, anarchists denounced the Bolsheviks and began to organize autonomously, leading to violence between the factions. Supported by the anarchist Nabat Federation, the Ukrainian Nestor Mahkno organized an army of peasants that began to seize and collectivize agricultural land. Mahkno and certain other anarchists collaborated with the Bolsheviks to defeat counterrevolutionary and invading armies from the summer of 1918 until November 1920, when the communists felt secure enough to liquidate their erstwhile allies. The following spring, radical workers in Petrograd called for a return to workers' control, while sailors at the Kronstadt naval base rebelled against the "commissacracy" established by the Bolsheviks. Anarchists aligned themselves with these upsurges and were targeted for complete elimination from the political landscape after the Red Army reasserted control and executed more than a thousand resistant soldiers and sailors. The highest profile anarchists, including Emma Goldman, Alexander Berkman, Voline, and (later) Mollie Steimer, were allowed to flee to Europe, while lesser-known activists were herded into makeshift prisons by the hundreds.[17]

News of the Bolsheviks' repression of left-wing and working-class critics had trickled into the United States since 1917, but it grew to a flood by the spring of 1922. U.S. anarchists sent Harry Kelly as their sole representative to an International Anarchist Congress held in Berlin in 1921. A steamer delay caused him to miss all but the final day, but he convened in Sweden with Emma Goldman and Alexander Berkman and relayed the revered duo's testimony upon his return to the United States. The pair published a series of exposés in major American newspapers, which were soon released as their books *My Disillusionment in Russia* and *The Bolshevik Myth*.[18]

The situation in Russia was not only politically, but also personally, compelling for Pesotta. Her father had been executed in 1920 by a general of the counterrevolutionary White Army. Yet only months later she received word that her lover, Kushnarev, had been imprisoned by the Bolsheviks.[19] Her hopes for the revolution eclipsed, Pesotta began to attend meetings of the Anarchist Red Cross. The organization had been founded in 1907 to support Russian anarchists imprisoned by the czar.[20] In the early 1920s, however, it provided aid to anarchists imprisoned or exiled to Siberia by Lenin's government. The macabre letters Pesotta and other member received from Russian prisoners and their families served as wedges dividing them from other radicals active in the unions.

The revolution in Russia fundamentally divided and reordered the American Left.[21] An invitation by Lenin for the left wing of the Socialist Party of America to join the international communist movement prompted a faction fight and the eventual expulsion of nearly sixty thousand radicals, including the majority of the party's foreign-language speakers. After jockeying over leadership and parrying with the Department of Justice for a few years, a unified, legal communist party emerged in 1921. It aimed to win control of existing labor unions and run candidates in local and national elections, with hopes of instigating armed revolution at an opportune moment. Following the loss of half its membership to the new organization, the Socialist Party struggled to retain momentum in the postwar years.

These tensions escalated into vicious faction fighting in the ILGWU during the 1920s. In 1922 Pesotta was elected as a delegate from Local 25 to the union's national convention, held in Cleveland, Ohio. She used this position to promote a variety of anarchist causes as well as those of the shop delegate movement she had joined in 1919. Pesotta and other anarchist delegates, such as Simon Farber, successfully lobbied the union to support the Sacco and Vanzetti defense campaign. Pesotta introduced another resolution, which stated, "Whereas, the Ferrer Modern School in Stelton, N.J. has after ten years of experiment and experience demonstrated that libertarian methods as applied to the education of children are far superior to authoritarian methods," the union should donate $300 to the school. It carried. Anarchists wrested another $150 dollars out of the coffers for the Kropotkin Publication Society and $100 for the Political Prisoners Defense and Relief Committee, aimed at freeing Red Scare victims still in prison. The *Fraye Arbeter Shtime* was granted $250 for its historical support of the labor movement, though it was cautioned for its "unjust criticism" and "undeserved attacks" on the ILGWU leadership.[22] The anarchists' work within mainstream unions clearly translated into at least modest material support for the movement's other efforts.

Pesotta and other members of the Shop Delegate League were far less successful in modifying the ILGWU's constitution than they were in securing funds for pet projects. Their caucus proposed an amendment allowing for the recall of officers of the general executive board, a system of proportional representation that would give the larger (Left-led) locals more power, and another to institute the shop delegate system itself. One after the other, each of these resolutions was defeated.[23] Moreover, cracks began to develop within the ranks of the insurgents as the convention wore on. Adroit supporters of the union's administration introduced a resolution to censure the Russian government, given that "there still are many political prisoners in Russia, while sections of the labor and Socialist movement are being suppressed, their leaders jailed and their members terrorized." The resolution sparked a vigorous debate. One Communist Party member moved for the resolution to be tabled, "owing to the unreliability of the news published regarding Russia." Another argued that the resolution would "aid the capitalistic world in crushing Russia." Concerned for their comrades and relatives, the anarchists attending the convention jumped into the fray. The proceedings record the following exchange:

> DELEGATE MISS PASETTA [*SIC*]: I amend it to read that this resolution apply only to anarchists, left social revolutionaries and social democrats.

> There was no second to the amendment.

> DELEGATE MISS PASETTA: If we request the capitalist governments to release political prisoners, it is no more than right to request the workers' government to release their political prisoners.

> DELEGATE LANCH: Why is it that Alexander Berkman and Emma Goldman, who were in Russia two years, were not put in jail although they had different opinions?

DELEGATE [SIMON] FARBER: Because the Soviet Government was afraid to arrest such famous people, who are known the world over.

Delegate Farber concluded his remarks by mentioning the names of several people who had been either executed or jailed because of their opinions and exhorted the delegates to pass the recommendation of the committee [demanding the prisoners be released].

Upon being put to a vote, the report of the committee was adopted. 129 voting for, 41 against.[24]

The anarchists' personal knowledge of the persecution of fellow anarchists, then, was an important factor in moving their union to inveigh against Soviet repression. Yet it greatly strained relations within the camp of union reformers.

The division between anarchists and communists in the shop delegate movement deepened after the convention. In 1920 the garment worker radicals had affiliated with the purportedly independent Trade Union Education League. By the end of 1922, however, it became clear that leaders of the league had secretly aligned it with the Communist International's union federation and begun to take funds and instruction from the Workers Party, as the Communist Party of America (CP) was then known. Following a directive to "bore from within," they worked to place communists in key leadership positions. Consequently, the anarchists bolted from the Shop Delegate League and the Trade Union Education League, forming their own caucus in the union and launching the weekly Yiddish-language newspaper *Der Yunyon Arbeiter* (The union worker).[25] A former IWW organizer, Morris Sigman, became president of the ILGWU in 1923 and deepened the fight with the communists by declaring the Trade Union Education League a "dual union," which allowed him to ban its caucuses, expel some members, and bar others from holding office.[26] Still, communists gained control of three New York City locals and held an unabashedly procommunist May Day rally in 1924. When Sigman suspended the executive boards of these locals, they organized a work stoppage by thirty thousand members to force reinstatement.

This upsurge put the anarchists in a torturous position. They opposed the political moderation and the antidemocratic practices of the union administration. Yet the news from Russia remained grim and they had experienced the CP's double-dealing firsthand in the Shop Delegate League. Left without sufficient numbers or resources to oppose both factions simultaneously, the anarchists eventually prioritized the struggle against communist control of their unions. When others, including leaders of the Socialist Party, leaned on Sigman to reach a settlement with the CP faction in 1924, a committee of four anarchists, including Simon Farber, "spent a whole night with Sigman vainly trying to dissuade him from signing the agreement."[27] Although the "right" eventually regained the upper hand, the CP continued to vie for control until October 1929, when the Communist International changed its labor strategy and ordered CP organizers to form independent unions rather than bore from within existing ones.[28]

Having sided with the moderate socialists, the anarchists came out on the winning side of the garment union "civil war." Anarchists such as Simon Farber, Louis Levy, Max Bluestein, Saul Yanovsky, and Anna Sosnovsky gained or retained staff positions as organizers, business agents, and editors of union periodicals in the 1930s and 1940s, sometimes even securing positions for their children. Rose Pesotta may have gained the most from the experience. She took a position as a staff organizer in 1933 and rose quickly through the ranks to become the first female vice president of the union.

Anarchists of other trades and ethnic groups, however, severely criticized the strategy adopted by the Yiddish-speaking anarchists during the conflict. In 1925, Stelton Colony resident Abe Blecher accused the anarchists grouped around the FAS of "revisionism" and of propounding "a type of anarchism which is ... rather liberalistic" and characterized by "its opportunism and conservatism."[29] A touch more sympathetically, the anarchist Sam Dolgoff later recalled,

> The *FAS* anarchists, with little or no reservations, swung their considerable influence to the "right wing" machine and became, in time, fully integrated into the class collaborationist "right wing" apparatus.... The defectors did not deliberately abandon their principles. Unable to formulate an independent, consistent anarchist policy alternative to both "right" and "left" factions and bewildered by the complexity of the situation, they became enmeshed in union factional politics.[30]

While criticizing the garment unionists' accommodation of moderate tendencies in their union, other anarchist groupings failed to offer an alternative strategy for outorganizing the communists. Meanwhile, they continued to accept much-needed union contributions to their Modern Schools, prisoner defense campaigns, and other projects. Beyond a plan to compete with the communists in particular unions, anarchists clearly needed to articulate a broader labor strategy relevant to the post–World War I context in which mass production and mass consumption were beginning to define life in the United States. Before the war, Italian organizers had attracted tens of thousands of miners and manufacturing workers to the anarchist fold. In the 1920s, however, contingencies led them to adopt priorities that differed from those of their forbears and their Jewish contemporaries.

DEFENDING SACCO AND VANZETTI
AND FIGHTING FASCISM

Italian anarchists in the United States had little time to lick their wounds following the raids and deportations of 1919 and 1920. Throughout the 1920s they concentrated on two central tasks: the fight to stop the executions of two of their own, Nicola Sacco and Bartolomeo Vanzetti; and strenuous opposition to the growth of fascism in Italy and the United States.[31] As before the war, they were divided into syndicalist and insurrectionist factions. The L'Era Nuova Group of Paterson never recovered from the raids and jailings its members faced during the Red Scare years.[32] Consequently, pro-union Italian anarchists tended to group around Carlo Tresca and his initiatives during the 1920s, while the circles formerly affiliated with *Cronaca Sovversiva* carried on independently. "After the Palmer Raids," historian Nunzio Pernicone writes, "dozens of Galleanisti went underground or into exile rather than risk deportation. Some never resurfaced, many restricted their activities, and still others became completely inactive."[33] For example, the Grupo Bresci of East Harlem disbanded after the raids. Some participants in the 1919 bomb plot, such as Emilio Coda, slipped out of the country and joined deported comrades in Italy and France. However, hundreds of "anti-organizzatore" remained active in the United States, if on a more discrete level. The Grupo Autonomo of Boston, among others, continued to meet weekly, and a number of papers arose to take the place of *Cronaca Sovversiva* on a stopgap basis.[34]

The Sacco-Vanzetti Defense Committee, based in Boston, was initially composed almost solely of Galleanisti. Despite long-standing tensions with the Galleanisti, Carlo Tresca arranged for Fred Moore, an able IWW lawyer, to head up a legal and political defense campaign for the prisoners. Tresca and his wife, Elizabeth Gurley Flynn, also swung into action raising funds and undertaking lecture tours to aid the prisoners.

The Galleanisti argued that Sacco and Vanzetti had been framed in retaliation for exposing the illegal detention of fellow anarchists Roberto Elia and Andrea Salsedo. By representing the pair as exemplars of heroic antiauthoritarianism, they hoped to use the case to rebuild support for anarchism in general. The committee was aided in this work when, in 1922, insurrectionists living in New York launched the newspaper *L'Adunata dei Refratarri* (The summoning of the unruly). The paper regularly published articles about the Sacco-Vanzetti case, urging readers to take militant direct action to save the prisoners' lives.[35]

Tensions quickly mounted within the defense committee. In letters to Tresca and Gurley Flynn, Moore complained that the Galleanisti's sectarianism and antiorganizational stance left them disconnected from labor unions and progressive organizations, which were vital sources of support. The lawyer hoped to organize a mass political defense for the prisoners on the pattern developed by the IWW in previous decades. In publicity for the English-language labor press, Moore, Flynn, and others significantly downplayed the defendants' anarchism, instead focusing on their status as unjustly targeted workers and labor organizers. The defense committee's continuing calls for workers to break the prisoners out of jail and exact revenge on their captors worked directly against this strategy. Moore hoped to use the case to indict the larger pattern of frame-ups and arrests that had incapacitated the IWW since 1917. In this way, two obscure Italian insurrectionist anarchists became symbols of the repression of working-class movements as a whole, and many perceived their defense as a final stand against the antilabor nativism of the Red Scare.

Sacco-Vanzetti defense committees sprouted up across the country, raising at least $365,000 for the defense between 1920 and 1925. Such efforts came at a cost, however. From the road, Flynn reported that "local groups feel that the Sacco-Vanzetti case is taking all their time, all their money, [and] stultifying their efforts along every other line."[36] For anarchists, who also felt compelled to support the victims of Bolshevik repression, prisoner defense work threatened to overtake other movement-building responsibilities in the 1920s.

By 1925, the case had attracted so much attention—nationally and internationally—that the Communist Party committed its own resources to winning the anarchists' freedom. Though Vanzetti personally welcomed its aid, the perception that the party was leveraging the case for its own purposes and downplaying the prisoners' anarchism created conflicts within the defense organizations. This created a tense situation in which loyalties were tested.

Jewish anarchists battled communists for control of the ILGWU, while some Italian anarchists accepted resources in a last-ditch effort to save the lives of their comrades. In July 1924, ten thousand workers rallied in Union Square to demand the pair's freedom, but a riot broke out between pro- and anticommunist supporters, prompting the police to disperse the gathering by force.

Despite his early assistance, the Boston committee soon excluded Tresca from participating directly in the defense campaign, owing to long-standing factionalism. As one New York anarchist put it, "The Italian movement in America was always dominated by personalities. Tresca had his groups and *L'Adunata* had its, and there was no cooperation between them."[37] Although personal loyalties played a significant role, the divisions also stemmed from the conflicting strategies of syndicalists and insurrectionists.[38]

The exclusion of the Italian syndicalists from the defense campaign allowed them to focus on other pressing matters. Throughout the 1920s, Tresca maintained his commitments to militant trade unionism, but he was forced to shift his primary focus to combating the growth of the fascist movement in Italy and the United States. Immediately after the war, the Italian Left grew dramatically through a series of factory occupations in the automobile plants of Turin, raising the hopes of Italian anarchists.[39] After Mussolini's March on Rome of October 28, 1922, however, Tresca recognized the serious threat posed by the fascist movement. Italian Americans established their own fascist groups in New York City and Philadelphia in 1921. Within two years, approximately twenty thousand fascists belonged to more than forty groups scattered throughout the country and coordinated by Mussolini. Scholars suggest that approximately 5 percent of the immigrant community, mostly working-class men, participated in Blackshirt activities, supported by significant sectors of the Italian American elite.[40]

Tresca soon became known as a leading figure of the antifascist resistance. Having steered his newspaper, *Il Martello* (The hammer), clear of censors during the war, Tresca made it a weekly in 1921, and circulation grew to a high of 10,500 copies in December 1924.[41] Articles in *Il Martello* both worked to discredit the heroic self-image fascists sought to cultivate and appealed to Italians living abroad to boycott business and services that supported the fascist government. Tresca and his allies denounced the fascists on crosscountry speaking tours, raised funds for resistance groups, and smuggled bundles of the paper into Italy, where the radical press had been suppressed.[42] Though he distrusted social democratic union leaders and had denounced Bolshevism after the Kronstadt rebellion, Tresca sought to build a pragmatic united front of leftists against fascism. Based on their own strategic assessment, the Il Martello Group collaborated with figures such as CP leader Vittorio Vidali to found the Anti-Fascist Alliance of North America. Unsurprisingly, conflict over communism in the unions destabilized the alliance from the outset.

The most ostentatious aspect of the resistance built on the anarchist commitment to take direct action. When dignitaries visited from Italy, or local Blackshirts mobilized publicly, antifascists organized enormous counter-demonstrations. Frequently, the antifascist crowds confronted their opponents physically. When the Italian deputy Giuseppe Bottai visited the United States in August 1921, Italian anarchists challenged him in New York City, Utica, New Haven, and Philadelphia. At Bottai's speech in Philadelphia,

> the audience included some 2,000 anti-Fascists. . . . Bottai spoke for ten minutes, repeatedly interrupted by shouts of *Abbasso Bottai* and *Morte a Bottai!* before police drove the anti-Fascists from the theatre with clubs. Outside, another 4,000 anti-Fascists joined the demonstration but were dispersed by mounted police who charged the crowd.[43]

When another politician, Antonio Locatelli, arrived in 1924, "3,000 anti-Fascists disrupted a banquet in his honor with a volley of tomatoes, rocks, and bricks."[44]

Blackshirt organizations sprung up alongside left-wing groups in Italian immigrant communities throughout North America, leaving them rife with tension. After immigrating to Detroit in 1920, Attilio Bortolotti learned about Sacco and Vanzetti and soon became a member of the Galleanisti Gruppo I Refrattari.[45] Bortolotti later recalled how his antifascist circle disrupted a meeting addressed by the Italian consul:

> I told the consul what they were—a bunch of killers, liars, and the rest. At my shoulder was a picture of the king. I tore it off the wall, crumpled it in my hands, and threw it in the face of the consul. That started a melee. In less than a minute the whole audience was fighting each other.[46]

At a Columbus Day parade in 1928, however, the Michigan antifascists were sorely outnumbered. Bortolotti recalled, "When the band began to play *Giovenezza,* the fascist hymn, we exploded in catcalls. . . . The man who held the fascist flag put it down, took out his gun, and shot two comrades, both anarchists."[47] One of them died, and the rest of the radicals barely escaped. Despite the high stakes, similar confrontations continued throughout the

1920s and 1930s. Actions such as these established a precedent for U.S. anarchists physically confronting fascists and white supremacist organizations, a practice that was revived in the 1990s under the auspices of the organization Anti-Racist Action.

LYING LOW IN RADICAL COLONIES

While many Italian anarchists experienced the 1920s as a period of heightened physicality and danger, other East Coast anarchists spent the decade in more serene environs, developing radical colonies in rural areas outside of New York City. As we have seen, anarchists associated with the Ferrer Center wanted to move the center's Modern School for children to a safer, rural environment before the war. They launched the Stelton Colony near New Brunswick, New Jersey, for that purpose. According to Joseph Cohen, "The primary object of the Colony, as conceived by Comrade Harry Kelly in the summer of 1914, was to secure a small tract of land and some buildings for the School out in God's open country. . . . Neither he nor any other influential member of the Francisco Ferrer Association was interested in colonization on its own account."[48]

In order to establish the school, the Ferrer Association purchased three contiguous farms, together constituting 143 acres. It divided this land and sold one-acre lots to members of the movement, retaining nine acres in common for roads, the school, and a boardinghouse for students with nonresident parents.[49] An early resident recalled that "all sorts of homes were built at Stelton, from neat two-story houses with modern plumbing, steam heat, and accessories to make them akin to a comfortable city dwelling, down to rough shacks that were used first as living quarters and later for chicken houses when the owners built more substantial structures for themselves."[50] By 1920, nearly 150 people lived at the colony year round. Russian Jews constituted approximately three-quarters of the colony's population, but Italians, Spaniards, Britons, and a sprinkling of people born in the United States also called Stelton home.[51] Residents primarily identified as anarchists; but the colony brooked no ideological test, and radicals of other stripes, including a few members of the newly formed Communist Party, settled there as well.

Although the initial colonists desired to build a life based on the principles of anarchist communism, they had no illusions that Stelton would be self-sufficient. Most adult residents traveled to New York, Philadelphia, or

New Brunswick by train each day, relying on factory work to support themselves. The colony did develop a number of cooperatively owned enterprises, however, including a taxi service to the nearest train stop, a grocery and ice service, and a small garment shop. Moreover, residents created a performance space in an old barn and erected a library named after Kropotkin. Members gathered for community dinners, at which they discussed concerns relevant to the colony and the broader movement. In the warm season, visitors eager to escape the city pitched tents on the weekend. Guests—including figures as diverse as John Dewey, Helen Keller, and Paul Robeson—lectured to adult members of the colony, helping to reproduce, on a smaller scale, the rich intellectual environment that drew many of the colonists to the Ferrer Center and to the anarchist counterculture in the first place.[52]

Although the Modern School provided the impetus that brought the colony together, it also at times threatened to tear residents apart. Raising their children with libertarian educational techniques became increasingly important to anarchists in the decade after Francisco Ferrer's execution, as this practice seemed to offer an alternative to the insurrectionary strategies of change that had proven unsuccessful to date. Kelly explains, "We wanted to give the children the best possible teaching, but above and beyond this was the social ideal behind the [Ferrer] Center, to rebuild society through the agency of schools for the young based on libertarian principles."[53] The goal, according to one historian of the school, was to raise "a generation of children uncorrupted by the commercialism and selfishness of the capitalist system and undisturbed by political repression and indoctrination in religion or government as taught in traditional schools."[54] However, residents rarely agreed on the details of libertarian education. Although it was generally accepted that students should not be graded or physically disciplined, the combination of topics and activities offered was subject to the whims of a revolving cast of instructors during the colony's first five years.

Stelton's most consistent educational program was initiated by Elizabeth and Alexis Ferm, who took charge of the school in 1920. The Ferms believed that raising children to be free human beings primarily entailed aiding them in a process of self-discovery and self-development. Yet the Ferms also aimed to train students to live as self-sufficient artisans or small farmers, in line with the vision Kropotkin sketched in his 1899 book *Fields, Factories, and Workshops*.[55] For this reason, they encouraged students to focus on manual trades, such as weaving and printing, rather than "abstract" and "academic" studies.[56] This pedagogical practice, however, did not sit well with many

Modern School parents, whose lives had been defined by industrial society and for whom intellectual pursuits, including a deep engagement with political theory, were important and gratifying.

Some parents were outraged that the Ferms refused to teach their children the rudiments of anarchist thought and ethics. Alexis Ferm argued that teaching such ideas would be as stultifying as the imposition of Christianity in religious schools. Yet the guidance offered by the couple was not morally neutral. Elizabeth Ferm, who spent her early life in a convent, promoted conservative sexual politics. She organized sex-segregated sleeping quarters in the school's dormitory, chastised children for masturbating, and discouraged the partial nudity that had become commonplace among the children before her arrival. In this sense, the bodily protocols observed at Stelton represented a reversal from the sex radicalism that prevailed in and around the Ferrer Center before the war. These issues added to the concerns of many working-class parents that their children would be limited by their lack of training in math, science, and other traditional subjects. As the sociologist Laurence Veysey astutely observes, "The parents of the Ferrer children had always tended to call for definiteness in the instruction, both morally and intellectually. In effect they demanded that the children be given the basic tools to enable them to rise in society at the same time that they be indoctrinated with the social consciences of militant revolutionaries."[57] The question of whether expanded freedom could best be achieved by practicing personal self-direction, or by teaching people how to define and fight for expanded rights and resources, would vex anarchists for decades to come. Under mounting pressure, the Ferms decided to leave Stelton in 1925.

In the early 1920s, Stelton residents also clashed over the nature of Russian society and communism. The colonists were at first wildly enthusiastic about the October revolution, even flying a red flag from the colony's water tower. Within a year, however, letters from friends and relatives began to arrive, carrying news of the growing centralization of power and the repression of anarchists and other Left dissidents. Community leaders read such letters aloud at public meetings, leading to "heated and often acrimonious argument over the merits and demerits of the economic, social, and political setup in Russia."[58] Similar disputes also wracked a second colony founded by anarchists early in the decade.

In 1923 Harry Kelly learned that a 450-acre wooded property on Lake Mohegan, forty-five miles north of New York City, was for sale. He called a meeting to assess interest in launching a second community-building effort. Kelly noted,

> Our purpose . . . was to establish another children's school, to be conducted along libertarian lines, to build a community wherein a larger measure of individual and social life . . . could be realized. We believed it possible to create a community life in that pleasant setting much better than anything we as individuals could hope for in a teeming city like New York. After all, as one of those present remarked, even workers are entitled to, and would prefer, a more aesthetic place to live in than the lower East side or even the Bronx. To which others said: Amen![59]

By the end of the year, twenty-five families had moved to the new colony. The Modern School opened its doors in 1924 and the new colony grew rapidly, attracting nearly three hundred families by 1930. Jews once again predominated, but immigrants from many European countries made their home in Mohegan. According to Paul Avrich, "Mohegan projected a more prosperous, more middle-class image [than Stelton], with professionals and even businessmen quite common among its inhabitants."[60] Though the Mohegan Association attempted to more stringently screen applicants than the founders of Stelton had, communists, socialists, and liberals again took up residence. Tensions flared when well-organized communists maneuvered to control the colony and encouraged their Young Pioneer youth groups to march around the grounds.[61]

Kelly's comments and the social character of Mohegan suggest that the colonists' initial desire to create social change through libertarian education was, by 1923, compounded by a plan to collectivize the process of social mobility. Anarchist colonies offered their residents more pleasant surroundings and greater freedom of expression in daily life, but also distanced them from opportunities to organize fellow workers and from the direct conflicts with authorities that characterized the lives of prewar urban anarchists. Nevertheless, Mohegan served as a home base to anarchists who played important roles in the interwar movement, including Valerio Isca, Simon Farber, and, after 1937, the revered German anarcho-syndicalist Rudolf Rocker. Like Stelton, Mohegan Colony regularly hosted lectures, conferences, and recreational excursions for comrades who continued to dwell in cities. The high density of radicals also made it possible for organizers to easily collect donations from each household. Large contributions from "Stelton" and "Mohegan" are recorded in the financial statements of most anarchist periodicals and prisoner defense organizations operating during the interwar years. Indeed, it was residents of Stelton who launched the first English-language anarchist newspaper of national scope after *The Blast* and *Mother Earth* were suppressed in 1917.

ENGLISH-LANGUAGE GROUPS AND
THE *ROAD TO FREEDOM*

Relative to the activity of Italian- and Yiddish-speaking communities, anarchist political work conducted in English was slower to revive after the Red Scare. When English-speaking groups and publications did resurface, they were predominantly composed of foreign-born individuals—most often Russian Jews—who recognized the importance of promoting anarchism in the official language of the country in which they lived. The most consistent and active English-speaking formations of the decade were based in Los Angeles, Chicago, and New York.

In November 1922, anarchists living in Los Angeles launched a new group called the Libertarians. Its most active members included Joseph Spivak, a Russian Jew; Jules Scarceriaux, a Frenchman; and Thomas H. Bell, who hailed from Scotland. Spivak noted, "At the beginning it was organized as a Jewish group but we soon realized the necessity of an English movement and changed into the above name."[62] The new group first focused on fund-raising for prisoner support, sending "$230 to the IWW and over $100 to the Russian Political Prisoners." After a year, the Libertarians began organizing a lecture and discussion series known as the Free Workers Forum. By 1927, the Libertarians functioned alongside an anarchist Workmen's Circle branch affiliated with the *Fraye Arbeter Shtime,* as well as a small Mexican formation, Libertario Centro, concerned with fund-raising and carrying out propaganda activities in Spanish. "With the three groups in existence, Los Angeles may be looked upon as the future central point of activity on the Pacific Coast," Spivak predicted.[63]

A similar pattern occurred in Chicago. It was "the arrival of distressing news from Soviet Russia[,] ... the anguished cries of our tortured brethren there," that prompted the formation of a new anarchist organization, the Free Society Group, in 1923, according to a prominent member, Boris Yelensky.[64] Initially the Free Society Group was composed solely of Jews and it conducted business in Yiddish. But as Yelensky recalled, "In the course of

The Free Society Group of Chicago, circa 1925. Rudolf and Millie Rocker, on a speaking tour of the United States, are seated third row from the front, fourth and fifth from the left. Courtesy of the Pacific Street Films Photographs Collection, Tamiment Library/Robert F. Wagner Labor Archives, New York University.

time the question arose as to what language we could most advantageously employ in continuing our propaganda activities. After extended debate it was decided that, inasmuch as our membership was no longer exclusively Jewish, we should conduct our agitation in English."[65] Beginning in 1926, the Chicago anarchists promoted monthly Free Society Forums, in which anarchists and progressive intellectuals debated economic and social issues at labor halls throughout the city. They distributed proceeds from these educational events and fund-raising socials to anarchist periodicals and defense campaigns in the United States and abroad. The Free Society Group also supported the publication of anarchist literature, such as G. P. Maximoff's account of the Bolshevik repression of anarchists, *The Guillotine at Work*. Maximoff was a Russian anarcho-syndicalist exile who settled with his wife, Olga, in Chicago in 1926. There he became active in the Free Society Group and the IWW while editing the Russian anarchist newspaper *Dielo Truda* (Labor's cause) and hanging wallpaper for a living.[66]

The relief efforts undertaken by the Libertarians and the Free Society Group were coordinated by a small group of Russian exiles operating out of Paris and Berlin. After fleeing the Bolsheviks' post-Kronstadt crackdown, Alexander Berkman, Mark Mratchny, Voline, and others established the Joint Committee for the Defense of Revolutionists Imprisoned in Russia. They attempted to track the whereabouts and condition of anarchists and other radicals taken into custody and to provide money, clothes, food, and moral support to every prisoner allowed to receive mail. Simultaneously, the committee attempted to mobilize international pressure against the regime through the publication of a bulletin in four languages. In December 1926, the Joint Committee was subsumed under the International Working People's Association, and Mollie Steimer and Senya Fleshin took on much of the relief work from Paris.[67]

The pages of the *Bulletin of the Joint Committee for the Defense of the Revolutionists Imprisoned in Russia* overflowed with missives from prisoners detailing their conditions.[68] A note from a prisoner held at the Solovetsky Monastery, which had been converted into a prison, plaintively stated, "We have reached a condition of physical exhaustion and we are now facing slow death from starvation." At Solovetsky, correspondents explained, female political prisoners were subject to systematic sexual assault. "They are forced to become concubines. . . . By degrees they are bereft of all human semblance, [and] are infected with venereal diseases."[69] Letters grew increasingly desperate over the course of the decade. However, the pages of the *Bulletin* also recorded regular contributions to the relief effort by anarchists throughout Europe and the United States.[70] Those making donations recognized that if they did not aid these prisoners, no one would.

In October 1924, a group of fourteen anarchists assembled at the Stelton Colony admitted, "There had been practically no activities in the anarchistic group of Stelton for what seems a long while."[71] Moreover, U.S. anarchists had not published in English since Marcus Graham's *Free Society* ran aground in 1921. That paper, like the other fly-by-night periodicals of the Red Scare years, lacked the scope and distribution of prewar ventures such as *Mother Earth*. Seeking to rectify this inactivity, the anarchists meeting at Stelton launched an eight-page monthly newspaper, the *Road to Freedom*. The fate of the Russian anarchists was clearly on the minds of these East Coast anarchists as well: "Road to Freedom" is the English translation of the title of the Nabat Federation's journal, *Put' k Svobode*.[72]

Upon being tapped as editor of the new periodical, Hippolyte Havel relocated from Mohegan to Stelton, where he was given free room and board by comrades until the 1940s. Havel's alcoholism grew in the postwar years, resulting in cycles of hard work followed by periods of incapacitated drunkenness. A younger man, Warren Starr Van Valkenburgh—known to friends simply as Van—officially replaced Havel as editor in 1928 but played a critical role even during the years Havel's name topped the masthead. Born in 1884, Van Valkenburgh hailed from Schenectady, New York, where he had distributed *Mother Earth* and *The Blast* before the war. As a young man, Van Valkenburgh had lost a leg while working for the railroad. In the 1920s, he and his wife, Sadie Ludlow, held clerical positions in New York City.[73] The paper also benefited from the energies of Rose Pesotta, who agreed to serve as secretary of the Road to Freedom Group in addition to her responsibilities in her union local, the Anarchist Red Cross, and Sacco-Vanzetti defense work. The Free Society Group held regular fund-raising events on behalf of the paper, while the Los Angeles Libertarians frequently contributed articles and money to the new periodical.

Early issues balanced commentary on current events with reprints of essays by anarchist luminaries such as Kropotkin and Malatesta. Havel declared "that monstrous bulwark of all our social iniquities—the State" to be the primary target of anarchist political activity; but regarding strategy he could only note, "By education, by free organization, by individual and associated resistance to political and economic tyranny, the Anarchist hopes to achieve his aims."[74] The Road to Freedom Group assumed working people to be its primary audience. "If we can give in every issue accurate reports of the main labor events all over the country," Havel assured readers, "we will secure a large number of genuine workingmen readers and a great moral influence with the working classes."[75] The editors, however, were never able to recruit enough correspondents to make the paper a reliable source of labor news. Although contributors consistently chastised AFL leaders for their timidity, they said little about the sweeping changes taking place in workplaces and the economy. Its monthly format, meanwhile, made it impossible for the *Road to Freedom* to be as comprehensive as the weekly and daily newspapers published by the Socialist and Communist Parties.

The *Road to Freedom* retreated from the discussion of gender and sexuality that *Mother Earth* and the "gruppi femminili di propaganda" developed before the war.[76] Contributors commented occasionally on the continuing oppression of "negros" in southern states, but made no effort to examine conditions within the rapidly growing communities of African Americans in northern cities, nor to consider the political appeal of organizations such as the Universal Negro

Improvement Association or the African Blood Brotherhood, which were on the rise in the 1920s.[77] Save for a short piece by Robert Henri in the debut issue, the *Road to Freedom* did not follow postwar developments in the world of arts and letters. Whereas *Mother Earth, The Blast,* and Havel's own prewar journal derived much of their punch from political cartoons and illustrations, the *Road to Freedom* was not illustrated in any way, giving it a drier tone. The *Road to Freedom*'s inattention to these issues suggests that prewar links between anarchists and bohemian intellectuals were severed during the Red Scare period and the subsequent departure of the "Lost Generation" of literati to Europe. Anarchists working to reestablish the movement in the 1920s either deprioritized or were unable to repair these connections.

Despite these literary and political limitations, anarchists began to regroup around the *Road to Freedom*. The constant need to raise funds for printing and mailing the paper prompted New York anarchists to resume organizing dinners and dances, which served both economic and community-building purposes. During the summer of 1925, for example, the paper advertised a "Concert and Dance at Danceland, Coney Island," to benefit the Anarchist Aid Society for Political Prisoners. The editorial group also initiated a mail order book service, as was common among publishers of prewar anarchist newspapers.[78] Although many titles were anarchist classics that offered increasingly dated analysis, the service likely provided the first means for curious individuals to obtain English-language anarchist books since 1917.

While most Americans celebrated the Fourth of July in 1925, the Road to Freedom Group hosted a two-day conference at the library of the Stelton Colony, with Spanish, Italian, Yiddish, and English speakers in attendance. The proceedings offer insight into what issues anarchists were and were not attentive to at mid-decade. In the first session, which addressed means of propaganda, Kelly argued that building colonies served as "a means of propaganda for an Anarchist mode of life." This drew criticism from other participants, who believed the "colony life engages the individuals in too much routine, diverting them from the general struggle of the movement." The conference passed six resolutions. Tellingly, three were pledges of support to imprisoned and exiled comrades, noting especially Sacco and Vanzetti. Another inaugurated an "International Group in New York, the said group forming a nucleus for all Anarchists in New York and vicinity, in the hope of being able to extend the Organization over the whole country." On the subject of the labor movement, the conferees could only "reaffirm their faith in the organization of the workers, insist in their right to propagate their ideas among the workers of all organizations, but repudiate most emphatically all dictatorship, dictatorship either on the part of the bureaucratic leadership or originating from political parties."[79] A high degree of concern for persecuted comrades, a low degree of unity on the matter of labor strategy, and an earnest desire to regroup: this was the state of U.S. anarchism in 1925.

Shortly after the conference, the new International Group established the Workers' Centre in lower Manhattan and organized a program of Friday evening lectures. Contributors to the newspaper also embarked upon lecture tours, selling subscriptions along the way. In April 1927, for instance, Marcus Graham spoke in Philadelphia; Washington, D.C.; New York; New Haven; Boston; Worcester; Rochester; Buffalo; Cleveland; Youngstown; and Detroit—most frequently on the topic of political prisons in Russia. Graham claimed that in several of the cities he visited, large halls were "overcrowded"—but many in the audience were communists, there to hear Graham debate with party officials. Graham's lectures primarily attracted immigrant workers. He noted that in Boston, "I was very pleased in having as one of the listeners, a colored man, the only one during my tour." A lecture organized by the local branch of the IWW in Buffalo, New York, brought a considerable crowd of "native-born" workers. With this exception, however, Graham lamented, there was an "almost complete absence of an American element in all the places I have been to."[80] Impressionistic as it is, Graham's tour report suggests that in 1927 the anarchist movement remained centered geographically in industrial cities of the Northeast and demographically among immigrant factory workers. Moreover, the Communist Party was gaining support among this base of supporters.

POTHOLES IN THE *ROAD TO FREEDOM*

The *Road to Freedom* assumed a tone less caustic and smug than that of prewar anarchist newspapers such as Berkman's *Blast* and Galleani's *Cronaca Sovversiva*. In this, it was the representative voice of a movement less sure of itself than its prewar counterpart had been.

The newspaper provided mixed signals about what types of tactics best served the anarchist cause. Havel and Van Valkenburgh de-emphasized propaganda of the deed and encouraged anarchists to expand efforts to promote propaganda of the word (through publishing and lectures) and libertarian education. Yet when a contributor suggested anarchists should explicitly reject violent methods in order to attract allies, he was roundly upbraided. Writing in 1925, D. Isakovitz argued that anarchists' fascination with expropriation and propaganda of the deed had "made our movement a nest for spies and provocateurs," divided anarchists from socialists, and alienated the "general public." Moreover, he argued, "every political, economical and social activity and reform that could not be considered as making the social revolution was ignored and labeled as a palliative, as a patch on the present rotten society and a hindrance to the millennium."[81] Contributor Theo L. Miles, however, insisted that Isakovitz's ideas amounted to "revisionism," plain and simple. "Every true anarchist," Havel added, "is a social rebel, awaiting with impatience the coming days of social revolution."[82]

Debates over forms of organization also continued to bog down anarchists. Tensions flared in 1928, when Joseph Spivak of the Los Angeles Libertarians asked readers to consider why the movement's influence remained "so negligible." After visiting comrades while traveling from the West Coast to the east, he concluded the problem lay with "the lack of interest in the English propaganda and the lack of the proper methods of organization." Spivak found that Italian anarchists, especially, remained averse to formal organization. "They do things spontaneously, when there is a call for it, in the eleventh hour of its need," he noted. Only with organization, he insisted, could anarchists develop an effective strategy and "become a movement of construction, a movement of planning and building in advance, not a movement of defense, of emergency, as it is now."[83]

Spivak insisted that such organization was in line with anarchist principles, because it would remain voluntary and federative. Resistance to formal organization, he added, often led to outcomes not representative of anarchist values:

> Activity and work carried out without a regular form of organization is breeding dishonesty, despotism and autocracy. The initiators of such a movement are only responsible to themselves not to a group, they are their own controllers, are not responsible to any particular individuals and have the best chances to become dishonest.[84]

The issue of informal, unaccountable leadership cropping up in purportedly egalitarian, collective efforts would recur with regularity throughout the century.

Despite the modest nature of his proposal, Spivak's article provoked strident rebuttals. Paul Boattini, an Italian anarchist based in Detroit, penned an indignant letter to the editor, asserting, "I think Spivak is trying to build a platform in America. . . . Anarchism is against platforms and you should understand the consequences if these articles do not stop." Boattini's letter suggests the ways anarchists in the United States remained attentive to international intramovement debates even as their movement sought greater traction among American workers. In the mid-1920s, Russian anarchists exiled in France and Germany launched a vigorous debate regarding the lessons to be gleaned from their deadly defeat at the hands of the Bolsheviks. One faction, led by respected organizers such as Petr Arshinov and Nestor Mahkno, published "The Organizational Platform of the General Union of Anarchists," which insisted that an anarchist movement capable of victory required greater theoretical unity and organizational discipline than had previously existed. Unsurprisingly, antiorganizationalists denounced "The Platform" as a deviation from anarchist principles, one that bordered on submission to Leninism.[85]

The *Road to Freedom* devoted little attention to discussing "The Platform," but Spivak's ruminations on organization sounded notes similar enough to provoke the ire of Boattini and others of the Galleanisti school. Intent on denouncing Spivak's organizationalism, however, Boattini missed the substance of his criticisms. He wrote, "We are conducting propaganda with five papers here and helping keep alive others in France. We are also helping hundreds of international victims, and not only Italians." Significant as this work was, it lent credence to Spivak's contention that the Italians devoted little effort to organizing English-speaking Americans; support for embattled anarchists abroad and maintenance of a sense of community among immigrants remained an absorbing priority.

Even beyond the Italian community, Spivak found there was little energy for a renewed organizing push. At a twenty-fifth-anniversary celebration for the *Fraye Arbeter Shtime,* Harry Kelly lamented, "Instead of the war being of short duration and bringing in its train a social revolution, it lasted long enough to kill a very large part of the youth and revolutionary forces of the world and so impoverish the rest as to create the weariness and pessimism of the present time."[86] Van Valkenburgh gloomily intoned that anarchism had become "an ideal to be achieved by posterity in ways unknown to us, unknown because unknowable."[87]

This mood of resignation only deepened with the execution of Sacco and Vanzetti in 1927. Like nearly every other radical organization in the country, the Road to Freedom Group had taken up the cause of Sacco and Vanzetti with increasing fervor as their case wound its way through the courts. Nearly apoplectic as the date of the execution approached, the editors covered the paper's front page with a desperate, accusatory cry for the nation's workers to save their comrades:

> Neither the Electric Chair—nor a Living Death!—But Full Freedom!! for Sacco and Vanzetti.... Give up appeals and use DIRECT ACTION! Only a GENERAL STRIKE will prevent this double murder and secure liberty for our two brothers and fellow-workers.... It's up to you to prevent this crime against humanity. Its YOU who are on trial today! History will judge YOU![88]

Thoroughly dispirited with their own inability to build a mass movement to save their incarcerated comrades, whether in Massachusetts or in the Solovetsky Monastery, much less rebuild the labor movement on libertarian footings, the editors, one senses, were actually concerned about history judging them.

Small in numbers and weak in analysis during the years of ballooning prosperity, U.S. anarchists were caught off guard by the crisis of overproduction that struck at the decade's end. None of the groups active in the 1920s had the organizational capacity to parlay the Great Depression into a boon for their movement. The Free Society Group redoubled its efforts to organize educational forums and debates in Chicago, catering to the desire of working people to better understand the factors contributing to mass unemployment.[89] The Road to Freedom Group recognized that in such a moment of crisis, "it is to the vast masses of the American people that we should speak."[90] Accordingly, the group replaced the *Road to Freedom* with a shorter weekly newspaper simply titled *Freedom*. From the outset, however, *Freedom* suffered from a scarcity of funds and contributors. It collapsed in June 1934, only eighteen months after it debuted, ending the larger publishing project initiated a decade earlier at Stelton.

STRETCHED THIN AND STRATEGICALLY DISORIENTED

While wartime repression created serious setbacks for U.S. anarchism, the movement might have regained momentum had it not been immediately beset with additional challenges. That the anarchist movement was placed in competition with, and came under attack by, the communists and the fascists immediately after having been repressed in the Western democracies was of grave significance. Beyond the conflicts in the garment unions and the streets of Little Italy, attacks on anarchists in Moscow, Berlin, and Barcelona also seriously affected the work of anarchists in the United States. Many felt a dire need to focus their efforts on providing spiritual comfort to comrades imprisoned abroad and to print literature to be smuggled into countries where publishing had become impossible. While the production of non-English anarchist newspapers in the United States spoke to the insularity of aging anarchist circles, it also indicates the endurance of their transnational commitments. Anarchists regarded the provision of such aid as a moral requirement, even if it proved a political liability by limiting local organizing work in their countries of residence during a period when resources were scarce.

Partly because of these international commitments, the U.S. anarchist movement of the 1920s failed to adapt to a class and racial landscape that had evolved substantially in the interwar years. According to Nunzio Pernicone, "By the Second World War, the anarchists were a dwindling element among Italian-Americans. The immigration laws of 1921 and 1924 had prevented any appreciable infusion of new blood from Italy, and the movement itself had failed to propagate a second generation."[91] This was just as true for Russians and Russian Jews, the other immigrant groups that had contributed large numbers of militants to the U.S. anarchist movement in the century's first decades. With the new immigration regime in place, it became more important than ever for U.S. anarchists to maintain their movement by organizing native-born workers and by passing their ideals on to their children.

Yet anarchists met with only limited success in reproducing political commitments among their own children during the 1920s. According to the San Francisco–based insurrectionist Domenico Sallitto, "Children of anarchists shied away from the movement because the parents themselves often failed to practice what they preached. The women seldom participated, and the Italian anarchist father was often an authoritarian at home."[92] To Sallitto's mind, the disinterest of some Italians in prefiguring egalitarian relations in the home hindered the development and continuity of their movement. However, the approach to education in the Modern Schools of the Stelton and Mohegan Colonies—refusing any doctrinal education, in order to allow the students to develop opinions freely—could be seen as a strict adherence to prefigurative principles, and it too failed to instill a deep commitment to anarchist organizing among most of the schools' students. The Modern Schools produced many bright students who excelled when they moved on to traditional public high schools and universities as teenagers; they did not, however, produce a new, larger, generation of anarchist militants ready to take the reins of the movement from their parents' hands.

The focus on education and the move away from factories and urban centers that had served as the flashpoints of earlier anarchist struggles implied a grudging acknowledgment among the colonists that the great social revolution was not imminent, as they had previously believed. In the end, the colonies may have contributed significantly to the upward mobility experienced by many anarchists in the interwar years. They provided an affordable means for workers to build single-family homes on their own plots of land—a process repeated by millions of working-class families moving to the newly built suburbs after the Second World War. Meanwhile the anarchists' intensive investment in education prepared many of their children to enter professional fields of which their parents never dreamed.

Despite these many setbacks and strategic dead ends, the U.S. anarchist movement did survive into the 1930s, a decade marked by dire economic circumstances but rife with opportunities for revolutionary anticapitalists. The demise of the *Road to Freedom* and *Freedom* cleared the ground for the emergence of two new major English-language periodicals, both edited by anarchists who had lived at Stelton during the 1920s. In this fashion, and in others, anarchist activism during the 1920s maintained a direct line of continuity for the movement.

FOUR

The Unpopular Front, 1930–1939

The stock market crash of 1929 sent shock waves through the United States and, soon, the rest of the world. As the value of investments in corporate stock plummeted, banks tightened terms of credit and businesses laid off workers or shut their doors completely. Unemployed wage-earners stopped depositing money in savings accounts and fell behind on loan repayments, leading to the collapse of small town banks. Farmers had already suffered from overproduction and low commodity prices for a decade when the Depression and a drought dealt them a brutal one-two punch. In the three years after Black Tuesday, unemployment climbed to nearly 25 percent of the workforce, leaving an estimated 30 million people without income.[1]

Here was the capitalist crisis of which Marxists had long warned. Socialists, communists, and the newly emergent Trotskyist movement scrambled to mobilize workers and their allies in trade unions, unemployed councils, and arts-oriented front groups. Business and political elites likewise recognized the depth of the crisis. They argued over the best way to save capitalism from its own instabilities and to stave off revolutionary alternatives. The New Deal, which crystallized out of myriad experimental programs and policies, offered some economic relief to the poor in the short-term and, over the longer run, fundamentally altered the scope of the state and the framework by which the economy operated. Both the Socialist Party and the Community Party endorsed government intervention and, during these years, most anticapitalists found some room to collaborate with one another under the banner of the Popular Front—a temporary alliance of political forces promoting the interests of working people. Taking advantage of new openings, the ranks of organized labor grew precipitously.

For these reasons, the 1930s continue to resonate as a high point of American radicalism, the defining decade for what has become known as the Old Left. Anarchists, however, proved an exception to this pattern. Given that antistatism was central to their political identity, anarchists, with few exceptions, advocated on behalf of victims of the economic collapse but rejected responses to the Great Depression that relied on public policy and government resources. Small in numbers, and unwilling to collaborate with the rest of the Left, they formed an unpopular front in the war against structural immiseration.

Throughout the decade, anarchists struggled to understand the seismic transformations of the state, and social relations more broadly, while proposing alternatives they believed would better serve working people in the long term. After 1932, insurrectionary and syndicalist camps became more pronounced, as they had been before the First World War. However, anarchists from both tendencies criticized the New Deal as a move toward fascism and condemned the reformist character of the emergent Congress of Industrial Organizations, showing little regard for the immediate benefits these new institutions provided working people. In a bid to support themselves during the crises, more than five hundred Jewish anarchists decamped to a farming commune in rural Michigan, but quickly found themselves entangled in debts and feuds. Meanwhile, a new political formation, the Catholic Worker Movement, linked anarchist ethics to Christ's teachings as they fed and sheltered the destitute. Despite the immediacy of the domestic crisis, U.S. anarchists remained deeply invested in European politics. Beginning in 1936, many became preoccupied with supporting their embattled comrades in Spain. Later they bitterly divided over whether the threat of German and Italian fascism warranted an exception to their traditional antimilitarism. Buffeted by constant crises, anarchists devoted little attention to the politics of race, gender, and cultural production, and made few attempts to reassess and update their core political philosophy during these years. Their failure to initiate mass political campaigns, coupled with theoretical stagnation, led to the dissolution of the traditional anarchist movement in the United States by 1940.

MAN!

The primary English-language organ of U.S. anarchism during the 1920s, the *Road to Freedom,* had never proven entirely satisfying to its readers, in part because contributors espoused different visions of anarchism and how to achieve it. Nevertheless, the intellectual forums, conferences, and networks of correspondence established under its auspices proved fertile enough that, by 1932, two of the tendencies sheltered under the *Road to Freedom*'s big tent were able to establish periodicals that expressed their political orientations more coherently and consistently. In April, young Jewish anarchists from New York organized themselves as the Vanguard Group, and brought out *Vanguard: A Libertarian Communist Journal* with the intention of rebuilding a syndicalist tradition among U.S. anarchists. The following January, Italian anarchists in San Francisco helped Marcus Graham to launch *Man!*, a monthly newspaper intended to revive the insurrectionist school of anarchism that had been promoted by Luigi Galleani earlier in the century. These publications, and the public events organized by their editors, served as the primary means for anarchists to reach English-speaking readers throughout one of the most volatile decades of the century.

After the *Anarchist Soviet Bulletin* (later titled *Free Society*) ceased publication in 1922, its editor, Marcus Graham, moved to the Stelton Colony, in New Jersey. During the 1920s, Graham occasionally contributed to the *Road to Freedom* and promoted the newspaper on speaking tours, as we have seen, but he never fully jived with the paper's editorial group or his neighbors at Stelton. The anarchist Abe Blecher recalled, "Graham was an individualist and naturist and raised his own vegetables."[2] He had developed a moral revulsion to eating "animal foods" after visiting a meatpacking plant as a young man. Graham was apparently a vegan at the time, eating "raw foods, mostly nuts and raisins."[3]

In the late 1920s Graham hitchhiked across the country to drum up support for political prisoners still languishing as a result of wartime repression, as well as to promote a book he had edited, *The Anthology of Revolutionary Poetry*. Through his travels, Graham grew close to Vincenzo Ferrero and other San Francisco Bay Area anarchists, who edited *L'Emancipazione* (Emancipation), a monthly newspaper aligned with Luigi Galleani's brand of insurrectionary anarchism.[4] In 1927, Galleani's former assistant, Raffaele Schiavina, had covertly returned to the United States and assumed editorship of *L'Adunata dei Refratarri* (The summoning of the unruly), issued out of Brooklyn. With *L'Adunata* cohering the Italian "Galleanisti," and the Depression showing no signs of abating, the L'Emancipazione Group decided to shift resources to promoting their ideas in English. Lacking facility in the language, they invited Graham to edit a new periodical. Temperamentally,

A Journal of the Anarchist Ideal and Movement

Mastheads of the newspapers *Man!* (1932–1939) and *Cronaca Sovversiva* (1903–1920). Courtesy of the Labadie Collection, University of Michigan Library (Special Collections Library).

he was an obvious choice. As one East Coast anarchist had it: "Marcus Graham was always spoiling for a fight. . . . He was supported mostly by Italian anarchists of the Galleani school, who admired his militancy, rather than by the more moderate Jews."[5]

In 1932 Graham leased a small fruit farm overlooking the San Francisco Bay and established an office above the restaurant Ferrero and his friend Domenico Sallitto owned in Oakland.[6] He later recalled that Ferrero "proposed the name for the new paper, *Man!,* as well as the subtitle, 'Man is the measurement of everything.'"[7] To support the venture, the Italians convened the International Group of San Francisco, which drew on the model of the International Group of New York and included English-, Yiddish-, and Mandarin-speaking comrades.[8] An eight-page tabloid with a visually appealing layout, the paper was, in many respects, a Galleanisti newspaper published in English. Its masthead declared as much to anyone familiar with movement history. A woodcut of a shirtless, muscle-bound man with a severed chain dangling from outstretched arms, it replicated the masthead of *Cronaca Sovversiva,* updated with art deco flair. Contributors advocated a mode of anarchist praxis that rejected formal anarchist organizations, labor unions, and a clear reconstructive vision, while celebrating personal forms of resistance.

For Graham and his collaborators, change required a personal process of coming to consciousness followed by steely acts of individual refusal. The debut issue advised, "The road to man's liberation lies in the breaking of every law, custom and sham creed in which he now finds himself trapped. Only thus can be brought about the inception of the great Social Revolution."[9] The editorial group, clearly, continued to believe a millennial-style revolution was on the horizon.

Strategic campaigns to win improvements in daily life had no place in this schema. Responding to an early critic, Graham happily declared, "Yes, indeed! Anarchists don't support the so-called sane, practical movements. . . . For the anarchist is the prophetic fiery denouncer of everything unjust and unfree, holding forth the Day of Liberation." Anarchists, he implied, should function as critics and visionaries, not organizers. To Graham's mind, the ideal revolutionary was a poet. For, who, he asked, "has it been in the history of mankind that rebelled foremost against the compromise of idealism to practicability—if not its greatest poets?"[10] In accordance with his fondness for the poetic, Graham dedicated the penultimate page of each issue to an "Arts and Literature" section. Surprisingly, the page celebrated classical art and romantic poetry rather than recent trends, such as Dadaism and Surrealism—another indication that U.S. anarchism had become divorced from the modernist art movement in the interwar years.

Like other papers in the insurrectionary tradition, *Man!* was decidedly anticapitalist, but it rejected the labor movement—including revolutionary syndicalism—as a means of achieving freedom. On this matter, Graham did not mince words: "The organized labor movement throughout the world is by its very nature and purpose a protective barrier against any spontaneous revolutionary action that may arise from among the exploited toilers."[11] To his mind, unions—whether affiliated with the revolutionary Spanish organization Confederación Nacional de Trabajadores or the liberal AFL—were by nature authoritarian.[12]

Graham saw union officials as self-serving "mis-leaders," and he reserved special scorn for anarchists who accepted such positions.[13] In the early 1930s the New York anarchists Rose Pesotta and Anna Sosnovsky had taken jobs as organizers with the International Ladies' Garment Workers' Union (ILGWU). After a string of successful campaigns, Pesotta rose through the ranks and eventually accepted a position as international vice president. In January 1934, Graham announced to readers, "Rose Pesotta has accepted a paid position to aid . . . in bringing back to power the same discredited officialdom of the International Garment Workers Union which she had at one time denounced and exposed as a band of careerists and crooks." Sosnovsky was likewise criticized for accepting a "paid position," which anarchists had long denounced as corrupting. "In mentioning these two instances," Graham explained, "*MAN!* wishes to show that the Anarchist movement holds no brief for such desertions from Anarchist principles. On the contrary, it stands ready at all times to expose and denounce them."[14]

While contributors to *Man!* expressed contempt for labor officials, working people who acted on their own behalf won admiration, encouragement, and financial support. The paper took particular interest in coal miners engaged in a series of bloody wildcat strikes in Kentucky, calling them "fierce," "sincere," and "brave."[15] Workers would have no need for institutionalized unions, Graham claimed, if, like the miners, they would act for themselves. Contributor S. Menico (an alias for Sallitto) likewise asserted that attempts to establish anarchist federations served only "a few individuals who are tickled by the aspiration of becoming omniscient potentates or illustrious bureaucrats."[16] Efforts to scale up the movement, from this perspective, reeked of self-aggrandizement rather than sincere desires to facilitate change. Fortunately, strategic planning was unnecessary, from *Man!*'s perspective, since anarchism was an essential "ideal of the human race." As contributor C. H. Mitchell argued, the movement could temporarily be repressed, but it could not be defeated, "unless someone discovers how to dissect a human animal so as to remove from him one of his race instincts which has motivated his ancestors' struggle for freedom through the ages."[17]

In all these facets, *Man!* recapitulated the perspectives Italian insurrectionaries had developed over the previous thirty years. Yet Graham also injected an anomalous critique of technology into the newspaper's politics. He claimed to subscribe to a "planless anarchy," believing, like Galleani had, that egalitarian structures could be conceived only after human nature had been freed.[18] Yet he often described anarchism in terms that looked to the past: "A society where all men and women shall have the equal opportunity to live as free artisans and natural human beings."[19] In this way, the editor gave voice to a romantic current within anarchism, present from the outset, that had competed, or functioned dialectically, with a celebration of science, technology, and modernization, as expressed by Peter Kropotkin and many anarcho-syndicalists.[20]

In a 1934 essay, Graham asserted that anarchists should reject modern technology. He argued that large-scale machinery greatly increases the power of those operating it to hurt and kill people, and he could not countenance the claim that humans willfully developed machines to escape the tedium of earlier times. Instead, it had been "commercialism, signifying, of course, exploitation and rulership, at the helm of fostering the machine." He also doubted machinery would promote happiness by alleviating toil, since he believed laboring for oneself was inherently joyful and rewarding. To Graham's mind, machines were "an attempt to mechanize life," to impose a rigid rhythm upon individuals.[21] "Every new device," he insisted, "becomes in turn a power to ensnare, mislead, delude and deaden man's need or possibility of employing his own thinking faculties."[22]

Graham advanced similar ideas on the lecture circuit. The *Albany News* of December 18, 1931, described a talk he gave under the heading "Machine Age Doom of Man, Poet Asserts—Marcus Graham Finds Civilization of Today Sterile—Speaks in Albany Tonight at Workmen's Circle Institute."[23] In presenting these arguments, *Man!*'s editor presaged anarcho-primitivist thought, which became influential in North American anarchism beginning in the 1980s. Like many contemporary "green anarchists" do today, Graham saw a silver lining in the catastrophic events roiling the world in which he lived.[24] He anticipated a second world war that would bring devastation. However, he believed, "out of these ruins humanity will evolve the pre-ancient, more experienced man, a self-reliant individual, striving to bring back the ancient civilization of the artisan, working out his destiny for the principles of voluntary cooperation, which in turn can only come through understanding, toleration and respect between human beings."[25] This was another brand of millennial thinking. If radicals could not initiate a fully transformative revolution on their own, social conflicts inherent in the system might incite a conflagration so severe as to prepare a tabula rasa upon which thoughtful anarchists might construct society anew.

While the Bay Area International Group waited for resistance to grow, they turned to the time-honored tradition of hosting monthly forums and social outings. These doubled as fund-raisers for labor defense campaigns, for *L'Adunata,* and for the Russian-language *Dielo Truda*. Supporters of *Man!,* in turn, held fund-raisers in Los Angeles, Chicago, Detroit, Paterson, Philadelphia, New York City, and a few smaller towns in the northeast.[26] But while the paper published news about fund-raisers, it contained few reports of demonstrations, organizing campaigns, the establishment of mutual aid organizations, expropriations of food, or other unruly activities, despite the Depression-era struggles taking place throughout the country. Insurrectionary anarchists had traditionally devoted significant coverage to the heroic acts of martyrs carrying out propaganda of the deed. But, save for the Appalachian miners, the decade apparently produced few acts of heroism legible to the editorial group.

Beginning in 1934, however, federal authorities began to subject the newspaper to a campaign of intimidation that allowed group members, themselves, to demonstrate techniques of resistance. On April 11, immigration officials "ransacked" the homes of Ferrero and Sallitto, arresting both men for violating Red Scare–era "criminal anarchy" statutes by providing office space to *Man!* Born abroad, Ferrero and Sallitto remained subject to immigration regulations that prohibited noncitizens from holding anarchist beliefs. A board of review recommended both men be deported to Italy, despite the likelihood that they would be jailed, if not executed, by Mussolini's government upon repatriation.[27] Anarchists, led by Graham, attempted to raise two thousand dollars in bail money to free the men pending an appeal; but given the period's chastening conditions, they fell far short. Rose Pesotta stepped in at this point. Despite being publicly castigated in the pages of *Man!* only months earlier, Pesotta phoned her union's joint board, which posted bail for both men the next morning.[28] Sallitto and Ferrero accepted the money despite their belief that unions only hurt the anarchist movement. Prosecutors eventually dropped Sallitto's case and put Ferrero's on hold. He quickly jumped bail, went underground and, going by the name "John the Cook," was harbored by comrades in Detroit and California for the rest of his life.[29] *Man!* did not modulate its position on unionism or acknowledge the singeing irony of how events transpired. Indeed, for the rest of the decade, supporters of *Man!* and *L'Adunata dei Refratarri* would verbally joust with the Vanguard Group, Italian anarcho-syndicalists, and other anarchists who continued to place great stock in labor unions as the primary means for bringing about anarchism.

THE VANGUARD GROUP

While Marcus Graham was tilling his plot at Stelton in the early 1920s, his young neighbor, Abe Bluestein, attended classes at the colony's Modern School. Abe's father, Max, was active in the anarchist faction during the ILGWU's "civil war" and nourished his son's interest in politics.[30] Morris Greenshner remembered, "In Stelton, they all thought that young Abe Bluestein would become a second Bakunin."[31] Later, the Bluesteins moved to the Amalgamated Co-ops in the Bronx and Abe enrolled at City College.

Soon after, he met his future wife, Selma Cohen, during a costume ball fund-raiser for the Modern School Association.[32] In the 1930s City College attracted many working-class and Jewish students who, like Bluestein, were the first members of their families to attend college. These budding New York intellectuals were attracted to Left politics of every hue and excitedly debated one another in the college's cafeteria.[33] When he arrived in 1932, Bluestein gathered a small anarchist contingent that alternately sparred with and collaborated with the hundreds of student socialists and communists.[34] He cofounded the Vanguard Group with his friend Sam Dolgoff the same year.

Born in Russia in 1902, Dolgoff had immigrated with his family to the Lower East Side at the age of three or four. After completing elementary school, he worked as a factory hand to supplement the income his father made painting houses. After a brief stint in a socialist youth group, Dolgoff spent the early 1920s as an itinerant laborer and soapbox orator for the Industrial Workers of the World (IWW). In 1926 he moved to Chicago and joined the Free Society Group, whereupon G. P. Maximoff became his mentor.[35] Dolgoff was impressed with the older man's perspective on the anarchist tradition: "For Maximoff, anarchism was not only a standard of personal conduct. Anarchism is a social movement—a movement of the people. . . . He insisted that we must work out a constructive, realistic approach to the problems of the Social Revolution and relate anarchism to the socio-economic problems of our complex society."[36]

In 1930, Dolgoff fell in love with Esther Miller, a Russian immigrant three years his junior and a member of the Cleveland, Ohio, Anarchist Forum. The couple moved to the Stelton Colony and gave birth to a son the next year. Sam contributed articles to the *Road to Freedom* but was dissatisfied with how the group functioned. "There were no qualifications for membership," he recalled. "People whom we did not know, anyone who happened to be passing through, participated in group affairs." In Dolgoff's opinion, "there was practically no coordination. The extreme 'individualists' who, in the pungent phrase of Luigi Fabbri, 'idealized the most anti-social forms of individual rebellion,' were against everything. Even a temporary committee of two or three comrades was denounced as a 'bureaucracy.'"[37] Dolgoff and Bluestein launched the Vanguard Group, in part, to circumvent these debilitating tendencies.

Vanguard's first members, most in their twenties and thirties, met one another through the *Road to Freedom* or via their parents' involvement in

New York's Jewish anarchist milieu. Early recruits included Bluestein's City College classmates Sidney Soloman and Roman Weinrebe, as well as Clara Freedman, whose father once served as secretary of the Jewish Anarchist Federation. Clara, in turn, was elected Vanguard's secretary and "did five times as much work as anybody else: correspondence, selling papers, organizing meetings, debates, and lectures."[38] The group also claimed a few Italians, a handful of Irishmen, and a single African American member, Glenn Carrington. Carrington, who was gay, worked as a parole officer and occasionally wrote short articles for *Vanguard* on "the negro question" under the name George Creighton.[39] Chinese anarchists Eddie Wong and Yat Tone sometimes attended meetings and hosted fund-raising dinners at their cooperatively owned Chinese restaurant.[40]

Mark Schmidt, an older man who had spent time in Russia shortly after the revolution, served as a "guiding teacher" to this relatively young group. Dolgoff acknowledged that Schmidt's "erudition, his knowledge of anarchist ideas and history, his revolutionary experience, all helped to clarify and work out the orientation of Vanguard."[41] Writing under the nom de plume Senex, Schmidt penned some of the sharpest essays published by the group. However, he also possessed personal traits that proved to be liabilities. Louis Slater remembered, "When someone made a mistake, he laughed mockingly."[42] Freedman recalled that "he would work on one person at a time and gain control of them.... He took a dislike to certain people, and he had contempt for women, whom he considered inferior."[43]

The primary work this group took on was the production and distribution of *Vanguard: A Libertarian Communist Journal*, which it issued monthly when funds allowed. Members were conscious that choosing the name "Vanguard" would be contentious given that communists were intent on claiming that mantle. "The idea of an active revolutionary Vanguard is not a specifically communist idea," they asserted. "The communists distorted it, degraded it to the level of a hierarchical apparatus. We anarchists also believe in the idea of a revolutionary Vanguard, but we do not claim any divine rights. We do not claim to be the only true mouthpiece of the dialectical process of history, or the vicarious representatives of the will of the proletariat."[44] Rather, they saw themselves as individuals devoted to the cause who would develop ideas and put in the hard work of organizing others.

Vanguard presented a considerably different vision of anarchism and how to achieve it than did *Man!* Dolgoff explained,

We wanted a paper which would ... present the classic anarchism of Kropotkin and Bakunin, and to some extent Proudhon, and the real anarchist movements that have roots among the people, among the masses and the labor movement, and that puts anarchism in the perspective as a part and parcel of the socialist movement. We considered ourselves to be the left wing of the socialist movement.[45]

While *Man!* supported a "planless anarchism" to be realized through spontaneous insurrection, *Vanguard* proposed a vision of anarchist communism so detailed it spanned three issues. Members debated a "transition program" that identified steps for transforming society over a period of decades.[46] At base, though, *Vanguard* advocated an anarcho-syndicalist approach, which prioritized organizing mass-based unions and well-coordinated federations of anarchists.

Unsurprisingly, given these affinities, the Vanguard Group developed a close working relationship with the Italian syndicalist Carlo Tresca. *Vanguard* rented an office in the building that housed his newspaper and the New York offices of the IWW, near Manhattan's Union Square. When the Vanguard Group was unable to fund its periodical in 1934, Tresca invited it to publish an English-language page in each issue of *Il Martello.*[47] Vanguard Group members, most notably Roman Weinrebe, also contributed to the legal defense of antifascists affiliated with Tresca, who continued to physically confront Italian American fascists.[48] In addition to support from elders such as Tresca and Maximoff, Dolgoff proudly recalled, "we had a very good staff of foreign correspondents."[49] Indeed, the journal featured regular contributions from Emma Goldman, Alexander Berkman, the German anarcho-syndicalist Rudolf Rocker, and officers of the French and Spanish syndicalist labor federations.

While the focus on class struggle made the journal's politics clear, it left the contents narrowly focused: anything smacking of "bohemianism," such as consideration of modern art or the promotion of progressive gender roles, was out.[50] Even with the international heavy hitters it published, *Vanguard*'s circulation topped out at three thousand to four thousand subscribers, a sizeable portion of them living abroad. The editorial group, composed primarily of the children of immigrants, believed they lacked a larger base because, "cooped up within the confines of little national colonies, broken up and fragmented into water-tight compartments of national movements, [the U.S. anarchist movement] never rose to the realization of the urgency of the youth movement. It could not think in terms of American life, its future and the place of the anarchist movement in it."[51]

For a number of years, members worked to change this. Bluestein recalled, "In addition to our magazine, we conducted forums and lectures and made soapbox speeches on street corners, getting into fights with the Communists all the time, protected by Wobblies with iron pipes wrapped with handkerchiefs."[52] Participants took short trips throughout the Northeast seeking to recruit new members and presenting lectures on anarchism to college students. In principle, the Vanguard Group was committed to organizing radical industrial unions and, simultaneously, a cadre of self-identified anarchists. However, the group made decisions that limited its ability to grow the ranks of either.

Early in its existence, Vanguard was handed an opportunity to influence the direction of the labor movement. Following the divisive "war" between communists and socialists in the 1920s, the ILGWU had begun to fall under the influence of organized crime. In 1933, the union's president, David Dubinsky, sought to rebuild the organization "on a new, clean basis" through a massive membership drive. Dubinsky requested that members of five leftist youth organizations, including the Young People's Socialist League and the Vanguard Group (but not the communist youth groups), serve as volunteer organizers during the campaign. At a meeting convened by Dubinsky, Vanguard members declared their approval of the organizing drive in principle. However, they demanded that the ILGWU leadership first create a document committing the union to "full worker's democracy within the union," "complete dissociation from any political clique," organization on industrial rather than craft lines, and development of revolutionary anticapitalist goals. The officials at the table politely agreed to give the proposal "careful consideration," then quietly dropped Vanguard from the campaign.[53]

Five years later, during an uptick in interest occasioned by the Spanish Civil War, Vanguard Group members strategized about growing the anarchist movement. "Practical work," they agreed, required more members and financial resources. Yet they decided, "We do not have the facilities at present to undertake mass propaganda or mass educational work among new-comers to the revolutionary arena." Therefore, members aimed to recruit "the many sincere and class-conscious revolutionists who are today disillusioned with the Marxist movements and who have libertarian tendencies."[54] Vanguard, in other words, called for more of the same: promoting its literature, organizing study groups, and hosting public discussions, with hopes of poaching militants from other small radical sects. These deliberations indicate the extent to which "Marxist movements" had overtaken anarchism since the

First World War, when the process of ideological conversion had operated in the opposite direction.

Reflecting back on his experiences forty years later, Sidney Soloman considered Vanguard's reluctance to engage in campaign work to be the group's biggest error. Soloman laid much of the blame at the feet of Mark Schmidt:

> He felt we were theoretically unprepared for action, such as labor organizing or forming cooperatives. He stopped us from organizing for the ILGWU.... Schmidt got us to decline. The YPSL [Young People's Socialist League] accepted and did useful work; hence their big reputation today. It was this failure to act that led to the collapse of our group and of the anarchist movement in New York.[55]

To Soloman's mind, the group had placed the cart before the horse. They assumed that action required theoretical closure, rather than seeing theory and organizing work as coinformative. Moreover, they mistook their goals for preconditions of participation. Rather than viewing the organizing drive as an opportunity for anarchists to influence others, they rejected the chance to discuss and debate ideas with fellow workers, believing that accepting union decisions would intolerably compromise their own principles.

Other factors, too, limited Vanguard's organizing efforts. Despite its intention to develop a style of anarchism relevant to the daily lives of Americans, the group devoted growing portions of its journal to analysis of events transpiring in Europe. This is not surprising, given the menacing rise of Nazi, Italian Fascist, and Stalinist power, which threatened the safety of whole societies as well as specific anarchists dear to the New Yorkers. In 1933 Rudolf Rocker and his wife, Millie, fled Germany under threat from the Nazis and settled at the Mohegan Colony. Hitler's rise to power also forced Mollie Steimer and Senya Fleshin to relocate from Berlin to Paris. As important as this international coverage was, consideration of novel developments and the struggle to survive in the United States—especially beyond the large East Coast cities—often took a backseat, likely diminishing the paper's appeal to a wider public. Still, Vanguard's efforts to drum up new support were not a total wash.

In 1933 the group established the Rebel Youth, a circle of anarchists "even younger" than the membership of Vanguard itself, sometimes also referred to as the "Vanguard Juniors." First, Irving Sterling, who grew up attending *Fraye Arbeter Shtime* dinners, pulled together approximately twenty junior and senior high school students in the Brownsville neighborhood of

Brooklyn.[56] Shortly thereafter, Audrey Goodfriend, the fourteen-year-old daughter of Jewish anarchists from the South Bronx, launched a similar group with her friend Sally Genn. Abe Bluestein, who lived nearby, led a Saturday morning study group and incorporated the South Bronx group into the Vanguard network. Goodfriend remembers, "We would read [Berkman's] *The ABC of Anarchism;* we would read an article from the *Vanguard* and discuss. And we read some Kropotkin or talked about Kropotkin."[57] Friendships developed, and eventually many of the Rebel Youth joined the Vanguard Group proper. In 1939, for example, Clara Freedman and Audrey Goodfriend hitchhiked from New York to Toronto to visit their heroine, Emma Goldman, who remained barred from the United States but had, in her twilight years, been granted admittance to Canada. Mentoring the Vanguard Juniors was, in the end, the group's most successful recruiting effort. It would have significant consequences for the future of U.S. anarchism, as we will see in the next two chapters.

Throughout the 1930s, then, the U.S. anarchist movement largely cleaved into an insurrectionist wing anchored by *Man!* and *L'Adunata dei Refratarri,* and a syndicalist wing grouped around *Vanguard* and *Il Martello;* neither wing proved successful at reestablishing anarchism as a mass phenomenon. While these factions rarely shared enough common ground to coordinate efforts, on certain matters—their assessment of the New Deal and the rapid growth of industrial unionism that followed in its wake—they found much to agree upon.

THE NEW DEAL, THE CIO, AND THE UNITED FRONT

During the presidential campaign of 1931, the patrician Democrat Franklin Delano Roosevelt instilled hope in a deeply shaken electorate by claiming "the forgotten man at the bottom of the economic pyramid" deserved a "new deal." During his famous first "hundred days" in office, Roosevelt proposed a flurry of new programs and policy changes aimed at reversing the downward spiral of the domestic economy, then already in its third year.

Anarchists approached the New Deal with their typical skepticism toward government initiatives heightened by suspicions stemming from the manipulative ways in which Mussolini and Hitler had recently ascended to power. In the April 1933 issue of *Man!,* Graham dubbed FDR's approach a "new hoax" and reminded readers that they could expect nothing from government but "deceit and treachery." He took particular umbrage with the Civilian Conservation Corps, the first experiment with a work-relief program, in which young men would be paid a modest wage to develop natural resources under the auspices of the War Department. "What this dastardly scheme really implies isn't hard to guess," Graham wrote. "It will be used for a two-fold purpose: first, to further lower the workers' wage scale; second to have a standing army ready to drown in blood any uprising that appears now so imminent." By August, Graham had concluded that the New Deal was a plot to introduce "American Fascism" under the guise of assisting the unemployed.[58]

In early articles on the subject, *Vanguard* focused more attention on Roosevelt's National Industrial Recovery Act (NIRA) but arrived at similarly pessimistic conclusions. The act suspended antitrust laws and created boards to establish "industrial codes" with the intention of raising commodity prices by limiting competition. The act affirmed the right to organize, called for labor to be represented on its industrial boards, and set a minimum wage and maximum hours for participating corporations.[59] Writing in May 1933, Mark Schmidt critiqued the "rigging and freezing up of prices" that the NIRA's industrial codes attempted, and predicted that the NIRA would dangerously increase the government's role in labor conflicts. "Democracy will become attenuated to the vanishing point, the powerful trusts merging with bureaucratic State apparatus, the workers' organizations deprived of any right to strike and act independently, 'coordinated' with the State.... This is the trend toward Fascism." Melchior Steele, a contributor to *Man!*, likewise believed that with the government acting as "a party to contracts," strikes would amount to "rebellion against the government," further disinclining patriotic workers from taking part.[60]

In actuality, a quite different scenario played out. Firms stridently resisted the NIRA's prolabor planks, refusing to abide by them and challenging their constitutionality in court. The president of the United Mine Workers, John L. Lewis, meanwhile publicly explained the new policy as a mandate from the president for workers to join unions as a means of combating the Depression. They responded enthusiastically, joining unions by the hundreds of thousands. The largest strike wave since the end of the Red Scare broke out the next year, as workers throughout the country fought to enact and defend via direct action the new labor rights that Congress had declared but had done little to enforce.[61] As Staughton Lynd and other historians have demonstrated, the labor upsurge of the early 1930s was driven by local unions that mobilized entire communities, frequently bridging racial and gender divides. Following the lead of former Wobblies and other radicals, many adopted democratic decision-making procedures and militant tactics to ward off strikebreaking police and replacement workers. Yet self-identified anarchists do not appear to have played significant roles.[62]

Having grown disheartened by the labor movement and distanced from less radical workers during the 1920s, anarchists often viewed the new unionism with jaundiced eyes. During the summer of 1934, to cite one example, communist longshoremen in California organized some 130,000 San Franciscans to halt work for four days in support of striking dockworkers. Marcus Graham dismissed the event's significance, telling readers of *Man!*, "There was no General Strike in San Francisco worthy of the name." Though Graham lauded the rank-and-file workers who had walked off the job, they had, to his mind, been betrayed in a predictable fashion by "despicable and treasonous" union spokesmen who had curtailed the strike. He could only hope the workers had learned their lesson: "never again to entrust their struggles in the hands of leaders."[63] Though the critique of overconciliatory representatives had merits, the pessimistic and critical commentary issued by anarchists in the 1930s won them few new blue-collar supporters, given that they offered no organizational alternative.

Although the Supreme Court eventually ruled that the NIRA's industrial boards were an unconstitutional interference with private business, the 1935 National Labor Relations Act bolstered the standing of unions. It declared collective bargaining not only legal but also a social good, and it established a government-monitored procedure by which a majority vote established a union as the sole representative of the entire workforce of a facility.[64] (New Deal politicians believed government backing would make it easier for workers to organize and command wage hikes. This would increase their purchasing power, redistributing wealth and reducing the threat of overproduction that had catalyzed the crisis in the first place.)[65] Bolstered by the new law, but faced with continuing employer recalcitrance, unionists launched major organizing drives among semiskilled workers in the steel, mining, automobile, and other industries that had become the centerpiece of the American economy.[66]

Much of this organizing occurred under the auspices of the Congress of Industrial Organizations (CIO), a new umbrella organization that broke away from the AFL in 1935. Like the IWW, the new CIO unions sought to organize industrially—uniting every worker in a given field of production, regardless of skill level and race. Unlike with the IWW, the abolition of capitalism was not a goal, and internal union democracy was not a priority. Indeed, John L. Lewis and other CIO leaders "preferred to act as labor generals who led their troops in battle, not as temporarily elected representatives who reflected the wishes of the ranks."[67]

To the publishers of *Vanguard,* the CIO was barely distinguishable from the AFL, an object of anarchist disdain since 1886. "A new unionism will not spring up as a result of those puny efforts," an October 1936 editorial assured readers. "The militancy of the great mass of unorganized workers will be stifled from the very beginning and whatever may be accomplished ... will be distorted by the monstrous centralization of power in the hands of an irresponsible bureaucracy."[68] The CIO did quickly move to consolidate many of the local unions formed in the early 1930s, and *Vanguard* was perceptive in anticipating the autocratic grip Lewis would exercise over the organization.[69] Yet the group misjudged the potential for a new, militant unionism to arise in the 1930s. The next years saw the invention of the mass sit-down strike in Akron, Ohio, and Flint, Michigan. Union membership grew by 5 million over the course of the decade, raising the percentage of the organized workforce from 7.5 to 19.2. Moreover, the CIO actively organized African American industrial workers and built multiracial locals with the intent of breaking the color line that still characterized many AFL unions.

In the wake of these advances, *Vanguard* published more nuanced considerations of the emerging social order. Contributor Joseph Zack argued in 1937 that the United States was becoming a "State Capitalist" system. Responding to the crisis features of traditional capitalism evidenced by the Depression, the government would henceforth take on "regulation of wages, prices, working hours, of 'social security' legislation and monetary manipulation"—in short, "the superstructural manipulation of capitalism for the purpose of defending its base." In Zack's view, the farsighted capitalists who favored this method of stabilizing the system could only overcome the resistance of traditionalist elites through the mobilization of working people. Roosevelt embraced the CIO to this end. In turn, Zack felt, "the aim of the C.I.O. leaders is to get an expanded, well implemented and regimented N.R.A. [National Recovery Administration], in the operation of which the new union bureaucracy will be the important and well paid servants of the new capitalism." Zack lauded the sit-down strike as a powerful new weapon developed by rank-and-filers, one that gave them greater leverage not only against their employers but also vis-à-vis the union bureaucracy. The sit-down strike, he concluded, "promises to be as much of a fighting instrument on the part of labor as the system of state capitalism is for the capitalist."[70]

Vanguard's developing perspective anticipated many points later elaborated by C. Wright Mills and other influential critics of mid-twentieth-century unionism.[71] Yet it may also have reinforced the anarchists' sense of paralysis. While hundreds of communists and socialists took up organizing responsibilities in the new CIO unions during the 1930s and 1940s, attempting to radicalize them in the process, anarchists largely continued to sit on the sidelines.[72] Likewise, they continued to shrug off entreaties to join a "united front against fascism."

In the fall of 1933, Graham argued that it would be foolhardy for anarchists to join a Left-liberal coalition, since the communists and socialists had yet to realize that "Fascism is in reality but an unveiled creature of the hidden monster, Rulership," and would themselves seek to rule once fascism was defeated. Here, Graham's proclivity to collapse political distinctions amplified his refusal to countenance strategic decision-making. For the Vanguard Group, the radical parties' diagnosis of fascism was less problematic than their plan to defeat it. "To the [fascist] counter-revolution must be opposed the gigantic powers which only the social revolution can generate," Dolgoff asserted in 1935. To his mind, the call by communist and socialist leaders for "the masses to unite with their bourgeois-democratic masters" to defeat fascism *delayed* rather than hastened anticapitalist revolution, dooming the united front strategy from the start.[73] Indicating their loose grasp on the concept, both newspapers insisted they would support a united front effort, but only if it was "permeated with the spirit and principles of libertarian communism."[74]

What, then, did anarchists suggest that those impoverished by the Depression do? Here the factions split in predictable ways. By late 1935, the Vanguard Group's Abe Bluestein could acknowledge that "Roosevelt's New Deal has lifted this country from the low depths of March, 1933." He felt its effects personally, as his wife, Selma, a painter, had taken a position with the Works Progress Administration. Nonetheless, Bluestein issued a pamphlet arguing that too many people remained unemployed, while those working for New Deal agencies remained scandalously underpaid. Reiterating that a complete solution required revolution, Bluestein nevertheless proposed a program to fight "for some measure of security from starvation." First, workers should demand "prevailing wages" for the unemployed and publicly employed, paid for by "the wealthy." Next, they needed to "get back into industry" by fighting for shorter hours with no reduction of pay, as a means to spread out the work. Winning these reforms, he believed, required the courage to break the law: "Let the unemployed show a little more respect for their persons and a lot less for private property, and the government and the wealthy will also begin to fear and respect their strength."[75] With little fanfare, then, a cofounder of the Vanguard Group acknowledged that despite a half decade of Depression, the final break with capitalism was not imminent and the federal government now represented a legitimate target from which anarchists might wring concessions, assuming they did so using disruptive direct-action tactics rather than elections and lobbying.

To Marcus Graham, however, "getting back into industry" was precisely the wrong approach. In late 1934, he wrote, "As it appears to me, the gravest of danger for mankind lies in the continued immense growth of industrialization of life to the point where the individual loses more and more of his significance as a self-reliant, self-creative and self-ingenuitive [sic] human being." Moreover, Graham believed the Depression was rooted in overproduction occasioned by industry's adoption of new technologies. With other countries following suit, the United States could not rely on expanded foreign markets to pull it out of the slump. War, he presciently asserted, would be the only way to eliminate oversupply and reverse the trend. For all of these reasons, Graham insisted, "the DECENTRALIZATION of every CENTRALIZED power and activity is the only safe assurance for the building up of a true and free society." To that end, in 1932 he urged an Austin, Texas, audience not to wait for federal assistance but to seize uncultivated land with the aim of supporting themselves. In Memphis, he was even more direct: "Abandon the cities; leave them as monuments to the folly of man."[76] It is impossible to know how many people—if any—took this advice. Any who did would have been forced to learn the rudiments of homesteading during one of the most severe droughts in the nation's history—one that sent thousands of "Okies" and other dust bowl residents fleeing to California.

A MIDWESTERN KIBBUTZ

While *Vanguard* and *Man!* theorized courses of action, other anarchists attempted to enact solutions to unemployment on their own. Marcus Graham was not the only anarchist who felt the best response to the Depression was for wage laborers to become self-sufficient farmers. But whereas Graham encouraged individual action, others put stock in group effort. In the fall of 1932, Joseph Cohen announced his intention to organize a cooperative agricultural colony. In a prospectus published in the *Fraye Arbeter Shtime,* he suggested purchasing a farm of at least a thousand acres on which approximately 150 families would live. Cohen explained,

> The land, the means of production and the things that are in common use must belong to the community as a whole; all the members must be provided for by the community, in accordance with its ability, with the necessities of daily life; the individual should own only objects of personal use (clothes, furniture, books, works of art) and share of the common income.[77]

Cohen had lived at the Stelton Colony with his wife, Sophie, until he became editor of the *Fraye Arbeter Shtime* in 1923. He was disappointed that the Stelton and Mohegan Colonies were composed of individually owned plots of land and hoped that a self-sustaining and truly collectivized community would promote anarchist ideals more effectively than the existing colonies had over the previous seventeen years. Members were "to live together as one large family, with a single common kitchen and dining room, carried on in the manner of a well-regulated restaurant." The new community, as he imagined it, would include "recreation rooms, libraries, gymnasium, theatre and instruction facilities," as well as "sleeping quarters, with modern conveniences," prepared before most participants arrived.

With nearly one-third of the U.S. population out of work, interest in the project grew rapidly. In February 1933, an anarchist living in Detroit discovered a ten-thousand-acre farm, replete with buildings, equipment, and livestock, selling for the low price of $170,000.[78] The planning committee moved quickly to gather a down payment, reducing the investment cost from $1,000 to $500 per family. Recruits were primarily Jewish and drawn from the ranks of organized labor, the Workmen's Circle, and other urban institutions. Most hailed from New York, Detroit, and Chicago, and few had ever worked in agriculture. They were not all anarchists, but, learning from previous experiments, the group excluded Communist Party members.

On June 27, the Sunrise Co-operative Farm Community was born, with approximately forty families taking over a working farm midseason. The theater, gymnasium, and library Cohen had envisioned were nowhere to be seen. To sleep, colonists crowded into an old farmhouse, a cramped rooming house built for migratory laborers, and small wooden shanties that dotted the property. They did quickly establish a rustic kitchen and dining room, in which they shared meals together. Despite their inexperience, this inspired crew managed to bring in a crop of peppermint, sugar beets, and grains worth

A barn at the Sunrise Co-operative Farm Community, Alecia, Michigan, circa 1933–1936. Courtesy of the Boris Yelensky Papers, 1939–1975, Labadie Collection, University of Michigan Library (Special Collections Library).

nearly fifty thousand dollars during the first season, following the guidance of hired advisors. New colonists continued to arrive, bringing the population in May 1934 to 150 adults and 56 children, as well as dozens of visitors volunteering their labor (and vacationing) at any given time. Three hundred people called Sunrise home in March 1935.[79]

Despite its promising beginnings, however, difficulties and conflicts quickly arose. Promotional meetings for the colony had been conducted in Yiddish, and many participants had assumed the colony would function with Yiddish as its primary language, as a means of retaining Jewish identity. Labor Zionism was growing in popularity; and to some, Sunrise surely appealed as an opportunity to experience kibbutz life. Yet Cohen, a longtime organizer of cross-ethnic anarchist projects, argued for English as the primary language, since the colony had "several" non-Jewish members and was home to dozens of children who spoke little Yiddish. He may also have been mindful of the anarchist movement's growing desire to appeal to native-born English speakers. Residents eventually agreed to conduct meetings and keep records in English, with language choice at other times a personal matter; but the debate remained an open sore.[80]

Sunrise members also struggled with how to fairly distribute the insufficient housing and divvy up the abundant amount of work required to make

Residents of the Sunrise Co-operative Farm Community, Alecia, Michigan, circa 1933–1936. Courtesy of the Boris Yelensky Papers, 1939–1975, Labadie Collection, University of Michigan Library (Special Collections Library).

the farm profitable. Debate flared for months over the management and decision-making structure the colony should adopt. Acts of nature also created unanticipated setbacks for Sunrise members. The colony's second season was severely marred by the same drought that uprooted farmers throughout the country. The following summer the farm faced the opposite problem: heavy rains that flooded the low-lying land. The spring rain was followed by an invasion of "army worms," or crop-eating caterpillars.[81]

All told, Sunrise was never able to gross much more than fifty thousand dollars a year, hardly a sufficient income for the two-hundred-odd people living there at any given time. As the nation's economy began to improve after 1936, a stream of colonists abandoned the farm to return to wage labor and the city life with which they were more familiar. Faced with financial disaster, the remaining colonists decided to seek a federal loan under the auspices of a New Deal agricultural program (likely the Resettlement Administration). By the time the loan was approved, however, so many problems had accrued that the colonists agreed to sell the entire operation to the government as a means of extricating themselves from the venture. A few dozen diehards, including Cohen, relocated to what they hoped was a more hospitable tract of land in Virginia, but within a year this venture, too, collapsed as a result of factional disputes.[82]

The Sunrise Colony was one of the most audacious projects U.S. anarchists embarked upon in the interwar years. It exemplified the anarchist strategy of building new institutions that modeled desirable social relationships—what has more recently been termed "building prefigurative counter-institutions." Its failure, however, hurt the movement in a variety of ways. First, it drew hundreds of dedicated activists away from the cities at just the moment when workers' struggles were rapidly expanding. Second, the Sunrise experiment increased conflict within the community of Jewish anarchists, as each faction at the farm sought support from friends and comrades in the cities. Finally, the realities of living communally on a limited budget challenged participants' convictions about the ease of self-management and desirability of collectivist living. Until the colonists moved to Michigan, anarchism existed more as an ideal than a daily practice structuring their lives. Even so, many Jewish anarchists continued to view kibbutzim as the best way to put anarchist values into practice, leading some to endorse the politically fraught settlement of Jews in the British Mandate of Palestine.[83]

THE CATHOLIC WORKER MOVEMENT

For all their talk of mutual aid, members of the traditional anarchist movement did not muster much direct assistance for individuals struggling to survive during the Depression. The dire conditions of the early 1930s did, however, inspire the establishment of the Catholic Worker Movement, a unique intellectual and political project that drew explicitly on anarchist thought and began to shape the broader U.S. anarchist movement in complex ways beginning in the 1940s. Philosophically, Catholic Workers synthesized a fairly literal interpretation of the Christian Gospels with French "personalist" thought and Peter Kropotkin's vision of a decentralized anarchist communist social order. In their practical activity, participants combined direct service to the hungry and homeless with nonviolent protest activity; they saw themselves working simultaneously in traditions established by Jesus Christ and the Industrial Workers of the World. It was an odd combination, to be sure, but one that was tactically timely and intellectually fecund. The Catholic Worker experiment generated more interest than the traditional schools of anarchism combined, and it pointed the direction the movement would develop in the coming decades.[84]

The Catholic Worker Movement was founded in New York City in 1933 by Dorothy Day and Peter Maurin. Day, thirty-five at the time, was raised in a white-collar, Protestant family with deep roots in the United States.

Inspired by the muckrakers as a Progressive Era teenager, she became a reporter for the socialist newspaper *The Call* after college and briefly edited *The Masses* before it was suppressed under the Espionage Act. The fifty-five-year-old Maurin was born to a large "peasant" family that had worked the same patch of land in southern France for fifteen hundred years. Educated in a Catholic boarding school, he joined a Tolstoyan youth movement, Le Sillon, before emigrating and working odd jobs in Canada and the United States. Day and Maurin both experienced religious awakenings in the mid-1920s that deepened, rather than eroded, their desire to foment radical change.[85]

The pair began by distributing a newspaper, the *Catholic Worker,* at a May Day rally in New York's Union Square. Interest in their religiously anchored anticapitalist politics grew quickly—circulation climbed from 2,500 to 110,000 in two years' time, outstripping the print runs of *Man!* and *Vanguard* by an order of magnitude.[86] Readers of the *Catholic Worker* were drawn, in part, to the manner in which Maurin condensed complex ideas into poetic, aphoristic "easy essays." One such essay, frequently reproduced, enumerates the group's activities while also revealing its anarchist inflection:

> The Catholic Worker believes
> in the gentle personalism
> of traditional Catholicism.
> The Catholic Worker believes
> in the personal obligation
> of looking after
> the needs of our brother.
> The Catholic Worker believes
> in the daily practice
> of the Works of Mercy.
> The Catholic Worker believes
> in Houses of Hospitality
> for the immediate relief
> of those who are in need.
> The Catholic Worker believes
> in the establishment
> of Farming Communes
> where each one works
> according to his ability
> and gets
> according to his need.
> The Catholic Worker believes

in creating a new society
within the shell of the old
with the philosophy of the new,
which is not a new philosophy
but a very old philosophy,
a philosophy so old
that it looks like new.[87]

The new movement wasted little time putting these beliefs into action. With donations from readers and clergy (some of whom saw the effort as an antidote to communism), they opened a storefront office, which soon doubled as a space to feed and shelter those in need of help. Maurin encouraged some of these guests to relocate to a farm donated to the growing movement, where they could learn agricultural skills and provide for themselves. Catholic Worker volunteers also regularly picketed in support of striking workers, against racist treatment of African Americans, and against German anti-Semitism.

The personalist philosophy that Maurin invoked was developed in the 1920s and 1930s by French intellectuals who opposed the consumerism, poverty, and war making that appeared endemic to capitalism, as well as the atheism and the totalitarian practices of the communists. "Capitalism," declared theorist Emmanuel Mounier, "reduces [people] . . . to a state of servitude irreconcilable with the dignity of man; it orients all classes and the whole personality toward the possession of money; the single desire which chokes the modern soul."[88] Personalism, in response, placed enormous value on the experience of dignity in human lives. It celebrated the unique characteristics of human beings at a time when Western societies felt increasingly "massified" and "faceless"—whether this took the form of fascism, Stalinism, or the bureaucratic "state capitalism" emerging in the United States. Yet personalists explicitly distinguished their ideas from liberal individualism, rejecting the idea of humans as autonomous, inherently self-maximizing agents. To them, a "person" was distinguished from an "individual" by the fact that persons developed skills, character, and a sense of self through the relationships they established with God and with other people in a community. Personalists committed themselves to the defense of individual dignity, whereas liberal "individualists" prioritized protection of individual rights, usually beginning with the right to amass property. It followed that decentralization into smaller communities was important to personalists' transformative vision.[89]

Personalism also entailed ideas about how to achieve a just and meaningful world—namely, that people should take "personal responsibility" for the well-being of others. As Nancy Roberts notes, the doctrine "stressed the importance of individual social action over broad, impersonal social movements." Catholic Workers, therefore, saw their houses of hospitality and farming communes as preferable to the creation of welfare programs, which passed responsibility on to distant, morally compromised state institutions. Catholic Workers placed greater emphasis on "pure means" than on the scale of the immediate impact of their efforts, following personalist Jacques Maritain's declaration "Victory or defeat with pure means is always victory." Dorothy Day insisted that personalism, pure means, and Christ's Sermon on the Mount required a staunch commitment to nonviolence. Since political states were based upon coercive violence, Catholic Workers minimized their interactions with the U.S. government. They avoided paying taxes, did not vote, and did not register for nonprofit status.[90]

Personalism, then, had much in common with anarchism, and Day and Maurin worked to amplify these affinities. As it grew, the Catholic Worker Movement evolved a structure remarkably similar to those of many secular anarchist organizations. It had no formal membership requirements, constitution, or defined positions. Groups of people could establish a community, house of hospitality, or farming commune without seeking permission from a central body, and no committee had the power to regulate or disband Catholic Worker communities. In other words, the movement was decentralized, like the society it sought to create. Yet while they were alive, Peter Maurin and Dorothy Day held enormous sway over other participants, exercising a form of informal leadership similar to Luigi Galleani's influence on readers of *Cronaca Sovversiva*.[91]

The combination of provision, protest, and institution-building advanced by the Catholic Worker was evidently compelling in the midst of the economic crisis. By decade's end, the Catholic Worker network included twenty-five houses of hospitality and communal farms operating in thirteen different states. Circulation of the newspaper topped out at 190,000 copies in 1938.[92] Despite their similarities and avowed affinities with anarchism, however, Catholic Workers do not appear to have interacted very extensively with the secular anarchist movement in the 1930s. Indeed, while Day and Maurin worked to highlight parallels in Christian and anarchist ethics, the attention of most American anarchists was focused on Spain. There, in the midst of a civil war, members of the country's large, working-class-based anarchist movement were gleefully executing priests and setting fire to Catholic churches.

THE SPANISH CIVIL WAR

On July 17, 1936, Spanish generals launched a coup against their country's republican government. Unable to seize control immediately, General Francisco Franco led a brutal war effort with the support of a coalition of conservative constituencies. The Spanish right resented the modernizing and democratizing reforms liberal and socialist politicians promoted, fearing loss of income, status, and cultural tradition. They clashed with a well-organized (if fractious) radical left composed of urban industrial workers and abjectly poor, landless peasants.[93] In contradistinction to the anarcho-syndicalist movement's dispiriting fortunes in the United States and most other countries, Spanish anarcho-syndicalism burgeoned into a mass movement during the First World War. A "militant minority" of some thirty thousand theoretically sophisticated anarchists, working under the auspices of the Federación Anarquista Ibérica (FAI), guided the half-million-strong Confederación Nacional de Trabajadores (CNT) in the years before the coup. The CNT-FAI wavered between uneasy alliance with and outright condemnation of the parliamentary left during the 1930s.[94]

Militias of armed anarchist, socialist, and communist workers defeated garrison uprisings in many parts of the country and scrambled to coordinate a force to oppose Franco's advancing army. Their challenge grew when, a week after fighting began, Hitler and Mussolini provided Franco with planes, tanks, and weapons, while England, France, and the United States refused aid to the elected Spanish government. As local authority collapsed amid the crises, anarchists in rural villages and cities, most notably Barcelona, declared a general strike and then seized land and factories in an effort to launch a social revolution behind the front lines.[95]

The Civil War captured the attention of radicals the world over, as it so directly—and gruesomely—staged the intensifying ideological conflicts of the day: revolutionary anticapitalist movements of varied stripes squared off against nationalist reactionaries, with the institutions of representative democracy caught in the crossfire. The Communist and Socialist Parties of the United States, as well as trade unions and ethnic associations, moved quickly to support the Spanish "republicans" by reporting on the conflict, organizing rallies, and sending funds to their counterparts. Together, they raised more than $2.3 million.[96] To assist more directly, the Communist Party organized the Abraham Lincoln Brigade—a troop eventually amounting to some twenty-eight hundred volunteers who covertly crossed the Atlantic to join the Spanish militias beginning in June 1937. Historians estimate that approximately forty thousand people, hailing from more than fifty countries, participated in the antifascist International Brigades.

When the Spanish Civil War broke out in 1936, U.S. anarchists were numerically puny, divided, and lacking in strategic initiative. However, recognizing that the conflict represented the movement's greatest hope for founding a new society based on antiauthoritarian principles, they mustered what energy they had to support their Iberian comrades. Anarchists in New York City organized an ad hoc group, the United Libertarian Organizations (ULO), to support the war effort. The ULO consisted of representatives from each of the anarchist organizations still active in the city: Cultura Proletaria, producers of a Spanish-language newspaper by the same name; the Spanish Youth Group; the remnants of the former Road to Freedom Group; the Libertarian Workers Group; the General Recruiting Union and the Marine Transport Workers of the IWW; Carlo Tresca's Il Martello Group; the Jewish Anarchist Federation; the Russian Toilers; and the Vanguard Group. For a short time even the L'Adunata Group participated. The ULO quickly launched a weekly English-language newspaper, *Spanish Revolution,* devoted to providing regular news and anarchist interpretations of the events as they unfolded across the Atlantic.

Helmed by former *Road to Freedom* editor W. S. Van Valkenburgh, the paper was published out of the office on West Seventeenth Street used as a meeting space by the Vanguard Group. *Spanish Revolution* relied on press releases issued by the CNT and the FAI and on reporting by anarchists at the front lines, such as Emma Goldman. The paper's most direct and reliable source of information, however, was the Vanguard Group's own Abe Bluestein.

In early 1937, Abe and Selma Bluestein contacted the Spanish anarchists via Mark Mratchny, the current editor of the *Fraye Arbeter Shtime,* who was personally acquainted with key figures in Spain and vouched for their commitment and abilities. The couple sailed to France in April 1937 and entered Spain through a border checkpoint staffed by loyalists, before making their way to Barcelona. There, Abe was assigned to work as an English radio announcer for CNT radio. In addition to making his radio broadcasts, which listeners throughout Europe tuned in to with shortwave radios, he sent written dispatches in English and Yiddish to the *Fraye Arbeter Shtime* and *Spanish Revolution,* as well as to the latter's British equivalent, *Spain and the World.*[97]

Back in the United States, the ULO raised money and collected supplies to send overseas. It held public meetings in anarchist halls and on street corners, sometimes in shaky coalitions with other sectors of the Left. As the number of refugees mounted, the CNT asked émigré Spanish anarchists to establish chapters of a new organization, Solidaridad Internacional Antifascista, to provide assistance to libertarians and republicans affected by the violence in Europe.[98] The Spanish anarchists of New York rented a hall on Broadway, a few blocks south of Union Square, which would be used by anarchist organizations for decades to come.

Solidarity committees formed in Philadelphia, Chicago, and Detroit as well. Detroit's International Libertarian Committee Against Fascism in Spain raised $8,702.97 in its first year. It sent $8,070.95 to the CNT-FAI and used the rest for expenses incurred hosting fund-raising "entertainments"—"Pic Nics, socials, dramas, etc."[99] Likewise, the Free Society Group convened "a special meeting of all Chicago libertarians" to coordinate support for the Spanish anarchists. The group's secretary, Boris Yelensky, proudly recalled:

> With the help of subscription lists, raffle tickets for art albums sent to us from Spain, eye-arresting posters, and special bulletins about the Spanish Civil War, we not only raised substantial funds for our beleaguered comrades who were resisting Franco, but also spread a great deal of enlightenment about the issues in that bloody conflict. Too, we organized several highly effective protest meetings, and sponsored the presentation of a dramatic Spanish anti-Fascist film in a downtown theatre for a whole week. Despite bitter cold weather that week, and the hostility of the Catholic church, we succeeded in raising—through the foregoing affairs and the sale of literature—nearly $9,000 for this cause.[100]

In 1938, communists in Spain turned their guns on the anarchists and other Left parties in hopes of centralizing military efforts and controlling postwar politics, should they win. In turn, communists began to clash openly with anarchists in the United States. In 1937 the ULO held street meetings where Van Valkenburgh and others addressed passersby from a small platform. In August, communists disrupted one such meeting by heckling the speaker, pushing through the crowd, and upending the platform. The ULO issued an urgent appeal for assistance:

Leaflet for a rally in support of Spanish anarchists, New York City, 1937. Courtesy of the John Nicholas Beffel Papers, Tamiment Library/Robert F. Wagner Labor Archives, New York University.

Our STREET MEETINGS must be protected. In spite of, and because of, the fascist tactics of Communist Party hoodlums in attempting to break up our street meetings, we have been gaining much sympathy and large audiences at our propaganda meetings. . . . ALL OUT FOR THE DEFENSE OF OUR RIGHTS AND THE RIGHTS OF OUR COMRADES IN SPAIN.[101]

After further pleading, Carlo Tresca and others sent some of their brawniest supporters. A few weeks later, a relieved Van Valkenburgh told a correspondent, "Our street meetings are keeping the local Stalinites standing on their hind legs. Each week more of the comrades come to protect the stand, which they smashed on one occasion. The most they do now is call us liars, Fascists, Franco 5th Column men and so and so."[102] Still, the incident revealed the movement's sluggishness and numerical weakness. An editorial in *Spanish Revolution* decried the anarchists' low level of agitational work, which, the writer felt, "flows from the mistaken notion now held by many a sympathizer with the Spanish revolution, that the only way to discharge his duty toward the latter is to send some money to the anti-Fascist forces of Spain."[103] The anarchists' modest efforts contrasted unfavorably with the Communist Party's ability to send hundreds of volunteer fighters to Spain under the auspices of the Abraham Lincoln Brigade. In the end, however, none of the left-wing forces fighting in Spain were able to hold off the combined military power of Europe's fascist movements. In March 1939, the last defenders of the Spanish republic laid down their weapons, while thousands streamed over the border to France in a bid to escape the executions and imprisonment sure to follow.

THE SECOND WORLD WAR AND THE COLLAPSE
OF CLASSICAL ANARCHISM

If the Spanish Revolution briefly aroused new interest in anarchism in the United States, this enthusiasm quickly dissipated after Franco's victory. In 1939, Vanguard began to come apart at the seams. "The fascist victory disastrously undermined not only the morale of the readers but the morale of the members of the Vanguard Group itself," Dolgoff later admitted.[104] Politically, Mark Schmidt drifted toward the Communist Party, and he urged the group to join united front organizations, which they refused to do. Later, he explained, "It was Russia's struggle against Hitler and fascism that led me to support it."[105] Beneath such political and strategic reconsiderations, however, lay more quotidian tensions—namely, sexual and romantic jealousy that arose from intragroup dating.[106]

Man! would not last much longer. After the attempt to deport Ferrero and Sallitto, federal agents interrogated and threatened the newspaper's subscribers.[107] These threats having failed to silence the newspaper, Marcus Graham was arrested in October 1937 on the basis of the now eighteen-year-old deportation order stemming from his first arrest in 1919. Graham appealed to subscribers and correspondents to organize a defense campaign in the style of the prewar Free Speech League. Agnes Inglis, one of Emma Goldman's former benefactors, with whom Graham corresponded, urged caution and apologized that she could not be of much assistance. "Somehow," she wrote, "organization work has been so overshadowed by defense that now defense has no backing."[108] During his trial, Graham was jailed for contempt of court but released on a one-thousand-dollar bond awaiting appeal.[109] The conviction was upheld; Graham failed to surrender to authorities, electing to give up *Man!* and to live clandestinely, like his erstwhile publishing partner, Domenico Sallitto.

With *Man!* and *Vanguard* both ceasing publication in 1939, the country was left without an English-language anarchist newspaper as war broke out across Europe. Small anarchist circles in New York and Chicago continued to publish newspapers in Russian, Spanish, Yiddish, and Italian, but they spoke almost entirely to aging immigrant communities, and the public activities of such groups ground nearly to a halt. The Second World War was a profoundly confusing and dispiriting experience for what remained of the U.S. American anarchist movement. "As antimilitarists we could not support the war," Abe Bluestein explained, "but we regarded Hitler and fascism as the greater danger."[110] During a nationwide speaking tour, Rudolf Rocker, a revered figure who had experienced fascism firsthand, encouraged U.S. anarchists to overcome their ambivalence. Bluestein later recalled,

> I remember him putting it this way: "We live in a house with many people who are not our friends, with whom we disagree and have always disagreed. I think of the British Empire, I think of the French government, I think of the American government. We have always opposed their policies and opposed their imperialism. I now see the Nazis across the table from us . . . threatening our lives. And I therefore say to you that it is better to work with opponents whom we can criticize and live than with opponents who will kill us as soon as they can get their hands on us." He defended very strongly the idea that we have to support a war against Nazi Germany . . . and we all accepted this.[111]

Shifts in opinion were often abrupt and adamant. In a letter to his anarchist pacifist friend Ammon Hennacy, Harry Kelly stated, "I am unregenerate and pro-war for, unlike you, my anarchism is and has always been based on self-defense."[112] The Vanguard Group's Irving Sterling joined the U.S. Army to contribute to the defeat of fascism.[113] Yet anarchist opinion was far from unanimous. Until its demise, *Man!* remained adamantly opposed to involvement, rehashing Galleani's position: "We are then: against war just as much as against the so-called peace under the present system. We are tho [*sic*] at all times for the social revolution, which is the only force able to wipe off from the face of this chaotic earth, the ignoble things of injustice called now peace or war."[114]

The outbreak of the war, then, further divided anarchism's already meager ranks. This was literally the case regarding the Stelton Colony. Although most of the remaining residents sided with Rocker and supported the war effort in principle, the entry of the United States into the conflict had unanticipated consequences. In 1941 the federal government bought a large tract of land immediately adjacent to the colony and quickly erected Camp Kilmer, an army base that at its peak housed seventy-five thousand troops. A series of robberies and sexual assaults committed by soldiers, above and beyond the general martial atmosphere, prompted most of the remaining Stelton residents to relocate, many of them to retirements in warmer climates.[115] While the Mohegan Colony remained intact, anarchists ceded control, and it, too, began to take on the airs of a retirement community.

If U.S. anarchists articulated their ideas more cogently than they had in the previous decade, their movement remained plagued by many of the limitations it had suffered since 1920. Stated bluntly, the 1930s pitted an organizing anarchism without organizers against an insurrectionary anarchism without insurgents. Those pursuing a utopian strategy at the Sunrise Colony largely ended up prefiguring deprivation and community discord. The focus on supporting Spanish anarchists in the late 1930s, likewise, echoed the priority anarchists had placed on defending comrades from fascism and communism throughout the 1920s.

Periodicals remained the primary outlet for anarchist ideas during the 1920s and 1930s. As we have seen, the interwar anarchist journals largely abandoned earlier analyses of gender, sexual, and racial oppression, as well as their engagement with emergent trends in philosophy and cultural production. They faithfully upheld varieties of class-struggle anarchism that assumed persistent immiseration would inevitably lead working-class-identified individuals to violently negate the whole of social relations in one swift, satisfying swoop. However, the survival of capitalism, the rise of the welfare state, the emergence of a reformist industrial unionism, and the harsh realities of ideologically driven total war overwhelmed the interpretive apparatus and the strategic options developed in the nineteenth-century anarchist classics.

The defensive posture that the movement assumed for more than two decades helps account for its theoretical stagnation in the years following World War I. The period just before that war had been one of intellectual excitement, generative debate, and new departures. In the interwar years, however, many of the movement's respected theorists were imprisoned, exiled to unstable living conditions, or killed. When they did have the opportunity to write, they focused their efforts on critiques of other political systems, rather than on refreshing their own. This is evident in the major books published by anarchists during this period. Berkman's *Bolshevik Myth,* Goldman's *My Disillusionment in Russia,* and Maximoff's *Guillotine at Work* all focus on exposing Bolshevik repression. Rocker's *Anarcho-Syndicalism: Theory and Practice* systemized the syndicalist position for the first time in English, though it was hastily penned in 1937 to explain the ideology of the Spanish anarchists then under heavy fire from Franco's troops.[116]

World War II proved a turning point in the lives of the generation—weary from twenty years of defeats—that had founded *Vanguard* and *Man!* Few remained politically engaged after the war. Within a few years, however, the U.S. anarchist movement reemerged in a substantially new guise. When it did, a number of the Vanguard Juniors were leading the way. The path they began to clear, to the surprise and dismay of their former mentors, had already been illuminated by the scandalously theistic, ideological syncretic Catholic Worker Movement.

PART II

The Rise of Contemporary Anarchism

FIVE

Anarchism and Revolutionary Nonviolence, 1940–1948

If the First World War shattered the U.S. anarchist movement, one could say the Second World War both splintered what remained of the movement *and* reestablished it on new footings. Much had changed in the intervening decades. As the United States joined the fray in 1917, anarchists, Wobblies, and socialists alike openly denounced the war. Collectively, they posed a significant enough threat that government, business, and vigilante organizations felt compelled to ban their publications, ransack their offices, jail their leaders, and deport rank-and-file organizers by the thousands. As the war progressed, the Russian Revolution cost the Entente Powers an ally and pushed revolutionary fervor in the United States and Europe to new heights. In contrast, as the United States edged toward war in 1941, the IWW, anarchist, and Socialist Party ranks were already decimated, the remaining militants at odds with one another over the war. The strongest Left formation, the Communist Party, had flip-flopped sharply and enthusiastically backed American entry after Germany invaded the Soviet Union. Following Pearl Harbor, American public support for the war became overwhelming; preemptive repression of the alleged domestic opposition focused on citizens of Japanese descent, not on organizations promoting proletarian internationalist dissent.

Although they lacked the capacity to influence war policy one way or the other, anarchists nonetheless caustically debated the *principle* of war resistance with one another, further dividing their already paltry numbers. As a result, U.S. anarchism was at a low point—perhaps the lowest since its inception—from the onset of World War II in 1939 until the mid-1960s, if judged by numbers of participants, organizations, and activities. Yet if anarchism was a tiny and marginal political current during the 1940s and 1950s, it was not at all static. As the last veterans of the nineteenth-century movement passed away, and as many of those active during the interwar years made peace with New Deal liberalism, a new generation of anarchists looked to radical pacifism and the cultural avant-garde to renew the libertarian socialist tradition.

During World War II, anarchist draft resisters befriended Gandhian pacifists in conscientious objector camps and federal penitentiaries, where they jointly resisted racial segregation and influenced one another's politics. Upon being released, pacifists who had embraced anarchism during the war launched new organizations to combat racism, economic injustice, and nuclear war using nonviolent direct action. Although workers' living standards were on the rise, anarchists sought alternatives to the alienating effects of early Cold War consumerist culture by immersing themselves in avant-garde cultural production, embracing sexuality and the natural world, and creating communities of like-minded individuals. During the 1940s and 1950s, then, anarchists served as a hinge linking radical pacifists with avant-garde artists and writers. They spent these years developing new political analyses, strategies, institutions, and aesthetics that shaped the Beat Generation, the civil rights movement, the 1960s counterculture, and the New Left. Writers drew on recent developments in social theory to broaden the anarchist critique of power beyond the movement's traditional focus on class oppression, while activists and artists explored nonviolent and representational techniques of self- and social transformation. From this milieu arose a conception of anarchism indebted to Henry David Thoreau and Leo Tolstoy that advocated individuals focus on living their own lives in a fashion that resembled their ideals as closely as possible. These "practical anarchists" sought to prefigure the world they hoped to live in rather than wait until after a revolution that now seemed impossibly far off.[1]

This chapter focuses on the encounter between anarchists and radical pacifists, primarily those based in New York City. Chapter 6 attends to the relationships developed between anarchists and groups of radical artists and writers—particularly those contributing to the San Francisco Renaissance. Together, they illuminate a series of major thematic, strategic, and demographic shifts that fundamentally shaped the course of U.S. anarchism over the second half of the twentieth century. As anarchist ideas contributed to midcentury pacifism, to the debates of the New York Intellectuals, and to canonical American expressive traditions, these influences, in turn, shifted anarchism away from mass organizing among industrial workers and toward a middle-class constituency. The ideology was upwardly mobile along with the young people who worked to maintain it during these difficult years. The early 1940s, rather than the late 1960s, should therefore be seen as the jumping-off point for contemporary U.S. anarchism.

After *Vanguard* ceased publication and the editors of *Man!* went underground in 1939, no English-language anarchist newspaper was published in the United States for three years. Periodicals had long served not only as a primary means of disseminating anarchist ideas but also as centers of activity around which anarchists organized other aspects of their political lives. U.S. anarchists had come to agreement in the mid-1920s on the need to prioritize recruitment of English speakers, since federal policies enacted in that period precipitated a decline in immigration from the countries that had previously supplied many of the movement's adherents. Given the scale of world crisis and the massive changes under way in U.S. society owing to the war, the need for an English mouthpiece felt especially urgent.

Everyday life changed rapidly in the early 1940s. The induction of approximately 10 million young men, combined with the demand for manufacture of war material of all sorts, spelled the end of the lingering economic depression. Full employment and temporary nationalization of the war industries proved an enormous boon for workers. Though the new CIO unions patriotically pledged not to strike for the duration of the war, they were free to recruit the millions of workers streaming into shipyards, canneries, and other workplaces. Moreover, the exigencies of war, coupled with timely and determined organizing campaigns, opened well-paid blue-collar positions to women and people of color for the first time, resulting in a second Great Migration of African Americans to cities in the North and West.[2] The war, the state's new role in the economy, the transformation of the American workforce, and many other developments all had serious implications for those who aspired to live in a free and egalitarian world. Silence in the face of such far-reaching changes could be disastrous.

In early 1942 a group met in New York to rectify the situation, with a number of Vanguard Juniors—young people who had been mentored by older members of the Vanguard Group during the 1930s—leading the charge. The first issue of the new anarchist newspaper *Why?* hit newsstands in April 1942, four months after the United States had officially entered the Second

World War. The founding group consisted of Audrey Goodfriend of the Bronx Vanguard Juniors; David Koven, former member of the Brooklyn Vanguard Juniors; *Vanguard* stalwarts Sam and Esther Dolgoff; a Wobbly merchant marine named Franz Fleigler; his wife, Bessie; and an older woman, Dorothy Rogers. Goodfriend had befriended Rogers when she and Vanguard member Clara Freedman hitchhiked to Toronto in 1939 to meet Emma Goldman. At the time, Rogers lived with the intrepid Italian anarchist Attilio Bortolotti and served as Goldman's personal assistant. After Goldman's passing, Rogers relocated to New York and took an apartment with Goodfriend, who was working as a bookkeeper after earning a degree in mathematics from Hunter College on a full scholarship.

This small group launched *Why?* at a moment of great change and historical uncertainty. Years later Franz Fleigler recounted, "I was the one who suggested the name. I looked back on the rise of fascism, on workers sitting on their ass, on the war, on Soviet Russia, where I had just been, and asked, 'Why? Why did all this happen?'"[3] Though the group desired to grapple with the big questions, the journal was a modest affair: it ran a mere eight pages, published monthly in a nine-inch-by-seven-inch magazine format. The first issues revisited much of the terrain covered by *Vanguard*. They included reprinted essays by Mikhail Bakunin and considerations of the nature of Soviet power, for example. Contributors, who wrote under pen names or initials during the war, argued, as had *Vanguard,* that the AFL and CIO's use of the 1935 National Labor Relations Act, in which the federal government legally recognized and regulated labor unions, amounted to a "great surrender" in which the labor movement became a tool of a sophisticated form of "state capitalism" that could more effectively manage working-class demands. The growing corporatist welfare state appeared to *Why?* to be a form of fascism growing within the United States itself. Still, the group saw a revitalized, militant, and independent labor movement as the best hope for achieving social justice.[4]

After only a few issues, *Why?* began to suffer from long-standing schisms within the American anarchist movement. Chief among these was the question of how anarchists should relate to the war. Rudolf Rocker, the highly respected German anarcho-syndicalist, had recently fled to the United States, where he urged critical support for the Allies as the only realistic means of defeating the fascist regimes that had gutted the Left in Europe.[5] All too aware of the fascists' ethnic cleansing of European Jews, the vast majority of Jewish anarchists supported this position. Many anarchists involved with the Spanish-language newspaper *Cultura Proletaria* and the Italian language *L'Adunata dei Refratarri,* however, upheld the traditional anarchist opposition to war. "Rudolf Rocker," explained the anarchist miner Guy Liberti, "was a good man but was wrong about World War II. Anarchism has always been antithetical to militarism. We must rely on people to rise up against dictators, not armies."[6] The Dolgoffs and Fleiglers supported Rocker's position and called for critical support for the Allies; they decided to break with *Why?* when the remainder of the group insisted on taking an antiwar position.[7]

Underlying the debate over the war lay simmering conflicts over political vision, strategy, and organizational forms that had divided anarcho-syndicalists and insurrectionary anarchists for decades. Tiny and marginal as the anarchist movement was in the early 1940s, this theoretical conflict appeared to some of the younger anarchists around *Why?* to be an absurd sectarianism. Owing to her friendship with Bortolotti in Toronto, Dorothy Rogers was embraced by the insurrectionary Italian group that published *L'Adunata dei Refratarri* in New York City, and she served as something of a bridge between the two camps.[8] The editors of *Why?* grew even closer to *L'Adunata* after Diva Agostinelli joined the group.

Agostinelli was born into a family of immigrant anarchists who worked as coal miners in central Pennsylvania. Even after World War I, the town of Jessup remained home to a significant community of Italian anarchists of the Galleani school. Agostinelli later remembered, "The young men in town had a pool hall called the Speedway and they would call me in—my mother said I was six or seven then. They'd take my shoes off, put me up in my stocking feet on the pool table and say, 'Tell us about the revolution' or 'Tell us about the strike' and I would make a speech." During the 1920s Agostinelli's uncle died tragically when a bomb he was preparing for use against Italian American fascists accidently exploded.[9] Diva relocated to New York City after earning a degree at Philadelphia's Temple University, paid for by her parents' comrades.

The trust born of Agostinelli's name and ability to speak Italian translated into crucial support for the English-language journal. When the printers who had brought out the first issue balked at *Why?*'s growing criticism of the war, the Italians agreed to print it in their own shop and to donate money toward other expenses. Beginning with the fourth issue, translations of articles originally published in *L'Adunata* appeared in *Why?* The English-language group promoted a fund-raising "Dance and Entertainment" at the

Galileo Club, the L'Adunata Group's social center at 118 Cook Street in the Bushwick section of Brooklyn, shortly thereafter.[10]

Exchanges with the L'Adunata Group helped nourish the antiwar stance of the remaining editors of *Why?* Seeds had already been planted, however, by the British anarchist newspaper *War Commentary.* Throughout the early 1940s, the editors of *Why?* exchanged letters and subscriptions with the London-based Freedom Group, who published *War Commentary.*[11] The Londoners pronounced the war an interimperialist conflict and argued that workers in each of the belligerent countries should seize the crisis situation caused by the war to depose their own governments, turning war into revolution as the Russians had done in 1917 and French workers had done with the formation of the Paris Commune in 1871. In December 1942, *Why?* published an article from *War Commentary* outlining this perspective under the heading "Our Policy in Brief."[12] This was similar to the concept of "revolutionary defeatism" adopted by the Trotskyist Socialist Workers Party, the only other faction of the U.S. Left that openly opposed the Second World War.

In 1944 the Why? Group published an English translation of *L'Adunata*'s Italian-language pamphlet *War or Revolution? An Anarchist Statement.* The pamphlet, penned by Raffaele Schiavina, argued that the First World War had ended when domestic social rebellion, inspired by the Russian Revolution, forced the Allies and Central Powers to cease hostilities in order to suppress the spread of revolution. According to Schiavina, fascism grew as a means of suppressing workers' movements, and it was supported by the democracies in this effort until fascist violence was directed against other "imperialist" states. While Left movements had opposed fascism from the beginning, liberal opposition to fascist politics could not be trusted. "The official war bulletins deal only with the battles and victories of the regular military fronts," claimed the pamphlet. "But the main factor of the struggle against fascism has always been and still remains the people's moral and physical revolt, and in the front ranks stand the militant workers who are the vanguard of the social revolution." This being the case, Schiavina reaffirmed the position declared by Luigi Galleani before the First World War: "Against war, against peace, for social revolution."[13]

As the decade progressed, members of the Why? Group moved from an antiwar politics toward an embrace of pacifism. Goodfriend and others were deeply impressed by *The Conquest of Violence: An Essay on War and Revolution,* published in 1937 by the Dutch anarchist and pacifist Bart de

Ligt. Influenced by utopian socialists as a theology student, De Ligt promoted feminist, anticapitalist, and antimilitarist ideas as a village church pastor beginning in 1910. He was jailed for his opposition to World War I and the draft, an experience of state repression that led him to study the anarchist classics. As the historian Peter van den Dungen explains, De Ligt recognized that "anarchism was grounded in a mystical-spiritual conviction which strove for the freedom, equality and brotherhood of all." Embracing this broader, humanistic spirituality, he gave up his church pastorship to devote himself to writing and organizing. De Ligt became a leading figure in the War Resisters International and collaborated with Mohandas Gandhi in the 1930s, all while continuing to promote anarchist principles. In 1931 he published a history of nonviolent resistance, *Peace as Deed: Principles, History, and Methods of Direct Action against War.* In choosing this name, he posited nonviolent direct action as a form of the traditionally violent anarchist practice of "propaganda of the deed." His second book likewise played on the title of Kropotkin's famous work *The Conquest of Bread.*[14]

The Conquest of Violence made important interventions that would have lasting repercussions for anarchist movements in the United States and Europe. First, De Ligt lambasted "the absurdity of bourgeois pacifism." A pacifism that opposed war but accepted capitalism and the maintenance of colonies was pointless, since "war, capitalism, and imperialism make a common chord, like the three notes, tonic, third, and fifth." Moreover, he asserted, "the capitalists make war, but the proletarians make it possible." Since workers continued to fight in wars, even against their own interests, the revolutionary antimilitarist had to recognize that factors deeply embedded in social life prompted them to do so. He concluded, therefore, that "the underlying cause of modern war is the character itself of modern society.... Our society is violent just as fog is wet."[15] Accordingly, those committed to abolishing war had to dedicate themselves to a long-term struggle to fully transform contemporary society, its culture, and its values.

Second, De Ligt questioned the assumption that social revolution required—and legitimized—the use of violence by radicals. Drawing from the experiences of the Russian Revolution and the Spanish Civil War, De Ligt introduced the maxim "The more violence, the less revolution."[16] The Dutchman argued that, given the scope of weaponry possessed by modern states, deposing a government by force would prove so destructive to the country's infrastructure and breed so much animosity that it would force the revolutionaries to establish structures of control indistinguishable from those they were seeking to abolish. He suggested that even the noble Spanish CNT had been caught in this trap:

> Strongly opposed to any form of military conscription, the Spanish anarchists accepted at the most "spontaneous violence for the revolution," and organized a free militia.... But the necessities of modern warfare made it imperative for the Revolutionary Army to be systematically militarized, the command to be centralized, conscription to be introduced and so on.... So that the longer the Civil War persisted, the more militarism and *étatism* began to grow, even in the most libertarian circles.[17]

De Ligt reasoned that it would have been preferable to allow Franco's forces to take control without opposition and for the people to then carry out a general strike and campaign of noncooperation. So confident was he in the power of nonviolent struggle that De Ligt concluded *The Conquest of Violence* with a detailed plan to defeat the looming invasion of fascist armies with a coordinated campaign of pacifist resistance. Unexpectedly, therefore, the pacifists and the Italian insurrectionists shared some ground: both rejected the use of national militaries to defeat fascism, and both were convinced that citizens self-organizing to resist authoritarian movements could provide a sufficient deterrent. They differed, of course, on whether violent or nonviolent methods would prove most effective.

De Ligt's anarchist pacifism proved influential in radical circles during the 1930s and 1940s. As van den Dungen notes, "De Ligt facilitated the growing together, especially in Holland, of religious-anarchist, libertarian-socialist, and revolutionary antimilitarist tendencies."[18] His writings helped unite a nearly identical set of constituencies in the United States over the next decade. Goodfriend later recalled how her own thinking began to change under De Ligt's influence. "At that time, thinking about Spain and how the anarchists entered the government, and all the things that beset the anarchists in Spain, and realizing how many people had been killed, had died—I just realized that change was not going to happen through violence. That was a very pivotal thing for me."[19]

Why?'s position on the war was more than a question of editorial line for the young men of the group; it directly affected their decisions about how to relate to the draft. During the Second World War, the federal government established a conscientious objector program to provide alternative service assignments to members of the peace churches—the Quakers, Mennonites, Brethren, and Jehovah's Witnesses—whose religious beliefs precluded them from fighting. Applicants found by a judge to possess religiously based pacifist convictions were assigned to Civilian Public Service (CPS) camps, where they worked in national parks, forests, and other infrastructure projects. Draft-age men who opposed the war, then, had to decide if they would seek conscientious objector (CO) status, which some saw as an accommodation to the war system, or refuse to cooperate at all and face a prison term of up to five years.[20]

Members of the *Why?* milieu parried with the Selective Service Board using a variety of strategies. Contributor Clif Bennett successfully dodged the draft for more than two years but was eventually apprehended and jailed. David Koven trained as a merchant marine medic to avoid military service. He, too, was briefly incarcerated, however, for refusing to respect the military discipline of a naval officer responsible for his certification.[21] Diva Agostinelli risked arrest by helping at least one draft resister flee the country, as Vietnam-era activists would do on a larger scale twenty years later.[22] Perhaps most significant for the future of U.S. anarchism, however, was the wartime experience of David Thoreau Wieck.

Wieck was born in the small community of Belleville, Illinois, to parents active in the Progressive Miners of America. Forced out of Illinois for political reasons, they relocated to the Bronx after Wieck's father landed a research job with the industrial relations department of the Russell Sage Foundation. In high school Wieck dabbled with the Young Communist League before attending Vanguard Junior meetings at the nearby Shalom Aleichem Houses, where he met Audrey Goodfriend and Abe Bluestein. Though named after one of the country's most prominent libertarians, Wieck later recalled, "it wasn't by reading Thoreau that I was persuaded to anarchism; it was Kropotkin and Emma Goldman whose lives were an effort to save the world from itself."[23] Wieck entered Columbia University at age sixteen, earning a bachelor's degree in philosophy. While in college, he researched the bureaucratization of the miners' union, and after graduating he contributed articles to early issues of *Why?*[24] When the United States declared war in December 1941, he refused to register for the draft, arguing that the effort to defeat fascism by war was leading the United States to itself become totalitarian.[25] Denied conscientious objector status, he was given a three-year sentence at the Danbury Federal Penitentiary in Connecticut after being apprehended during a poorly planned attempt to flee to Mexico in the spring of 1943.[26] Wieck was resigned to serving time in order to honor his conscience; he could not have predicted the extent to which imprisonment would open doors to new ideas, allies, and opportunities for resistance.

With many of the group's men in jail or on the lam, *Why?* was edited and distributed predominantly by women during the course of World War II. These included Goodfriend, Rogers, Agostinelli, and Sally Grieg, who joined the group along with her journalist husband, Michael. In addition to assuming editorial responsibilities, these women regularly wrote news items and analytical articles, marking a departure from the domination of anarchist publishing by male writers after *Mother Earth* was suppressed in 1917.

RETORT

During the period when Wieck, Bennett, and Koven were parrying with the Selective Service Board, *Why?* was joined by *Retort*. Styling itself "a journal of art and social philosophy," *Retort* was issued quarterly by editor Holley Cantine Jr. from a small cabin in Bearsville, New York, just outside of Woodstock. Unlike the editors of *Why?*, Cantine came from wealth. His maternal great-grandfather served as the first president of Panama and later as ambassador to the United States, while his father owned Cantine's Coated Papers, a major employer in the Hudson River town of Saugerties, New York.[27] Although Cantine had not participated in anarchist circles as the members of the Vanguard Juniors had, his mother moved in left-wing social circles and he spent his childhood in Woodstock, a flourishing left-wing "artist colony" that attracted anarchists such as Hippolyte Havel and Stella Ballantine in the 1920s.[28] He attended Swarthmore College and Columbia University, concentrating on anthropology, but abandoned the academy before completing a doctoral dissertation in order to live a self-sufficient Thoreauvian life. Cantine and his partner, the painter Dorothy Paul, built an eighteen-foot-by-thirty-two-foot cabin on family-owned land and began raising goats. There, Cantine set up an old pedal-driven printing press and devoted himself to a life of politics and literature.[29]

Since he believed "all free societies have always been artistic societies," Cantine sought to intersperse original political thought with provocative poetry and fiction in each issue of the journal. *Retort* served as an early outlet for a variety of respected literary figures—Kenneth Patchen, Saul Bellow, and Robert Duncan among them—as we will see in the following chapter. However, the journal's most notable nonfiction essays emanated from Cantine's own pen. Beginning with its first editorial, *Retort* marked a departure from left-wing politics, including much of the anarchism, of the previous

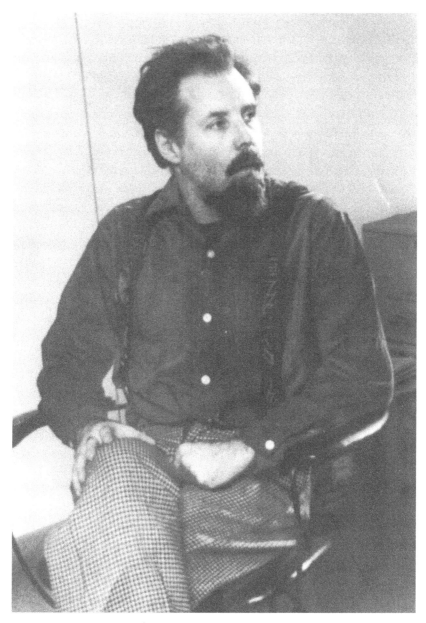

Holley Cantine Jr., 1940s. Courtesy of Antonia Weidenbacher.

decades. Despite their long-standing feuds, anarchists often shared with orthodox Marxists certain fundamental assumptions: the struggle between economic classes formed the basis of the revolutionary project; a materialist viewpoint provided the conceptual tools radicals needed to make sense of the world; revolution was an inevitability in the progressive march of history; when it occurred, it would do so at the hands of masses of workers—organized or inspired by self-conscious radicals—who would dispense with the old and initiate new institutions in one fell swoop. *Retort* boldly set itself against all these positions. "We enter the arena with few, if any illusions and no certainty that our cause will be victorious. Overconfidence is one of the few weaknesses that our opponents cannot accuse us of," Cantine acidly admitted.[30] As one verity of the Left after another was disproven in the twentieth century, he had seen most radicals either grow despondent or retreat into a delusional sectarianism. "However," the editor asserted, "we cannot persuade ourselves that an absolutism which claims that success is impossible is any more reasonable than the old absolutism of inevitable success."[31] The task of committed intellectuals, then, was to propose tenets of a new radicalism at the same time that they thoroughly debunked the old.

Cantine could see that "human motivation is more complex than the theorists of the last century realized."[32] He hoped that applying the insights offered by the "sciences" of psychology and anthropology—disciplines he had studied at Columbia—to the social crisis of the contemporary world would help leftists establish a more accurate understanding of human nature and new strategic directions. Cantine drew on the writings of Sigmund Freud to consider why ordinary people, instead of acting for themselves, continued to place their faith in great revolutionary leaders despite so many betrayals.[33] In *Retort*'s second issue, Cantine delved into anthropological accounts of early societies to conceptualize the origins of the myriad forms of oppression existing in his own day. "Social stratification is deeply rooted in human society," Cantine wrote, "and can take a number of different forms—all of them inimical to the establishment of a really free and stable social order. Therefore, before a decent society could be brought into existence, all factors—political, economic, religious—that make it possible for a minority to rise to a position of predominance must be eliminated."[34] Cantine's anthropological approach and his conclusion that anarchists must seek to root out not only economic exploitation but also all forms of social domination, anticipated by three decades ideas that became central to U.S. anarchism in the 1970s.[35]

Cantine's thought, which outlined what might be called an "anarchism without guarantees," paralleled that of his contemporary Antonio Gramsci, whose theory contravened the strict economic determinism of more orthodox Marxists and suggested that the complexities of modern forms of power made old revolutionary strategies obsolete.[36] At points, similarities in their writings are striking, such as when Cantine states, "We believe that certain institutional forms, by their very existence, preclude the possibility of desirable social change, but that these institutions—the state, for instance—have too many subtle psychological ramifications to be destroyable by a direct frontal assault. The problem of achieving a decent society is vastly more complex and roundabout than the 19th century imagined."[37]

This very complexity convinced Cantine that radicals must select the means for attaining their goals "with great care." The Russian Revolution had proven that "the mere overthrow of a decadent ruling class is but an incident in the real revolution. . . . Indeed, it may be the prelude to a worse reaction than before."[38] The instrumentalist means enacted by earlier militants needed to be carefully parsed, given the degree to which they were implicated in the further oppression of those they promised to liberate. "In the name of a vague and distant future of Triumphant Socialism the worst exploitation and persecution have been condoned," Cantine wrote. For this reason, he argued, no future movement should be considered revolutionary if it sacrificed the lives of individual humans for the promotion of an abstract system. While such realizations led many former leftists to experience paralysis, they encouraged Cantine to consider different routes to revolution.

Cantine's interpretation of history prompted him to eschew "placing very much reliance in benevolent leadership," since leaders of previous revolutions had either turned on one another or grown detached with privilege and power from the people they claimed to represent, undermining the goals originally fought for. Furthermore, he argued, "It is the radical movement's present-day emphasis on politics—the idea of achieving control of the government, either by election or insurrection—that is perhaps the greatest single reason why the movement is so thoroughly stratified." An organization that "expects to achieve its goal by taking over the state, must be highly centralized, and dominated by a hierarchy of trained specialists."[39]

Cantine believed that another strategy was possible:

Since both violent revolution and parliamentary activity seem to lead away from the realization of fundamental liberty, a realistic radical movement should concern itself with building up a nucleus of the new society "within the shell of the old." Communities and various other kinds of organization must be formed, wherein the ideals of the revolution are approximated as nearly as possible in daily life. The new society must be lived out by its advocates; both as a way of influencing the masses by example, and in order to iron out weaknesses of theory by actual experiment.[40]

Retort's editor claimed no credit in originating such a critique of social democratic and Leninist forms of radical politics. "This tradition," he noted, "found probably its clearest expression in the writings of Thoreau and Tolstoi . . . and today provides the driving impulse for most conscientious objectors. . . . It is present, at least by implication, in the writings of Eugene Debs and nearly all anarchist thinkers."[41] To an extent, Cantine was correct. Bakunin's followers in the First International had fiercely criticized Marx because they feared his centrally directed and disciplined model of organizing would translate into a dictatorial society once it achieved success. Yet earlier anarchists had also oriented their activities with reference to an anticipated moment of swift revolutionary transition that was likely to occur sometime within their lives. When the IWW spoke of building the "new world in the shell of the old," they referred to radical labor unions that would coordinate mass production in the place of government after a period of rupture brought on by a general strike. Cantine, however, was rearticulating the concept, shifting its meaning slightly by urging radicals to practice their revolutionary values in communities of like-minded individuals and in the various aspects of daily life. Although he mobilized syndicalist language, Cantine was, in fact, advocating a departure from both the mass organizing and the insurrectionary strategies that dominated pre–World War II anarchism, to support a deeper investment in the strategy of prefiguration, or what Mohandas Gandhi described as "being the change you want to see."

A pacifist himself, Cantine was impressed by the antiwar stands that Thoreau and Tolstoy had taken in their times. He reprinted Tolstoy's famous 1898 essay "Cathargo Delenda Est," in which the Christian anarchist had argued, "Every man, in refusing to take part in military service or to pay taxes to a government which uses them for military purposes, is, by this refusal, rendering a great service to God and man."[42] Cantine intended to personally resist the draft during the Second World War. However, the local draft board classified him "4-F," unfit for service on mental health grounds. Cantine believed the board willingly disqualified him to maintain its otherwise spotless record of compliance.[43]

Through words and material practice, however, *Retort*'s editor suggested that anarchists should extend Tolstoy's strategy of individual refusal beyond participation in war to other aspects of the social order that they found odious—including industrial production. Cantine took pride in setting, printing, and binding the journal by hand rather than having it produced in a commercial printshop. He saw his efforts as promoting the merits of small-scale artisanal production and a rejection of the spread of automation and mass production. In this, he shared much in common with Marcus Graham, the anti-industrial editor of *Man!*, and he anticipated the critique of technology by U.S. anarchists in the 1970s. Sam Dolgoff, sure that worker control of heavy industry through radical unions was the only way forward for humanity, dismissed Cantine as an "oxcart anarchist." On the other hand, the editors of *Why?*—who were of the same generation as Cantine, mostly college-educated like him, and opposed to the war—quickly embraced *Retort*.

DWIGHT MACDONALD AND PAUL GOODMAN

Retort and *Why?* grew to see each other as kindred spirits that differed mainly in emphasis: *Why?* focused on shorter, newslike items, while *Retort* interspersed long, theoretical considerations with literature. Soon the periodicals were cross-promoting one another. They also encouraged readers to subscribe to the journal *NOW*, edited in London by Freedom Group member George Woodcock, and to *politics,* published in New York by Dwight and Nancy MacDonald.[44] Dwight, a former editor of the highbrow, Trotskyist-oriented *Partisan Review,* had been forced out for his own antiwar commitments. He and Nancy launched *politics* in 1944 with a donation from Margaret de Silver, the widow of Carlo Tresca. The eminent anarcho-syndicalist had been gunned down on the street in 1943, likely by Mafiosi, spelling the end of his newspaper, *Il Martello,* and further contributing to the decline of the old immigrant anarchist movement.[45]

The journal *politics* would go on to publish a remarkable array of European and American social thinkers, including Albert Camus, Hannah Arendt, Simone de Beauvoir, and C. Wright Mills. As Dwight MacDonald began to carve out a contemporary libertarian socialist and pacifist politics in his own contributions to the journal, Nancy MacDonald embarked on a practical effort that the anarchists responsible for *Why?* and *Retort* could enthusiastically endorse: the creation of the Spanish Refugee Aid Committee, an organization that provided material support and immigration assistance to exiled partisans of the civil war living precariously throughout war-torn Europe.[46]

These shared intellectual commitments developed into friendships. Audrey Goodfriend recalled, "David [Koven] and I went up to Woodstock and we walked over . . . to meet Holley." Later, the Why? Group bought a small hand-printing press in case the government sought to repress antiwar voices as it had done in 1917. Goodfriend recalled, "David and I lived at 635 E. Ninth Street [just east of Manhattan's Tompkins Square Park]. Across the street in the basement, we had the printing press. So Holley actually taught us how to print, and he lived there for a while too when he came down and lived in New York."[47] (The group was never forced to print the journal this way, but they did use the press to issue occasional leaflets and pamphlets.)

It was on one such trip to New York that Cantine met the MacDonalds' editorial assistant, Dachine Rainer, on a visit to the *politics* office. Rainer, born Sylvia Newman in 1921, was the daughter of leftist Polish Jews. She grew up in the Bronx and was touched as a young child by the executions of Sacco and Vanzetti. Having read Tolstoy and Kropotkin as a teenager, she already counted herself an anarchist pacifist by the time she enrolled at Hunter College, on scholarship, in 1938.[48] Cantine had by this time separated from Dorothy Paul. After an awkward courtship, Rainer returned with Cantine to Bearsville and became coeditor of *Retort*. She contributed poetry and helped print the journal while earning money for the household by reviewing books for liberal magazines.

In November 1944, recognizing that others beyond their small circle were taking interest in their ideas, the Why? Group began hosting weekly lectures and discussions. The meetings took place on Saturday afternoons at the Solidaridad Internacional Antifascista, the anarchist hall maintained by aging Spanish-speaking anarchists on the second floor of a building on Broadway, two blocks south of Union Square. Speakers ranged from the German émigré council communist Paul Mattick to the novelist James Baldwin. Dwight MacDonald spoke, as did A. J. Muste, chairman of the Christian pacifist organization the Fellowship of Reconciliation.[49] *Why?*'s influence also grew beyond New York by 1945. In addition to supplying its local readership of aging Italian-, Spanish-, and Russian-speaking subscribers, the group mailed bundles of each issue to distributors in cities such as Phoenix, Arizona, and San Francisco. The radical poet Kenneth Rexroth hawked issues of *Why?* and *Retort* among a circle of writers, artists, and war resisters in California's Bay Area, some of whom ventured East to meet the papers' editors.[50] After the war, the Why? Group and the Libertarian Circle helmed by Rexroth would develop tighter bonds, as we will see in chapter 6.

Through these meetings and other activities, *Why?* attracted additional recruits to the group, including Sally and Michael Grieg, the poet Jackson Mac Low, and an African American Brooklyn College student named Dan DeWeiss. Perhaps the most influential person to join the milieu in the mid-1940s was Paul Goodman, a poet and essayist who had returned to New York after earning a doctorate at the University of Chicago. Like MacDonald, Goodman had burned bridges to the city's Marxist-literary community through his staunch criticism of the war and efforts to craft an antiauthoritarian politics relevant to current conditions. Goodman brought an interest in sexual politics to *Why?* through his promotion of the theories of the Austrian psychoanalyst Wilhelm Reich and via his personal life as a husband and father who also openly pursued sexual relationships with younger men. He would become a mentor to campus radicals in the 1960s, following the publication of his best seller *Growing Up Absurd*.[51]

During the spring of 1945 Goodman wrote a series of essays that would prove to be his most significant contributions to anarchist theory. Though later issued jointly as *The May Pamphlet,* the material was first published in sections spread across issues of *Retort, Why?* and *politics*. Goodman's perspective had a good deal in common with that of Cantine. "A free society," he wrote, "cannot be the substituting of a 'new order' for the old order; it is the extension of spheres of free action until they make up most of the social life." Goodman then posited a simple maxim: "Free action is to live in the present society as though it were a natural society." The libertarian

> does not look forward to a future state of things which he tries to bring about by suspect means; but he draws now, so far as he can, on the natural force in him that is no different in kind from what it will be in a free society, except that there it will have more scope and be persistently reinforced by mutual aid and fraternal conflict. Merely by continuing to exist and act in nature and freedom, the libertarian wins the victory, establishes the society; it is not necessary for him to be the victor over any one.[52]

Goodman, then, articulated a vision of anarchist politics that radically deemphasized organizing and collective confrontation. It was gradualist rather than millenarian, and it implicitly posited conscription and antigay discrimination, rather than hunger, as the primary threats to freedom and well-being that should concern anarchists. These ideas thrilled members of the Why? Group who had grown increasingly dissatisfied with traditional anarchism yet remained alienated from the world of weapon production, war bonds, and victory gardens that had grown up all around them. Koven later called Goodman the "ferment" in the Why? Group that "made our meetings the most vital and exciting in New York. He introduced us to . . . the contemporary world of psychology and sociology."[53]

RADICAL PACIFISTS

Owing to his arrest, David Wieck missed the early *Why?* forums as well as the new ideas and friendships that grew out of them. However, upon arrival, he was happy to learn that Danbury Federal Penitentiary had been designated as one of the East Coast centers for detaining war resisters. In a letter home, he insisted that his mother "quit worrying," since "the physical side is abundantly cared for" and he had met "several COs in quarantine [the section of the prison for new inmates] who are decidedly good and interesting company."[54] Wieck's new companions were some of the nearly 6,000 conscientious objectors and war resisters imprisoned during the Second World War. Historian James Tracy explains, "Of these, 4,300 were Jehovah's Witnesses with little or no political agenda. . . . The remaining seventeen hundred, however, constituted the most militant distinct group of pacifists in the country."[55] Indeed, a new form of pacifism, with broader commitments and more confrontational tactics, was on the upswing in the early 1940s.

Before World War II, the U.S. pacifist movement was anchored by the peace churches and two organizations based in New York City: the Fellowship of Reconciliation (FOR) and the War Resisters League (WRL). Founded in 1915, the FOR functioned as a nondenominational center for Christian antiwar organizing. By 1943 the organization counted 450 local chapters, and FOR membership included many ministers who preached a message of "universal brotherhood" to their congregations, counseling young men not to fight should war arise. The War Resisters League was organized in 1923 as a secular alternative to the FOR. It attracted significant numbers of Jewish pacifists and shared members with the Socialist Party and a variety of feminist organizations. The membership of both organizations was predominantly white and middle class, and both shied away from protest activity and issues beyond war, such as poverty and racial inequality.[56]

This had begun to change in the late 1930s under the leadership of A.J. Muste and the inspiration of Mohandas Gandhi. Muste, a Congregational minister, joined the FOR during World War I but dedicated his energies to labor and the Left for the next two decades. Muste considered himself a socialist and maintained friendly relations with anarchists during the 1920s and 1930s. He was a leader of the 1919 Lawrence textile strike alongside Carlo Tresca; directed the Brookwood Labor College, where Rose Pesotta was a student in the 1920s; and lectured at the Stelton and Mohegan Colonies later in the decade. Muste was appointed chair of the FOR in 1940 after securing a reputation as a brilliant speaker, organizer, and strategist during the Depression. While critiquing orthodox Marxism, he steered the FOR toward fighting class and racial inequality in addition to war, declaring forthrightly that a world without violence—social as well as military—required revolution.[57]

The FOR's adoption of a broader conception of violence, along with the tactical experimentation that would soon follow, owed largely to members' growing appreciation of Gandhi's principles of nonviolent struggle for social justice. Although African American newspapers and college professors had trumpeted the innovations of the anticolonial leader since the early 1920s, the FOR was among the earliest and most consistent advocates of Gandhian nonviolent direct action within white, progressive Christian circles. Richard Greggs, a Quaker and member of the FOR's National Committee, for example, penned *The Power of Nonviolence,* a widely read account of Gandhi's philosophy and method, a book that proved highly influential for many World War II war resisters.[58]

Like De Ligt, Gandhi argued that class- and caste-based societies were structured in violence, even when not officially at war. For more than twenty years he had demonstrated ways in which nonviolent means of struggle could prove more effective than reliance on bloodshed. His method emphasized the importance of individuals withdrawing their participation from ethically corrupt institutions, including sovereign states, even when this was likely to incur great personal hardship. In addition to Hindu and Christian theology, Gandhi drew on diverse traditions of political thought, including the anarchist writings of Peter Kropotkin, Leo Tolstoy, and Henry David Thoreau.

David Thoreau Wieck's experience in prison was significantly enlivened by the rising interest in Gandhi's ideas. In 1940 two former missionaries to India established the Harlem Ashram, a multiracial intentional community whose members shared resources and worked to combat the racism and poverty that structured life in Harlem's African American and Puerto Rican communities, using techniques inspired by Gandhi. A group of white students from the nearby Union Theological Seminary, including David Dellinger and George Houser, joined the ashram and later launched a second ashram in Newark, New Jersey. Embracing Gandhi's pacifism, they refused draft exemptions offered to clergy and, dubbed the Union 8 by the press, landed in Danbury for a year. The group refused to bend to the prison's policy of racial segregation and other offensive regulations, earning themselves long stays in solitary confinement but also the grudging respect of fellow inmates.[59] Born in 1915 to a patrician Boston family, Dellinger began developing an egalitarian worldview through a social gospel Christian organization at Yale University. After experiencing the Spanish Civil War firsthand and running messages between dissidents in Nazi Germany, Dellinger joined the FOR and the Socialist Party while studying to be a minister. George Houser was the son of Methodist missionaries and chair of a social action committee at Union Seminary. The experience of prison only deepened both men's commitment to radical social transformation.

Though the Union 8 had already been released when Wieck began his sentence in 1943, they had set the tone for dozens of other war resisters who followed them into the prison. Shortly after Wieck arrived, approximately two dozen Danbury draft resisters launched a successful strike against racial segregation in the prison cafeteria—an attempt to apply Gandhian techniques within a controlled setting in the United States. Wieck took part in the four-month strike—refusing to work, take his allotted time in the yard, or eat meals in the segregated cafeteria. Through the strike he befriended a number of young men, including Jim Peck and Ralph DiGia, who would dedicate their lives to radical politics. He also met Lowell Naeve, an anarchist painter from Iowa. The pair coauthored a memoir of life at Danbury and smuggled it out in a papier-mâché picture frame.

Hoping to prevent the protest from spreading, the warden at Danbury housed the nonviolent militants together in a secluded section of the prison, where they were allowed to interact in a common space. A letter Wieck wrote to his mother indicates the sense of community that quickly developed among strike participants. "I have been having a swell time up here in my new quarters," he explained. "We have very interesting discussions, debates and arguments on a variety of subjects, currently, primarily 'the beard,' the label one of the infidels here plastered on God. But [also] the labor movement . . . and even racial segregation."[60] With the aid of outside supporters, including

Adam Clayton Powell, the Danbury strike attracted national media attention and resulted in the full desegregation of the mess hall beginning in February 1944.[61]

The Danbury strikes against Jim Crow regulations sparked a wave of similar actions in prisons and CPS camps throughout the country. In the Lewisburg Federal Penitentiary in central Pennsylvania, thirteen war resisters launched a hunger strike to protest their prison's segregation policies in May 1943. Among them was Bill Sutherland, an African American pacifist and socialist who had lived at the Newark Ashram before refusing the draft. The Lewisburg strikers were later joined by Dellinger, who was returned to prison as a recidivist war resister after his release from Danbury. When DiGia was transferred from Danbury to Lewisburg as punishment for his intransigence, he participated as well.

A similar protest broke out among COs in the summer of 1945 at the federal prison in Ashland, Kentucky, under the leadership of the experienced pacifist organizer Bayard Rustin. Rustin had grown up as an African American Quaker and had worked with the Communist Party before embracing pacifism and joining the staff of the FOR. Before the draft board caught up with him late in the war, Rustin helped develop the FOR's Committee on Racial Equality.[62] The committee was established in 1942 by former Harlem Ashram members James Farmer and George Houser, following Houser's release from Danbury, with the intention of combating racial segregation with nonviolent direct action. It would soon be renamed the Congress of Racial Equality (CORE).

Conscientious objectors also protested conditions in the CPS camps. One of the most prominent was Igal Roodenko, a socialist-Zionist from a Ukrainian American family, who was assigned to the Powellsville, Maryland, camp in February 1943. There he conducted hunger strikes in sympathy with two COs who were protesting the government's right to conscript them with a "fast unto death." Roodenko later transferred to a camp in Colorado, where he helped organize work stoppages and protests to increase the paltry stipends COs received. He later abandoned the camp altogether, choosing to accept jail time rather than continue to collaborate with the CO system.[63]

Mail flowed fairly freely between CPS camps and the federal penitentiaries, allowing war resisters to communicate with one another. Anarchist periodicals also helped spread information and bolster a spirit of resistance. As some of the few radical publications that opposed the war, *Why?*, *Retort*, and *politics* left a significant impression on many COs. The May 1945 issue of *Why?* saluted COs who were bucking the "forced labor" they were required to perform in Civilian Public Service camps. The article quoted Roy Kepler, a pacifist stationed at the Germfask camp in Michigan, as claiming, "More and more CPS men are beginning to oppose the State and its power to make war."[64] After his release, West Coast CO Paul Lieber Adams wrote to Holley Cantine:

> When I was in CPS camp from January to Thanksgiving, 1944, I liked *Retort* very much. As you can guess, most of the men in those labor camps who could be considered politicized at all are men in the libertarian socialist position. Even in the backwoods camp to which I was assigned there were some philosophical anarchists and many younger fellows who have gone down the line from CP membership to sympathy with the IWW and the SP. *Retort* is a good influence for such people.[65]

The resistance paid off. In addition to successfully desegregating and liberalizing the polices of federal penitentiaries, the wave of nonviolent direct action united the radical pacifists and prompted them to discuss the potential for a broad movement of "revolutionary nonviolence" against war, racism, and economic inequality in the United States. Imprisonment also led the dissenters to modify their beliefs. Wieck later wrote, "I did not go to prison as a pacifist but rather as an objector to war and conscription. (I take words seriously.) It was in prison that I learned the methods of nonviolence. If I didn't dislike hyphenations I would characterize myself as an anarchist-pacifist."[66] In turn, the influence of prisoners such as Wieck and Naeve helped move other COs and pacifists, such as DiGia, Peck, Dellinger, and Sutherland, in the direction of anarchism.[67]

NEW ALLIANCES

The war encouraged anarchists to develop new partnerships beyond the walls of the prisons, as well. Although members of the Why? Group had considerable differences of opinion with religiously motivated radicals, they recognized them as some of the few allies available during the war and found ways of working with them. Audrey Goodfriend remembered that the Why? Group "would do street corner meetings, stuff like that. There was one time we were scared shitless that we would be hurt because we were near Hell's Kitchen and a bunch of Catholics were coming out. But the Catholic Worker was antiwar, and we were having meetings with all groups of people like that—War Resisters League, Catholic Worker—and so we were safe! These kids came out and saw a Catholic paper and they backed off!"[68]

As made evident in chapter 4, the Catholic Workers drew heavily on Tolstoy's and Kropotkin's anarchism but did not forge close bonds with the Vanguard Group, the Jewish Anarchist Federation, or the editors of *L'Adunata*. In the 1940s, however, the gregarious anarchist Ammon Hennacy devoted considerable energy to bridging the Catholic Worker and secular anarchist movements. Born in 1893, Hennacy was a Socialist Party member when World War I broke out. He refused to enlist, owing to his belief in working-class internationalism, and was imprisoned for two years at the Atlanta Federal Penitentiary. There he met Alexander Berkman, serving his own term for counseling draft resistance. Shortly after Berkman converted the midwesterner to anarchism, Hennacy was placed in solitary confinement with nothing but a Bible to occupy him. He was released a self-declared "Christian Anarchist," believing Jesus's Sermon on the Mount to be the "most revolutionary statement ever written."[69]

Hennacy spent much of his time over the succeeding decades as an itinerant laborer in the West and Southwest. He wrote occasionally for the anarchist newspapers the *Road to Freedom, Freedom,* and *Man!* In 1943 he began to distribute *Why?* and *Retort* in the Phoenix area. Cantine published Hennacy's essays in *Retort* and even ran a poem written by his daughter, Sharon, who lived with Hennacy's estranged wife. Although he was too old to be drafted for the Second World War, Hennacy still felt compelled to publicly resist. He picketed the nearest Federal Building daily and wrote a letter each year to the IRS declaring his refusal to pay taxes during a time of war. He urged other anarchists and pacifists to be similarly outspoken and to bravely accept the consequences. Dorothy Day portrayed Hennacy's self-motivated acts of personal refusal as exemplary of the Catholic Worker approach to change and convinced him to join her movement.

Although Hennacy's enthusiasm for bold acts of resistance was infectious, he often exalted symbolic protest by individuals to the exclusion of collective action. Like the Italian insurrectionists of earlier years, Hennacy distrusted organizations and discounted the efficacy of collective action by workers or any other group. In 1948 he wrote to Cantine and Rainer:

Ammon Hennacy, Phoenix, Arizona, 1951. Courtesy of the Department of Special Collections and University Archives, Marquette University Archives.

There is another matter on which I expect we agree, that is that we do not suffer from the illusion that what we say or write will move the masses. [Fred] Thompson of the Wobblie paper [the *Industrial Worker*] recently wrote me that great numbers of workers were wise to this system but were unorganized. I don't believe it, and even if they were organized that would likely spoil them into some party line that would limit their growth. You two living on the land, approximating the simple life (even with Holley's wine and tobacco) and myself doing productive work and denying the tax man and the other war mongering bastards have an influence much greater than thousands of voters and union members who gain 2 penny victories but are bound to the same capitalist wheel of misery.[70]

Later in life, Hennacy would publish *The One-Man Revolution in America*, a book of biographical sketches of figures who stood against the dominant thinking of their times, further indicating his individualistic conception of how change occurs.[71] Nevertheless, Hennacy's enthusiasm helped congeal an anarchist pacifist coalition that outlasted the war itself.

The Why? Group, the Catholic Workers, and the War Resisters League jointly picketed Danbury prison in February 1946 alongside parents of COs who remained incarcerated after the armistice (including Wieck's parents). On that occasion, Why? Group members distributed a leaflet that read in part: "The war is over, but the government fears that if these men come out, they will influence others to resist the government's power to bring us into war, a power in which your children will be sacrificed. Wars are not stopped by preparing for them. . . . Only such action as these men have taken, joined by workers who refuse to produce any war materials, can secure peace."[72] The picketers were not well received. "It was scary!" Goodfriend recalled. "We were practically run off the road by Danbury residents!"[73] Soon after, the Why? Group raised funds to mail packages of food and clothing to European anarchists left destitute by the war. When they discovered that regulations severely limited what they could send, they picketed the U.S. Post Office.[74]

NONVIOLENT REVOLUTIONARIES
AGAINST WAR AND RACISM

David Dellinger, too, began to seek out new allies from his cell in Lewisburg Federal Penitentiary as the war ground to a close. In an October 1944 letter, he told Holley Cantine, "Dwight MacDonald performs an excellent service in *Politics*. So do you in *Retort*."[75] Dellinger promoted the journals to other pacifists as well, inquiring of CO Roy Finch, for example, "Have you been reading *Politics*? What is your reaction to it? What of *Retort*?"[76] Dellinger especially appreciated the ways that *Retort* departed from prewar leftist publications. "Much of my gratitude for *Retort* lies in the fact that it is taking a free approach to contemporary issues at a time when it is clear that we must develop a new ideology and methodology if we are to keep alive," he told the editor.[77] Throughout his incarceration, Dellinger thought deeply about what such a new ideology and methodology would entail, sharing his ruminations with Cantine and other correspondents. For a time Dellinger considered creating "a radical—and nonviolent—caucus which would try to work in and through the Socialist Party," but by 1945 he had started to sketch organizational precepts incompatible with a traditional leftist party. Dellinger resigned from the FOR in April 1944, because, he told Cantine, "it is pretty well solidified as a little religious cult of the privileged classes—with no prospect of meeting the needs of workers, farmers, artists, revolutionaries, and returning soldiers."[78] Dellinger saw the need for pacifism to be reestablished on a more radical basis. "Personally," he explained, "I believe that if there is to develop a new movement which is to be historically relevant it must be unequivocally nonviolent. Of course the nonviolence that we know today is a bourgeois phenomenon with a terminology and attitude that are unsatisfactory. But just as Marxian socialism developed into a fairly hard-headed practical movement out of its early utopianism, so I think pacifism can outgrow its origins and early manifestations."[79] Though he clearly drew on both, these comments echo the emphases of De Ligt more than Gandhi.

Dellinger's letters to Cantine demonstrate that by the mid-1940s, anarchism played a formative role in his thinking, and that Dellinger saw the anarchist Cantine as a potential collaborator in the political work he planned to do upon release. "Naturally I have read quite a lot of Marx, Engels, Lenin, Kropotkin, de Ligt, and Trotsky," Dellinger explained in one letter, but he asked Cantine to suggest other relevant political theory for him to delve into.[80] The experienced organizer was not seeking a unilateral form of mentorship from the editor, however. In February 1945, Dellinger challenged what he perceived to be overcorrections in Cantine's analysis, suggesting there were alternatives to completely abandoning political organizations and campaigns:

> I think that some kind of communal associations—from each . . . ability, to each . . . needs [sic]; and, so far as possible with a non-monetary scale of values—is a great help toward avoiding the pit-falls of intellectualism and professional radicalism without being exhausted by "the life of a worker." . . . I think a revolutionary organization should operate somewhat similarly. Its full-time workers should be men who have left their other work for 6 months, a year, or so, and will return to it again. I think this would increase the value of this work as well as avoiding some of the problems of a centralized "leadership" that tends to become sterile, self-perpetuating and conservative. . . . Not only would their [leaders'] effectiveness be increased, but others would be developed who are now kept undeveloped or are alienated.[81]

Dellinger hoped that communal life could be balanced with confrontational organizing campaigns—indeed, that the two practices might support and amplify the impact of each other. The concepts that Dellinger was developing not only meshed with the outlook of the younger generation of anarchists but also suggested organizational principles that later became important to sectors of the civil rights movement, especially the Student Nonviolent Coordinating Committee, as we will see in chapter 7.

Dellinger was emboldened and inspired by the experience of resisting conscription and of combating segregation in prison; he hoped to broaden the struggle, in collaboration with other COs and allies, outside the prison's walls. During his last days of incarceration, Dellinger wrote Cantine that he was eager to meet in person so that they might discuss in more detail "the kind of left-wing libertarian socialist movement in which we are both interested." As his biographer, Andrew Hunt, asserts, "Once a Christian socialist, Dellinger had evolved into a secular anarchist in Lewisburg."[82] Released in April 1945, Dellinger drew on the network of anarchists, writers, and pacifists that had developed during the war, in order to get his life together.[83] The poet Kenneth Patchen and his wife, Miriam, arranged for David and his wife, Elizabeth, to share a property with them in Mount Pleasant, New York, near Woodstock. Dellinger recalled, "On the first or second weekend, Betty and I walked about ten miles to visit Holley Cantine, an anarchist who, doing his own printing, published a small magazine that I liked, *Retort*. It was in *Retort* that I had first read one of Kenneth Patchen's poems, after my first release from prison and just before he showed up at a meeting at which Paul Goodman and I were speaking."[84] Cantine informed Dellinger that James Cooney, former publisher of *The Phoenix,* a pacifist and avant-garde literary journal, had a printing press for sale and helped arrange for him to purchase it.

With the press in hand, Dellinger and his CO comrades Bill Kuenning, Ralph DiGia, and Roy Kepler produced the first issue of a new militant pacifist journal, *Direct Action*. It featured an essay, "What to Do Now," by anarchist poet Robert Duncan and a forum on postwar unemployment with comments from George Houser. The journal's most powerful article, however, was "Declaration of War," penned by Dellinger in the aftermath of the atomic bombing of Japan. It is worth quoting at length:

> The "way of life" that destroyed Hiroshima and Nagasaki . . . is international and dominates every nation of the world. . . . With this "way of life" ("death" would be more appropriate) there can be no truce nor quarter. . . .

> The fight against military conscription cannot be separated from the fight against the economic conscription involved in private ownership of the country's factories, railroads, and natural resources. . . . *The enemy is every institution which denies full social and economic equality to anyone. The enemy is personal indifference to the consequences of acts performed by the institutions of which we are a part.* . . .

> *The war for total brotherhood must be a nonviolent war carried on by methods worthy of the ideas we seek to serve. . . .* There must be strikes, sabotage and seizure of public property now being held by private owners. There must be civil disobedience of laws which are contrary to human welfare. But there must be also an uncompromising practice of treating everyone, including the worst of our opponents, with all the respect and decency that he merits as a fellow human being. . . . Every act we perform today must reflect the kind of human relationships we are fighting to establish tomorrow.[85]

Dellinger's essay sought to infuse radical pacifism with an anarchist sensibility at the same time that it called upon anarchists to adopt pacifist principles. By describing capitalist property relations as a form of economic "conscription," Dellinger pushed pacifists to incorporate class struggle into their politics and to view the state and the economy as a coercive complex, like classical anarchists had. He also blurred the lines between traditional anarchist and syndicalist forms of direct action, which held little regard for elite property and life, and Gandhian nonviolent direct action, by encouraging "sabotage" while insisting that opponents be treated with respect.[86] Yet Dellinger also endorsed ideas developed by Gandhi, De Ligt, and others that called for significant shifts in anarchist praxis. Like De Ligt, Dellinger indicted the entire Western "way of life" in perpetuating organized violence and inequality; in doing so, he implied that radicals must struggle to alter accepted values and forms of everyday life that allow suffering to continue. This suggests that people in a variety of social positions, not just the "elite," have some degree of responsibility for perpetuating injustice. By defining the enemy as *all* institutions that deny "full social and economic equality" to any person, he broadened the parameters of anarchist critique beyond the church, state, and capital (while shifting attention back to the principle of *equality* rather than *freedom*). Taken together, Dellinger's insistence that means must align with desired ends, and his call to refuse complicity with the actions of bureaucratic institutions, laid the moral foundations for the focus on alternative lifestyles and prefigurative action that became central to postwar U.S. anarchism. Finally, the "Declaration," began to carve out a new avenue of antistate criticism.

For Dellinger, the atomic bomb made clearer than ever the need for political power to be "decentralized" away from the modern nation-state. The bombing led to similar conclusions by other World War II resisters whose interest in anarchism had been piqued in the preceding years. In the August 1945 issue of *politics,* Dwight MacDonald argued that the federal government's willingness to use atomic weapons meant, simply: "We must 'get' the modern national state, before it 'gets' us."[87] In 1946, Lewis Hill, a West Coast CO, asserted, "The modern state is the first enemy."[88] The San Francisco–based anarchist poet Kenneth Rexroth pithily remarked, "The bomb is the state—transubstantiate."[89]

Postwar antistatism shared ground with the traditional anarchist critique of sovereign power but shifted its focus in significant ways. While nineteenth-century anarchists opposed states for their hand in the exploitation of the working class, many postwar anarchists argued that nation-states threatened the immediate annihilation of humanity, as a whole, through their production and use of nuclear weapons. The creation of a technology as complicated and destructive as the atomic bomb required a level of financial commitment and a scale of organizational apparatus that could be mobilized only by a massive, centralized nation-state. This analysis contributed to an expanding vision of who would benefit from the anarchist reconstruction of society, and who might be compelled to participate in anarchist activism, broadening the movement's potential base from "workers" to "humanity." Moreover, by arguing that state power threatened life in general, anarchism was articulated in moral terms. Accordingly, campaigns against nuclear weapons (and later against nuclear energy production) became central to anarchist organizing in the United States and parts of Europe from the 1950s to the 1980s.[90]

Direct Action also contained a "Call to a Conference" to consider how to collectively act upon the principles expressed in the "Declaration of War." The editors and a handful of collaborators, including Roy Finch and Lewis Hill, mailed copies of this call to hundreds of former COs just as they were exiting prison and CPS camps, deciding what steps to take next in life. Approximately one hundred attended the conference, held in Chicago in February 1946.[91] Although neither the original call nor the conference resolutions contained the word *anarchist,* anarchist concerns, ideas, and practices were central to the proceedings. One participant, David Platt, wrote to the conveners, "I believe an anarchist and syndicalist direction is the very thing we should aim at, and I hope that an alignment along this line will come out of the conference." George Houser, on the other hand, expressed concern that the group "has narrowed itself to an infinitesimal group of persons who have anarcho-syndicalist tendencies on the one hand and a belief in nonviolence on the other." Others correspondents remained close to the Socialist Party and wrote to defend the use of electoral and legislative strategies on certain matters.[92]

After four days of debate, the conferees launched a new organization, the Committee for Nonviolent Revolution (CNVR). The committee subsumed differences between nominal "anarchists" and "socialists" under the mantle of an emerging politics of revolutionary nonviolence. Participants adopted a resolution calling for "decentralized democratic socialism." This entailed worker self-management and a rejection of Soviet-style nationalization of industry; equalization of income and guaranteed access to food, health care, and other basic goods; and a reorganization of government authority to vest greater power in the hands of ordinary people and to make decisions closer to home.[93] The CNVR, then, did not call for the complete abolition of the state and of laws, as anarchists did, but promoted a decentralization of power and a deepening of democracy.

The CNVR also articulated a specific vision of nonviolence. While individual objection to war was important, the group emphasized the need for a "coordinated resistance program." But war was only the tip of the iceberg. The group argued that "the present economic and social system are inherently violent in so far as they deny people access to the means of production and to the necessities of life, except under conditions imposed by private owners and other external authorities." In fact, they argued that the social order as a whole was "founded on might or the threat of it." Then, reversing the equation, the group asserted, "Violence is ultimately dictatorial. Nonviolent power is ultimately democratic."[94] This conceptual linkage (or conflation) prompted members of the CNVR to pursue new, egalitarian models of organization.

Time did not permit the group to plan structure or set priorities in a detailed way. However, they agreed to form local groups with a national "coordinator" that would help groups "exchange information and plans" without having the power to set policy. While this structure looked back to those of the nineteenth-century international anarchist organizations, other aspects of the CNVR program anticipated central concerns of contemporary anarchism. "The revolutionary program must involve continual agitation to attempt to promote the revolutionary situation," wrote the CNVR. "It also involves beginning to form immediately demonstrations of alternatives to the present system. The growth of these alternatives will hasten the collapse of existing institutions and point the way out." Members were perhaps most eager to experiment with intentional communities, but they also saw co-ops as important counterinstitutions. Finally, the group adopted the Gandhian attitude that change was an inward- as well as an outward-directed process.

"We must work on ourselves at the same time as we work for the revolution," they explained.[95] Whereas CNVR members sought to eliminate their own "vindictiveness," late-twentieth-century anarchists would seek to check "internalized" habits of sexism, racism, and homophobia.

Dellinger and other CNVR members expected that large sectors of U.S. citizens would share their revulsion to the bombing of Hiroshima and hoped they could channel such sentiments into a powerful social movement. Accordingly, they jumped into the fray on a number of issues. They picketed the newly formed United Nations, calling it a "3-Nation circus" meant to divert people from challenging the real sources of international conflict. The New York City chapter mailed postcards to supporters encouraging them to join a picket organized by CORE (now known as the *Congress* of Racial Equality) to "stop jimcrow [*sic*] at the Palisades Amusement Park swimming pool"—an action that succeeded in desegregating the pool.[96] The Philadelphia branch of CNVR reported to the national coordinator that sixteen people attended its monthly meeting in May 1946. After evaluating their recent demonstration for the release of still-incarcerated COs, they turned to theoretical study. "The principle discussion of the evening was on the article 'The Root Is Man' in the April issue of Politics magazine," recorded chapter secretary Kenneth Ives. "Parallels between Dwight MacDonald's present position and that of the Anarchists such as Kropotkin were noted."[97]

In August 1947, CNVR members convened for a conference at the Catholic Worker farm in the Hudson River town of Newburgh, New York. The next issue of the *Catholic Worker* newspaper noted points of unity, as well as differences, in the ideas espoused by CNVR, anarchists, and the Catholic Worker organization itself:

> Both The Catholic Worker and the Committee for Nonviolent Revolution have a great distrust for the State. Most States in history have been founded on violence, and continue to operate by violence. And while we of the C.W. would not go the length of complete anarchism . . . there is an obligation to go pretty far along the anarchist road. . . . We are also at one with the committee in regarding the capitalist system as inherently evil.[98]

Meanwhile, CNVR members made good on their dream of establishing an intentional community of radical pacifists that might get a jump on reinventing the American way of life. Together with three other former COs and their families, the Dellingers purchased a twenty-acre farm in northwestern New Jersey, built additional houses, and named it the Glen Gardner World

Citizens Community. At Glen Gardner, Dellinger and former CPS rebel Igal Roodenko established Libertarian Press: A Worker's Cooperative. They printed leaflets, periodicals, and books for movement organizations, as well as enough commercial contracts to provide a steady, if modest, income for their families and the community as a whole.[99] One priority was a four-page monthly newsletter, *Alternative,* that replaced *Direct Action.* The publication's masthead explained it was published by an "association of libertarian individuals" that included Ralph DiGia and Roy Finch, in addition to Dellinger and Roodenko.[100]

NEW TACTICS, STRATEGIES, AND ORGANIZATIONS

David Thoreau Wieck was released from prison in May 1946 and quickly gravitated back to the Why? Group. There he met and began a romance with Diva Agostinelli that would endure for the rest of their lives. In 1947 the Why? Group decided to change the publication's name to *Resistance,* indicating the greater clarity they now felt about the social order and how to respond. The group's name changed accordingly. Brimming with postprison energy, Wieck took on increasing responsibility for producing the periodical. He expanded the size and page count, drawing on new printing technology to add photographs and original artwork. Beginning with the first issue, *Resistance* devoted considerable space to chronicling and promoting the activities of radical pacifists, especially their expanding efforts to subvert Jim Crow segregation. The group also handed printing responsibilities over to Dellinger and Roodenko at the Libertarian Press. Over the next few years, the Libertarian Press would also issue Naeve's prison memoirs, *A Field of Broken Stones,* as well as a novel by Paul Goodman and Ammon Hennacy's autobiography. The Resistance Group continued to hold weekly political discussions in the Solidaridad Internacional Antifascista Hall and to collaborate with New York–area radical pacifists, even as founding members Audrey Goodfriend and David Koven relocated to San Francisco, joining that city's literary anarchist pacifist milieu, as we will see in the next chapter.

The beginning of 1947 was a busy and exciting time for the nonviolent revolutionaries grouped around the CNVR, WRL, FOR, and CORE. On February 12, Dellinger, Muste, MacDonald, and Rustin led a ceremonial draft-card burning—the first of its kind—in New York. Sixty-three men, including David Wieck, participated locally, while approximately four hundred young men living elsewhere returned cards to draft boards as part of the demonstration. Two months later, members of the nonviolent revolutionary community embarked on the Journey of Reconciliation, an interstate direct-action campaign that served as the model for the 1961 Freedom Rides. As coordinators of CORE, Rustin and Houser constructed a plan to test enforcement of a 1946 Supreme Court ruling prohibiting segregation on buses and trains that crossed state lines. They gathered a planning committee that included the anarchist pacifist Bill Sutherland as well as the dynamic NAACP organizer Ella Baker. When the Journey commenced in April 1947, with pairs of white and black men riding at the front and the back of buses, Jim Peck and Igal Roodenko were on board. Journey members were arrested on six separate occasions, and Peck was beaten by taxi drivers in Chapel Hill, North Carolina. Despite the attack, Peck became a CORE stalwart, serving as editor of its newsletter, *The CORElator,* for years. Rustin and Roodenko, meanwhile, were sentenced to work on a chain gang.[101]

The same year, CNVR members ran for seats on the WRL's executive committee as a means of pushing its nearly ten thousand members in a more radical direction. At the time, the executive committee was composed largely of liberals who wanted to focus on antiwar education and counseling poten-tial draft resisters. Members of the CNVR recognized that gaining access to the WRL's membership lists, newsletter, and funds would prove crucial to helping them promote their more expansive vision of Gandhian resistance to the culture of violence and inequality. Voting as a bloc, they elected Dave Dellinger, Roy Finch, Igal Roodenko, Dwight MacDonald, George Houser, and Jim Peck to the committee.[102] Of the six, only Dwight MacDonald had not served a term as a war resister. Dellinger, Finch, Roodenko, and MacDonald were, at the time, avowed anarchists, and Houser and Peck were personally and politically close to the anarchists.[103] David Wieck also became active in the WRL at that time.[104]

In the three years after they began trickling out of penitentiaries and CPS camps, the radical pacifists initiated or rejuvenated publications, established supportive intentional communities, pioneered new tactics, and launched one radical organization and commandeered another, all with the intent of facilitating far-reaching cultural and economic shifts in the postwar world. Shifts did take place in these years, but not in the directions radical pacifists desired. America's position of dominance with respect to other national economies at the war's conclusion enabled the rapid growth of consumer spending power. By the millions, Americans chose to establish new types of communities, but these were overwhelmingly commuter suburbs, soon to be notorious for their race and class segregation and isolating tendencies, rather than the simple-living communes promoted by the pacifists.[105] Politically, 1947 marked the beginning of the Cold War, with president Harry Truman supplying U.S. aid to contain Soviet influence abroad and initiating loyalty reviews of federal employees. In October of that year, the House Un-American Activities Committee began its investigation into communist influence in Hollywood that would result in a notorious industry blacklist.[106] In this atmosphere, CNVR leaflets and demonstrations—creative as they were—gained little traction among the broader population.

In April 1948, radical pacifists regrouped in Chicago to create a new institutional vehicle better keyed to national sentiment. The meeting of nearly three hundred radical pacifists established Peacemakers, a new organization that included CNVR members such as Dellinger, Rustin, and Houser, and which attracted additional pacifists, including Muste, MacDonald, Juanita and Wally Nelson, and Marion and Ernest Bromley. Peacemakers did not explicitly bill itself as a successor to the CNVR, but the latter group faded away as members shifted their attention to new projects and campaigns.

Although it toned down its rhetoric, Peacemakers continued to advocate broad social transformation and to tout the strategic value of direct action campaigns paired with the establishment of exemplary intentional communities.[107] Anarchists held less sway, and Peacemakers placed greater emphasis on spirituality than had CNVR—the organization's name, for instance, was drawn from the Beatitudes of Jesus's Sermon on the Mount. Nevertheless, the formation, which was active into the 1960s, is significant to the development of contemporary U.S. anarchism. Peacemakers continued the search for organizational forms distinct from those of mass political parties and liberal membership organizations. It had no staff or office, and participants were encouraged to join the movement as "cells"—what would later be called local "affinity groups"—rather than as individuals. Cells initiated their own political projects and coordinated with others through a newsletter and a yearly meeting. Peacemaker projects ranged from picketing segregationist restaurants and establishing interracial living situations to encouraging tax resistance during wartime. The group also adopted the practice of making decisions by consensus rather than by majoritarian voting. Consensus decision-making had been developed by the Quaker church and adopted in the early 1940s by intentional communities and a number of liberal organizations. However, Peacemakers appears to be the first radical political organiza-

PROTEST THE DRAFT

A Public Rally Against Conscription

Program

Chairman, Roy C. Kepler

THE FAILURE OF OBEDIENCE ....Newton Garver

MAN CHALLENGES THE STATE ....David Wieck

WAR WITHOUT VIOLENCE ....Bayard Rustin

Songs by Bayard Rustin, Bill Sutherland,
anb Harkie McCallum

CAN PRISON STOP US? ....David Dellinger

WHAT CAN NON-DRAFTEES DO? ....Audrey Goodfriend

WHY I WILL REFUSE TO REGISTER ....Robert Bone

Open Discussion

LABOR TEMPLE

242 East 14th Street
(Near Second Avenue)

Sunday, August 29 at 8 P. M.

Admission Free

Sponsored By:

Resistance Group, Box 208, Cooper Station, New York 3
Peacemakers, 2013 Fifth Avenue, New York 25
Committee for Non-Violent Revolution, Box 827, Church St. Station, New York 8

LIBERTARIAN PRINT SHOP, A WORKERS' CO-OPERATIVE, NEWARK, N. J.

Leaflet for an antidraft rally organized by anarchists and radical pacifists, New York City, 1948.
Courtesy of the David Thoreau Wieck Papers, Swarthmore College Peace Collection.

tion, and the first with anarchist members, to embrace consensus as an organizational tool. In sum, the group functioned as a decentralized pacifist cadre organization, a banner under which deeply committed individuals could dedicate themselves to peacemaking as a whole way of life—even in a period when mass social movements were nowhere to be seen.

This ethos—and this sense of isolation—united radical pacifists, antiracist organizers, and anarchists as the decade wound to a close. Such interconnections are clearly displayed in a leaflet announcing a "public rally against conscription" issued in 1948. Chaired by *Direct Action* editor Roy Kepler, the program included speeches by David Wieck and Audrey Goodfriend of *Resistance,* as well as by David Dellinger and Bayard Rustin. Bill Sutherland provided entertainment alongside Rustin. The event was cosponsored by *Resistance,* the recently organized Peacemakers, and the soon to be defunct Committee for Nonviolent Revolution. Dellinger and Roodenko's Libertarian Press, unsurprisingly, printed the leaflet.[108]

Less obvious in this leaflet, although no less significant, were the bonds forged between radical pacifists, anarchists, and avant-garde artists during the same years. Centered in the San Francisco Bay Area, but maintaining outposts in Greenwich Village and elsewhere, a collection of anarchist poets, playwrights, and painters embraced pacifism and rejected central tenets of midcentury American culture alongside, and in conversation with, the circles surveyed in this chapter. They injected serious considerations of sexuality, ecology, and the transformative potential of art into these conversations, leaving a distinct imprint on U.S. anarchism as they did so. We must carefully consider the contributions of these midcentury literary anarchists, then, before we can accurately assess how significantly anarchism evolved during the supposedly "dead" period of the 1940s and 1950s.

SIX

Anarchism and the
Avant-Garde, 1942–1956

During the Second World War, and throughout the 1940s, anarchists crafted alliances not only with radical pacifists but also with avant-garde cultural workers. Anarchist, pacifist, and personalist ideas deeply informed the creative output of poets, playwrights, and novelists living in New York and California. Though marginal at the time, many participants in these networks—including Kenneth Rexroth, Gary Snyder, and Jackson Mac Low—have since been widely recognized for their contributions to twentieth-century American literature.

The literary anarchists of the 1940s drew ideas and inspiration from a variety of disciplines, religious practices, and world literatures. Their deep interest in sexuality, psychology, and the natural environment injected new themes and theoretical resources into anarchist discourse that have had an enduring impact. This small group found fault with the emerging postwar culture of abundance, particularly its mass scale, its stultifying moral conventions, its technological rationality, and its remove from the natural world. Largely abandoning the tactics of pressure politics, radicals of this generation sought to alter social relations through their own practices of cultural creation. There was a twofold quality to this activity. Anarchists produced critical and searching cultural works—especially poems, plays, and paintings—while establishing new ways of living in communities of like-minded people, which they hoped would inspire imitation.

The immediate results were disheartening for those anticipating a quick revival of mass dissent. However, the new themes and the basic contours of cultural resistance carved out in these years have had an enormous impact on the priorities, the practices, and the demographic base of anarchism—and radical politics more generally—ever since. Literary anarchists of the 1940s self-consciously reestablished the bohemian anarchist tradition, which had flourished in belle epoque Europe and Progressive Era America but had lain dormant during the interwar years. This bohemian anarchism expanded in significance through a series of transmissions and amplifications that took place over the second half of the twentieth century. This process began in the early 1950s, when anarchists and their radical pacifist allies established bookstores, performance spaces, and other venues that, taken together, provided a vital institutional seedbed for the writers dubbed the Beat Generation. In the mid-1960s, Beat-inspired radicals would recover anarchist source traditions and use them to craft a mass counterculture, bestowing on contemporary anarchism its marked subcultural character.

WARTIME CONNECTIONS

As we saw in chapter 5, the Second World War prompted a generation of young anarchists to ally with radical pacifists and explore new currents of social theory in the pages of the journals *politics, Why?/Resistance,* and *Retort.* At the same time, anarchists began to express greater interest in literature as a source of insight and as a vehicle for promoting their values. From the outset, Holley Cantine aimed for *Retort* to provide an outlet for new literary energies as well as political ones. Throughout the 1940s, the hand-printed journal served as an important early-career venue for a variety of now canonical figures, including Norman Mailer, Saul Bellow, and e.e. cummings. Significantly, the journal's first issue featured a poem by Kenneth Rexroth, a rising star of the West Coast literary scene. Rexroth's contribution eulogized the recently deceased Emma Goldman and the antimilitarist stand she took during the previous World War.[1]

Born in 1905, Rexroth received only five years of formal schooling but educated himself about art and politics at Chicago's Bughouse Square and Dil Pickle Club, where his "favorite people were the anarchist and former IWW freelance soapboxers."[2] A fierce autodidact, Rexroth imbibed the writings of nineteenth-century anarchists alongside literature, philosophy, and religious thought published in a half dozen languages. In the 1930s he joined the Community Party–affiliated John Reed Clubs while penning guidebooks for the Works Progress Administration, but he denounced the clubs' Stalinism and artistic ineptitude by the time the United States entered the war. By 1940, he had published an award-winning book of poetry, ripe with anarchist themes and references, and become one of the most respected literary talents on the West Coast.[3]

Rexroth expressed considerable affinity with the political vision Cantine was carving out in his essays and editorial decisions. "From the looks of Retort #3," he wrote, "you are out for another synthesis, Kropotkin, Rosa [Luxemburg], Geo[rge] Fox—which is pretty much my point of view too."[4] The poet ordered copies of *Retort, Why?* and *politics* in bulk to distribute in the Bay Area. It may have been Rexroth who connected Cantine with David Dellinger. After receiving the first issue of *Retort,* he suggested Cantine "try getting something out of the CO camps, thru Dorothy Day, the FOR . . . and similar sources."[5]

Rexroth had himself reached out to William Everson, a younger poet who had organized a fine arts program at the Civilian Public Service (CPS) camp at Waldport, Oregon. Everson ran the Untide Press, which issued hand-printed poetry books, including a collection by the anarchist pacifist Kenneth Patchen. Everson also contributed to a literary journal, *The Illiterati,* edited by fellow COs.[6] He had convinced the pacifist Church of the Brethren, which administered the camp at Waldport, to sponsor such projects, arguing, "These are the years of destruction. We offer against them the creative act. . . . It is because of the inherent sympathy between the purposes of pacifism and the purposes of art that a pacifist artistic movement seems capable of wide influence." Everson held up the work of a new generation of British poets as a model: "They are not writing pacifist propaganda, but the ideology of pacifism, its conception of human nature, its values and attitudes which are being drawn upon and exhibited in their work."[7] This desire to create an engaged but nondidactic mode of expression took root outside the CPS camp as well.

Rexroth wrote encouraging letters and invited Everson and other West Coast COs to visit him in San Francisco during the weeklong furloughs they were afforded. The line between pacifist and anarchist ideas soon blurred in Waldport publications. The cover of the journal's fourth issue, for example, read, "The Illiterati Proposes: Creation, Experiment and Revolution to Build a Warless, Free Society." It contained a poem from the British anarchist Alex Comfort and an essay by the anarchist novelist Henry Miller. As the war dragged on, a loose literary milieu of visiting COs and younger men began to congeal around Rexroth in San Francisco.

Some of the young poets from this group helped cement ties with anarchists on the other side of the country. Philip Lamantia, born into a family of Sicilian immigrants in 1927, discovered the Surrealist movement while in high school. As inheritors of the European avant-garde tradition, Surrealists associated with the communist and Trotskyist movements during the 1930s. However, André Breton, one of the movement's founding theorists, later argued that the Surrealist vision was most compatible with anarchism.[8] In 1943, the art journal *View* published poems Lamantia had penned at the age of fifteen. Breton, sitting out the war in New York alongside other Surrealists, struck up a correspondence with the young talent and printed three additional poems in his own journal, *VVV*. In 1944, Lamantia traveled east and met with his idols but was disappointed to find the community of émigré intellectuals dissipating as the war drew to a close. However, Lamantia socialized with the editors of *Why?* and *Retort* before returning to San Francisco in 1945.[9]

The poet Robert Duncan followed a similar trajectory. Duncan joined a circle of literary radicals while attending the University of California at Berkeley, but left school to follow his male lover to the East Coast in 1939. Though the relationship did not survive, Duncan solidified his appreciation of anarchist politics while meeting the Surrealist exiles and sharing a New York City apartment with Jeff Rall, son of a Wobbly, who maintained a personal "library of anarchist literature."[10] Duncan also lived, for a time, in Woodstock with James and Blanche Cooney, editors of the literary journal *The Phoenix*. The Cooneys published some of Duncan's poetry and introduced him to other contributors, including Henry Miller and Anaïs Nin. Duncan visited Holley Cantine in nearby Bearsville and later contributed to *Retort*.[11]

It was a tight-knit community of writers and radicals that welcomed Robert Duncan to New York. According to Robert Bertholf, "Duncan met Jackson Mac Low at an anarchist meeting, September 1943, and that meeting began a political association between the two poets that lasted for many years."[12] The meeting was organized by the Why? Group, of which Mac Low was a member. Duncan attended regularly and "surprised his radical associates by taking them to the Gandhi ashram in Harlem"—the organization frequented by David Dellinger, George Houser, and James Farmer—"which he had discovered earlier."[13] During the same period, Mac Low and the writer William Humphrey sought out the editor of *Retort* on a trip up the Hudson River. After their visit, Cantine's partner of nine years, Dorothy Paul, left him to marry Humphrey.[14] Owing to serendipity or insularity, however, Cantine met and fell in love with another woman, Dachine Rainer, during a visit to New York in which he taught printing techniques to members of the Why? Group. After the war, Cantine arranged for James Cooney to sell his printing press to David Dellinger, who used it to issue the journal *Direct Action.*

At the time she met Cantine, Dachine Rainer was working as an editorial assistant for Dwight MacDonald's *politics.* Robert Duncan also established connections with MacDonald. After exchanging a series of letters, MacDonald published the young poet's essay "The Homosexual in Society." The article was especially bold because Duncan not only outed himself in a period during which homosexuality was punishable by imprisonment but also sharply criticized the gay community in the process. Duncan experienced the "camp" style of gay New Yorkers as "loaded with contempt for the human." He found it frustrating that gays and lesbians had not yet linked their struggles for dignity with the broader struggle for human freedom and equality. Finding himself dually alienated, Duncan called for grounding gay politics in broader anarchist-personalist efforts.[15] After publishing "The Homosexual in Society," however, he found his literary aspirations blocked, and he returned to California at the end of 1945.

East Coast anarchists became more enmeshed in literary circles as the war ended. In 1946 Rainer and Cantine published *Prison Etiquette,* a collection of essays and illustrations about incarceration penned by recently released draft resisters.[16] Rainer asked W. H. Auden to bless the collection with an introduction, but he passed the task off to his friend, the openly gay British novelist Christopher Isherwood.[17] Around the time the journal *Why?* was renamed *Resistance,* in 1947, Paul Goodman began work on a series of novels, and Jackson Mac Low deepened his interest in experimental poetry. The composer John Cage began to identify as an anarchist after living and working among the small community of radical artists linked to the Why?/Resistance Group.[18] Yet, as diligent as New York artists were during this period, they could not match the creative energy emanating from the San Francisco Bay Area.

THE LIBERTARIAN CIRCLE

Back in San Francisco, Duncan and Lamantia attended boisterous dinner parties organized by Rexroth and impressed him with tales of the Why? Group meetings they had experienced while in New York. The trio decided to launch a similar, informal anarchist group of their own. In 1946 Rexroth informed Rainer and Cantine, "We seem to have got together a very healthy little 'Circle.' The first English speaking one since [Alexander] Berkman was out here." The Libertarian Circle, as it was called, held discussions on the top floor of a house in the Fillmore District owned by a branch of the old Jewish Workmen's Circle. Meetings sometimes drew fifty or more participants, including William Everson and other veterans of the CPS camps, such as Adrian Wilson and George Reeves, who settled in San Francisco after being released from service.[19]

During early meetings, the Libertarian Circle studied the anarchist tradition extensively. Each week a presenter spoke about a historical event or theme before opening the floor to discussion. Topics included the Kronstadt rebellion, "Andalusian Agricultural Communes," "communalist groups in the United States," and figures such as Kropotkin, Goldman, and Voltairine de Cleyre. "Our objective," Rexroth recalled, "was to refound the radical movement after its destruction by the Bolsheviks and to rethink all the basic principles . . . [, as well as] to subject to searching criticism all the ideologists from Marx to Malatesta."[20] This required placing the "classics" in conversation with new ideas.

"Our bunch," Rexroth wrote Rainer in 1946, "are not precisely up the same anarchistic alley—it's a trifle orgiastic and apocalyptic out here. In theory of course, no impurities. But lots of [Wilhelm] Reich and [D. H.] Lawrence and not so much of that fine rational air of Condorcet or whoever it is you read."[21] This was a bit presumptuous, as the editors of *Retort* were also champions of literary modernism, and Diva Agostinelli of the Why? Group remembered that the first time she met Paul Goodman he was on the floor demonstrating a "Reichian orgasm."[22] Rexroth's comments do, however, place a time stamp on a historically significant departure in U.S. anarchism: a moment when a new generation of anarchists began to draw on an array of intellectual traditions previously marginal to anarchist theory, to subject society to new lines of criticism, and to place much greater emphasis on cultural strategies of change. Rexroth's own interests and writings highlight many of these shifts.

Rexroth interpreted the defeat of the Spanish anarchists and the carnage of World War II as signs of "collapsing cultural values," and he insisted on linking these catastrophes to daily life in modern America. In his 1944 book *The Phoenix and the Tortoise,* the poet derided a process of history whose "goal is the achievement / Of the completely atomic / Individual and the pure / Commodity relationship."[23] Rexroth spoke often about "the Social

Lie"—the idea that behavioral norms and an accumulation-obsessed economy served the best interests of everyone, not just the elite. Because people were increasingly alienated from themselves in industrial society, he thought, they were losing their ability to connect with and care for others. The deployment of atomic bombs only confirmed Rexroth's intuition that Western culture's devotion to technical rationalism was profoundly dangerous to human bodies and souls. If people were to find their way back to one another, he believed, they needed to develop a critical consciousness and to restore a proper balance between the logical, the sensuous, and the intuitive aspects of life.[24]

Members of the Libertarian Circle viewed themselves as progeny of a tradition of twentieth-century literature that saw its apotheosis in the figures of D. H. Lawrence and Henry Miller. Both authors critiqued dehumanizing aspects of modernity and wrote sexually explicit novels that broached subjects such as homosexuality and incest, leading to obscenity trials and legal suppression of their work. Miller had been a devotee of Emma Goldman in pre–World War I New York.[25] After more than a decade abroad, he settled near Big Sur, California, in 1944, denouncing modern America as "an air-conditioned nightmare" in a book by the same name the following year.[26] In a 1947 essay, Rexroth celebrated Lawrence's attack on the taboos and sexual guilt instilled by Christian morality, "the insane dynamic which has driven [man] across the earth to burn and slaughter, loot and rape."[27] Lawrence's literary fusillade against sexual repression was neatly complemented by the work of the Austrian psychoanalyst Wilhelm Reich.

Beginning in the 1920s, Reich synthesized Freudian psychoanalysis with Marxist theory, arguing that "neurotic" behaviors were actually responses to economic exploitation, sexual repression, and other aspects of the social order.[28] Reich's consideration of authority aligned with classical anarchist thought while drawing generative new linkages. His book *The Sexual Revolution* argued that the male-dominated nuclear family was central to the reproduction of capitalist states, and vice versa. Reich pointed to ways in which governments and churches of all sorts promoted monogamous heterosexual marriage in a manner verging on compulsion, punished homosexuality, and suppressed adolescent sexuality through public schools and other channels. In *The Mass Psychology of Fascism,* he argued that working people had acceded to Stalinism and Nazism because they had first been acclimated to authoritarian order when their sexual impulses were suppressed by their parents.[29] Taken together, Reich, Miller, and Lawrence taught that violating

sexual norms not only was fun but also might potentially generate antiauthoritarian ripple effects. They did not, however, carefully attend to the ways
in which conservative sexual politics burdened and endangered women in
distinct and more intensive ways than men. Therefore, the sexual revolution
inherited by 1940s anarchists was not directly feminist.

The literary anarchists explored religious mysticism at the same time they
came to emphasize sex, rejecting the idea that the practices were contradictory. Rexroth introduced the group to the Jewish mystic Martin Buber, who,
in his 1923 book *I and Thou,* suggested that God (or meaning in life) was
present when people established direct, mutual, and noninstrumental relationships with one another.[30] A relative latecomer to the San Francisco circle,
Gary Snyder, translated literature from Chinese and Japanese and promoted
Zen Buddhist meditation among his friends. Snyder saw the Buddhist perspective as commensurate with the anarchist belief in mutual aid and the
possibility of social harmony. Another prominent booster, Alan Watts, promoted Zen as an alternative, potentially reparative worldview among the
literary pacifists aghast at their country's nuclear bombing of Japan. Religious
scholar James Brown has argued, "Those poets who adopted Zen did so in
large part because the critique of Western culture it offered confirmed their
antiauthoritarianism and provided an alternative to what they saw as the
deadening effects of rationalism on the human spirit, evident in postwar U.S.
culture's technocracy and alienation."[31] Though few embraced the trappings
of institutional religion, the exploration of heterodox spiritual traditions
helped San Francisco's pacifists and poets refocus the anarchist critique of
capitalist society on the challenges of achieving authenticity and personal
connection in daily life, rather than on direct material deprivation. This
would remain a central and consistent theme for anarchists living in high-
income industrial societies.

A final component of the emerging Bay Area sensibility, crucial for understanding the ways U.S. anarchism developed in later decades, was the
community's embrace of the natural environment. The contemplative and
naturalistic aspects of Buddhism and Asian poetry reinforced an appreciation
for the outdoors cultivated in many members of the Libertarian Circle by the
years they had worked in secluded CPS camps (and, earlier, in New Deal
conservation programs). The nearby Sierra Nevada, like Big Sur and other
wilderness areas, offered an accessible refuge from the booming industry and
highway construction then reshaping the country. Beginning with his first
book of poetry, Rexroth frequently contrasted the despair brought about by

political defeats (he directly invoked the suppression of the Kronstadt uprising and the defeat of the Spanish anarchists) with the sense of wonder, and the recognition of the unity of living things, inculcated by spending time in the woods. In one poem, Rexroth recalled mountain climbing with his wife, Marie, on the tenth anniversary of Sacco and Vanzetti's execution. Even while "crossing the brilliant mile-square meadow," he could not shake his memory of Vanzetti "in the sour prison light." The poet consoled himself, writing,

> Some day mountains will be named after you and Sacco.
> They will be here and your name with them,
> "When these days are but a dim remembering of the time
> When man was wolf to man."[32]

Rexroth credited the anarchist geographers Peter Kropotkin and Élisée Reclus for having instilled in him this propensity to distill moral principles from his studies of nature.[33]

Having grown up in the Pacific Northwest logging country, Gary Snyder directly challenged human despoliation of ecosystems. As Paul Messersmith-Glavin has noted, he sought "to express the importance of nature, beyond the concerns of humans, even adopting wild nature's standpoint, in his poetry."[34] In a series of poems crafted between 1952 and 1956, Snyder reflected, "San Francisco 2x4s / were the woods around Seattle / Someone killed and someone built, a house / a forest wrecked or raised / All America hung on a hook / & burned by men, in their own praise."[35] Although his parents had both been members of the IWW, Snyder saw their generation's acceptance of environmental destruction as a tragic flaw in their politics. "You bastards," he seethed in a later poem. "My fathers / and grandfathers, stiff-necked / punchers, miners, dirt farmers, railroad-men / killd off the cougar and grizzly."[36] Working men and women, from this perspective, could no longer automatically be assumed innocent and noble.

Rexroth, Snyder, and their comrades evoked California's natural beauty so frequently in their verse that critics later branded them the "Bear Shit on the Trail" school of poetry.[37] Their writings "in defense of the earth" (as Rexroth named a 1956 volume of poetry) also served as a direct inspiration for the ecological turn that U.S. anarchism took in the late 1960s. For that to be possible, however, San Francisco's literary anarchists had to find readers outside their own insular salons.

A series of new initiatives helped build the Bay Area's reputation as a literary hotbed in the late 1940s. Former Waldport COs established an avant-garde theater troupe, the Artist's Workshop. After a few months of historical and philosophical discussion, the Libertarian Circle began to host a biweekly Poetry Forum, where members presented their work for friendly criticism. Meanwhile, Robert Duncan initiated a poetry workshop on the campus of the University of California, and public readings at art galleries and cafés multiplied.

In the spring of 1947, the Libertarian Circle produced a literary magazine, *The Ark,* that featured poetry by established writers such as e.e. cummings and William Carlos Williams, as well as contributions from a panoply of younger anarchists: Duncan, Goodman, Lamantia, Rexroth, and Everson. Ammon Hennacy and George Woodcock, editor of the British anarchist journal *NOW,* contributed essays about their visions of anarchism. *The Ark*'s editorial statement announced its personalist credo in words that could have appeared as easily in the *Catholic Worker.* "In direct opposition to the debasement of human values made flauntingly evident by the war," the editors wrote, "there is rising among writers in America, as elsewhere, a social consciousness which recognizes the integrity of the personality as the most substantial and considerable of values."[38]

The East Coast and West Coast anarchist communities became further enmeshed when Audrey Goodfriend and David Koven of the Resistance Group traveled to San Francisco in the fall of 1946. Taken with the energy around the Libertarian Circle, Goodfriend and Koven decided to stay permanently and convinced Resistance Group mainstays Dan DeWeiss and Michael and Sally Grieg to join them. The five transplanted New Yorkers decided they "should start a co-operative community of some sort" so that they might "withdraw from the system."[39] They rented a large house together with an eye toward practicing the types of relationships they had long discussed.

There was much to enjoy about postwar San Francisco. In November 1946, Rexroth sent Dwight MacDonald an update: "Big party last week. Big party this week for Philip Lamantia's new book of poems. Big Parties all the time. The way to run a successful revolution is on alcohol."[40] Nor was alcohol the only organizing tool on hand. Former Waldport CO Adrian Wilson later characterized the editors of *The Ark* as "a group of literary anarchists and marijuana addicts" who did their composing in a "dank kitchen."[41]

This bacchanalian atmosphere suggests another departure from prewar anarchism. While consumption of alcohol was common in earlier periods, it had not been assigned a positive political value (even if half in jest), and illegal drugs were rarely used or discussed. Perhaps more significant than the use of intoxicants is the way in which readings, performances, and exclusive parties moved to the center of anarchist praxis. Picnics, balls, and performances had been a consistent feature of anarchist life up through the 1930s. Historically, however, they supplemented organizing drives, political rallies, and physical assaults on authority figures. In the 1940s Bay Area scene, participating in such revelatory events became the primary activity expected of an anarchist. Indeed, we might interpret this as the time and place where an anarchist "scene" emerged—exciting and socially rewarding to participants, but easily perceived as insular and exclusionary to those less connected.

In April 1947, the Libertarian Circle gained national notoriety when *Harper's Magazine* published an exposé of the "New Cult of Sex and Anarchy" that had blossomed on the streets of San Francisco and the beaches near Big Sur.[42] "Around [Rexroth], as around [Henry] Miller," wrote University of California professor Mildred Brady, "there collected a group of young intellectuals and writers who met weekly in self-education sessions, reading the journals of the English anarchists, studying the old-line anarchist philosophers like Kropotkin, and leavening the politics liberally with psychoanalytic interpretations from Reich."[43] Poetry readings, she emphasized, took pride of place in this new "bohemia": "Thirty or forty at a time can be found crowded together listening gravely to language patterns that are all but incomprehensible to the uninitiated. Poetry is far and away the most popular medium of these young writers, and their poems make no compromise with old standards of communication."[44] Brady's description hints at the significance of these events to the development of anarchism in the second half of the twentieth century. If the word *poetry* were replaced with *punk music,* and the word *songs* swapped in for *poems,* the passage could as easily describe one of the thousands of anarcho-punk shows that have disseminated radical ideas throughout the world since the late 1970s. Poetry served the same functions for the movement in the 1940s that music would in later decades. By decade's end, San Francisco poets began to read their poetry aloud over live bands playing the new bebop jazz.

While the *Harper's* article salaciously played up the erotic aspects of the milieu, some participants did attempt to overcome jealousy and sexual monogamy. Shortly after the New Yorkers arrived, David Koven entertained a brief romantic relationship with Marie Rexroth, Kenneth's wife. Although both couples were purportedly in open relationships, Kenneth and Audrey Goodfriend were hurt. The tryst left a residue of tension at the same time it added a romantic layer to linkages between the New York and San Francisco

David Thoreau Wieck, circa 1948. Courtesy of the David Thoreau Wieck and Diva Agostinelli Papers, Tamiment Library/Robert F. Wagner Labor Archives, New York University.

anarchists.[45] The East Coasters intended to raise children together in their communal home, though it is unclear if they were sexually intimate with one another. However, when Sally Grieg later became pregnant, the Griegs left the house to raise their child more traditionally, a decision that again proved painful to Goodfriend. Meanwhile, Dan DeWeiss, a black man, felt compelled to return to New York after experiencing heightened racial discrimination on the West Coast.[46] Reinventing social relations, it turned out, was harder than the group had imagined.

In the mid-1940s, San Francisco was still home to many of the aging Italian anarchists who had supported the newspaper *Man!* in the 1930s. Under the mantle of "Gruppo Libertario," they hosted regular fund-raising socials for *L'Adunata dei Refrattari,* which continued to appear until 1971. In her portrait of the milieu, Brady recorded Rexroth's attempts to collaborate with these older anarchists. "At meetings of the Libertarians, today," she noted, "you will be apt to find young intellectuals sprinkled among the mustachioed papas and bosomed mamas who, until recently, had no such high-toned cooperation."[47] Yet relations between the city's two "libertarian" groups were at first tentative, owing to language and political differences. It was not until later in the year that they found a go-between that both groups trusted: *Resistance* editors Diva Agostinelli and David Wieck.

Enticed by the *Harper's* article and their friends' upbeat missives, David Wieck and Diva Agostinelli decided to experience the San Francisco Renaissance for themselves in the summer of 1947. Like Goodfriend and Koven had done the previous year, the editors of *Resistance* made the trip by bus, stopping to meet subscribers and give talks about anarchism along the way. Atomic bombs had flattened Hiroshima and Nagasaki less than two years earlier. In New York, Wieck's draft-resisting comrades were busy establishing the Committee for Nonviolent Revolution (CNVR) and experimenting with civil disobedience to desegregate public swimming pools. Optimistic about these new efforts, the couple was eager to learn what dissidents were doing in other parts of the country. Yet a series of letters mailed to Wieck's parents from the road records their growing realization that the Lower East Side existed as a sort of radical bubble, while most of the country had settled in to a comfortable complacency.

In Detroit, Agostinelli reported she was "disappointed" with the event she and Wieck had organized. "No one even seemed to know what I was talking about," she admitted. "One kid simply said, 'Why should I get all excited about the world, the way people work and live? . . . I'm satisfied.'" Agostinelli was likewise shocked by the way U.S.-born miners accepted conditions of life in Johnson City, Illinois, in contrast to the rebellious, immigrant-heavy mining town in which she had grown up. Chicago did not offer much hope either. "I was very disappointed with the 'comrades' we met there," Agostinelli wrote. "After a while you get fed up with people whose radicalism is pure intellect—that is something to discuss and talk about but which has not one bit of reality in their lives."[48] The traditional forms of anarchist movement centered on class struggle, the couple quickly realized, had very little traction in a postwar economy that delivered rising living standards—embodied in the form of cars, appliances, and single-family homes—to blue-collar factory workers. It would take nearly another decade, however, before many anarchists paid close attention to the racially discriminatory ways in which this new wealth was distributed.

After the shock of middle America, San Francisco gleamed even more enticingly. Upon arrival the couple rented a house, and Agostinelli quickly found a job as a bookkeeper; but Wieck discovered that San Francisco employers seldom hired men to complete the clerical work he was accustomed to performing in New York.[49] It did not take long to make friends, however.

Writing to his parents in December 1947, Wieck explained that the "comrades" he and Diva had met in San Francisco "fall into two groups—the old Italians, and the young "bohemians." The Italians welcomed the young New Yorkers, owing to Agostinelli's family connections, their ability to speak Italian, and their close bond with the editors of *L'Adunata* in New York. Wieck described the challenging position this put them in:

> Most all of both groups are nice people. But the Italians expect Diva and I to be "propagandists" and neither of us has any inclination for it. They expect us to straighten out the young intellectuals about what anarchism is, and hell we're as confused as anybody. On the other hand the young intellectuals are up somewhere in a semi-religious sub-stratosphere (all of them, I guess, are beardy in an unorthodox non-Christian way).[50]

The poets' emphasis on creativity and lifestyle had proven confusing to the aging Italian anarchists who sometimes attended Libertarian Circle events. Many felt the neophytes were straying too far from anarchism's roots in workplace issues, and some resented the fact that the younger group had associated anarchism with sexual freedom. In a letter to his parents, Wieck recounted a moment in which these conflicting visions of anarchism came to a head:

> When I met Rexroth for the first time, at an Italian dance, we chatted awhile till I made a chance remark that led him to think I was on the side of the Italians and their anti-Bohemianism. He started shouting and raging and insulting about these sectarians who think nobody is any good except proletarians, and how they crucified Emma Goldman because she was too literary, and how they crucified LaSalle . . . because Marx had accused LaSalle of being a spy just because he looked like an intellectual and dressed like an artist.[51]

Wieck's account is remarkable for the manner in which it depicts the reemergence of a self-consciously bohemian strain of anarchism—the likes of which had not been seen in the United States since the First World War. It also illustrates how cleavages reappeared among anarchists that were at the same time generational, ethnic, class-based, and reflective of different priorities and strategies. As we saw in chapter 1, Goldman was indeed criticized (if not *crucified*) by other anarchists for her growing investment in the politics of literature and sexuality after 1905. Yet, in the Progressive Era, déclassé artists sought to support the militant unionism of the IWW and other working-class initiatives. They saw their exploration of stigmatized sexual practices and new forms of expression as running parallel to labor's attack on traditional property relations, even if only a minority actually built lasting relationships across class boundaries.

In 1948, by contrast, Wieck wrote of the community around Rexroth: "No contact at all with any workers. The Commies have the same tight hold on radical workers here; and, as elsewhere, those who get disillusioned with the CP are usually disillusioned about everything. But that's all an old story."[52] The older Italian anarchists were, by the late 1940s, an isolated remnant, unable to play the bridging role that Big Bill Haywood and others had in the second decade of the twentieth century. Their lack of a base in the working class—or other specially burdened sector of society, for that matter—was apparently not particularly troublesome to the locals.

For many of the Bay Area anarchists, art was not a mere supplement to political struggle but was seen as its highest form. Rexroth bragged to Cantine and Rainer: "As for Patchen, Everson, Goodman, Miller, Duncan, myself and a few others—Lamantia for instance for the past year—*we* are the freedom you are fighting for. Frankly, I think one poem by Kenneth Patchen worth all the possible theoretical journal articles that ever have been and ever will be published—and I don't think Patchen the greatest poet."[53] William Everson later described the bond he shared with Duncan in similar terms: "The important thing was that we both saw art as insurrectional, revolutionary: the *real* revolution."[54]

Beneath their remarkable hubris, comments such as these did contain an underlying logic. Literary critic Morgan Gibson suggests that, to Rexroth, "poetry [was] not merely a literary game of skill . . . but [was] instead an act of human communion, the source of community."[55] Writing poetry was, like Zen meditation, a contemplative search for enlightenment and authenticity; sharing it was an act of direct communication that built respectful I-thou relations. In this sense, the San Francisco group saw their poetry as profoundly contributing to the work of reestablishing relationships of understanding and solidarity between people. Instead of vainly throwing themselves against the old order, they would turn their backs on it and create anew. Like later generations of anarchists, they managed to be earnest and arrogant at the same time.

Wieck found the West Coast focus on art and lifestyle partly compelling but ultimately unsatisfying, for it seemed to downplay the importance of strategic political engagement. Coming from his experience of successful resistance to Jim Crow regulations at Danbury Federal Penitentiary and his associations with the direct-action enthusiasts of the CNVR, Wieck was more optimistic about the impact activism could make.[56] Upon Agostinelli and Wieck's arrival in December 1947, Agostinelli informed Wieck's parents that the Libertarian Circle "seemed to have broken up for a while but now want to start something. Dave is scheduled to open the meeting with a short talk." Yet returning focus to more traditional politics proved to be an uphill battle. By March, Wieck could report to his parents, "Last Friday at the discussion group we finally got to something concrete: The [Korean] War. As a result, before the regular discussion next week we will have a kind of 'action' meeting to discuss what can be done to promote anti-war activity on the University of California campus. There is talk of leaflets, street-meetings, etc."[57] To his chagrin, however, the antiwar activity never materialized. Frustrated by this inaction and his continuing inability to land a job, Wieck returned with Agostinelli to New York City later that spring.

Nor were they the only ones to leave the Bay Area. The bolt of postwar energy seems to have waned toward the end of the decade. In 1949, Rexroth received a Guggenheim award and used it to travel around the world. Robert Duncan, meanwhile, traveled to England and later taught briefly at Black Mountain College, in Tennessee. Snyder went to Japan. This was only a brief hiatus, however. A new round of institution building and an infusion of new talent would raise the area's political and literary output to new heights in the mid-1950s.

COLD WAR ANARCHISM

After Wieck and Agostinelli returned to New York they resumed publishing *Resistance* and organizing weekly discussions at the Solidaridad Internacional Antifascista Hall on Broadway. Wieck took on primary editing responsibilities; under his influence the magazine addressed a broader range of topics, at greater length, and with more theoretical sophistication than *Why?* had managed. In part, this owed to the fecund exchange of ideas between anarchists in different countries that began after the war. *Resistance* continued to exchange subscriptions and letters with the Freedom Group in London. David Wieck and Paul Goodman became particularly close with a younger member, Colin Ward, who would go on to found the important journal *Anarchy* in 1961. Wieck also established a friendly correspondence with the Noir et Rouge Group in France and the publishers of the Italian journal

Volontà. Together, writers from each of these small collectives puzzled over what it meant to be anarchists in advanced capitalist societies as the Cold War began to take shape.

In 1947, President Harry Truman had announced that the United States would intervene throughout the world, beginning with Greece, to prevent communists from coming to power. The House Un-American Activities Committee began its dramatic purge of Hollywood communists the same year, and in 1949 eleven leaders of the Communist Party were imprisoned for violation of the wartime Smith Act, which had recriminalized advocating the overthrow of the government. By 1950 this new Red Scare found its namesake in Wisconsin's cynical and blustery senator Joseph McCarthy.[58]

Despite the anarchists' long-standing antipathies to the Communist Party, the editors of *Resistance* spoke out early and stridently against government prosecution as a clear violation of the rights of individuals to free speech and political association. Anarchists themselves seem to have survived the tide of repression unscathed, in stark contrast to their treatment during the previous Red Scare. In the main, this suggests how unthreatening the movement had become over the previous three decades. It is also notable that some respected anarchists, nearing retirement from movement activity, lent verbal support to the United States in the Cold War. In *The World Scene from the Libertarian Point of View,* a long pamphlet issued in 1951 by the remnants of Chicago's Free Society Group, G. P. Maximoff lamented,

> Since we cannot destroy both warring factions simultaneously . . . [we must] side with those whose victory will give us our best chance to unite the proletariat and overthrow the victors. That side, strange as it may seem, is the capitalist bourgeoisie, not the Communist dictatorship represented by a new class of bureaucrats. Such is the paradox of history.[59]

Although Rudolph Rocker and other eminent figures agreed with Maximoff, the pamphlet also included a brief dissent penned by David Wieck that again highlighted generational differences in the movement. Wieck rejected becoming a "realist" if that required anarchists to "argue the relative merits of a bomb now or two years from now." Instead of proffering hypothetical strategies for leading the masses in the distant future, he explained, "We have learned that as groups living the ethics and meaning of Anarchism we create an Anarchist community in and as our movement, and demonstrate by this new society our ideas, and their practicality."[60]

Wieck's response bore the influence of the San Francisco poets, Cantine's "Thoreauvian" life in the woods, and Goodman's *May Pamphlet*. Indeed, the idea of modeling alternative forms of society in intentional communities took many forms in the late 1940s. The Resistance Group drew upon the work of the School of Living, a small organization founded by a former business executive dismayed by the growing scale of U.S. society. Ralph Borsodi and his collaborators taught that decentralization—"the organizing of activities in smaller units, both efficient and voluntary, in which all participants involved develop initiative and responsibility"—provided an array of benefits, including increased self-worth and a greater consideration of how one's actions affected others.[61] The School of Living felt obliged to promote these ideas without itself adopting centralizing practices—such as building a mass political party. To this end, it established a series of small communities throughout the Northeast and Midwest. Audrey Goodfriend recalled, "We would go out there frequently to talk to them. None of them called themselves anarchists, but their ideas were definitely ideas that all of us could subscribe to."[62]

Theoretical treatises also had an impact. In 1947, Paul Goodman coauthored *Communitas* with his brother Percival, an architect. The book ruminated on the history of urban planning and suggested ways of organizing life around principles other than profit maximization.[63] Two years later, Martin Buber published *Paths in Utopia,* an attempt to recover a non-Leninist revolutionary tradition.[64] The book emphasized the ideas of one of Buber's mentors, the German anarchist Gustav Landauer, whose writings were previously unknown to most English speakers. Like Buber himself, Landauer highlighted the importance of personal relations. In a line that would become a touchstone of late-twentieth-century anarchism, he declared, "The State is a condition, a certain relationship between human beings, a mode of behaviour; we destroy it by contracting other relationships, by behaving differently toward one another. . . . We are the State and we shall continue to be the State until we have created the institutions that form a real community and society of men."[65] Taken together, these many influences reoriented midcentury anarchism toward a strategy that contemporary anarchists often term "prefigurative politics."

This strategic shift emerged not in isolation from other aspects of anarchist social theory but as a considered response to historic events and in conjunction with important philosophical reconsiderations. These broader ruminations are captured in a 1948 essay, simply titled "Anarchism," that was penned by Wieck but adopted by the *Resistance* editorial committee as a statement of its position.

The Resistance Group assured readers that it remained "in complete agreement" with the basic goals and values of the anarchist tradition. "Freedom is the core of a society of healthy, happy human beings; that State and Government—that is, law; institutionalized violence; war; individual, group and class domination—are the antithesis of freedom and must be destroyed."[66] However, the group expressed grave doubts about the traditional methods anarchists had employed to reach their goals. The editors of *Resistance* woefully abandoned their former faith that the majority of people were becoming increasingly immiserated and, therefore, radicalized. "The mass of the people is increasingly indifferent to radical ideas—indifferent even to thinking," Wieck tartly asserted. Therefore it was incumbent upon anarchists to recognize the following:

> The revolution is not imminent, and it is senseless to expend our lives in patient waiting or faithful dreams: senseless because the revolution of the future requires active preparation: not the preparation of conspiracy and storing of arms, but the preparation of undermining the institutions and habits of thought and action that inhibit release of the natural powers of men and women. . . . The revolution as a "final conflict" exploding out of the condition of man is an illusion; revolutionary growth is necessarily the hard-won learning and practice of freedom.[67]

In short, the group rejected the teleological view of history and economistic assumptions about liberation that many classical anarchists shared with orthodox Marxism. This was a highly significant theoretical turn—one that required a deep reconsideration of the nature of power, the timeline of change, and which activities to prioritize.

While the *Resistance* statement shared key themes with earlier essays by Cantine, Goodman, and others, it addressed the question of "what is to be done?" in a more specific and multifaceted fashion than had previous contributions to the conversation. First, it recognized the importance of winning "concrete victories" and "improving existing conditions"—in other words, reform struggles. To this end, Wieck's "Anarchism" suggested that direct action campaigns should be prioritized in the workplace and against militarism and racism. Second, the anarchist movement should function as a communal sphere of freedom. As Wieck put it, "Perhaps our strongest achievement and our strongest propaganda is a movement where . . . people can find a refuge of sanity and health, where they can learn in practice what anarchism and an anarchist society are."[68]

Finally, the statement argued for greater emphasis on education. Rather than another round of newspapers and forums, however, anarchists needed to focus on educating the young and reconstructing relationships within the family. "We believe the present state of 'human nature' is largely responsible for the present state of human society, and that this 'human nature' is formed in the early part of life when the family and morality and discipline (and not economic or political institutions) are the dominant facts in the life of the individual."[69] In this discussion of the formation of "human nature" (in scare quotes), we can glimpse the group's growing recognition that power not only functions restrictively, from outside the human personality, but also works in an educative and formative capacity. The group's readings in psychology only compounded their doubts about an imminent and sweeping revolution. Given the ways they had been raised and conditioned, the group reflected, "it is not at all certain that we would be able to live in a free society."[70]

Members of the Resistance Group, and the larger milieu around the journal, worked to carry out each of these planks over the course of the next decade. Despite the theoretical unity achieved with the statement, however, the community of anarchists, pacifists, and poets established during the war soon began to splinter. In 1951, Dachine Rainer left Holley Cantine, and *Retort* ceased publication. Cantine turned to writing short stories and playing music but maintained ties to the anarchist and pacifist movements into the 1970s. David Dellinger and other draft resisters departed for Europe in a quixotic attempt to defuse East-West tensions by distributing pacifist literature while biking from Paris to Moscow. A few years later, Audrey Goodfriend and David Koven launched a libertarian educational center—the Walden School—in Berkeley, that drew on the pedagogical theories of A. S. Neill, another disciple of Reich. Public events at the Solidaridad Internacional Antifascista Hall wound down in the early 1950s. According to Wieck, they became "depressing. . . . The only people we were attracting were the crazies." In 1954, *Resistance* ceased publishing. "The Climate of the time," Wieck recalled, "was infinitely dreary, and everything that could be said had been said." He returned to school, earned a PhD in philosophy from Columbia University, and moved with Diva Agostinelli to Troy, New York, to teach at the Rensselaer Polytechnic Institute in 1960.[71] In 1952, Goodman titled an autobiographical novel *The Breakup of Our Camp*.

The new ideas Goodman, Wieck, and others were generating nearly died on the vine under the harsh light of McCarthyism and 1950s somnolence. Yet it is clear that the themes developed in the 1940s—sexual freedom, intentional communities, nonviolent direct action against war and racism—fundamentally informed the mass movements of the 1960s. This relay was made possible by a series of linked institutions—the Living Theatre, Pacifica Radio, and City Lights and Kepler's Bookstores—established by the postwar anarchist pacifist milieu in the early 1950s.

In New York, bohemian anarchism survived the early 1950s largely thanks to the frenetic energy of the Living Theatre, a pioneer off-Broadway repertory company created by a young couple named Judith Malina and Julian Beck. Malina had been placed on *Why?*'s mailing list while studying drama at the New School for Social Research. In the late 1940s, she met Goodman and began attending Resistance Group forums at the Solidaridad Internacional Antifascista Hall. Malina's diary records one such meeting addressed by the émigré council communist Paul Mattick. In response to Mattick's argument that change was impossible while the workers' movement remained fragmented, Malina recorded herself as saying, "We stand outside of wars. Our personal example is a useful political action in spite of Mattick's contention that it is a limited expression. Gandhi's action, and Christ's too, began as limited expressions."[72] Malina convinced Beck to join her, and soon the couple was asked to lead a discussion on pacifist strategies of transformation.[73]

In December 1951, they established the Living Theatre on Cherry Lane in Greenwich Village. Alongside works by Gertrude Stein and T. S. Elliot, early productions included Kenneth Rexroth's verse drama *Beyond the Mountains* and Paul Goodman's *Faustina*.[74] When not writing or acting in his play, Goodman was developing, with Fritz and Laura Perls, the practice of Gestalt therapy—which attempted to synthesize Martin Buber's philosophy with Reichian psychoanalysis and other influences. Malina became one of his early patients. A few years later, Malina befriended Dorothy Day of the Catholic Worker when both women were incarcerated for resisting Cold War civil defense drills. The anarchist pacifism that Malina and Beck imbibed from Goodman and Day shaped the content and form of the couple's performances, as well as the way they ran their company.

Julian Beck (left) and Judith Malina (center) of the Living Theatre, with an unknown actor (date unknown). Courtesy of the Living Theatre Records, Yale Collection of American Literature, Beinecke Rare Book and Manuscript Library.

KPFA-Pacifica Radio, the country's first listener-supported radio station, began broadcasting from Berkeley in April 1949. Pacifica was the brainchild of Lewis Hill, the former CO who had helped found the CNVR with David Dellinger and others in 1946. After growing frustrated with the New York pacifists, Hill moved to the Bay Area and began associating with the Rexroth circle. Dissatisfied with the limited reach of the pacifist Left, he urged his friends to begin making use of modern communication technologies by founding a nonprofit radio station. Hill recycled the name from a CPS publication, *Pacifica Views,* after that journal was merged with Dellinger's *Direct Action* to become the four-page monthly *Alternative*. Goodfriend and Koven helped raise funds. Once KPFA was operational, Rexroth began recording a weekly book review program that aired back-to-back with a show about Buddhism hosted by Alan Watts. Theodore Roszak, a California pacifist who later penned a classic text on the 1960s counterculture, remarked that KPFA "turned this area into a real cultural and political community."[75]

That community was also crucially nurtured by a publishing house and trio of bookstores that shared similar anarchist pacifist roots. City Lights, the first and most famous of them, opened near San Francisco's Chinatown in 1953. Though associated today with the Sorbonne-trained poet Lawrence Ferlinghetti, the store was cofounded by Peter Martin, son of the late, highly revered anarcho-syndicalist Carlo Tresca.[76] City Lights quickly became a favorite haunt of Bay Area poets and served as a rare outlet for anarchist publications. Ferlinghetti recalled that the neighborhood's Italian garbage man was a regular customer. "Each week he'd jump off as the truck passed, pick up the Italian anarchist papers *L'Adunata* and *L'Humanitá Nova,* and jump back on."[77] In 1955, City Lights also launched a small publishing house that issued small, oddly shaped books of contemporary poetry that replicated exactly the format of the book of Kenneth Patchen poems produced by the Untide Press at Waldport, Oregon.

That same year, Roy Kepler opened another smartly curated bookshop near the campus of Stanford University, forty-five minutes south of San Francisco. Kepler was another former World War II conscientious objector who had become close with anarchists such as David Dellinger and Bill Sutherland. He had worked as executive secretary of the War Resisters League for two years following the CNVR takeover of that organization's executive board, before a stint on the staff of Pacifica Radio. Kepler helped Fred and Pat Cody establish a third radical bookstore, Cody's, in Berkeley. More than just commercial ventures, the stores served as physical locales where people not satisfied with life in the 1950s could discover new ideas and meet one another. Galleries and performance venues served a similar function.

At the end of 1952, Robert Duncan and his lover, an expressionist painter who went by the single name Jess, converted a San Francisco carriage house into the King Ubu Gallery. They named the space after *Ubu Roi,* a play by the nineteenth-century French anarchist Alfred Jarry, which railed against the ways in which "governments inhibit the free expression of individual feeling and impulse."[78] The play was a favorite among the Surrealists, and the Living Theatre had staged a performance earlier in the year.[79] Duncan and his collaborators declared they would maintain the gallery for only one year, to mitigate the temptation of profiting off of avant-garde art. During that time, they hung over a dozen exhibits and hosted readings by the likes of Rexroth, Lamantia, and Weldon Kees, a transplant from New York who had been close to the Why? Group in the 1940s.[80] Although Duncan made good on his word, the gallery had proven so vital to the San Francisco scene that another group of artists took over the space, renaming it the Six Gallery.

If the Beat Generation was symbolically inaugurated by Allen Ginsberg's first public reading of "Howl" in 1955, as literary critics have come to agree, then it was born of the collision of a circle of queer, drug-addled New York hipsters and the Bay Area's community of anarchist poets. Ginsberg debuted "Howl" at the Six Gallery and shared the stage with Surrealist anarchist Philip Lamantia and the Buddhist anarchists Gary Snyder and Phillip Whalen. Kenneth Rexroth, the man who had worked tirelessly for over a decade to meld anarchism and poetry into something new and ecstatic in San Francisco, played master of ceremonies.

By 1956 the Libertarian Circle had disbanded, but connections between anarchists and experimental poets endured. In April, David Koven launched a short-lived libertarian journal called *The Needle.*[81] Koven wrote, "The revolutionary masses seem to have dwindled to a handful of individuals like ourselves, grimly holding out against the onslaught of growing totalitarian forms." With little hope of organizing, he saw *The Needle* simply as a forum of expression for those "not yet captured by our statist culture."[82] To this end, he devoted considerable space to the new poetry, securing contributions from older associates such as Robert Duncan and Gary Snyder, as well as from leading voices of the emergent Beat movement such as Gregory Corso and Allen Ginsberg. Soon these authors would be publishing in much weightier periodicals.

By keeping the tradition of a politics-tinged avant-garde and bohemian community alive, San Francisco and New York City created the atmosphere and institutional framework from which the larger Beat subculture could emerge. In 1959, the poet Chris Nelson recalled, "One thing about the Village, it had a tremendous tradition, and that was the first thing that hit you.... There was a folk group, mostly Stalinists.... And all the old anarchists. There was an anarchist hall on Broadway. There was the Spanish anarchists, there was the Catholic anarchists who had a soup kitchen down near the Bowery on Christy Street.... The anarchist group was the most powerful group at that time. It was the intellectual force of the Village—and it fell apart suddenly."[83] Disintegration, however, could promote dissemination. Stuart Perkoff, a Korean War draft resister and a member of the Resistance Group in the late 1940s, moved west and helped establish the Venice Beach Beat community in the 1950s.[84]

ASSESSING MID-TWENTIETH-CENTURY U.S. ANARCHISM

Anarchism evolved in fundamental ways during the 1940s. The period is notable for the profound number of new thinkers, concepts, strategies, and tactics taken up by U.S. anarchists. While interwar anarchists largely clung to nineteenth-century theoretical frameworks despite their declining correspondence with social conditions, post–World War II anarchists drew deeply from anthropology, psychology, literature, and urban planning. The range of spiritual influences—Social Gospel Protestantism, Catholicism, Quakerism, Jewish Mysticism, and Zen Buddhism, among them—is perhaps the most surprising development, considering the centrality of atheism to classical anarchism. In this voracious search for new ideas, the desire to make up for lost time, to elaborate an anarchism relevant to an era of shocking brutality and monumental change, is palpable.

The extent to which anarchism evolved in the 1940s becomes clear upon reviewing table 1, "Components of Social Anarchist Politics," in this book's introduction.

Theorists of the 1940s complicated earlier anarchist accounts of human nature and began to focus on the ways in which the social and psychological environment that a child grows up in shapes his or her values, character, and priorities. They also acknowledged that forms of domination were more extensive and more difficult to overcome than previous anarchist theorizations of "the state and capital" suggested. Strategy changed fundamentally—toward effecting cultural transformation—once these theorists surrendered the belief that revolution was likely to occur soon and decided that an insurrectionary upheaval would not, in itself, lead to a new society. Thinkers of this period also extended earlier anarchist analysis of the means-end relationship, especially regarding violence. Focusing on sexual repression, cultural alienation, and the catastrophic potential of atomic warfare suggested that anarchism might find adherents outside of its traditional working-class base (even if activists found few new recruits in practice).

Despite all of these reconsiderations, postwar U.S. anarchism did not mark a complete break from earlier incarnations. Prominent postwar anarchists (Rexroth, Goodfriend, Koven) had been active in anarchist circles in the 1930s. While they became estranged from some older anarchists, they continued to seek mentorship from others, such as the Italian editors of *L'Adunata dei Refrattari* and members of the British Freedom Press Group. Rather than reinvent anarchist strategy and tactics wholesale, the postwar generation adapted older precepts. They upheld the traditional anarchist emphasis on taking "direct action" but decided that it was more effective when conducted nonviolently.

The new generation also adapted the prefigurative element of anarchist politics. The IWW's call to begin building the "new world in the shell of the old" was widely touted in the 1940s by figures such as Cantine, Goodman, and Maurin. In the Wobblies' vision, the structure of their democratic, industrial unions prefigured the organizational form that would stitch together all of postcapitalist society. Postwar anarchists developed the metaphor in new directions, however. They urged anarchists to begin creating the new world in all aspects of their daily lives—including the types of communities they lived in, the sorts of family relationships they maintained, and the ways they treated fellow humans in need. Earlier anarchists had created their own cultural worlds, as attested to by the nineteenth-century anarchist singing and drama societies and the interwar anarchist colonies. In the postwar period, however, anarchists' prefigurative lifestyles and communities were less and less embedded in broader working-class traditions and neighborhoods, and they were not paired with confrontational class struggle.

The midcentury period has bestowed a mixed legacy on liberation movements that have followed. The milieu's commitment to gender equality, for example, was uneven but an improvement over that of the previous generation of U.S. anarchists. Men continued to dominate the front lines of direct action and to produce the most respected theoretical writings, but women took on prominent roles in editing and contributing to publications. The exploration of Reich's ideas marked the first substantial engagement with the politics of family and sexuality by anarchists in the United States since 1917. This led to experimentation with open relationships and communal living, which sometimes ended painfully, but which also helped make the anarchist and pacifist Left a relatively safe and supportive environment for gay, lesbian, and bisexual individuals.

Yet the anarchism of the 1940s also became divorced from working-class struggles. The ideology was upwardly mobile along with the few young people who worked to maintain it during these difficult years. Key figures of this period—Wieck, Goodfriend, Agostinelli, Duncan, and Goodman among them—benefited from the expansion of federal support for higher education in the 1930s and 1940s, becoming the first members of their families to attend college. That experience helped expose them to the worlds of literature, psychology, anthropology, and other disciplines. Ironically, federal repression of war resisters introduced these working-class radicals to pacifists from more affluent backgrounds (Dellinger, Peck) who had arrived at an anarchist position more from their opposition to violence than from their opposition to class exploitation.

Because of conservative tendencies in the leadership of the labor movement and the perceived acquiescence of working people in the face of expanded postwar consumer opportunities, anarchists largely gave up hope for the working class as a collective agent of change. These anarchists were not able to muster the long-range vision needed to anticipate later shifts in capitalist development that would again leave workers in precarious conditions that compelled them to more forcefully fight back. Anarchists of the period were also ambivalent about organizing. This stemmed partly from concerns—born of recent historical events—about re-creating hierarchies and delegating power to leaders that could then be turned against the movement itself. But it was also due to the promotion, by some participants, of artistic expression and the maintenance of resistant lifestyles as the highest form of activity for social rebels to engage in. In sum, participants' educational trajectories combined with a de-emphasis of labor organizing to shift the demographic and cultural norms of anarchism away from the working class.

Despite these shortcomings, the writers and activists of the 1940s and early 1950s adapted the anarchist tradition to the disheartening historical circumstances they found themselves in. By doing so they were able to keep the libertarian socialist current alive during a period of total war, McCarthyism, and declining labor-movement militancy. Perhaps counterintuitively, the aversion to organizing and the inward focus of many participants insulated them from the dismal political climate of the late 1940s and the first half of the 1950s. Not expecting inspiration to come from the masses, they flourished by sharing new ideas and visions with one another.

The anarchist-pacifist-poet milieu of the 1940s and early 1950s diverged into two distinct streams after 1955. In the first of these streams, anarchist pacifists contributed tactics, organizational techniques, and institutions to the historic Black Freedom Movement, as we will see in the next chapter. The second stream devoted itself to the invention and promotion of new values, life priorities, and senses of identity, in the form of the Beat counterculture. As chapter 8 demonstrates, these streams reconverged in the mid-1960s, profoundly influencing the tenor of the counterculture, antiwar, student, and women's movements.

SEVEN

Anarchism and the Black Freedom Movement, 1955–1964

While anarchists experienced the decade after Hiroshima as an isolating period of quiescence in American life, hopeful signs of change began to emerge in the mid-1950s. The February 1956 issue of the anarchist newsletter *Views and Comments* declared, "All over the world the submerged peoples are rebelling against the imperialist exploitation which is based in large part on the false doctrines of racial superiority. The struggle of the Southern Negroes is part of that movement."[1] Indeed, a wave of decolonization struggles after 1945 had checked the ambitions of France, the United Kingdom, and the Netherlands to reassert power in the territories they had controlled before the war. India, Burma, Indonesia, the Philippines, Vietnam, Laos, and Cambodia had dislodged their historic colonial governments by 1956; Algerians were escalating attacks on French *pieds-noirs;* and in less than a year Ghana would emerge as the first independent African nation-state. In the United States the landmark Supreme Court ruling on *Brown v. Board of Education* legally overturned nearly a century of Jim Crow racial segregation. Facing a campaign of "massive resistance" to integration by southern whites in and out of office, African Americans quickly developed campaigns to test compliance with the ruling and to force local authorities to actually desegregate public facilities, businesses, workplaces, and neighborhoods.

As *Views and Comments* presciently noted, each of these geographically distant struggles attacked the ideology of white supremacy and the specific forms of economic exploitation it enabled. Out of these confrontations emerged new insights into the nature of capitalism, racism, state power, and the best means of resisting them. Many participants would come to view their local campaigns as fronts in a larger movement against what they called *imperialism:* a racialized and global capitalism fundamentally structured by the asymmetrical deployment of state-based military force. Decolonization and domestic antiracism played out in a world organized around Cold War polarities: nuclear-armed superpowers struggling for control of vital resources and military placements (and thereby developing forms of *neo*colonialism), mirrored in an ideological battle between authoritarian communism and liberal democratic capitalism.

This set of conditions marked an exceedingly complex situation for anarchists to act in and upon. Since 1919, anarchists had struggled, with little success, to articulate and popularize a "third camp" politics that offered a humane social vision superior to both major systems (as well as to fascism). Always concerned with means as well as outcomes, anarchists of the 1950s and early 1960s championed the independent initiatives of people of color who sought greater autonomy, but they equivocated when those movements sought assistance from the U.S. government, on the one hand, or communist organizations, on the other. Though the number of anarchists active in the country during these years was minuscule—a few hundred at most—they did not always agree on how to relate to these struggles.

This chapter compares the ideas and efforts of anarchist pacifists who worked in organizations such as the War Resisters League, Congress of Racial Equality, Peacemakers, and *Liberation* magazine with those of the anarcho-syndicalist Libertarian League. The encounter between anarchists and civil rights organizers affected both parties more than historians have recognized, though the black freedom struggle likely had a greater transformative impact on the U.S. anarchist movement than vice versa. While anarchists promoted nonstatist direct-action tactics and horizontal organizational forms, the fight against Jim Crow helped anarchists previously focused on class struggle to move beyond economistic thinking and reinvest in strategies based on mass organizing. In the momentous desegregation and decolonization fights of the mid-twentieth century, the anarchist belief that government was inherently a corrupting force of domination chaffed against groups of historically oppressed people marshaling the resources and authority of government to blunt the coercive, often deadly, force of other centers of power, be they racist mobs or foreign corporations backed by imperialist governments. These real-world tests of political principle challenged both the pacifism and the antistatism of some midcentury anarchists, dividing and disorienting the already weak anarchist camp in the early 1960s, just as the New Left was emerging.

As indicated by chapters 5 and 6, the experience of spending years in Civilian Public Service camps and federal penitentiaries for refusal to join the armed services during World War II fundamentally shaped the lives and political commitments of hundreds of men in the postwar years. Those entering prison with commitments to socialism, anarchism, and Gandhian pacifism emerged as nonviolent revolutionaries eager to grow a new movement based on points of unity within the anticommunist Left.

Having successfully overturned racial segregation policies in federal prisons through organized acts of noncompliance, the anarchist pacifists and other nonviolent revolutionaries designated the fight against white supremacy a top priority. The relationships and institutions that the nonviolent revolutionaries developed in the decade after the war became vital to the Black Freedom Movement that fundamentally transformed American life beginning in the 1950s. For more than a decade, the pacifists had bravely experimented with tactics of nonviolent direct action against racial segregation, notably on the 1947 Journey of Reconciliation, and had trained others in these techniques. In 1956 they contributed a platform for debating movement strategy and theory in the form of *Liberation* magazine.

Shortly before being released in 1945 from his second draft resistance sentence in Lewisburg Penitentiary, David Dellinger had written to Holley Cantine, editor of the anarchist journal *Retort,* "I have decided that I would like to establish a monthly magazine that will help build up a left-wing pacifist socialist mov't [*sic*] and body of thought."[2] A decade later, his own publishing attempts having floundered, Dellinger accepted an invitation from A. J. Muste to co-edit a full-size monthly magazine alongside Bayard Rustin and Roy Finch.[3] At the time, Muste served as chair of the Fellowship of Reconciliation (FOR) while Rustin was lauded as an intrepid antiracist organizer and co-founder of the Congress of Racial Equality (CORE). Finch had served time in a Civilian Public Service camp in California, emerged an anarchist, and moved east to throw himself into work with the Committee for Nonviolent Revolution, Peacemakers, and the War Resisters League (WRL). Aided by a larger circle of collaborators, this editorial collective produced a wide-ranging and accessible, yet intellectually rigorous, journal that served as a movement resource for more than two decades. By 1959, circulation reached approximately 2,000 copies per issue.[4]

Liberation's debut editorial acknowledged that traditional Left arguments no longer inspired hope and that the world needed fresh vision. The editors encouraged contributors and readers to develop such vision by drawing on four "root traditions." These included the "Judeo-Christian prophetic tradition, which gave men a vision of human dignity and a reign of righteousness, equality, and brotherhood on earth" and an "American tradition" that "asserts that government rests upon consent, and institutions are made for man, not man for institutions." In addition to Jefferson and Paine, the editors included Eugene Debs, Randolph Bourne, and the abolitionist movement in this tradition. Third, they looked to "the libertarian, democratic, antiwar, socialist, anarchist and labor movements" that fought for a "class-less and war-less world." Finally, they celebrated the tradition of nonviolence, especially noting the contribution of Gandhi, who "joined nonviolence and revolutionary collective action."[5] Despite the breadth of these ideological wellsprings, the editors agreed on the following:

> We do not conceive the problem of revolution or the building of a better society as one of accumulating power, whether by legislative or other methods, to "capture the state," and then, presumably, to transform society and human beings as well. The national, sovereign, militarized and bureaucratic State and bureaucratic collective economy are themselves evils to be avoided or abolished.[6]

While less certain than earlier anarchists that government could be jettisoned completely, the editors of the new magazine clearly sought to critique the dangers posed by state power while continuing to search for nonauthoritarian strategies of change.

In many respects, *Liberation* picked up where *Resistance* left off when it had ceased publication two years earlier. Like that magazine, *Liberation* mixed news reports about a wide variety of international social-justice struggles with long essays analyzing movement strategy and evaluating recent trends in social theory and popular culture. The new magazine drew upon a wider stable of writers than had *Resistance,* including Michael Harrington and other socialists, radical academics like Sidney Lens, and international leaders such as Kwame Nkrumah and Julius Nyerere. Nevertheless, anarchists retained a distinct presence in the pages of *Liberation,* with figures such as Kenneth Rexroth, Paul Goodman, George Woodcock, and David Wieck serving as regular contributors. Moreover, anarchist labor made the periodical possible at a material level: for its first ten years, each issue was printed by Dellinger and Igal Roodenko's Libertarian Press.[7] In its early years, then, *Liberation* served as a big tent for the anticommunist Left, including the now relatively dispersed community of pacifist-minded anarchists who came of age politically in the 1940s.

Liberation debuted, coincidentally but fortuitously, just months before a boycott of segregated city buses in Montgomery, Alabama, inaugurated a thrilling new phase in the struggle against white supremacy. While securing funds and dispatching advisors in their roles as board members of pacifist organizations, the editors opened the pages of the magazine to African American organizers, providing the new movement with a ready-made forum in which to debate strategy and a simple means of reaching supporters throughout the country. The magazine likewise provided an early outlet in the United States for the perspectives of national liberation spokespeople who would later command much greater attention—Nkrumah and Nelson Mandela among them. Since two of the editors and many contributors were anarchists, *Liberation* was able to consistently inject anarchist ideas into these debates. After 1954, the pacifists were joined by a new formation of anarcho-syndicalists, who also paid considerable attention to civil rights struggles developing throughout the country.

THE LIBERTARIAN BOOK CLUB AND
THE LIBERTARIAN LEAGUE

After withdrawing from the Why? Group in 1942, Sam and Esther Dolgoff focused their energies on working and raising their children. Sam plied his trade as a housepainter and, as an IWW member, remained an oppositional force pushing for greater radicalism within the House Painters Union. In 1945, at the urging of G. P. Maximoff, the Dolgoffs gathered a group of comrades from the *Road to Freedom* and *Vanguard* days to establish the Libertarian Book Club in New York City. The club rented a room from a Workmen's Circle branch to host monthly "forum discussion meetings and socials." Meetings of the Libertarian Book Club served, in large part, as social events that held together the small community of aging immigrant anarchists. The club did, however, publish a few volumes and organized a mail-order service to make classic books, pamphlets, and foreign anarchist newspapers available to readers across the country.[8]

Ten years after it was founded, the Libertarian Book Club was supplemented by a new organization. The Dolgoffs and another seasoned anarchist,

Russell Blackwell, formed the Libertarian League in New York City in 1954. A communist in the 1920s, Blackwell joined the Trotskyist movement in the 1930s and traveled to Spain during the Civil War to fight with the Workers' Party of Marxist Unification (the party with which George Orwell was also aligned). Although he had been "converted to anarchism in Spain," where he participated in the Friends of Durruti group, Blackwell took leave from the radical movement to focus on his family and his career as a cartographer during the 1940s and early 1950s. By 1954, however, he felt eager to return to public activity.[9]

In "What We Stand For," a brief public statement of the new group's politics, the Libertarian League placed its activities in the context of the Cold War. "Two great power blocs struggle for world domination. . . . Their conflict threatens mankind with atomic destruction." The league suggested an alternative, however:

> The exploitative societies of today must be replaced by a new libertarian world which will proclaim—Equal freedom for all in a free socialist society. "Freedom" without socialism leads to privilege and injustice; "Socialism" without freedom is totalitarian. The monopoly of power which is the state must be replaced by a world-wide federation of free communities, labor councils, and/or co-operatives operating according to the principles of free agreement.[10]

Dolgoff later summarized the group's politics as "essentially anarcho-syndicalist, with a nostalgia for anarchist-communism."[11]

In its first years, the league attracted only a handful of members. They included two couples: Phyllis and Robert Calese, and Richard and Patricia Ellington. The Caleses worked as librarians; Richard Ellington was a professional printer and Patricia's occupation is unknown. Another participant, Bill Rose, came from a prominent family and was introduced to anarchism by underground members of the Confederación Nacional de Trabajadores while studying literature in Spain. Notably, for an organization promoting industrial unionism, members' skewed middle class in their levels of educational achievement and career choices. While others would cycle in and out of the organization over its thirteen-year existence, meetings rarely attracted more than a dozen people.

The league began by organizing weekly political discussions and distributing its blandly titled periodical, *Views and Comments*. Issued first as a mimeographed newsletter, *Views and Comments* grew into a twenty-to-forty-page, 5.5″ × 8.5″ monthly journal, with an aesthetic strikingly similar to that of the photocopied fanzines that would become popular in the 1980s. Sensitive to the lingering atmosphere of McCarthyism, contributors often wrote anonymously or marked their contributions with initials or pseudonyms. For the first years of its existence, the Libertarian League met in the same Solidaridad Internacional Antifascista Hall that had hosted public events organized by the Resistance Group in the 1940s.

By the mid-1950s, Greenwich Village had begun to attract a new generation of young bohemians, many of them participants in the American folk music revival.[12] Like others in the folk scene, Dave Van Ronk, a guitarist and singer who had grown up in Queens, was attracted to leftist politics but was unimpressed with the Communist Party members he met in and around Washington Square Park. While out drinking one night, a friend encouraged him to check out the "libertarian center" at 813 Broadway. Van Ronk remembers that "the center turned out to be a big loft on the corner of 12th Street, which they would set up on forum nights with long trestle tables and folding chairs for about thirty people." The young musician was impressed that league meetings drew a few "genuine firebrands who had fought in the Spanish Civil War, people who had been forced to flee Europe because of their revolutionary activities, veterans of the IWW strikes."[13] The first Libertarian League meetings Robert Calese attended left a striking impression on him as well. "Sam," he recalled, "looked like he combed his hair with an eggbeater. His eyeglasses were covered with paint. His teeth were rotten and he mispronounced every other word. But he made the other speakers look like junior high school students."[14] Van Ronk was impressed with the determination he saw in these older radicals and joined the group. He recalled that, "unlike the Marxists, who expected 'History' to descend like a deus ex machina and pull their chestnuts out of the fire, the anarchists knew how long the odds were, and they went about their business with a kind of go-to-hell, cheerful, existential despair."[15]

Views and Comments provided an avenue for the Libertarian League to maintain contact with scattered sympathizers throughout the United States and with more developed syndicalist organizations in Europe. However, its circulation remained tiny, topping out at just over three hundred subscribers, "many of them in American colleges and universities."[16] Russell Blackwell and Sam Dolgoff took brief lecture tours through the Northeast and Midwest in an attempt to develop league chapters in other cities. In May 1959 the organization held its first and only conference in Youngstown, Ohio.

Anarchists from Cleveland, Detroit, and Milwaukee attended, but the assembled group acknowledged that not enough energy existed to establish regularly functioning chapters outside New York, much less a nationally coordinated organization.[17] Still, a number of individuals living outside New York City, such as the poet Robert Duncan, counted themselves as members. With such limited capacity, the only organizing campaign the Libertarian League initiated was an attempt to raise international publicity on behalf of members of the Confederación Nacional de Trabajadores threatened with execution by the Franco regime in Spain.[18]

While the league maintained a distinct organizational existence, members expressed an affinity for and willingness to collaborate with the anarchist pacifist and radical pacifist groups based in New York. In June 1955, Dorothy Day and Ammon Hennacy of the Catholic Worker, Muste and Rustin of the FOR and WRL, and Judith Malina of the Living Theatre, were arrested with others for deliberately refusing to take cover during a public air raid drill as symbolic resistance to the absurdities of Cold War social conditioning. The following issue of *Views and Comments* carried a front-page article lauding "our pacifist friends" for their protest against the "authoritarianism, control, and militarism" that marked the city's Civil Defense campaigns.[19] (Day and collaborators repeated the Civil Defense demonstrations each year until the early 1960s.)[20]

The Libertarian League also welcomed the launch of *Liberation* in early 1956. "On final objectives and basic attitudes we find ourselves in substantial agreement with these comrades," wrote an anonymous member. The league's principle objection was to *Liberation*'s insistence on the superiority of non-violent tactics in all situations. Still, the reviewer acknowledged, "We will agree with our anarcho-pacifist comrades that all possibilities of non-violent resistance must be explored first."[21] Comments such as these indicate the extent to which *Liberation,* in its early years, was acknowledged as a contribution to the anarchist movement in a period of severely diminished activity.

Holding to the tenets of anarcho-syndicalism, league members assumed that political change would arise through a radicalized labor movement. Yet the early rumblings of a more overt struggle against racism in the Deep South elicited the respect the anarchists reserved for individuals willing to take exemplary, self-sacrificing action. An unsigned October 1955 *Views and Comments* editorial, for example, denounced the exoneration of the white men accused of murdering the black adolescent Emmett Till (the men soon admitted to the crime) and honored the black men who testified against them despite threats to their own safety. "We salute their heroism even while we tremble for their lives," proclaimed the league.[22] In the eyes of league members, such heroism contrasted markedly with the behavior of the American labor movement.

The Dolgoffs and Blackwell launched their group the same year that the American Federation of Labor merged with its former rival, the Congress of Industrial Organizations, to form the joint AFL-CIO. Union density had peaked immediately after World War II, with nearly one in three employed Americans belonging to a union. With international competition minimized by the wartime destruction of rival industrial stock, profits for American corporations soared. The Keynesian theory driving policy in Washington suggested that unions could be a stabilizing force in the economy, assuming they were limited to acting within certain bounds. The 1947 Taft-Hartley Act had tamped down many of the rights extended to labor unions in the 1930s and banned communists from holding elected leadership positions, leading to a purge of radicals.[23]

The Libertarian League extended the traditional anarchist critique of liberal unions to address this new era. As Dolgoff argued in a 1958 pamphlet, the accommodationist "business unionism" of the 1950s might lead to better compensation for workers, but it did so at the price of withdrawing labors' moral critique of capitalist property relations and quashing the activity of rank-and-file members in favor of the unions' paid staff. Where others saw a heyday for American labor, the league saw a movement lured into a disarming trap and largely oblivious of its own fate.[24]

Kathy Ferguson has argued that U.S. anarchists placed little stock in African Americans as agents for change in the early twentieth century because their demands and forms of action did not comport with anarchist notions of radicalism or reach the heights of militancy characteristic of dynamiters and IWW unionists.[25] In the 1950s, however, with labor mollified and black Americans boldly experimenting with new strategies, anarchists of various stripes looked for ways to promote and contribute to their efforts.

Between 1955 and 1965, *Liberation* and *Views and Comments* devoted hundreds of pages to analyzing these movements. Though both periodicals promoted nonstatist and direct action strategies, they differed significantly in depth of analysis, tone, and the stature of the writers they were able to attract.

By examining what these periodicals had to say about four flashpoints that shaped the course of the Black Freedom Movement in the years between 1955 and 1964—namely, the Montgomery bus boycott, the Little Rock Nine crisis, Robert F. Williams' armed self-defense, and the growth of the Student Nonviolent Coordinating Committee—we can better understand how anarchist ideas and the groups of activists struggling to overcome white supremacy mutually influenced one another.

ANARCHIST VIEWS OF CIVIL RIGHTS FLASHPOINTS

Despite decades of earlier struggles that made possible the confrontations of the 1950s, the 1955–1956 boycott of the segregated city bus system in Montgomery, Alabama, is often seen as marking the beginning of a new and heroic phase of the Black Freedom Movement in the United States.[26] As is widely known, on December 1, 1955, the civil rights activist Rosa Parks refused to follow segregationist seating policies on a city bus in Montgomery, Alabama, with the intention of launching a campaign of resistance to the broader Jim Crow social order. When Parks was arrested for her defiance of the ordinance, local African American organizers and ministers launched a protest campaign centered on a boycott of the bus system by the African American community. The campaign lasted for more than a year and resulted in hundreds of arrests and many acts of violence against participants. By the time it was over, the boycott had succeeded in desegregating public facilities and services in Montgomery and in making the campaign's most compelling spokesperson, Martin Luther King Jr., a figure of national and international renown.[27]

Views and Comments enthusiastically endorsed the Montgomery desegregation movement. The boycott not only advanced the struggle for equality, but also confirmed the convictions of Libertarian League members about how social transformation could and should occur. The campaign in Montgomery, one member wrote, "shows the power of direct mass action and possibilities which go far beyond the channels of legalistic action. It shows that the people themselves are fully capable of initiating, organizing and coordinating complex social functions by free agreement, not only without but even against the opposition of the state."[28]

While the Libertarian League lent verbal support to the fight in Alabama, anarchist pacifists contributed to the bus boycott in a more direct way. As the campaign heated up, the WRL dispatched Bayard Rustin to Montgomery to help the local leaders strategize. Rustin placed the knowledge he had accumulated from twenty years of nonviolent struggle, much of which he had developed collaboratively with anarchist pacifists such as Dellinger, at the disposal of the ministers organizing the boycott. King's own training made him receptive to such suggestions. The young minister had first learned of Gandhi and his innovative anticolonial campaigns from lectures delivered by A. J. Muste and Howard University president Mordecai Johnson at Crozer Seminary in 1949 and 1950. As a seminarian, King also imbibed personalist interpretations of Christian gospel similar to those pervading Catholic Worker practice.[29] Beginning with the Montgomery campaign, Rustin helped King translate Gandhian principles into a strategic plan of civil disobedience geared to the conditions of the American South. After returning to New York, historian James Farrell recounts, "Rustin consulted King by telephone and maintained King's connections with pacifists like A. J. Muste and David Dellinger."[30]

Rustin might have never advised King and other southern organizers had it not been for New York's anarchist pacifists and the network of organizations they established after World War II. In January 1953, Rustin had been arrested in Pasadena, California, when he was caught having sex with two other men in the back seat of a car. At the time, he was employed as a field secretary for the FOR while continuing to serve on the executive committee of the WRL. Fearing fallout from the revelation that its most prominent staff person was gay, FOR secretary A. J. Muste threatened to fire Rustin if he did not immediately tender his resignation. Rustin did so and, without prompting, also wrote a letter of resignation from the WRL.[31] In 1953, however, the anarchist conscientious objector Roy Finch served as chairman of the WRL (and coeditor of *Liberation*), while nonviolent revolutionaries, including the anarchists Dellinger, Ralph DiGia, Dwight MacDonald, and Igal Roodenko, constituted a majority of the organization's executive committee, following their 1947 takeover of the organization.

Since the mid-1940s the broader anarchist pacifist milieu had functioned as a relatively safe haven for gay and bisexual men such as Robert Duncan and Paul Goodman. The anarchist press advocated greater sexual freedom, as journals such as *Mother Earth* had done before the First World War.[32] Dellinger's younger brother had recently been murdered after making a pass at another man. Evidence gathered by biographer Andrew Hunt suggests that Dellinger, too, had engaged in relationships with men and had been charged with a "sexual misdemeanor" similar to Rustin's in 1951.[33] Not surprisingly, then, the WRL refused to accept Rustin's resignation. Instead, the executive committee supported Finch's decision to hire Rustin as the WRL's full-time program director.[34] In this way, anarchists promoted to a position of leadership a man who would become one of the most important figures in the civil rights movement at precisely the time other veteran organizers were ready to drum him out of politics owing to his sexuality. Their fund-raising efforts (along with those of the WRL's nonanarchist members) paid for Rustin's trips to Alabama, which in turn established a link to the New York–centered radical pacifist community.

Rustin also served as a direct link between the Montgomery movement and *Liberation* magazine. The second issue, released in April 1956, opened with an account of the ongoing conflict in Montgomery signed by King, which announced the nonviolent basis of the campaign. The article concluded with a personalist declaration that fully accorded with midcentury anarchism: "We must not try to defend our position by methods that contradict the aim of brotherhood. . . . We do not wish to triumph over the white community. That would only result in transferring those now on the bottom to the top. But, if we can live up to non-violence in thought and deed, there will emerge an interracial society based on freedom for all."[35] It was later revealed that Rustin had ghostwritten the essay, indicating the extent to which King relied on Rustin.[36]

In these ways, the anarchist ideas of Kropotkin, Tolstoy, and De Ligt filtered down—via Gandhi, Christian personalism, and anarchist pacifist advisors—to the leadership circles of the early civil rights movement. There, anarchist tenets such as the equal liberty of all people, the importance and validity of individual resistance to social evil, and direct action by the oppressed became mixed with the social justice traditions of liberalism, the African American church, black nationalism, and the below-the-radar contributions of communist activists.[37]

In contrast to *Liberation, Views and Comments* never gained the clout to solicit contributions from central figures of the Black Freedom Movement. Despite their opposition to white supremacy, members of the Libertarian League had little firsthand knowledge of conditions in the U.S. South or previous experience working with civil rights groups in New York City. Following a pattern established by early generations of anarchists, league members appear to have never ventured across the Mason-Dixon line during speaking tours. And though it convened only six miles south of Harlem, the "cultural capital of black America" and a hub of black radical politics, the league remained a preserve of European immigrants and white Americans, despite the cordial relationships members developed with figures such as Rustin and with black labor organizers.[38]

In September 1957, segregationists organized to prevent the integration of Little Rock Central High School. Crowds of white citizens threatened and spat on black students trying to enroll, while Arkansas governor Orval Faubus mustered the state National Guard to block their entry. After some equivocation, President Dwight Eisenhower ordered federal troops to Arkansas to escort and ensure the safety of nine African American teenagers as they attended classes. Weighing in on the Arkansas crisis, the league asserted that Little Rock would henceforward serve as "the symbol of the shame of the United States." However, the league criticized Eisenhower's decision to deploy the army, claiming it set "an extremely dangerous precedent" for federal intervention in labor disputes and should be considered a "step toward complete state control—toward fascism."[39] After all, an anonymous writer pointed out, Eisenhower defended his decision as a means of upholding federal authority, not as a means of pursuing integration. Since the league also saw Faubus's tactics as "fascist," however, it condemned both politicians. The certainty with which members denounced both the "Arkansas racists" and Eisenhower's intervention stemmed from core beliefs that shaped their interpretation of the crisis. They wrote,

> The racists are effectively hiding the real enemies of the people, their economic exploiters and the political lackeys of these exploiters in both the State and Federal governments. "Divide and Conquer" has always been the slogan of our overlords, and the situation in Little Rock was manufactured and is being skillfully used by them for their own ends.[40]

Statements such as this indicate that in 1957 the league held to an economistic perspective, which saw class relations as determinant of inequality and social conflict as a whole. From this angle, capitalist exploitation was the true form of injustice, and white working people in Arkansas had been tricked by the ruling class into expressing racism against workers of color.[41] The Libertarian League supported integration but believed there was only one antiauthoritarian way to achieve it: "The only cure for the problem of race discrimination is making [the people] see that all who are economically exploited should unite firmly in their struggle against their common enemies. This can best be effected through militant unionism. The color bar falls on the picket line."[42] Unionism, in this view, was a tactic much preferable to federal intervention, which, the league pointed out, tended to unite moderate whites against civil rights efforts. Yet there was a hitch. "When we say unionism," the league clarified, "we mean real, militant, democratic unionism, which is the very antithesis of the shameful racketeering and low 'Politicking' of those who dictate to the AFL-CIO."[43] Since the anarcho-syndicalists viewed the AFL-CIO as hopelessly conservative, their position effectively meant that black freedom would have to await the reconstitution of the labor movement on new, radical footings—something even they admitted was not likely in the near future.

Instead of issuing a definitive position, the editors of *Liberation* published a forum exploring the dilemmas raised by the Little Rock conflict, in which they included contributions from a spokesperson for the NAACP, a reporter beaten by the mob during the standoff, the novelist Lillian Smith, and the anarchists David Wieck and Paul Goodman. Wieck's essay shared points of commonality with the Libertarian League's position but also diverged in ways indicating differences both ideological and temperamental between the syndicalists and pacifists. Wieck admitted that as the conflict unfolded, he favored Eisenhower's deployment of troops, despite the pacifist and "libertarian, anti-state philosophy" that he held. "One branch of government was suppressing a mob incited by another branch of government; the soldiers were giving the adolescents the chance, within the school, to discover their way to each other," he rationalized.

However, Wieck recognized that the use of troops set a bad precedent for the growing civil rights movement. First, he noted, "if the Federal government is, in an objective sense, a kind of ally to the struggle against racism, it is the most uncertain kind of ally: not from conviction but from the pressure of an immediate situation (especially as bears on the 'prestige abroad')."[44] Since Eisenhower's support for integration was driven by a variety of political calculations, the movement could not predict when he would seek compromise or withdraw from the conflict entirely. Better, then, to depend on the actions of those motivated by their deeply held antiracist convictions. Wieck also argued that use of the military allowed southern whites to avoid resolving the moral dilemma of their own racism. Like Gandhi and King, he believed that in addition to its impact on the oppressed, the psychology of domination "maimed" the personality and degraded the humanity of the oppressor, so methods that forced a conscious reckoning, rather than merely coerced people, would be more transformative. The question, then, was how antisegregationist forces, especially whites, might be induced to take "responsibility."[45]

In contrast to the Libertarian League, Wieck explained that he did not feel entitled to prescribe concrete alternative tactics, "if only because I am a 'white' northerner, whose relationship to the case is emotional rather than personal, and who cannot expect to know what is the exactly appropriate act in the given circumstances." Wieck's position was more modest and less doctrinaire than the league's. He recognized the limits of his knowledge about the particular social conditions present in Arkansas and resisted the temptation of the politically savvy outsider to attempt to impose enlightened leadership from afar. Instead of declaring that the use of troops to promote integration was wrong, as an ideological absolute, he explained why a local, popular strategy would have been *preferable.*

The conflict in Arkansas continued despite the forced integration of Little Rock Central High School. Governor Faubus was reelected by a wide margin, and segregationist forces organized a statewide effort to remove white students from public schools and install them in segregated private schools. In September 1958, Wieck and fellow pacifist Al Uhrie were appointed by Peacemakers to travel to Arkansas so that northern activists might learn more about the situation. In two additional articles for *Liberation* based on the trip, Wieck provided a more incisive analysis of racial dynamics than the Libertarian League's class-struggle assumptions made possible. He found that resistance to integration was led at the political level by the class of rural planters in eastern Arkansas. In the city, however, its most impassioned opponents were working-class whites. He suspected that wealthy white residents felt secure in their superiority and might be willing to accept gradual desegregation. "For lower-class whites, however, the existence of Negroes is a very ambiguous fact; their entrance into 'white schools' raises the possibility that individual Negroes (or the whole body of Negro students) will excel [beyond] one's own child, and thereby demonstrate that one is inferior to the group whose inferiority is so emphatically asserted."[46] Developing new theory grounded in the analysis of local conditions, Wieck pointed to psychological factors that might encourage racist attitudes and behaviors among white workers distinct from those of the upper class. His perspective attributed more agency to working-class whites than the league's did, even if, ironically, it was the agency to discriminate.

As campaigns developed in cities throughout the country, anarchist pacifists and anarcho-syndicalists alike found ways to participate.[47] Jim Peck, who had been Wieck's cellmate during World War II, edited CORE's house publication, *The CORElator,* as well as the WRL newsletter without compensation. Members of the Libertarian Youth Club organized by the Libertarian League participated in the Second Youth March for Integration held in Washington, D.C., in October 1958. Members also participated in a successful sit-in against segregated apartment complexes, organized by CORE.[48]

In an article published in the April 1959 issue of *Views and Comments,* a league member noted, "The Negroes and their organizations have displayed magnificent discipline and excessive restraint in the recent months of struggle. One cannot help but wonder at what point the policy of non-violent resistance practiced so far in Alabama will have to be reinforced by realistic actions of self-defense."[49] Before a month was up, one of the early conflicts in the black freedom struggle between nonviolence and armed self-defense exploded into public consciousness. In May, a Monroe, North Carolina, jury acquitted a white man who had very clearly assaulted a black women. In response, Robert F. Williams, the independent-minded head of the local NAACP branch and a former U.S. Marine, publicly declared that without the protection of the courts, blacks would have to "meet violence with violence."[50] When the local branch of the Ku Klux Klan attacked the house of the Monroe NAACP's vice president, Williams and his followers returned fire, driving them away.

Moderate civil rights leaders and a variety of pacifists rebuked Williams for the fear his words and action stirred among segregationists and federal officials; NAACP headquarters suspended him from his position. The league, however, came out squarely in favor of Williams. The February 1960 issue of *Views and Comments* reprinted an article from Williams's newsletter, *The Crusader,* and noted, "We recommend this publication to all those interested in following the struggles of the militants among the Negro people, those among them who, unwilling to limit their struggle to prayers, petitions, and pacifist action, propose instead a policy of militant direct action, with an insistence on the elementary right of self-defense by all means available."[51] If, for Wieck, nonviolent tactics promised some manner of redemption, league members seem to have shared with Malcolm X and Frantz Fanon a belief that violence enacted by oppressed individuals carried its own benefits.[52]

The editors of *Liberation* deemed the issues raised by the Williams controversy worthy of careful ethical consideration. The magazine ran a long article by Williams, "Can Negroes Afford to Be Pacifists?" which made a powerful case for armed self-defense. "Nonviolence is a very potent weapon when the opponent is civilized, but nonviolence is no match or repellent for a sadist," Williams cautioned. While passive resistance was a useful tool in "gaining concessions from oppressors," he argued that if Mack Parker, a black man recently murdered by white racists, "had had an automatic shotgun at his disposal, he could have served as a great deterrent against lynching." Williams concluded by forthrightly criticizing "cringing Negro ministers" and NAACP lawyers, whom he viewed as overreliant on the government to make changes and protect black citizens. While legal work had its place, he called for the "acceptance of diverse tactics."[53]

Liberation provided the NAACP with space to present its position on the Williams controversy and called upon King to reiterate the moral and tactical benefits of nonviolence. David Dellinger, however, took a different tack in an editorial titled "Are Pacifists Willing to Be Negroes?" The vigilante violence faced by the black citizens of Monroe tested the stalwart pacifist's moral commitments. Dellinger noted that the movement had hit a wall of opposition and was nearly at a standstill. With violence against African Americans unabated, Dellinger claimed it would be "arrogant" for white pacifists to criticize men like Williams for practicing armed self-defense:

> Gandhi once said that although nonviolence is the best method of resistance to evil, it is better for persons who have not yet attained the capacity for nonviolence to resist violently than not to resist at all. Since we have failed to reach the level of effective resistance, we can hardly condemn those who have not embraced nonviolence.

To Dellinger's mind, white pacifists had no room to criticize others' responses to injustice when they were not themselves doing all that they could to end it. He encouraged them to envision themselves in the position of southern African Americans, and to act as they would in that situation. Yet Dellinger also took a sly anarchist jab at Williams's eagerness to counterpose armed self-defense to the "cringing" strategy of those who looked to the state to secure civil rights. Dellinger reminded readers, "The power of the police, as the power of the F.B.I., the courts, and the Federal government, is rooted in violence. The fact that the violence does not always come into bloody play does not alter the fact that the power of the government is not the integrating power of love but the disintegrating power of guns and prisons."[54] The alternative to both types of violence, Dellinger reiterated, was that of the brave, imaginative, and active practice of nonviolence that had been effectively arrayed against the mob and state violence in Montgomery.

THE STUDENT NONVIOLENT COORDINATING COMMITTEE AND ANARCHIST ORGANIZATIONAL MODELS

In 1960 African American youth took the sit-in desegregation tactic, first developed by CORE in the 1940s, to new locales and new extremes. The student sit-in movement began as a local action when four black college students asked for service and refused to move from the segregated lunch counter of a Greensboro, North Carolina, Woolworth's department store in February. Within days, students across the southern states began to emulate the action with hastily planned lunch-counter sit-ins of their own. By June an estimated fifty thousand students had joined the fray in more than a hundred cities across South Carolina, Tennessee, Maryland, Virginia, Mississippi, and other states.[55] The sit-in movement was exactly the type of activity many anarchists and radical pacifists, as well as a subset of civil rights organizers, had been longing for since the victory in Montgomery. In May 1960, the Libertarian League explained that the surge of activity "shows how a genuine people's movement arose spontaneously, produced its own organization, devised its own tactics and inspired everyone to participate creatively and valiantly in a common cause." Instead of counseling reliance on a great leader, "it arouses people from apathy and restores their belief in their own power."[56]

In April, the experienced antiracist organizer Ella Baker arranged a meeting of students who had participated in the sit-ins with the hopes of launching an organization that could coordinate and sustain their activism. Baker's sense of urgency arose from an understanding of the process of social change that shared much in common with that held by anarchists.[57] From decades of experience working in black political organizations, Baker felt that reliance on the highly educated lawyers of the NAACP and on charismatic preachers like Martin Luther King Jr. reduced poor and working-class black people's confidence in themselves and their own power. Since the civil rights movement was intended to combat the sense of dependency and powerlessness that southern African Americans felt in relation to the white power structure, Baker found it perverse that the movement itself should suggest they depend on "saviors" of one sort or another. It was her bedrock belief that "strong people don't need strong leaders."[58]

Baker helped the student sit-in leaders develop a political organization, the Student Nonviolent Coordinating Committee (SNCC), which distinguished itself from existing civil rights formations by its dedication to the use of nonviolent direct action and through its efforts to invent egalitarian forms of organization, participatory decision-making processes, and what Baker termed "group-centered leadership." Historian James Farrell claims, "SNCC's own organization followed a communitarian anarchist model." Clayborne Carson likewise notes that the student activists "strongly opposed any hierarchy of authority such as existed in other civil rights organizations."[59] Instead of carrying out a program designed by a few leaders, SNCC members collectively engaged in long discussions in which those not used to speaking up were supported and gently urged to participate alongside the more loquacious. On all major questions, the organization attempted to reach consensus—that is, make plans that all participants could agree upon. This was a technique introduced by participants such as James Lawson, who were affiliated with CORE and influenced by Peacemakers.[60]

Although developing strategy by consensus was a time-consuming and often frustrating process, sociologist Francesca Polletta has argued that by drawing in more people, it built the leadership capacities of those involved.[61] This process was fundamental to Baker's understanding of social change. She believed that "instead of the leader as a person who was supposed to be a magic man, you could develop individuals who were bound together by a concept that benefitted the larger number of individuals and provided an opportunity for them to grow into being responsible for carrying out a program."[62] Baker's ideas were strikingly similar to those elaborated by Dellinger in the course of his imprisonment during World War II. In 1945 he had argued that staff positions in revolutionary organizations should be rotating rather than permanent. This would help solve "some of the problems of a centralized 'leadership' that tends to become sterile, self-perpetuating and conservative. . . . Not only would their effectiveness be increased, but others would be developed who are now kept undeveloped or are alienated."[63]

During its first year, SNCC members built up a network of contacts and carried out additional sit-ins to desegregate restaurants and other public facilities. Inspired by their activity, CORE launched a series of "Freedom Rides" in April 1961 modeled on the 1947 Journey of Reconciliation. They, too, were violently attacked as they traveled through Mississippi and Alabama. Jim Peck, the only Freedom Rider who had participated in the 1947 actions, was beaten nearly to death by Klansmen while FBI agents and police silently looked on.

After the Freedom Rides, SNCC members devoted themselves to a voter registration campaign. In their patient organizing work, members sought ways to extend the process of perpetual leadership development beyond the staff to the people they worked with in voter registration efforts. SNCC developed in its day-to-day organizing work an ideal of participatory democracy that demanded ordinary people be able to make the decisions that affect their lives. Bob Moses, a high school teacher from New York who was recruited for the southern movement by Rustin and mentored by Baker, exemplified and promoted this approach within SNCC.[64] Moses remarked about SNCC's organizing process: "How are you going to, as early as possible, move in the direction of [local] people taking ownership? You get into what has come to be called participatory democracy . . . in which the people who are meeting really get more and more of a feeling that this is [their] meeting."[65] This, Moses hoped, would be a step toward people taking ownership of the various institutions shaping their daily lives. For Moses, as for Baker, freedom was not to be found only in policy changes, important as those were, but was also found in the perceptions of ordinary people that they were competent enough to direct their own lives. This emphasis attracted not only the anarchist pacifists but also the anarcho-syndicalists to SNCC in its early years.

By 1963, the Libertarian League had softened its line regarding the institutional sources of progress. An unsigned article, later claimed by league member David Sachs, acknowledged, "The church, which has been for years the Negro's major social gathering place, naturally was to become, with the changing times, a lever for social change. As much as we may wish its replacement in this role by the union hall, it must be considered an important factor in today's civil rights outlook."[66] Nevertheless, Sachs went on to say, "The civil rights ministers, despite their long fiery speeches favoring direct action, too often have carried the preacher-preached relationship into the human rights movement." Sachs warned that "as long as the intra-organizational tendencies toward control-from-above are not persistently counterbalanced by libertarian tendencies, there is a great potential danger of bureaucratic ossification and the sell-outs and stagnation this implies." Rather than continuing to insist on a single *type* of organization (labor unions), the league, as seen here, began to support of a set of *principles* of organization consistent with the anarchist tradition.

By the summer of 1964 the league had moved even further in its thinking about the sources of progressive change. In a short article titled "Bigots," it denounced the "shameful" tradition of racial discrimination within the U.S. labor movement. Pointing to a recent instance in which a local of the Plumber's Union refused to accept an African American and three Puerto Rican plumbers, the league editorialized, "Only the magnificent, around-the-clock demonstrations of civil rights organizations FORCED the union to consider the applications of the four men."[67] This incident raised "disturbing" questions that cut to the quick of some of the members' political assumptions. "Why did not the rank and file protest this outrageous discrimination?

Can all the blame be placed exclusively against the officials of the union?" asked the article. The answer, painfully, was *no*. "The sad fact is that the officials, in this instance, echoed the racist sentiments of the members."

Aspects of league members' economistic thinking were breaking down. Dolgoff and other anarchists had long held that conservative union policies stemmed from the misleadership of officials compromised by their positions of power. In contrast, they believed rank-and-file workers would instinctually fight to overturn inequality if their energies were not diverted.[68] Yet in "Bigots," the league admitted that workers were themselves at least partly responsible for divisive racism within the unions. "In exposing these social sores," they wrote, "the civil rights demonstrators are performing a great service towards the moral regeneration of the unions."[69] Whereas in 1957 the league had believed unions would defeat segregation, by 1964 they could admit that civil rights demonstrators might save the labor movement, and hence the class struggle, from a hopeless conservatism.

The strategic and organizational alignment between SNCC and the anarchists, however, would be short lived, as events in the summer and fall of 1964 led SNCC to sharply change course. The organization brought hundreds of white and black college students to the South in an all-out voter registration push known as Mississippi Freedom Summer. The initiative met with intense backlash, including the murder of three volunteers. SNCC organized a Mississippi Freedom Democratic Party that vied to replace the state's official, white-only, delegation to the party's national convention, but was rebuffed by President Lyndon Johnson.

The continuously virulent opposition of white citizens and politicians, the intergroup difficulties engendered by the influx of new volunteers, and the influence cast by writers such as Malcolm X and Frantz Fanon, led some SNCC organizers to centralize leadership, renounce nonviolence, and dismiss white staff and volunteers, with the aim of becoming a revolutionary nationalist organization. These changes were designed as an explicit departure from the priorities of the group's earlier years. The new leadership valued the perceived advantages of a disciplined programmatic focus and strategic nimbleness derived from centralized leadership over the grounding and developmental benefits of the nonhierarchical, participatory organizational model. Cleveland Sellers, for example, denounced the decentralist faction, which included Moses, as "philosophers, existentialists, anarchists, floaters and freedom-high niggers." His centralist faction, he acknowledged, was urging a departure from SNCC's "freewheeling, anarchistic origins."[70]

The Libertarian League did not endure long enough to comment on these developments, having dissolved in the summer of 1965. However, league members would likely have found the Marxism and the nationalism of the final years of SNCC disturbing. Importantly, however, many younger anarchists who gained political consciousness in the early 1960s were inspired and influenced by African American militants who called for "Black Power." As we will see in chapter 8, that influence led them to embrace tactics and racial politics quite different from those advanced by SNCC during its first five years.

NATIONAL LIBERATION

The politics of Black Power that SNCC leaders such as Stokely Carmichael, James Forman, and Cleveland Sellers began to articulate in 1964 drew sustenance from the struggles of people of color in Africa, Asia, and Latin America to achieve independence from European and American colonial governments. Like many African American militants, U.S. anarchists eagerly monitored and analyzed the unfolding of national liberation movements during the 1950s and early 1960s. Anarchists had opposed colonialism since the movements' inception in the 1860s. Indeed, Benedict Anderson argues that in the final two decades of the nineteenth century, anarchism "was the dominant element in the self-consciously internationalist radical Left," a "gravitational force" linking "militant nationalisms on opposite sides of the planet."[71] Yet anarchists never developed a systematic account of how power functions at the international scale. Moreover, the actual processes by which groups of people overturned colonial domination frequently clashed with anarchist notions of freedom and how change should come about. As advocates of local, direct political decision-making, anarchists universally opposed the control of people by a faraway state apparatus. However, successful movements against colonial domination had, to date, established new nation-states that tended to mirror the Western political models anarchists stridently rejected. Anarchists, then, looked for ways to abet anticolonial struggles, but on their own terms and reserving the right to criticize national liberation movements should they achieve power. Both *Liberation* and the Libertarian League struggled to strike the right note regarding anti-imperialist struggles in the 1950s and early 1960s.

Decolonization had been central to the political vision of the radical pacifists grouped around *Liberation* magazine ever since Gandhi had elaborated his nonviolent strategy and philosophy as a means of throwing off British colonialism in India. The editors were aware, however, that not all anti-imperialist movements would follow the Mahatma's lead, and that such movements would be insufficient, in themselves, to establish enviable social orders. "Seizure of the war-making and repressive machinery of the State," they wrote in the publication's debut editorial, "cannot be a step toward transforming society into a free and humanly satisfying pattern."[72] The magazine, therefore, published essays by anticolonial leaders that emphasized indigenous egalitarian traditions and questioned the tendency to mimic Western social structures. The magazine's premier issue, for example, included an essay by Gandhi disciple Vinoba Bhave, who argued, in opposition to the emerging postcolonial state, for common ownership of land and the decentralization of political power to the village level.[73]

As in the case of domestic antiracist struggles, the Libertarian League took a more programmatic approach to the issue than did *Liberation,* publishing an official position on imperialism and colonialism in *Views and Comments.* Unsurprisingly, the group unequivocally endorsed movements against "imperialism." But it went on to say,

> Once the colonial countries are free from foreign domination, however, our position should change, for independence from foreign control is meaningless to the people unless they have economic independence also. Replacing a colonial government with a native government does not accomplish anything of real value for the people. A native government can be—and usually is—just as oppressive as that of a foreign imperialist power.... Partial struggles must be supported, with libertarian participation always aimed at carrying a "national" revolution into more progressive social stages; if possible, into a libertarian revolution.[74]

The organization's members understood colonialism primarily as a form of political and economic domination designed to extract wealth from the colonized people. They paid less attention to the changes in cultural practices, sexual norms, and belief structures demanded by imperial officials and settlers who justified their domination by claiming it as an attempt to civilize racially inferior people. This could lead to an arrogant-sounding undervaluation of the significance of decolonization in everyday life.

Yet, the league was clear-eyed in declaring that "independence" did not prevent the rise of authoritarian forms of government or obviate the pressures of international capital markets.[75] Such warnings were prescient, given the history of dictatorship and violence that has plagued many postcolonial states since the late 1950s.[76] Their perspective had the advantage of acknowledging authoritarian developments within the postcolonial states that some other sectors of the Left minimized owing to their anti-imperialist sympathies. Yet league commentary often verged on gloating that the anarchists' pessimistic assertions about statist means of struggle had come true. In the absence of antiauthoritarian movements achieving better results, this generally critical perspective likely served as a deterrent to movement-building in the United States.

These questions among third-camp radicals about how to relate to postrevolutionary states eventually sharpened into a conflict over the nature of the Cuban revolution and the ways anarchists should relate to it. On New Year's Day 1959, the July 26th Movement, an armed band of socialist revolutionaries led by Fidel Castro, succeeded in overthrowing the dictatorship of Fulgencio Batista. Batista had deep ties to U.S. businessmen and organized crime families, as well as military support from the U.S. government.

After traveling throughout Cuba for two weeks in the fall of 1960, David Dellinger penned an article for *Liberation* sympathetic to the revolution. By the time of his trip, U.S. officials and major media outlets regularly claimed Cuban society was being made over in the style of Soviet-bloc nations. Dellinger, however, saw marked improvements in the lives of rural Cubans under government-run agricultural co-operatives and remarked, "I was convinced that there is no present evidence of overweening state control, thought control, or suppression of meaningful freedom." Dellinger criticized the regime for executing opponents and urged it to begin preparing for elections. Overall, however, he saw the Cuban experiment as a "humanistic" revolution distinct from either pole of the Cold War.[77]

The article was hailed by many on the anti-Stalinist Left—the *New Left Review* and the *Catholic Worker* reprinted it, for example. However, members of the Libertarian League and *Liberation* editor Roy Finch found much to fault in it. In the early months of 1961, approximately two dozen Cuban anarchists left the island and resettled in Miami and New York, claiming they would have been jailed, or worse, for their objections to Castro's government had they remained. In February, Finch participated in an interview with twelve of the Cubans, facilitated by the league's Russell Blackwell, and published part of the dialogue in the March issue of *Liberation*. The exiles claimed nearly all of the country's unions had been taken over by communists, anarchists had been expelled, and "real wages" had decreased. The exiles approved of Castro being deposed, even by conservative forces. Based on this information, Finch and members of the league concluded that the "Cuban Revolution has all but been stolen from the Cuban people."[78]

The exchange brought a flurry of letters from anarchist readers of *Liberation*. Jim Peck, Dachine Rainer, and former Dil Pickle Club proprietor Jack Jones lined up with Finch. In a rejoinder, Dellinger provided evidence contradicting many of the claims made by the Cuban Libertarians. Although he reiterated his concerns about violations of civil rights by the new regime, he felt that by denouncing the revolution alongside right-wing "counterrevolutionists" they only "helped their predictions that Cuba was moving towards the Communist camp become a self-fulfilling prophecy."[79] In May, Roy Finch resigned as a coeditor of *Liberation*. In a parting statement, he noted that *Liberation* had begun with a dedication to third-camp politics and a clear denunciation of dictatorship of any kind. Whether beneficent or not, Castro was a dictator, and by the spring of 1961 it was clear that he would not remain neutral in the Cold War. Since four out of five editors supported the Cuban government, Finch felt he had to resign to remain true to his principles.[80]

While the exiles and members of the league stewed, Dellinger was invited to the 1964 May Day celebration in Cuba. Upon his return *Liberation* published another favorable article and sponsored a speaking event in which its founding editor was to share his experiences and perspective. Viewing his continued support of the Castro regime as a betrayal of anarchist principles, the Libertarian League picketed the event and distributed a leaflet calling vaguely for "support" of the Cuban people against domination by either of the Cold War blocs. Sam Dolgoff recalls, "I, and a few other comrades, denounced him as a liar and a turncoat. I challenged him to debate the issue anywhere, anytime, at our expense."[81] The demonstration and criticism by former allies hurt and dispirited Dellinger. In an October 1964 letter to David Wieck, Dellinger sarcastically snipped, "I was sorry to miss you and Diva this summer although I understand that you and all true anarchists were at a conference, which I might have attended if I had been qualified."[82] Wieck responded to his old friend that he found "the Blackwell-Libertarian League thing . . . monstrous," but that he harbored his own criticisms of Dellinger's position on Cuba.[83]

In a 1965 essay published in *Liberation*, Wieck argued that it was untenable to claim, as the Libertarian League had, that the Cuban regime was totalitarian and that conditions were worse for the majority of its citizens than they had been under Batista. Yet it was also wrong to describe the society as free and socialist, as Dellinger had done. Wieck believed "the Cuban state presents the unusual phenomenon of the paternalistic and generally benevolent rule of a group of individuals." Wealth was being redistributed, but Wieck saw little indication of the growth of "initiative from below, the delegation of responsibility by the working people themselves, and control over the persons to whom responsibility was dedicated." The idea that authority should rest with the people as a whole, he maintained, was a defining principle not only of anarchism but also of the broader socialist tradition from which it had sprung. Wieck noted that the positions taken by tiny libertarian socialist formations in the United States would have little impact on Cuba. The point, rather, was to maintain a clear vision of the type of world that radicals were fighting for, so they would not misdirect their own efforts while working to achieve that vision.[84] Writing to Finch shortly after the article was published, Wieck added, "I think it's rather important to define the Cuban situation accurately because there are analogies between the enthusiasm for Castro and enthusiasm for the N.L.F. [National Liberation Front] in Vietnam and I expect there will be more of this."[85] He was right.

As the war in Vietnam escalated after 1965, Dellinger began advocating that Americans support the communist regimes of North Vietnam and China, while still criticizing their abuses. With the black freedom struggle entering a new phase, and the student movement growing rapidly, Dellinger was again traveling constantly and serving as a mentor to a new generation of radicals. Dellinger's tone in letters he exchanged with Wieck in the mid-1960s indicates that although he continued to view himself as an anarchist, he felt increasingly estranged from the small community that had carried the anarchist mantle since the Second World War. The personal animosities that arose in the debate over Cuba help explain why Dellinger refrained from openly declaring himself an anarchist during the height of his influence in the late 1960s.[86]

Bayard Rustin also marked a break with the anarchist pacifist milieu in these years. In 1965, Rustin famously called for the civil rights movement to move "from protest to politics," meaning, in part, a concerted effort by organizers to integrate themselves into the Democratic Party and to build influence by strategically allying with existing liberal institutions.[87] In response to Rustin's shift, David Wieck remarked privately to Dellinger:

> The thing that bothers me most about the Rustin business is that I believe that certain attitudes, a certain tone, that are customary in most all politics,

including most all radical politics, have no place in an anarchist or a pacifist movement. Anybody who seriously calls themselves a personalist, or an anarchist, or a pacifist, should have a different style of politics, and a different style of relating to people even in political and conflict situations, than other people do.[88]

Wieck's remarks underscore the extent to which midcentury anarchist pacifists viewed "personalism" and "anarchism" as congruous, if not synonymous, terms, as well as the degree to which they had considered Rustin within that fold until his move toward the center.

AFFIRMATIONS AND RECONSIDERATIONS OF ANARCHIST THEORY

Resistance to racial segregation in the federal penitentiaries helped call the midcentury anarchist pacifist movement into existence. In turn, this movement and its "third camp" radical pacifist allies influenced the strategies and organizational style of the black freedom struggles of the 1950s and 1960s. Anarchists helped invent and promote forms of nonviolent direct action against racial segregation during and after the Second World War, and they lived in multiracial intentional communities during the politically hostile years of the early Cold War. Anarchists staffed institutions such as the War Resisters League that served the movement by paying the salaries of controversial but skilled leaders, such as Bayard Rustin, and providing tactical advice and support for nonviolent campaigns in the South. They also established media outlets, notably, *Liberation* and *Views and Comments,* that promoted black freedom struggles and served as important forums in which to debate strategy, forms of leadership, and other issues of consequence to the movement. In the pages of these periodicals, in the nonviolence trainings they provided, and in other interactions, anarchists and their radical pacifist allies advocated nonstatist, mass-based, and direct-action-focused strategies in antiracist struggles. In words and in deeds, they promoted and exemplified decentralized, egalitarian, and prefigurative forms of organization that prioritized community building. The organizations and individuals that constituted the civil rights and Black Power movements drew from myriad political and religious perspectives, including liberalism, Marxism, black nationalism, Southern Baptism, and Christian personalism. Alongside these influences, the anarchist precepts of direct action, decentralized organization, and belief in the leadership capabilities of ordinary people, formed one significant, but not overriding, thread. Very rarely were these influences explicitly perceived as deriving from the anarchist tradition.

Despite the various contributions anarchists made to the Black Freedom Movement, it is likely that this movement had more of a transformative impact on U.S. anarchism than anarchists had on it. Anarchism, after all, remained a tiny, marginalized political current in the 1950s, probably claiming no more than a few hundred adherents nationwide and boasting very limited funds and institutional resources with which to promote civil rights organizing. The Black Freedom Movement, in contrast, encompassed a political upheaval carried out by millions of people. New styles of organizing and forms of organization, new examples of bravery and militancy, and new political expectations arose from the energy that it unleashed. Mass movements for national liberation in formerly colonized areas of the world also forced U.S. anarchists to reevaluate deeply held convictions.

Activists such as David Dellinger, who embraced anarchist pacifism at the beginning of the 1950s, were persuaded by the exigencies and accomplishments of these movements to adopt a more flexible set of politics by the decade's end. The anarcho-syndicalists affiliated with the Libertarian League changed in different ways. The group's early ruminations on civil rights initiatives indicated that they remained tied to theories of social change that privileged struggles over economic class. The growth and success of black freedom struggles over the course of the next ten years, however, challenged league members to begin thinking in a more multidimensional way about oppression and liberation. By 1964 they recognized that social movements based on racial identity and demands for racial justice had the potential to inspire large numbers of people to take militant action that had the potential to reconstruct fundamental social relations, including the class structure of the country. These reconsiderations of traditional anarchist perspectives were another step in the transformation of anarchist thought from a classic tradition that focused primarily (though never exclusively) on class struggle to a more contemporary form that set itself against all forms of "social domination."

The Black Freedom Movement, and especially SNCC, came to represent a new historic model of a successful *mass* movement that relied on direct action, eschewed authoritarian leaders in favor of "group-centered leadership," as Ella Baker termed it, and worked to expand the democratic control of ordinary people over the institutions that ordered their daily lives. Not since the IWW lost its mass base as a result of repression during the First World War had U.S. anarchists witnessed a movement that seemed to confirm their beliefs about the process of social change. It provided a tangible example of people making change through self-organization, mass mobilization, and direct action, with a focus on the poorest. SNCC organized primarily around racial identity rather than class identity, but it nevertheless contributed to class struggle. It fought for working-class power and economic justice through the demand for racial equality and constituted a class struggle within the race struggle, by placing the priorities of the poorest African Americans before those of the middle class.

Of significance for later generations of anarchists, SNCC was not, in its early years, an effort to "smash" the capitalist state, with the assumption that a new society would arise the day or the week after. Rather, it became an attempt to reconstitute the very idea of democracy in day-to-day life—by extending decision-making power to those previously excluded from it, and by defining democracy as all persons having a say in all the decisions that affect their lives. This vision of democracy taking place at the lowest possible level, and directly involving as many people as possible, shared much in common with the anarchist vision of popular self-rule. For these reasons, SNCC proved attractive and inspirational to the small number of anarchists active in the United States in the 1960s. More important, the example of SNCC served as an important nodal point in the transmission of horizontal styles of organizing between the traditional, labor-based anarchists of the prewar period, and the ecology- and antinuclear-focused anarchist campaigns of the end of the twentieth century. Tom Hayden, a leader of Students for a Democratic Society, would later claim that Bob Moses "created the pattern of non-leadership that affected many of us for years."[89] SNCC's influence on that organization, the women's liberation movement, and other sectors of the New Left would bode well for anarchism, in that antiauthoritarian and participatory democratic ideals would circulate widely during the 1960s and help spark, by decade's end, a renewed interest in explicit anarchist politics that still infuses movements today. SNCC's example was only one route among many by which anarchist ideas and values came to inform the mass movements of the 1960s, however. In the book's final chapter, we will see how the nonviolent-organizing tradition of anarchism both clashed and fused in a powerful alchemy with the prefigurative and dissociative tradition that developed in the San Francisco Libertarian Circle and spread throughout the country under the auspices of the Beat Generation.

EIGHT

New Left and Countercultural Anarchism, 1960–1972

Numerically, anarchism nearly became an anachronism during the 1940s and 1950s. Yet by 1971, major publishing houses were rushing the works of Kropotkin, Bakunin, and Goldman back into print. Professors issued volumes of "essential" anarchist texts, while *Village Voice* reporter Paul Berman presented *Quotations from the Anarchists,* a collection of choice invective from the likes of Errico Malatesta and the Haymarket martyrs, perhaps intended to rival the quotations of Chairman Mao.[1]

Interest in anarchism grew in tandem with the constellation of radical social movements that fundamentally altered American society during the "long 1960s."[2] Yet standard accounts of the New Left tend to downplay anarchist contributions, while scholars of twenty-first-century anarchism credit movements of the 1960s with bringing anarchism back to life.[3] More likely, a virtuous circle existed: anarchists provided theories, values, tactics, and organizational forms, which activists in the antiwar, countercultural, and feminist movements took up; in turn, these mass movements radicalized hundreds of thousands of people, a portion of whom adopted anarchism as their ideological outlook.

Journalists, scholars, and activists writing as the decade unfolded clearly recognized the contributions of anarchist thought on the growing student and antiwar movements. In 1966, *Village Voice* editor Jack Newfield explained, "The New Radicalism is pluralistic, amorphous, and multilayered. Its three political strands—anarchism, pacifism, and socialism—mingle in different proportions in different places." A 1970 volume, *"All We Are Saying . . .": The Philosophy of the New Left,* featured chapters by anarchists Murray Bookchin and Fredy Perlman. The next year, a worried Communist Party weighed in with *The New Radicalism: Anarchist or Marxist?*[4]

Later minimizations of the role of anarchism may stem from the ways it has been conceptualized. If one looks for the influence of prewar, class struggle anarchism, one will find little discernable impact. However, if one looks for traces of the thinkers and forms of anarchism that emerged in the early 1940s, as described in the previous three chapters, the influences loom large. It is also likely that anarchist impacts have been difficult to assess because they came diffusely, through many channels. No single national organization or publication consistently promoted anarchist politics throughout the decade. Instead, smaller enclaves of artists and activists rediscovered parts of the anarchist tradition and experimented with them. In contrast to the experiences of young socialists and communists coming into the movement, they encountered few movement elders attempting to impose orthodoxy.

This chapter begins to recover the specific ways anarchist ideas, goals, and methods crept or crashed into the communal storehouse of ideas animating the period's "movement of movements."[5] Anarchism came to influence the New Left through multiple transmission routes; most important were Students for a Democratic Society, the counterculture, radical pacifism, and feminist initiatives. Though each contributed unique elements, these strands of activity were never fully distinct; they came to shape one another in complex ways. Because interest in anarchism expanded so rapidly and took so many forms, the narrative becomes more telegraphic here than in previous chapters. I aim primarily to schematize these points of transmission, leaving to future studies the task of considering the ways in which anarchist ideas were incorporated, modified, and defeated when put in play alongside the other ideological tendencies—democratic socialism, Third World Marxism, cultural nationalism, feminism, and gay liberation among them—that also greatly shaped the period's radical culture and politics.

STUDENTS FOR A DEMOCRATIC SOCIETY

Postwar U.S. anarchism shaped and, in turn, was transformed by the largest campus-based organization of the 1960s. In January 1960, members of the near moribund Student League for Industrial Democracy, a holdover from the prewar social democratic Left, renamed themselves Students for a Democratic Society (SDS) and sought ways, as college students in the North, to support the black freedom struggle. The lunch-counter sit-in movement that erupted in Greensboro the following month and the Student Nonviolent Coordinating

Committee (SNCC) became major inspirations to SDS.[6] Members worked with SNCC in the summer of 1961 and absorbed political lessons from Ella Baker and Bob Moses. SDS built chapters on campuses across the Northeast and Midwest, providing an institutional vehicle for young people to join the struggle against racism and to discuss other concerns.

In June 1962, sixty members drafted the Port Huron Statement, a powerful declaration of the group's values and aims. The statement mixed a declaration of decentralist and radically democratic values with a concrete program focused on social democratic reforms, reflecting the students' attempts to synthesize ideas inspired by SNCC and *Liberation* with those promoted by the Socialist Party.[7] Though no self-identified anarchists are known to have helped draft the document, the section of the Port Huron Statement focused on values reads as if intended to contribute to the project of reworking anarchist theory that had played out over the previous twenty years.[8]

Echoing the personalist declarations of the *Catholic Worker, Liberation,* and *The Ark,* the statement explained, "We oppose the depersonalization that reduces human beings to the status of things—if anything the brutalities of the twentieth century teach that means and ends are intimately related."[9] The statement also took a nuanced position on the tension between individual freedom and social equality that has animated anarchism from the start. Feeling the burdens of mass society and demands for conformity, the assembled students called for a renewed individualism to resist consensus politics and quiescent lifestyles. They also clarified what this meant: "As the individualism we affirm is not egoism, the selflessness we affirm is not self-elimination. On the contrary, we believe in generosity of a kind that imprints one's unique individual qualities in relation to other men, and to all human activity."[10]

From this declaration of ethics, the statement proceeded to its most famous assertion: "We seek the establishment of a democracy of individual participation" in which "the individual share[s] in those social decisions determining the quality and direction of his life." The students explained that "in a participatory democracy, decision-making of basic social consequence [would] be carried on by public groupings." Because the form of such groupings was not spelled out, it was possible to imagine them as versions of workers' councils or citywide assemblies, which accorded with anarchist projections of a free society.

The authors of the Port Huron Statement went far beyond democratic socialist and Leninist calls for nationalization of industry when discussing economic vision. "Work should involve incentives worthier than money or survival," the statement insisted. "It should be educative, not stultifying; creative, not mechanical; self-directed, not manipulated, encouraging of independence, a respect for others, a sense of dignity, and a willingness to accept social responsibility."[11] This was an economic vision that rejected the ways work life in actually existing socialist economies had come to mirror that in capitalist nations and addressed the sense of alienation to which postwar anarchism had become increasingly attentive.

Making a society truly democratic, according to these criteria, required both the transformation of political processes and the extension of the principle of egalitarian self-governance into all spheres of life. Yet participatory democracy was an ambiguous concept. Paul Booth, a National Secretary of SDS later opined, "If everything could be restructured starting from the SNCC project in McComb, Mississippi, then we would have participatory democracy."[12] Greg Calvert, another SDS National Secretary, acknowledged that for SDS members, participatory democracy "probably covered a spectrum of belief from radical democrats to anarchists and anarcho-syndicalists through democratic socialists and even some social democrats."[13] Although SDS allowed communists to attend meetings and demonstrations, the group's founding philosophy rejected authoritarian government and central planning as attractive alternatives to "corporate liberalism" and imperialism. At the center of SDS's and SNCC's politics was the desire to eliminate asymmetries in decision-making power and to inculcate initiative in ordinary people—goals that all anarchists endorsed.

SDS members debated whether participatory democracy was an end goal or a practice that had to be implemented within the organization itself. Questions about how to implement it arose in the 1963 Economic Research and Action Projects (ERAP), which planted members in poor neighborhoods of northern cities with the intent of helping poor people fight for better housing conditions, work, and income support. ERAP organizers faced the same dilemmas that SNCC organizers did: they wanted to help people who had traditionally been given little decision-making power gain more of it, but they found this often required telling these people what to do. Sociologist Wini Breines notes that while these theoretical hang-ups about leadership were often paralyzing, "the instinct of wanting to encourage indigenous leaders, of wanting to be a catalyst but not a directive or manipulative leader, sprang from a rejection of authoritarianism and of the use of middle-class skills for manipulation and exploitation."[14]

The same principles had structured anarchist debates about strategy and political leadership since the 1870s and had become a running concern for the editors of *Retort, Resistance,* and *Views and Comments,* especially following the rise of communism. Unsurprisingly, some ERAP organizers also looked to exemplary activity as a solution to the conundrum. One member of a New Jersey project noted, "It is important to make real what kind of society we want and we think is possible.... The real power relationships in the society will become apparent as we create a new 'counter-society.'" Breines found that by modeling egalitarian relationships in shabby offices, ERAP rarely bolstered the participation of community members. However, organizers who shared living accommodations often grew close and found ways of practicing participatory democracy among themselves; this contributed to the idea of radical activists living in urban communal houses, which has endured to the present day among U.S. anarchists.[15]

Most ERAP projects were abandoned after a year or less, as the student movement shifted its attention in the wake of the Free Speech Movement at the University of California, Berkeley. A mass movement, led by students just returned from the Mississippi Freedom Summer, emerged there in the fall of 1964 after administrators attempted to ban political organizing and fundraising on campus. The students' victory, covered by national media, led to a ballooning of campus organizing just as the federal government was drastically ramping up its military campaign in Vietnam. In April 1965, SDS led the first national march on Washington to oppose war in Southeast Asia and was happily surprised when twenty thousand people attended. This crowd would pale in comparison to the size of antiwar demonstrations that would be staged only a few years later as the student and antiwar movements continued to expand exponentially.

FROM BEATNIKS TO COUNTERCULTURAL ANARCHISTS

As southern civil rights organizers braved mobs and police dogs, and the northern student movement gained momentum during the first half of the 1960s, a mass counterculture took shape in cities across the United States. The coalition of anarchists, radical pacifists, and avant-garde artists that emerged during the Second World War had planted the intellectual seeds of this phenomenon during the 1940s and 1950s, as we saw in chapter 6. Mass media depictions of beatniks, distorted as they were, spread nonconformist, communal, environmental, and sex-positive values widely in the late 1950s and early 1960s. A new generation of cultural rebels then traced these traditions back to anarchism and worked to reinvigorate the tradition.

As the literary stars of Jack Kerouac, Allen Ginsberg, and their associates rose in 1957, Kenneth Rexroth acted as an interpreter and friendly critic of the new school. In an important essay, "Disengagement: The Art of the Beat Generation," he noted, "Politically they are all strong disbelievers in the State, war, and the values of commercial civilization. Most of them would no longer call themselves anarchists, but just because adopting such a label would imply adherence to a 'movement.' Anything in the way of an explicit ideology is suspect."[16] Indeed, Kerouac made his debt to the San Francisco literary anarchists clear in his second published novel, *The Dharma Bums*. Rexroth makes an appearance as the "old anarchist fuddy-duddy Rheinhold Cacoethes," before the narrator breathlessly follows a young poet, Japhy Ryder, into the Sierra Nevada. Ryder, much like Gary Snyder, "had learned Chinese and Japanese and discovered the greatest Dharma Bums of them all, the Zen lunatics of China and Japan. At the same time, being a Northwest boy with idealistic tendencies, he got interested in old-fashioned IWW anarchism and learned to play the guitar and sing old worker songs to go with his Indian songs and general folksong interests."[17]

In a 1961 essay, "Buddhist Anarchism," the real Gary Snyder suggested the Zen idea that "the universe and all creatures in it are intrinsically in a state of complete wisdom, love and compassion; acting in natural response and mutual interdependence" was consummate with the anarchist belief in social harmony and mutual aid. However, in a call for greater political action by Buddhists, he concluded, "The mercy of the West has been social revolution; the mercy of the East has been individual insight into the basic self/void. We need both."[18] Following his lead, a loose network of young cultural radicals began working to mold a growing community of hipsters, freaks, and hippies into an anticapitalist and revolutionary force. While anarchists were by no means the only progenitors of the 1960s counterculture, they played outsized roles in circulating ideas, building international relationships, and encouraging "dropouts" to participate in the freedom struggles being waged by other social groups. Counterculture anarchists were simultaneously inspired by ideas developed by European ultraleft groups and by the turn to militancy by growing numbers of African Americans. Believing that, in affluent societies, alienation derived from ordinary people accepting social conventions unthinkingly, they experimented with means of denaturalizing everyday life and modeling alternatives. As the decade wore on, they turned from poetry, jazz, and theater (the cultural forms privileged by midcentury anarchists) to rock 'n' roll, and from meditation to drug use, as means of finding ecstatic communion.

Chicago

In the working-class suburb of Maywood, Illinois, high school sophomore Franklin Rosemont learned of Jack Kerouac in 1958 from a magazine article he read at a dentist's office. After devouring *On the Road* and *The Dharma Bums,* Rosemont and his multiracial circle of friends launched a literary magazine, which earned them reputations as communists and beatniks. In 1960 Rosemont traveled to San Francisco to experience the scene that had grown up around City Lights bookstore. His reading and travels opened additional horizons. Rosemont recalled, "Only with my discovery of the Beat poets, did I begin to appreciate the vitality and richness of African-American culture, and particularly jazz."[19] Reading Philip Lamantia and the other proto-Beats of the 1940s led Rosemont to study the French Surrealists. In their writings he found a set of ideas that tied together his love of poetry and jazz and his growing interest in radical politics. "As early as the 1950s," he claimed, "some of us recognized the new jazz as the auditory equivalent of Surrealism in painting. . . . Our most extravagant revolutionary dreams were summed up, renewed and expanded in the untrammeled loveliness" of the music of John Coltrane, Thelonious Monk, and Archie Shepp.[20]

Rosemont met like-minded students, such as Penelope Bartik, whom he would later marry, at Chicago's Roosevelt University.[21] Joffre Stewart, an older anarchist poet and member of Peacemakers, encouraged the young writers, most from working-class families, to learn about the Industrial Workers of the World.[22] At the IWW General Headquarters, still located in Chicago, they were welcomed by old-timers happy to see renewed interest in the struggling organization. After becoming official Wobblies, they attempted, unsuccessfully, to organize migrant farmworkers in southwest Michigan during the summer of 1964. In the fall, as the Free Speech Movement was erupting in Berkeley, the group opened Solidarity Bookshop, a prototype of the modern infoshop. The store sold castoffs from the IWW's Work People's College, anarchist classics, and a large selection of radical periodicals from abroad, in addition to literature and comic books.[23] Penelope Rosemont recalled, "My first days at Solidarity I began reading all the books on anarchism in the place." The speeches of the Haymarket martyrs, who had haunted the same neighborhood eighty years before, made a lasting impression.[24]

Later in the year, the bookstore group launched a journal, the *Rebel Worker*, using the IWW mimeograph machine. It broke new ground by pairing worker-centered politics with considerations of the revolutionary potential of high art, popular culture, and urban riots. The Rebel Worker Group learned about revolutionary unionism from Wobblies like Fred Thompson, who had been imprisoned under the criminal syndicalism laws passed during the Red Scare of the World War I era. However, their labor analysis also benefited from friendly exchanges with Facing Reality, an unorthodox Marxist group based in Detroit, and with the British libertarian socialist organization Solidarity.[25]

Facing Reality and Solidarity both fit the mold of ultraleft organizations. The term has come to signify a constellation of small groups formed after the Second World War by former communists, Trotskyists, and socialists disillusioned with their parties' policies and disgusted by what passed for socialism in the Soviet bloc. Such groups have generally consisted of a few dozen members—typically a smattering of salaried professionals and intellectuals collaborating with a handful of self-educated wage-laborers—whose primary focus is the production of a theoretical journal. They earned their reputation as ultraleft owing to their consistent criticism not only of capitalist culture and economics but also of the theory and strategies extolled by the traditional Left—the Socialist and Communist Parties, and their trade union affiliates, which enrolled millions of people in many European countries. These small organizations had a character similar to anarchist formations such as the Resistance Group. Both functioned as amateur think tanks seeking to reconstruct radical praxis in light of changing social conditions; but whereas the latter sought to rethink classical anarchism, the former began with orthodox Marxism.

The Chicago Rebel Worker Group sent copies of their journal to Solidarity and Facing Reality, printed letters from their members, and stocked their publications at Solidarity Bookshop. Each of these organizations developed a criticism of "democratic centralist" vanguard revolutionary parties, argued that labor unions had become incorporated into the postwar capitalist production system, and promoted forms of rank-and-file action, worker self-management, and council democracy.[26] The influence of Facing Reality and Solidarity could be seen in *Rebel Worker* articles critiquing the role of

Sketch of an IWW rock band by Tor Faegre, illustrating the Rebel Worker Group's pamphlet *Mods, Rockers, and the Revolution*, 1965. Courtesy of the Labadie Collection, University of Michigan Library (Special Collections Library).

mainstream union officials in quelling workers' independent acts of shop-floor resistance. However, articles about the point of production competed for space with essays such as Franklin Rosemont's "Mods, Rockers, and the Revolution," a defense of rock 'n' roll music as an expression of working-class youth's "refusal to submit to routinized, bureaucratic pressures."[27] If class struggle was not limited to the practice of union organizing, they reasoned, it could also take place outside the workplace and be expressed in the desire to "slack off."

While the Rebel Workers were invested in post–British Invasion youth culture, they were also attentive to shifts taking place within the black freedom struggle. In the spring of 1965, SNCC did away with its decentralized structure and practice of consensus decision-making. After SNCC leader Stokely Carmichael declared the need for "Black Power" the following year, the organization also shed its commitment to nonviolence and to maintaining a multiracial staff.[28] These changes marked a response to the intransigence and violence of southern racists and the federal government's reluctance to support civil rights organizers. In July 1964 a massive riot, or "uprising," took place in Watts, a poor African American neighborhood in Los Angeles. It set a precedent for more than a hundred such conflagrations in the black ghettos of northern and western cities over the next five years. Most were touched off by incidents of police brutality but expressive of the generalized hostility of communities suffering from segregation, discrimination, and unemployment.

Seeking an adequate response to such conditions, SNCC leaders looked to national liberation struggles in Africa, Asia, and Latin America.[29] From writers such as Frantz Fanon, Amílcar Cabral, and Che Guevara, they ingested a Third World Marxist politics that counseled tighter organization, strong leadership, and, eventually, the pursuit of armed struggle.[30] While older anarchists such as David Wieck and Sam Dolgoff were dubious of these developments, fearing a slide toward authoritarian forms of communism, many in the new generation looked upon them favorably as signs of a growing radicalism and, perhaps, a coming revolution.

The *Rebel Worker* published a firsthand account of the "Harlem insurrection" of 1964 (penned by Robert Calese of the Libertarian League) and hailed a similar rebellion that broke out in Chicago two years later. Franklin Rosemont later noted, "Just as our labor perspective focused not on 'leaders' but on 'actions by the workers themselves, in or out of the unions' so too we identified ourselves strongly with the masses of black proletarian youth who outgrew the increasingly conservative older civil-rights groups and took up direct action in the streets."[31] Yet, even as the movement for racial justice grew in new directions and the antiwar movement heated up, the Chicago group remained invested in cultural radicalism.

In 1966 Penelope and Franklin Rosemont traveled to Europe to meet with *Rebel Worker* readers and some of their intellectual heroes. André Breton and his cohort of aging Surrealists welcomed them into the fold.[32] They also visited with Guy Debord of the Situationist International (SI), a unique group of intellectuals that sought to marry ultraleft ideas with the arts. The SI worked to extend the critique of everyday life in capitalist societies developed by generations of avant-gardists, beginning with the romantic poet Comte de Lautréamont and extending through Dada to Surrealism. Debord and others in the SI argued that with the invention of television, sophisticated marketing techniques, and other features of postwar society, capitalism had reached a new stage where "spectacles" rather than commodities had become the most important products of capitalist social relations. (In French, the term *spectacle* indexes an array of concepts including performance, illusion, and appearance.) In this new environment, the SI argued, complacent citizens merely consumed representations of events and emotions that they had once experienced directly. The Situationists argued that the working and middle classes of Western countries, who had supposedly gained the most from postwar prosperity, in fact had lost what was most significant—self-knowledge, genuine connection to other people, and unmanipulated feelings.[33]

This critique of alienation echoed points made by the California literary anarchists in 1940s, but with key differences. The SI grounded their claims in the thinking of Western Marxists, such as Georg Lukács and Henri LeFebvre, rather than in religious mysticism. In place of poetry, Situationists wrote in an obscure style that added élan to the group while making their ideas difficult to comprehend. Moreover, rather than counsel disengagement from the world, as Rexroth had, the SI suggested activism should now target the realm of representations. Members invented means of intervening in the routines of daily life—playing pranks and creating extraordinary "situations" that denaturalized the social roles (especially "consumer") that people unwittingly played.

The Rosemonts did not fully gel with Debord when they met in 1966, owing to personality conflicts and the Frenchman's dismissal of the continuing relevance of Surrealism. Still, they returned to the United States with a box of Situationist literature. Solidarity Bookshop was among the first distributors of the SI journal in the United States, though most of the group's writings remained untranslated until the 1970s.[34] After 1968, Situationist ideas would exert an enormous influence on the anarchist movement in the United States.

Upon their return, the Rosemonts focused their energies on opening an exhibition space, the Gallery Bugs Bunny and publishing the journal *Arsenal: Surrealist Subversion*. Franklin played in a short-lived rock band, the Enragés. Yet they also contributed to SDS, briefly forming a chapter, working in the organization's printshop, and helping produce the journal *Radical America*. Though the *Rebel Worker* proved short-lived, it had provided a means for the Chicago group to communicate with like-minded cultural radicals throughout the United States and around the world. It played a significant role in transmitting the ideas of C. L. R. James and his collaborators to new generations and in carving out a place for Surrealism in late-twentieth-century anarchism.

San Francisco Bay Area

In the San Francisco Bay Area, KPFA-Pacifica Radio and the trio of bookstores established by anarchist pacifists in the 1950s provided an institutional base from which cultural radicals could strike out in new directions. Roy Kepler's bookstore in Palo Alto served as a bohemian "free space."[35] Kepler, the World War II draft resister and cofounder of the Committee for Nonviolent Revolution, let customers drink coffee and play music in the store while his gregarious cashier, Ira Sandperl, schooled patrons on pacifism and other political issues. Stewart Burns, a nonviolent radical who moved to the area in the 1960s, explained, "Kepler's Books became the anarchist, radical pacifist, and then later Marxist-Leninist hangout, a hotbed for the whole [area that would become known as] Silicon Valley. It was not a very attractive space back then, but large enough to have meetings; and so all kinds of things were incubated there."[36] Notably, Kepler's served as a meeting place for the Merry Pranksters—a collection of Beat-influenced writers who traveled across the country in 1964 promoting hippie values and lifestyle, including the consciousness-expanding effects of LSD—and the iconic psychedelic rock band the Grateful Dead.[37]

Thirty minutes north, in San Francisco, Beat-influenced artists began to migrate from the North Beach neighborhood centered around City Lights Bookstore to Haight Street, near Golden Gate Park, following a wave of commercialization and police harassment in 1962. Members of the new community adopted the "hippie" moniker by 1965, as shops, bands, and newspapers promoting psychedelics began to proliferate. The same year, members of the San Francisco Mime Troupe, an avant-garde theater group, began performing free antiwar and anticapitalist plays in the park, developing the concept of "guerrilla theater" as they went.[38] In the fall of 1966, approximately twenty Mime Troupe members broke away to form the Diggers. This loose association of writers, actors, and theorists borrowed their name from a band of seventeenth-century British rebels, frequently described as proto-anarchists, who opposed the enclosure of commonly farmed land and sought to abolish private property. The San Francisco Diggers took inspiration and a number of important cues from a new Dutch anarchist movement called Provo.

The Provos formed in Amsterdam in 1965 as a collaboration between anti-nuclear protestors and organizers of outdoor art "happenings." Provo founder Roel van Duijn wrote for the Dutch anarchist newspaper *De Vrije* (The free) and drew inspiration from Bakunin and the Dutch libertarian socialist Ferdinand Domela Nieuwenhuis. After abortive attempts at organizing factory workers, he concluded, "We were not going to get any revolution from the proletariat. We would need something else: the 'provotariat'—the masses of rebellious youth, the idle riffraff, who were not afraid of a little rough-and-tumble."[39] The Provo manifesto called for rebellion against a "capitalist society . . . whose members are being brought up to worship Having and despise Being," a bureaucratic society "suppressing any form of spontaneity," and a militaristic society that threatened death. "PROVO," the statement concluded, "wants to renew anarchism and bring it to the young." Provos created various "provocations" that challenged the sanctity of private property and exposed the repressive nature of the police. Famously, they painted hundreds of bicycles white and proposed that they be used as free, communal transportation in place of private cars, which would be banished from the city.[40]

Like their Dutch contemporaries, the San Francisco Diggers believed rebellious youth, specifically those congregating in growing numbers on Haight Street, might serve as a revolutionary "base." And like the Situationists and the Provos, the Diggers devised interventions in daily life that would challenge cultural preoccupations with status and accumulation.[41] Digger Peter Berg termed these interventions "life-acting" and explained that the process should aim "to create the conditions you describe."[42] Historian Michael William Doyle notes the term "punned on the dual meaning of the verb 'to act,' combining the direct action of anarchism with theatrical role playing."[43] They began by serving food every afternoon in Golden Gate Park. It was free—the Diggers refused to accept payment—but those partaking were asked to first walk through a large, yellow, wooden rectangle deemed "a free frame of reference." The group soon opened a store, Trip Without a Ticket, in which all items were up for grabs, and volunteers intentionally subverted the roles of employee and customer.

Diggers also used life-acting to create "free" public space and to subvert the authority of city police. They organized hippies to partake in mass street theater, using giant puppets, coffins, and other props to demonstrate that a city street could become a playground or dance floor anytime people chose. Digger Peter Coyote later explained, "Our hope was that if we were imaginative enough in creating social paradigms as free men and women, the example would be infectious and might produce self-directed (as opposed to coerced or manipulated) social change."[44] Diggers shunned personal notoriety, often deploying pseudonyms, and took the long-standing anarchist critique of domineering leaders to new heights, referring to themselves as the "fuck-leader youth."[45]

Digger initiatives were unified by their concept of "the Free," which conflated the meanings "costing nothing" and "the ability to do as one pleases." The Free, as deployed by the Diggers, was a deeply anarchist concept, in that it attempted to demonstrate that liberty and equality were directly linked, rather than contradictory, goals. When necessities were provided free of cost, individuals gained a much broader purview to choose how to spend their time and how to behave. Digger projects depended, financially, on theft, donations from the Grateful Dead and other local bands, repurposing of welfare checks, and donations from wealthy individuals.[46]

Although they competed with other denizens of the Haight-Ashbury District who saw psychedelic and mystical experiences as the path to a new society, the Diggers fundamentally shaped the San Francisco counterculture. They helped organize the first Human Be-In in January 1967, which helped establish the neighborhood as a new countercultural mecca. As legions of young dropouts flooded the area a few months later, in what became known as the Summer of Love, Diggers established tenuous "crash pads" and pushed the city to provide free medical clinics. The public information arm of the Diggers, the Communication Company, made use of state-of-the art Gestetner machines to add multicolor printing and photography to the group's posters and publications, influencing countercultural and anarchist aesthetics for years to come.[47]

The Diggers also served as a conduit between the hippie community and the Black Panther Party, which formed in nearby Oakland in 1967. The party began by organizing armed patrols to stem the tide of police brutality against African Americans. It quickly grew into a nationwide organization that demanded black liberation and socialism, immediately facing intense repression by the FBI.[48] The Communication Company printed the first issues of the Black Panther newspaper, and party leader David Hilliard credits the Diggers' free grocery service as inspiring the Panthers' free breakfast program for children.[49] Peter Coyote notes the Diggers "were not 'serving' black causes out of ideological loyalty." Rather the groups were "allied by territory and a common love of freedom," leading them to "forge an alliance."[50]

Still, like many of their white countercultural contemporaries, Diggers gave voice to an implicit racial politics that celebrated, but also tended to romanticize, black masculinity and Native American culture in general.[51] Indeed, the group's name itself indexed reverence for indigenous lifeways. The term *digger* had served as a slur against indigenous peoples who foraged for food during the era of the California gold rush. As scholar Timothy Hodgdon notes, "If *digger* named a group whose 'crime' lay in living without money or private property, yet within the limits of the ecosystem, then the hippie collective found the name all the more appealing."[52] In articulating their critique of midcentury American culture, Diggers often drew upon Gary Snyder's poetic formulations, which linked whiteness with a war-making technical rationality opposed to both "wildness" and "Wilderness."[53] Placing high value on these terms, they served as an important link in the development of an explicit anarcho-primitivism in the 1980s.

By the summer of 1968 many of the original Diggers began to leave San Francisco and to take up residence in rural communes.[54] Counterculturalists had begun establishing a new generation of intentional communities as early as 1965. Young people interested in the practice often looked to the School of Living and the Catholic Worker for advice, given that both organizations had practiced the art of low-income cooperative living in rural areas since the 1930s.[55]

Yet as Digger activity faded in San Francisco, cultural radicals in New York, Detroit, and cities further afield reproduced and reworked practices the Diggers had pioneered. Notably, a group centered on Abbie Hoffman, Jerry Rubin, and Paul Krassner called themselves the New York Diggers for a few months in 1967, before renaming themselves the Youth International Party, or Yippies! Abandoning the principle of anonymity, the Yippies would adapt Digger techniques to attract television coverage in an attempt to harness the power of mass corporate media for revolutionary ends.[56]

Over the longer term, the Diggers (and their international counterparts, such as the Provos) can be seen as a source of inspiration for many practices and tactics that became fundamental to late-twentieth-century U.S. anarchism such as making events free or as cheap as possible, the distribution of food and other items for free, radical puppetry, the establishment of "temporary autonomous zones," and the turn to carnivalesque forms of protest.

New York City

If the IWW General Headquarters helped young Chicago radicals connect to the anarchist tradition, and City Lights and Kepler's Bookstore served a similar function in the Bay Area, New York could boast multiple sites in which the anarchist tradition might be passed from one generation to the next. As the 1960s dawned, the Libertarian League remained the only explicitly anarchist English-speaking membership organization functioning in the United States.[57] As indicated in chapter 7, the league's half dozen or so members focused on corresponding with foreign radicals, circulating the publication *Views and Comments,* and hosting political discussions on Manhattan's Lower East Side. In the early 1960s, a handful of younger radicals gravitated to the organization. David Sachs moved to New York City from Baltimore in 1962, after participating in socialist, civil rights, and peace activism in high school. He found his way to the league though involvement with the Congress of Racial Equality and the General Strike for Peace.[58] Walter Caughey was so impressed with a lecture that Sam Dolgoff had given at Antioch College, in Ohio, that he moved east to join the group. Jonathan Leake was still a high school student when he began attending meetings.

Newcomers absorbed revolutionary lore from Blackwell, the Dolgoffs, and the aging Spanish exiles who sometimes attended meetings. This new blood enabled the league to expand the size of *Views and Comments* and to support activities of the Congress of Racial Equality in the early 1960s. Yet the younger members' growing interest in cultural transformation led to tensions that eventually dissolved the Libertarian League. In 1964, Leake and Caughey began to produce *Resurgence,* a mimeographed magazine that promoted Surrealism, drug use, and Third World liberation, billing itself as the organ of the Resurgence Youth Movement, which did not exist (at least by that name). To Sam Dolgoff's mind "a new element of crazies, nuts, acidheads, and junkies, some with authoritarian tendencies, came in.... Their talk was dominated by sex, drugs, and violent action.... The group collapsed amid bickering and quarrels."[59]

While Dolgoff's account is likely exaggerated, a cultural as well as strategic rift had clearly opened. The first issue of *Resurgence* called for "permanent insurrection: :antipolitics: :cultural sabotage: .... :subversive fantasy and science fiction: :juvenile delinquency."[60] Not content with dreary analyses of social forces, they playfully sought to will a new movement, or at least a new language and greater personal freedom, into existence. David Sachs later recalled that he drifted away from the league at about the same time, explaining, "My increasing interest in psychedelics and amphetamines made the idea that I had a role to play in changing the world less tangible. Drugs opened areas of interest that made anarchism less compelling." Yet, other changes also took a toll on the Libertarian League. Russell Blackwell devoted more time to civil rights organizing and the Ellingtons moved to California.

New York also boasted other points of connection to the anarchist tradition. The avant-garde repertory company The Living Theatre, active since 1947, reached new peaks of recognition and popularity as the decade progressed, performing some of its most explicitly antiauthoritarian plays. *The Brig,* for instance, depicted the casually cruel discipline meted out to members of the armed forces. Meanwhile, the Living Theatre's anarchist directors, Julian Beck and Judith Malina, continued to participate in antiwar activity and politicize younger artists. In 1964, the troupe decamped to Europe for four years, choosing Amsterdam as base of operations and bringing performances of their orgiastic, pro-sex show *Paradise Now!* into the streets.

Still, the Lower East Side continued to boast other resources. In 1962, the social theorist Murray Bookchin convened a new anarchist study group, the East Side Anarchists, consisting of a handful of artists, students, and civil rights activists. Bookchin was born in the Bronx in 1921 to a family of radical Russian Jews. A young communist during the 1930s, he became a Trotskyist on the heels of the 1939 Hitler-Stalin Pact and organized with the Socialist Workers Party while working in iron foundries and the automobile industry until 1947.[61] During the 1950s he participated in a small ultraleft organization, the Contemporary Issues Group, which formed as a libertarian offshoot of the German Trotskyist movement after World War II.[62]

The Contemporary Issues Group decided that the labor movement could no longer be relied upon as a force for radical change, as unions had traded their autonomous power for wage hikes and a measure of respectability in the late 1940s. It criticized both camps of the Cold War and suggested future leftist movements promote more direct and participatory forms of democracy. Bookchin penned essays for the group's journal and, in 1962, issued a book warning about dangers posed by pollution and other "synthetic" outputs of modern industry, such as chemical additives in mass-produced food.[63] Exploring the idea of "decentralization" as a corrective to urban and industrial problems led him to investigate the anarchist tradition. As the New York branch of Contemporary Issues disintegrated in the late 1950s, Bookchin met anarchists at demonstrations organized by the Congress of Racial Equality and antinuclear protests convened by members of the Catholic Worker and the Living Theatre. He attended meetings of the Libertarian League for a time but found their perspective outdated.[64]

His new group, the East Side Anarchists, explored potential points of overlap between anarchist theory and the emerging field of ecology. Bookchin's first essay of this period, "Ecology and Revolutionary Thought," published in 1965, warned that the inherently expansive nature of capitalism threatened to devastate the natural world and imperil human health—a novel concept at the time. Ecology framed problems in terms of imbalances, but Bookchin claimed these imbalances extended into the social world. "The notion that man must dominate nature emerges directly from the domination of many by man," he argued. If the problems were interlinked, so were the solutions. Bookchin noted that both ecology and anarchism supported the idea that a thriving whole (whether a watershed or a society) depended on a diversity of interdependent components rather than domination and homogenization. A decentralized, smaller-scale anarchist society, then, was required, "not only to establish a lasting basis for the harmonization of man and nature, but also to add new dimensions to the harmonization of man and man."[65]

Over the next five years, he continued to explore what anarchism might offer affluent, or "postscarcity," societies in which technology had obviated the need for humans to focus their lives on competing in order to secure basic needs. In a series of essays, he began to focus anarchist critique on the multiple and co-reinforcing systems of domination at work in the world, theoretically displacing class as the overriding human antagonism. Bookchin's thinking built on ideas of the Frankfurt School critical theorists Theodor Adorno, Max Horkheimer, and Herbert Marcuse, who had developed the concept of *domination,* criticized humans' destructive relationship to the natural world, and contemplated the possibilities afforded by a postscarcity social order, beginning in the 1940s.[66]

Bookchin, already in his forties, benefited from interactions with younger members of the group. He would later gratefully acknowledge that, from member Allan Hoffman, "I acquired a broader sense of the totality sought by the counterculture and youth revolt."[67] Their energy and experimental projects provided some basis for the utopian visions of social reorganization he was developing. Beyond their theoretical work, the East Side Anarchists carried black flags in antiwar demonstrations, published one issue of a journal called *Good Soup,* and opened a short-lived radical bookstore, the Torch.[68]

While significant strains of late-twentieth-century anarchist thought can be traced back to Murray Bookchin, recent anarchist aesthetics and tactics also owe a debt to the magazine *Black Mask,* another project emanating out of lower Manhattan in the mid-1960s. *Black Mask* was the brainchild of Ben Morea, a painter in his twenties who came to anarchist politics in a trajectory similar to that of Franklin Rosemont. Growing up in Hell's Kitchen, Morea immersed himself in the local bebop jazz scene (Thelonious Monk lived nearby) until he was imprisoned for heroin use. Morea explained, "After I quit heroin, when I was about nineteen, I already had this subcultural context, so I struck up a friendship with a lot of beatniks. Especially, first, the Living Theatre. Judith Malina and Julian Beck—they're the ones who put the name to the way I felt, [gave me] the term *anarchist*."[69] Over the next few years, Morea attended meetings of both the Libertarian League and the East Side Anarchists. "I felt more comfortable with the Libertarian League in terms of political consciousness," he recalled. "They were working class. I liked Murray, I liked him a lot. [But his group] was more intellectual, . . . more removed."[70]

Readings in the history of Dada, Surrealism, and other radical artistic currents also proved crucial to Morea's education.[71] After collaborating with Aldo Tambellini and others involved with the Group Center space, Morea and his friend Ron Hahne launched *Black Mask,* a four-page broadsheet devoted to avant-garde art and radical politics, in 1966. Allan Hoffman, of the East Side Anarchists, contributed, as did the poet Dan Georgakas. The group also befriended Valerie Solanas, author of the radical feminist *SCUM Manifesto.*[72]

The name *Black Mask* resonated in a number of ways for Morea. He later recalled, "There was a book written by Frantz Fanon, *Black Faces, White Masks.* Well, I always thought, 'White faces, black masks.' I was also friends with the black nationalists, and some of them used an African mask as a symbol. The color black was an anarchist symbol, but the mask fit the art side more than, say, *Black Flag*."[73]

Since they identified as artists, the editors of *Black Mask* felt it their responsibility to subvert museums and other symbols of high culture, which, they argued, concealed the brutality of U.S. society, exemplified by the war in Vietnam and the treatment of African Americans. The journal's first issue reprinted a flier from the Lowndes County Freedom Organization, an off-shoot of SNCC, which first used the black panther as a symbol of its members' willingness to defend themselves. *Black Mask* enthused, "A new spirit is rising. Like the streets of Watts we burn with revolution. . . . The guerrilla, the blacks, the men of the future, we are all at your heels."[74]

Fanon's ideas, the urban uprisings, and the turn toward armed self-defense by the Black Freedom Movement drew Morea and his friends away from the

Demonstration by the Black Mask Group, New York City, 1967. © Larry Fink.

pacifism embraced by their Beat friends. "I liked Allen [Ginsberg] a lot," Morea recounted, "but at some point I became antipacifist. So he'd say, 'Om,' and I'd say, 'Arm!' That was a mantra we had. He'd go, 'Ommm,' and I'd go, 'Aaaarrrrmmm!'"[75]

During the mid-1960s the editors of the *Rebel Worker, Resurgence,* and *Black Mask* corresponded and promoted each other's publications. Morea traveled throughout the United States, visiting with the Diggers in San Francisco, the Rebel Worker Group in Chicago, and members of Facing Reality in Detroit. Dutch Provos and members of the Japanese student movement, the Zengakuren, visited him in New York.[76] The Situationist International briefly encouraged *Black Mask* to affiliate, but retracted the offer after member Raoul Vaneigem determined Allan Hoffman to be too "mystical" during a short visit to New York.[77] (After they definitively broke off contact with *Black Mask,* three other members of the New York radical milieu—Tony Verlaan, Bruce Elwell, and Robert Chasse—were officially recognized as the American section of the SI.)

Like the Diggers and Provos, the Black Mask Group specialized in creating public interventions. In February 1967, contributors literalized the publication's name when they marched through the financial district in black ski masks and clothes, bearing skulls on poles and a sign that read "Wall Street is War Street." This stark demonstration against the Vietnam War appears to be the first deployment of the "black bloc" aesthetic that would become an internationally recognized symbol of anarchism by the 1990s.[78]

In October, contributors participated in mass demonstrations at the Pentagon in Washington, D.C. They handed out leaflets, headlined "Anarchism Is the Theory of Urban Guerrilla War," which suggested means of self-defense against riot police and offense against television reporters sure to misrepresent the demonstrations ("Hair spray or spray paint disables cameras").[79] Black Mask participants and their associates managed to briefly fight their way into a less-guarded side door of the Pentagon while most demonstrators amassed in front.[80] The group clearly recognized it was marking a significant departure from the tactics, ethics, and representational strategies shared by most of the Left. In a follow-up leaflet, Black Mask announced, "This has nothing to do with moral witness, peaceful demonstration or even resistance—this is aggression, the beginning of revolutionary struggle."[81]

In the wake of such actions, the group grew to include more than a dozen core members, including Osha Neumann, the stepson of Frankfurt School theorist Herbert Marcuse. Early in 1968, as the New Left and counterculture swelled, the group theatrically dumped garbage on the steps of the Lincoln Center for the Performing Arts, signing an explanatory leaflet "Up Against the Wall, Motherfucker." The line was drawn from a poem penned by black nationalist LeRoi Jones during an urban uprising that had convulsed Newark, New Jersey, the previous year.[82] The name stuck, and the group ceased publishing *Black Mask* in favor of wheat-pasted broadsides and more direct modes of confrontation.[83]

Billing themselves "a street gang with an analysis," Up Against the Wall / Motherfuckers (UAW/MF) organized hippies, dropouts, and Puerto Rican youth to squat in empty buildings and instigate small-scale riots. The turn to trashing and brawling with the police was informed by the black ghetto uprisings, the street-fighting tactics of the Zengakuren, and militant confrontations by students and workers that brought France to the brink of revolution in the spring of 1968.[84] The group intended to push members of the white counterculture to increase the intensity of their confrontations with authorities, in order to serve as another "front" in the struggles being waged by people of color in the United States and anticolonial forces abroad. "The hip community poses a way of living rather than simply a way of life," Morea declared at the time. "The existence of our community represents both an alternative to the present system and a means for its destruction."[85]

LSD became a significant aspect of that way of living. "We felt like in order to change the world, you had to change yourself," Morea later explained, and psychedelics seemed to offer that opportunity.[86] For these reasons, the group insisted that "the hippie is a threat"—one more potent than traditional leftist "political" organizations could hope to be.

For hippies to remain a threatening alternative, however, UAW/MF believed it was imperative to resist the commodification of the counterculture—a practice also important to the Diggers. Members fought for a "free night" at the premier rock venue in New York City and used bolt cutters to clandestinely dismantle fences at the historic August 1969 Woodstock Festival, allowing thousands of people to enter without paying. Morea proudly recalled, "We stormed the entrance to the Pentagon—the only people in history to actually penetrate into the building. *And* we cut the fences at Woodstock. So here you've got this cultural thing *and* this political thing. And that was us."[87] As Osha Neumann put it, "We advocated a politics of rage and tribal bonding, 'flower power with thorns.'"[88] In other words, the group attempted to combine a prefigurative cultural strategy with an insurrectionary strategy.

UAW/MF's efforts to resist commercialization and co-optation by the media and cultural industries distinguished them from the better-known Yippies, who also concertedly pursued cultural revolution from the Lower East Side beginning in 1968. Yippies instead attempted to co-opt the co-opters, playing pranks that would prove irresistible to television reporters as a means of securing free "advertisements for the revolution." While they succeeded at reaching a much larger audience, their strategy of playful self-parody and tricksterism left many confused as to how committed they were to realizing goals beyond self-expression.[89] While the Yippies are often remembered as the beginning and end of a politicized counterculture, they formed three years after the Rebel Worker Group, directly adopted ideas from the Diggers, and were less steeped in revolutionary traditions and had fewer international connections than *Black Mask*. These differences, along with personality clashes, created a measure of animosity between organizations. Years later, Neumann could acknowledge that he and other members of UAW/MF "were both envious and contemptuous of the Yippie media stars."[90]

UAW/MF remained an overwhelmingly male group whose members evinced a swaggering macho posture that they equated with revolutionary commitment. This prickly style, paired with the group's strategy of frontal attack, came with significant consequences, both political and personal.

UAW/MF declared themselves a chapter of Students for a Democratic Society in early 1969 but used that status primarily to berate student radicals for what they regarded as physical timidity and intellectual posturing. Some members of the Columbia University SDS, such as Jeff Jones, would soon form the Weather Underground and take the Motherfuckers' attempt to weld counterculture and violent confrontation to another level.[91] Yet the core members of UAW/MF left New York City in 1971 to escape the escalating cycle of violent protest, drug use, and incarceration they found themselves becoming trapped in. Some made their way to rural communes or other types of political work, while others dipped deeper into underworld activities. The group dissolved soon afterward but left a significant legacy.[92]

One could argue that the "thorns" UAW/MF imposed on "flower power" represent the first disjunctive sprouts of the punk counterculture that would emerge a decade later. In fact, British radicals imbued with Situationist ideas and Black Mask's attitude established the groups King Mob and the Angry Brigade, which in turn informed Malcolm McLaren's and Jamie Reid's infamous experiment with spectacular politics, the Sex Pistols.[93] It is unclear whether Black Mask's Wall Street procession influenced the development of the black bloc tactic in Europe, but the group's approach to the Pentagon demonstration marks an important break in action tactics. Their rejection of moral witness in favor of the attempt to physically damage institutions of power; their advice to minimize rather than court television coverage of such activity; and their intention to avoid arrest rather than embrace it as a symbol of commitment, instigated a heated debate on what makes a street protest successful. That debate continues to the present day.

Detroit

The counterculture evolved in Detroit along the pattern established in Chicago, San Francisco, and New York. Though the Detroit scene did not incorporate an explicitly anarchist politics until the early 1970s, developments in that city would have their own enduring impact on late-twentieth-century anarchism. In the early 1960s, local beatniks John Sinclair and Leni Arndt opened the Artists Workshop, a performance space that hosted poetry readings and jazz shows.[94] In 1965, a teenager launched an underground newspaper, *Fifth Estate,* in a storefront adjacent to the Artists Workshop. The newspaper featured a column by Sinclair and attracted writers such as Peter Werbe, a former SDS leader and antiwar organizer.[95] As LSD became readily available in 1966, Sinclair transformed the Artists Workshop into a production company and commune called Trans-Love Energies. He began to manage the MC5, a local rock band who distinguished themselves with performances that were increasingly sex- and feedback-laden. Trans-Love borrowed a page from the Diggers, providing free services to the neighborhood's growing counterculture. Commune member Pun Plamondon later noted, "I always thought of Trans-Love Energies as the link between the beatniks, which was the Artists Workshop, and the hippies."[96]

For a time, Trans-Love Energies, the MC5, and the *Fifth Estate* functioned as a semicoherent whole. Werbe recalled, "Those of us around the *Fifth Estate* were into the cultural scene as well as politics, with its rock 'n' roll, psychedelic drugs, and art. Detroit's seminal rock band, the MC5, used to practice in the basement of the *Fifth Estate* while we were doing layout. They came to demonstrations and all that, but weren't steeped in the revolutionary traditions and knowledge that we were."[97] MC5 guitarist Wayne Kramer explained the assumptions that defined the period: "That the music could represent the possibility that we could change the world. That we could stop the war, that we could change the reefer laws, that we could reinvent ourselves and that we didn't have to go along with the program."[98] This mostly white counterculture was shaped by the massive 1967 urban insurrection in Detroit and collaborated fitfully with the diverse but powerful local Black Power movement.[99]

Shortly after the MC5 performed at the Yippies' August 1968 Festival of Life, Trans-Love Energies announced that it was transforming itself into the White Panther Party (WPP). Earlier that year Black Panther chairman Huey Newton had suggested (perhaps in jest) that white people who supported the Black Panther Party could form their own White Panther Party. Sinclair and the MC5 took him at his word and attempted, awkwardly, to meld the Black Panther's party form and revolutionary nationalist politics to countercultural strategies. They adopted a ten-point program whose first point was an endorsement of the Black Panther Party's own program. The next nine points, however, built upon the Digger concept of "the Free."[100]

The MC5's first album, released by Elektra Records, featured a manifesto beneath a gatefold photo of the band sporting WPP buttons on their bare chests and carrying rifles alongside their guitars. The new organization declared, "Our program is cultural revolution through a total assault on the culture. . . . We are LSD-driven total maniacs in the universe. We will do anything we can to drive people out of their heads into their bodies. Rock & roll music is the spearhead of our attack because it's so effective and so much

Left to right, Peter Werbe of the *Fifth Estate,* Pun and Genie Plamondon of the White Panther Party, and Jerry Rubin of the Yippies at an underground press conference, Madison, Wisconsin, 1968. © Leni Sinclair.

fun."[101] While neither the band nor the party identified as anarchists (they read Fanon and Mao in their study groups), they clearly amplified the strategy of cultural revolution promoted by U.S. anarchists since the 1940s. In 1946, Kenneth Rexroth had bragged that his circle of young draft resisters and artists were "a trifle orgiastic and apocalyptic." In 1969, John Sinclair saluted draft dodgers and called for "Dope, guns, and fucking in the streets."[102] The connections were not lost on the individuals involved. In 1969, a young counterculturalist named Ken Knabb circulated a letter to fellow Bay Area anarchists encouraging them to attend a poetry reading benefit for John Sinclair, then facing criminal charges. "The poets," he explained, "are Gary Snyder, Lew Welch, Lawrence Ferlinghetti, and Michael McClure, all anarchists of sorts, and all beautiful poets."[103]

Wall-of-sound rock music proved more lucrative than the "indecipherable" poetry readings of the 1940s. For a time, the MC5 funneled their earnings into the political initiatives of the WPP. Although they maintained an alliance with the Yippies, at least some White Panthers took seriously the goal of building an actual membership organization. Pun Plamondon recalls that the group decided to "organize ourselves along the Black Panther model, with a Central Committee (CC), ministers and such. Everything was to come and go from the center; the CC was to direct and control all Party activity."[104] Yet White Panther statements on authority and leadership were never consistent, revealing the project's inherent tensions. A newspaper produced by the New England branch of the WPP relied on an anarchist vocabulary in describing its aims: "To take collective responsibility for one's own affairs, that is self-government. To destroy all hierarchies which merely serve to paralyze the initiative of groups and individuals. To make all those in whom any authority is vested permanently responsible to the people."[105] Similarly, the first version of the WPP's ten-point program concluded with the plank "Free the people from their 'leaders'—leaders suck—all power to all the people—freedom means free everyone!"[106] At some point before the end of 1969, however, point ten was altered to read, "Free the people from their phony 'leaders'—everyone must be a leader—freedom means free every one! All Power to the People!"[107]

The evolution in this language is indicative of the competing conceptions of "leadership" circulating in the late 1960s. If "leaders suck" was the cry of the Diggers and *Rebel Worker,* "everyone must be a leader" rang closer to the position sounded by the early incarnations of SNCC and SDS. Yet by changing the first phrase to "free the people from their phony 'leaders,'" the program implicitly made room for the more genuine leadership that members of the WPP Central Committee, emulating the Black Panthers, felt compelled to provide.

Like its counterparts in other cities, the WPP was short-lived but influential. Unsurprisingly, the attempt to synthesize prefigurative cultural revolution with disciplined party organizing and armed struggle soon proved unworkable. In July 1969, Sinclair was sentenced to ten years in prison for giving two joints to an undercover officer. He and Plamondon were also indicted for bombing a CIA office and weapons-research laboratory. Plamondon decided to go "underground" to avoid prosecution, spending time in rural communes with Diggers and eventually in Algiers with exiled Black Panthers. The WPP increasingly devoted its energies to legal battles, losing organizing momentum. The MC5, meanwhile, distanced itself from direct involvement in politics and became more involved with drugs.[108]

Nevertheless, the idea that a music group could anchor a political project by disseminating radical ideas, generating income, and building community proved irresistible. Over the next decades, hundreds of punk groups throughout the world would promote anarchism through their lyrics and aesthetic choices. Some of the most significant, such as the British bands Crass and Chumbawamba, would live communally and stuff their record sleeves with manifestos, as the MC5 had done.[109] Such groups would endlessly debate the politics of seeking funds and a mass audience by collaborating with capitalist record labels, like the MC5 did, or by seeking to decommodify their music and culture in the tradition of Up Against the Wall / Motherfuckers. For these reasons, the MC5 and White Panther Party collaboration should be seen as a milestone and pivot point in the evolution of anarchist cultural politics. This was not the only legacy of the Detroit counterculture, however.

As the decade wound to a close, the editors of the *Fifth Estate* began to distance themselves from the WPP and move in a new political direction. "In the paper we dutifully reported on Sinclair's slogan of 'dope, rock 'n' roll and fucking in the streets,'" Werbe recalled. "But those seemed like pretty silly political demands."[110] Over the next few years the editors began exploring ideas and thinkers that would lead them to embrace anarchism later in the decade. According to Werbe, "What really got us going was Fredy and Lorraine Perlman."

The Perlmans had met in New York in the 1950s, where they socialized and demonstrated with the founders of the Living Theatre. After Fredy earned a PhD in Marxist economics in Yugoslavia, the couple founded the journal *Black and Red* in Kalamazoo, Michigan, where Fredy held a teaching post. Invited to lecture in Italy during the spring of 1968, he boarded a train for Paris when student demonstrations there spread to involve factory workers. Lorraine notes, "During these action-filled weeks . . . Fredy learned about ideas and histories which influenced him in the decade which followed: the texts of the Situationist Internationale, anarchism and the Spanish Revolution, the council communists."[111] Back in Michigan, he composed essays that built upon Situationist and Provo themes. "Men who were much but had little now have much but are little," he wrote in a widely circulated essay, "The Reproduction of Daily Life."[112]

In August 1969, the Perlmans relocated to Detroit and befriended the remnants of the *Fifth Estate* editorial collective. Together, they launched a cooperative printshop, which produced *Radical America* and other Left periodicals. Black and Red evolved from a monthly journal into a publishing house that issued pamphlets and books. In 1970 the Perlmans and some friends translated Guy Debord's *Society of the Spectacle* into English for the first time, circulating the text as an issue of *Radical America*. The SI harshly denounced the project, claiming that errors of translation and the theoretical eclecticism of *Radical America* would prove misleading to readers.[113] Despite this falling out, the relocation of Black and Red had a major impact on the Fifth Estate Group. Werbe remembered that in the early 1970s, "we were affected, both theoretically, and in terms of action, by the Situationists and 1968 in France."[114]

The Perlmans introduced local radicals to other schools of European ult-raleft thought as well. "They shared books with us that, at first, we couldn't even understand, such as Jacques Camatte's *The Wandering of Humanity,*" Werbe explained. Drawing on Camatte, Jean Baudrillard, Gilles Dauvé, and other French thinkers, *Fifth Estate* and Black and Red began to articulate a critique of the industrialist and economistic assumptions of traditional Marxism, as well as the authoritarian tendencies of revolutionaries they had celebrated only a few years before. By 1971, according to Werbe, "Everyone in the New Left was exhausted after a decade of activism. People were going off to live in rural communes and 'getting in touch with their feelings.' The other underground papers all collapsed; people weren't interested in them any longer. But we were fired up by these ultraleft ideas!"[115]

At first the circle identified its politics not as anarchist "but rather [as] Left Marxism, Left communism, council communism."[116] However, in the mid-1970s, veterans of the old L'Adunata dei Refrattari Group, now mostly retired, contacted the Fifth Estate Group and inspired them with their unwavering passion for revolution. Federico Arcos, an anarchist Spanish Civil War veteran living in Detroit, also made an impression. Lorraine Perlman notes, "In the 1970s, the designation 'anarchist' came into increasing use when people referred to recent Black and Red books."[117] Likewise, though *Fifth Estate* preferred the designation "antiauthoritarian," the magazine became a mainstay of the post-1960s U.S. anarchist milieu, serving as a key forum for neo-Luddite positions that would blossom into anarcho-primitivism in the 1980s.[118]

ANARCHIST PACIFISM AND THE RESISTANCE

While some of the young radicals who drew inspiration from anarchists, such as UAW/MF and the WPP, gravitated toward armed conflict, another segment of the New Left upheld the traditions of anarchist pacifism and revolutionary nonviolence that had momentarily shined during the Second World War. Roy Kepler was happy that his Palo Alto bookstore provided a meeting ground for hippies. Yet he suspected that cultural rebellion had its limits, so chose to focus his own energies on rekindling interest in radical nonviolence. Roy Kepler and Ira Sandperl's best-known protégé was the folk-singer Joan Baez, who grew up near their store, and whose father joined anti-nuclear protests organized by the pair.[119]

In 1965, already wealthy from tours with Bob Dylan, Baez invited Kepler and Sandperl to help her establish the Institute for the Study of Nonviolence, a school offering visitors intensive classes on revolutionary nonviolence.[120] The intellectual links pacifists had forged with anarchism in the 1940s remained intact. Stewart Burns, who studied and then taught at the institute later in the decade, explained, "[At the institute] we would have workshops where we wouldn't just read Gandhi and Barbara Deming. . . . We would read Martin Buber, maybe Kropotkin, and Proudhon." Dwight MacDonald and Paul Goodman were also included on reading lists. Moreover, Burns notes that after 1968, "the institute staff would have identified first and foremost as anarchists. We might not have wanted to use that term, but that's what we were reading and discussing, that's what we were learning about, that's what we were trying to prefigure in our structures that we were building."[121]

Joan Baez's husband, David Harris, had been elected president of the Stanford student body before dropping out to focus on politics. In May 1967 he cofounded the Resistance, which grew quickly into a national network of draft resisters.[122] Burns, who helped organize the group, later explained, "We were very committed to Gandhian nonviolence, but I would say in the Palo Alto Resistance, which was kind of the flagship for the whole country, we were more anarchist or libertarian socialist than pacifist. They were very conjoined, but the accent mark would be on the anarchism more than the pacifism."[123] This was the case elsewhere, as well. The artist Ernest Larsen notes, for instance, that he and his wife, Sherry Millner, "met as conscious anarchists (I was a draft resister active in the Resistance and she was a member of Anarchos, the affinity group centered around Murray Bookchin) who also happened to think of ourselves as artists."[124]

David Harris's anarchist politics are evident in his writings from the period. In *Goliath*, published while he was incarcerated for refusing induction, Harris posited, "In making life, we must do our future in the present." According to his strategy, "A community is organized. . . . As it grows, it becomes an alternative to the state." This new form of life and politics must operate differently, Harris insisted. "Men must govern themselves in common association based on consensus. It is an arrangement of resources according to need."[125] This vision of change clearly bears the imprint of Paul Goodman's World War II–era essays.

Goodman was a major intellectual presence throughout the decade. After languishing in obscurity during the 1950s, he published *Growing Up Absurd* in 1960.[126] The book, which lamented the obstacles to living an authentic and fulfilling life for young men (it implied young women had no such needs), became a best seller. Goodman also took on duties as an editor of *Liberation* in these years, following the departure of Roy Finch. As the student and antiwar movements grew, Goodman traveled the campus lecture circuit, dishing out advice, once again, about "drawing a line" beyond which one would not compromise his or her values.[127] David Dellinger, likewise, served as a tireless itinerant organizer for the antiwar movement, releasing a collection of essays, *Revolutionary Nonviolence,* via a major publisher.[128]

As a new generation of war resisters came to the fore, younger members of the Catholic Worker Movement, such as Karl Meyer, staked out some of the most uncompromising positions.[129] Over the course of the 1960s, the Catholic Left expanded. Priests such as Daniel and Philip Berrigan took up Dorothy Day's call to use direct action in the service of an egalitarian and pacifist interpretation of Christ's word.[130] Other denominations also mobilized anew. After working with Martin Luther King Jr., members of the Society of Friends formed A Quaker Action Group to oppose the war in Vietnam. In 1971 they reorganized as Movement for a New Society, a feminist radical pacifist network that significantly shaped the face of anarchist and direct action politics throughout the 1970s and 1980s.[131]

IDEOLOGICAL DISPUTES IN STUDENTS FOR A DEMOCRATIC SOCIETY

By 1967, SDS had grown exponentially, based largely on its resistance to the draft and the war in Vietnam. At its peak it counted approximately a hundred thousand official members, but staff found themselves unable to keep up with the flood of applications, and many students associated or identified with their local SDS chapters without ever officially seeking membership. With the rapid growth of black militancy (and new Chicano and American

Indian movements), the antiwar movement, and the counterculture, SDS's politics evolved rapidly and unevenly. Existing accounts have emphasized tensions in SDS after 1966 between factions supporting different varieties of Marxist politics. However, as early as 1965, anarchists and libertarian socialists also began articulating distinct perspectives and proposing strategic directions for SDS.

At the University of Texas–Austin, SDS members embraced the emerging counterculture. They smoked marijuana liberally, grew their hair long, and emphasized personal authenticity. Chapter delegates saw themselves as representatives of a "prairie power" turn in SDS more expressive of the views of the organization's chapters from the South and the Great Plains. "Old guard" SDS leaders from the northern Midwest and the Northeast, such as Todd Gitlin, sensed that "they were instinctive anarchists, principled and practiced antiauthoritarians."[132] The historian Doug Rossinow has argued, "The Austin leftists were not unhappy to be called anarchists, associating this label with liberation and antiauthoritarianism. Although they were not doctrinal anarchists, they saw a marked looseness of organization—indeed, a minimum of ongoing, centralized bureaucracy—as the real meaning of participatory democracy."[133] Echoing David Wieck's and Kenneth Rexroth's late 1940s pronouncements, they argued that SDS and other New Left organizations should prioritize establishing meaningful and egalitarian relationships between their members, even if efficiency in organizing and mobilizing was sacrificed in the process. Other chapters emphasized different aspects of the anarchist tradition.

At the end of 1967, Penelope Rosemont and other Chicago radicals affiliated with Solidarity Bookshop organized the Louis Lingg Memorial Chapter of SDS. Lingg was the most intransigent of the eight anarchists convicted in the Chicago Haymarket Affair of 1886; he blew off the side of his face with a dynamite cartridge smuggled into his jail cell to deprive the state of its ability to execute him.[134] The Lingg Memorial Chapter of SDS was organized in this spirit of total resistance. Its hastily composed statement of purpose announced, "This chapter is formed in unrelenting opposition to 'law and order' . . . which means the rich before the poor, white before black, and old before young. . . . 'Law and order' which seeks only to suppress or contain social revolution, maintain imperialism and refine the repressions of daily life."[135] Though it sent a representative to the spring 1968 SDS National Convention in East Lansing, Michigan (where both red and black flags flanked the speakers' podium), the Lingg Memorial Chapter does not appear to have had a long life.

The SDS chapter at the Massachusetts Institute of Technology also leaned heavily in a libertarian socialist direction. Students there were advised by a young linguistics professor named Noam Chomsky. As a teenager in the 1940s, Chomsky had visited a radical uncle in New York City who exposed him to the *Fraye Arbeter Shtime* and books by Rudolf Rocker and other anarchists.[136] While Chomsky was also influenced by classical liberals, labor Zionists, and others, the writings of the anarcho-syndicalists left a distinct imprint on him.[137] In *American Power and the New Mandarins,* his first book on politics, Chomsky excoriated American intellectuals for their tacit or explicit support for the war in Vietnam and lionized the Spanish anarcho-syndicalist movement.[138] Students also gained support from Howard Zinn, a Boston University historian who had been an early supporter of SNCC and expressed sympathy with anarchism.[139]

Chomsky and Zinn worked with a variety of talented student-activists, among them Michael Albert, George Katsiaficas, and Robin Hahnel. The group blockaded a campus recruiting session held by representatives of Dow Chemical (producers of Agent Orange) and organized antiwar demonstrations that drew upward of a hundred thousand people. Members' diverse influences were put on display when the chapter decided to rename itself. As Albert later wrote, "We voted among Ho Chi Minh SDS, Sacco and Vanzetti SDS, and Rosa Luxemburg SDS." Sacco and Vanzetti would have been appropriate, given the students' location in Boston, while the Viet Cong leader was a hero to most SDS members by 1968. However, Albert explained, "We went for Rosa for her gender and her anti-Leninism."[140]

In 1968, Albert was elected student body president. In the school yearbook, he encouraged graduates to join the revolutionary struggle. With many forms of radicalism on offer, he gave specific advice. "The movement for achieving [a better world] is itself the embryo of the new society. Any defects that it might have will appear in full grown horror in the world we are to build.... Revolutionary violence must be self conscious and seek its own dissolution. Revolutionary leadership must be anti-authoritarian, it must come from the initiative of the people. Revolutionary discipline must be offered and not demanded. Revolutionaries must always struggle against their own tendencies toward racism, chauvinism, and the accumulation of the power of privilege."[141] Despite this clear promotion of anarchist values, Rosa Luxemburg SDS is less significant for what it accomplished in the 1960s than for the contributions core members of the group made later in life, including development of the theory of participatory economics, as noted in this book's epilogue.

In 1967, Murray Bookchin organized the Anarchos Group as a successor to the East Side Anarchists. The group created a journal (also titled *Anarchos*) primarily composed of Bookchin's essays on anarchism, ecology, and libertarian organizational forms, which in 1971 would be issued as his influential book *Post-scarcity Anarchism*. Following the Democratic National Convention of 1968, Anarchos saw a need for more coherence in the movement, and determined that SDS was the most likely vehicle for achieving that aim. Members also recognized, with alarm, the growing tendency of some SDS members to adopt the tactics, organizational forms, and posture of old-line Marxist-Leninist groups.

The Anarchos Group decided to participate in the June 1969 SDS national convention with hopes of organizing a libertarian caucus that could lead the student movement in an anarchist direction.[142] "We were trying to wed the potentially utopistic visions of the counterculture with the socialistic visions of the New Left and with anarchism, basically relying on an ecological perspective to make this marriage," Bookchin would later explain.[143] It is unclear how many members of the Anarchos Group attended the convention. However, they distributed two thousand copies of Bookchin's anti-Leninist polemic, "Listen, Marxist!" and found many delegates receptive.[144] The group invited supporters to a meeting at the IWW General Headquarters, where they constituted themselves as the Radical Decentralist Project and adopted two resolutions drafted by Bookchin.

The resolutions first challenged the notion that a "tightly disciplined 'vanguard' organization is indispensible to the success of a revolution."[145] The Radical Decentralist Project argued, instead, that "deep-seated historical forces" compel people to spontaneously take action in revolutionary situations. The project believed revolutionary organizations were necessary, but only as "catalysts" that could help individuals develop "consciousness" and learn how to act as "libertarian human beings." To shift SDS in this direction, their proposals called on SDS members to adopt more libertarian lifestyles as a means of shaking off patterns of bourgeois authoritarianism and to "reawaken imagination [and] spontaneity." Structurally, the proposal called for chapters to reorganize themselves "on an assembly basis, based on direct democracy with no formalities."[146]

Bookchin claims that on the basis of these proposals, the decentralists built a caucus of approximately 250 people at the convention and convinced a number of genuine students to run for national-level offices in the organization.[147] Despite this significant presence, the decentralists were outnumbered by the Progressive Labor Party faction and the Revolutionary Youth Movement. The convention quickly became a chaotic contest, with the latter group eventually walking out of the convention en masse and then expelling the Progressive Labor Party faction the following day. Yet the Revolutionary Youth Movement faction would itself subdivide into groupings that would soon give rise to the Weather Underground and what would become known as the "new communist movement."[148] Unprepared for this level of political maneuvering, the Radical Decentralist Project withdrew to reconsider its strategy. In the wake of this faction fighting, however, SDS never recovered as a stable national organization and the Radical Decentralist Project dissolved.

After the national convention debacle, the Anarchos Group called for anarchists to gather independently with hopes of creating a new organization that might serve as an alternative to SDS. Anarchists based in Madison responded and helped organize a gathering that would take place September 5–16, 1969, in Black River Falls, Wisconsin.

Approximately ninety individuals from the United States and Canada attended.[149] By all accounts, the results were disappointing. Louise Crowley, of Madison, stated gently, "The essential process of getting acquainted, of beginning to understand each others' varied emphases and styles of revolutionary work, consumed nearly all the time allowed us."[150]

Bookchin later complained, "We were obliged to sit in a 'non-hierarchical' circle, which meant that instead of a coherent discussion we had a drifting stream of consciousness."[151] (Ironically, the Radical Decentralist Project's organizational proposal to SDS had called for the abandonment of parliamentary procedure in favor of free-flowing conversations of this sort.) Bookchin's resentment may have been colored by the gathering's refusal to adopt versions of statements the Anarchos Group had prepared ahead of time, citing the need for a collective writing process. The conference broke up without having established an anarchist-oriented student organization and without issuing a statement of principles. Participants agreed only to continue discussions through a mailing list and a newsletter.

According to Bookchin, participants were divided between the Anarchos Group's interest in an ecology-oriented movement and the desire of others to focus on Situationist-inspired politics. After the conference broke up, Crowley and another Madison activist, Michael Brownstein, attempted to draft a compromise statement that could speak to points of "common agreement." The attempt to blend Situationist language with Bookchin's "social ecology" perspective is striking: "The historic contradiction between the utopian possibilities in desire and the tragic actualities imposed by material scarcity has entered its ultimate crisis. The new technology prepares conditions for resolving the contradiction: an end to want and toil, unleashing the latent exuberance of human imagination and creativity." Though light on strategy, the statement concluded, "The future must take on a palpable life in the present; the revolutionary movement prefigures the postrevolutionary society."[152]

Reactions to the draft statement ranged, according to Brownstein, "from rapture to disgust."[153] Three issues of the newsletter appeared between September and December, but the "Black River Movement" soon collapsed.

The Black River project indicates that, like other sectors of the Left, anarchists' expectations about the possibilities of change in the late 1960s were far out of step with their ability to realize such goals. Despite their biting critiques of the repercussions of authoritarian behavior and factionalism in other sectors of the Left, anarchists were unable to overcome divisiveness themselves, as allegiances began to harden around a new set of big name theorists and master texts. An additional pattern set by the rest of the New Left appeared within the anarchist movement as well: at the same time male-dominated antiwar, antiracist, and countercultural efforts began to fracture, women took on more public roles and reworked movement concepts to articulate a powerful critique of gender and sexual oppression.

ANARCHISM, FEMINISM, AND GAY LIBERATION

Given the diversity of organizations and initiatives that promoted versions of anarchism in the 1960s, it is remarkable how little attention they paid to issues of gender equality. Although a few women, such as Penelope Rosemont and the Living Theatre's Judith Malina, played prominent roles, men predominated as organizers, theorists, and performers. Moreover, anarchist-influenced groups, such as UAW/MF and the WPP, consciously worked to "toughen up" the counterculture and promoted forms of masculinity and sexual freedom that reinforced traditional power relationships as often as they challenged them. (During the student occupation of Columbia University, to take one blatant example, UAW/MF circulated a leaflet with an illustration that showed the slogan "All Power to the Communes" being ejaculated out of an erect penis.)[154] Hardly limited to anarchist sectors of the movement, sexism pervaded the New Left and was a major impetus for the emergence in 1967 of women's liberation organizations.[155]

While plumbing history for precedents and useful theories of gender and sexual oppression, feminists quickly recovered the writings of Emma Goldman. In 1971, historian Alix Kates Shulman marveled at the fact that "Emma Goldman's name has re-emerged from obscurity to become a veritable password of radical feminism. . . . Her face adorns T-shirts, her name headlines posters, her words are repeated on banners."[156] Radical women's groups also reworked guerrilla theater and other cultural tactics. The Women's International Terrorist Conspiracy from Hell (WITCH) placed a hex on Wall Street, whereas UAW/MF had only marched on it.[157] In turn, the new autonomous women's movement soon reshaped the face of anarchism, at first in subtle ways. In 1969, Louise Crowley coauthored the Black River draft statement. In 1970, the Yippies and White Panthers sent an all-female delegation to Vietnam. In 1972, Su Negrin, a former participant in the Anarchos discussion group, authored *Begin at Start: Some Thoughts on Personal Liberation and World Change* and published it through her own Times Change Press. The book is an early attempt to integrate feminism and gay liberation with the politics of ecology and "hip culture."[158] Women in Chicago produced ten issues of *Siren: A Journal of Anarcho-Feminism* between 1971 and 1973.[159]

The Gay Liberation Front, which formed in New York shortly after the landmark Stonewall Riot of 1969, was also linked to the anarchist milieu. Jim Fouratt, a gay member of the Yippies and the short-lived New York Diggers, advocated ongoing street confrontations and collaboration with other movement sectors as an early participant.[160] On marches, members frequently chanted, "Two, four, six, eight, smash the church, smash the state!"[161] The group adopted what one member called "a structureless structure" that "embraced participatory democracy and the ideal of consensus." Members grouped themselves into small cells based on interests and tasks. Not all participants appreciated this arrangement, however, with one Marxist member denouncing it as "some Murray Bookchin inspired notion."[162] Though many members of the Gay Liberation Front turned to more traditional campaigning, radical queers have maintained an affinity with, and presence within, U.S. anarchism to the present day.

The debate over "structure" was not limited to the Gay Liberation Front. Anarchist-minded feminists began to locate one another as they responded to a heated discussion regarding what organizational structures were appropriate to the women's movement. In 1972, radical feminist Jo Freeman published "The Tyranny of Structurelessness," which pointed to faults in supposedly "leaderless, structureless" feminist groups. As feminists had dissected the ways men dominated New Left organizations, some had come to argue that hierarchical organizations with designated leaders were masculinist by nature. Suggesting small, loosely networked, and egalitarian forms as a feminist alternative, they unconsciously reiterated long-standing anarchist critiques and purported solutions to organizational matters. However, Freeman argued that the alternatives often unintentionally produced unaccountable, informal leaders, as well as resentment among members. Many on the Left recognized that her criticisms might apply equally to anarchist formations. Attempts to reckon with these issues by anarcha-feminists such as Cathy Levine, Peggy Kornegger, Carol Ehrlich, and Marian Leighton marked out an anarchist tendency within feminism, and a feminist tendency within anarchism.[163] These formations would grow and challenge the heterosexist priorities and practices of the anarchist movement throughout the 1970s, just as anarcha-feminists such as Goldman, Voltairine de Cleyre, and Maria Roda had challenged them early in the twentieth century.

CONTEMPORARY ANARCHISM COMES INTO VIEW

Historian David Farber has insightfully argued, "Whereas the New Left staked its fortunes on the belief that through new or recovered forms of political organization like local organization, collectivities, consensual decision making, and direct rather than mass-mediated information processing the People could regain sovereignty over their own lives, the Yippies staked their political fortunes on the primacy of consciousness over social forms and structure."[164] I extend his argument to suggest that not just the Yippies but the entire countercultural Left staked its fortunes on "consciousness." Moreover, the dual emphasis on new forms of organization and transformation of consciousness succinctly marks the ways in which midcentury anarchism fundamentally shaped the movements of the 1960s. Both were strategic hallmarks of the anarchist–pacifist–avant-garde coalition that developed in the 1940s and 1950s. Turning decidedly away from the route of labor organizing and electoral politics pursued by the socialist and communist Left, the predominantly white sectors of the New Left amplified the concerns (addiction to war, sexual repression, consumerism, alienation from nature) and the approaches (nonviolent direct action, communal living, cultural production, decentralized and egalitarian organizational forms) that anarchists and pacifists had experimented with and theorized during those years.

Chronologically, this level of influence makes a certain sense. Classical anarchism was already in steep decline as communism came to the fore during the interwar years. As a result, anarchists were ready to reinvent their tradition sooner; they began cobbling together the elements of a new Left in the early 1940s, a decade and a half before a significant number of communists felt the need to fundamentally reorient their movement. Like the Marxist tradition, anarchism sprouted a contingent of New York intellectuals in the century's middle decades. This group established personal and intellectual ties to an additional crowd of San Francisco intellectuals. Unlike the Marxists, few members of either contingent lurched toward conservatism later in life.

If anarchism contributed important components to the movements of the 1960s, those years of struggle also fundamentally reconfigured the tradition. The late 1960s can be seen as a threshold in the history of U.S. anarchism—a moment of transition between the periods I term mid-twentieth-century anarchism and contemporary anarchism. In the twenty years after the outbreak of World War II, U.S. radicals developed what might be termed a "valley time anarchism"—an adaptation of the movement's values and practices to a period of relatively scant social-movement activity, focused on contemplation, self-expression, symbolic acts of dissent, and self-selecting communities living by shared values. The 1960s, by contrast, were a "mountain time" for radical movements, to use the terminology of the revered trainer Myles Horton—a period of political ferment and movement expansion.[165] When the terrain first began to change, anarchists generally attempted to adapt their valley times practices to broader, newly receptive constituencies rather than to recall and recalibrate the mass-organizing practices the tradition had developed during previous mountain times.

In the early 1960s, three faint strands of anarchism were present in the United States. The Libertarian League represented a residual anarcho-syndicalism, which had begun to reorient under the influence of the early civil rights movement. Yet as radicalism grew, it was unable to articulate a new labor strategy *or* embrace rebellious youth as a collective revolutionary subject. Though sidelined in the 1960s, new syndicalist and councilist formations would emerge in the early 1970s. They continued to struggle for traction, however, given their largely middle-class composition.

The anarchist pacifist strand that operated through the War Resisters League and *Liberation* magazine during the 1940s and 1950s proved important to the development of Students for a Democratic Society and the

Resistance during the following decade. Though SDS members focused on organizing college students and draftees in these years, antiracism and processes of collective decision-making remained central to their analyses. At the end of the decade they readily incorporated feminism into their framework. Gregory Calvert, former SDS national secretary, later asserted, "The notion of participatory democracy . . . laid the groundwork for a reexamination of the concept of direct democracy that the world inherited from 5th century Athens and that had not been seriously reevaluated since Rousseau in the 18th century."[166] Such a reexamination of the general assembly, town hall meetings, and participatory economic systems became central to the anarchist and near-anarchist thought developed in the late twentieth century by figures such as Murray Bookchin, Noam Chomsky, and David Graeber. This represents a significant shift from the categorical rejection of political democracy by early-twentieth-century anarchists and the hesitancy of midcentury anarchists to think beyond the scale of community. The movements of the 1960s, in other words, posed a crucial question, which has not yet been satisfactorily resolved: Is anarchism (now) a form of radical democracy, and if so, what are the ramifications?

The third, culturalist, strand of anarchism took perhaps the most complex itinerary through the decade. Beginning in the late 1950s, the Beat subculture introduced many young white Americans to African American hip culture and to European avant-garde traditions. Taken together, these influences convinced them of the desirability and possibility of cultural revolution and prompted some to embrace an anarchism focused on toppling social conventions and embracing pleasure. Marxist-derived critical theory and ultraleft thought became central to these anarchists' praxis in a way it had not to their predecessors. This subtendency, more than any other, revolutionized anarchist graphics and aesthetics as it embraced the era's more versatile printing technology.

Although pacifism predominated among anarchists in the United States between 1940 and 1965, that commitment was challenged over the next five years. While members of the Resistance and the Catholic Worker held fast to the principle of nonviolence, groups such as UAW/MF encouraged new forms of sabotage and direct confrontation with authorities. Struggles against racism and colonialism influenced both camps. While the nonviolence of Mohandas Gandhi and black southerners inspired the anarchist pacifism of the mid-twentieth century, the rioting and turn to armed self-defense by African Americans in the northern and western states after 1964 inspired a revival of insurrectionist thinking by decade's end. For the first time since the second decade of the twentieth century, black and Latino city dwellers seemed to represent a social group large, dispossessed, and volatile enough that it might tear the social order down in one quick swoop. That did not happen, and since that time urban rioting seems to have implicitly replaced eighteenth- and nineteenth-century-style (and -scope) social uprisings in the strategic imaginary of insurrection-minded anarchists living in the United States.

As the New Left splintered in the early 1970s, anarchism was in a contradictory position. It is evident that the number of people in the United States sympathetic to anarchism grew by thousands during the course of the decade. However, by the time anarchists found one another and rallied publicly under the black flag, government repression was again on the rise and the mass movements were losing momentum. Moreover, it is likely that by decade's end anarchism had never meant more things to more people. What emerged in the early 1970s was not a unified anarchist movement as such but an array of small groups excited by communalism, syndicalism, situationism, libertarian socialism, ultraleftism, revolutionary nonviolence, anarcha-feminism, and social ecology. Expecting more mountain times ahead, many entered the 1970s viewing the wrong-headed analyses of other factions of the Left as the biggest obstacles in the path to achieving fundamental social change. They were forced to moderate their ambitions quickly when they ran headlong into the emergent New Right and a business elite furiously organizing a neoliberal counterattack against the achievements of the 1960s.

Conclusion

I have endeavored in the eight preceding chapters to compose a *prehistory* of contemporary U.S. anarchism. Anarchism has, of course, continued to develop in complex, sometimes contradictory, ways since the early 1970s and to affect life in the United States (and beyond) in the process. Yet it is useful to note that activists and theorists in these later years have tended to define their ideas and practices in comparison to the movements of the 1960s, which continue to serve as a high-water mark of radical politics internationally. *Unruly Equality,* then, has traced the evolution of U.S. anarchism from one plateau—the Progressive Era—to another, the "long 1960s." In some respects this history shows anarchism coming full circle, from the No Conscription League and the sex radicalism of the Ferrer Center community in 1916 to the Resistance and the emergence of anarcha-feminist formations in the early 1970s. In many other aspects, however, the movement of the 1970s would appear nearly unrecognizable to an old militant like Luigi Galleani or Alexander Berkman. In this conclusion, I compile the historical claims I have made throughout the book and offer a few points of consideration for those seeking to advance the linked values of liberty, equality, and solidarity today. In the epilogue that follows, I venture a rudimentary sketch of the development of U.S. anarchism from the early 1970s to Occupy Wall Street, which I hope will serve as a jumping-off point for future studies.

The most fundamental points I have argued are the following:

1. Anarchists have been continuously active in the United States since the 1880s.

2. Anarchism has been a far more complex phenomenon than is generally known or acknowledged.

3. Anarchism has significantly shaped the broader U.S. Left, including the movements of the 1960s.

While anarchists have never dominated the Left numerically, they have been consistent experimenters and innovators in the realms of theory, art, and tactics. They have frequently served as a moral compass, declaring that facets of society (sexual oppression, the nuclear arms race, and more recently, prison) are so wrong that they must be abolished, even if that requires reordering nearly everything. Scholarship on the history of U.S. radicalism has frequently neglected or minimized the contributions of anarchists. This does a disservice even to those strongly opposed to anarchist ideas, since it prevents precise dissection of their faults.

The U.S. anarchist movement expanded between 1905 and 1917 owing to (1) its ability to attract industrial and extractive laborers via its affiliation with the Industrial Workers of the World, and (2) its capacity to simultaneously interest middle- and upper-class supporters through anarchists' bold work in favor of civil liberties, women's and homosexuals' liberation, novel forms of education, and modernism in the arts. The Red Scare of 1917–1920 reversed this momentum. It did so by imprisoning and deporting the de facto leadership of the movement and by making possible an ethno-racial restructuring of the U.S. working class that dissolved the traditional base of U.S. anarchism: poor European immigrants.

A series of additional threats and crises added to the difficulty of rebuilding the movement during the 1920s and 1930s. The decline of the IWW created a need for anarchists to develop a novel labor strategy. Yet prisoner defense campaigns and efforts to combat communism and fascism left them little time or energy to do so, much less to build on their prewar feminist and artistic initiatives. Their most concerted efforts in these years, such as the creation of modern schools and intentional communities, marked a shift toward gradualist modes of change. Anarchists abstained from the major organizing drives and leftist coalitions of the 1930s, and the traditional movement all but collapsed as leading figures clashed over how to respond to the Second World War.

As classical anarchist priorities and strategies faded out, contemporary anarchist practices and interests came to the fore. The tipping point of this cross-fade occurred in the early 1940s, when a new generation of anarchists largely abandoned labor organizing and established enduring relationships with radical pacifists. Drawing on varied religious traditions and new schools of social theory, some shifted their energies toward a long-run strategy of cultural transformation. These anarchists recovered the focus of some Progressive Era anarchists on education, arts, sexuality, and living "otherwise." Others devoted ideas and resources to the momentous struggles to dismantle white supremacy and the system of formal colonialism in the 1950s.

Anarchist *ideas* were highly influential to the mass movements of the 1960s, even though, as organizers, anarchists were disjointed and institutionally weak. The principles of decentralization, self-governance, and antiauthoritarian leadership informed the concept of participatory democracy as a goal and a practice within Students for a Democratic Society. The central themes of postwar anarchism—sexual liberation, psychological deconditioning, environmentalism, and rejection of alienating consumer society— became the driving concerns of the counterculture. The same can be said regarding methods: hippies, like the postwar anarchists, placed significant stock in the consciousness-transforming power of music and other arts, enlightenment through meditation or drugs, and exemplary communal living. In figures such as Emma Goldman and in the movement's critique of domineering leadership styles, second-wave feminists found their own uses for the anarchist tradition.

During this period, anarchism was such a marginal current that it was largely passed down in a face-to-face manner, through family ties and personal mentorship relationships. If we view the Haymarket martyrs and Johann Most as the first generation of social anarchists in the United States, *Unruly Equality* suggests that four additional generations made their own contributions to the movement by the end of the 1960s, each operating in a different social context. The following chart gives a sense of these generations, based on the dates of birth and death of figures central to my narrative.

I have also suggested a framework for analyzing anarchist strategies and cultural practices. From its nineteenth-century origins until today, anarchism has relied on three general strategies: insurrection, mass organizing, and prefiguration. Insurrectionists attempt to bring on fast, far-reaching change by encouraging mass violent revolt, often through propaganda of the deed. Italian American insurrectionaries attempted to trigger an uprising of this sort via their bombing campaign during World War I. After they were defeated, U.S. anarchists sidelined insurrectionism until Up Against the Wall/Motherfuckers promoted rioting in solidarity with black urban

Birth and death dates of representative U.S. anarchists, organized by activist "generation"

Name	Date of Birth	Date of Death
GENERATION 1		
Johann Most	February 5, 1846	March 17, 1906
Albert Parsons	June 20, 1848	November 11, 1887
Lucy Parsons	c. 1853	March 7, 1942
Louis Lingg	September 9, 1864	November 10, 1887
GENERATION 2		
Luigi Galleani	August 12, 1861	November 4, 1931
Emma Goldman	June 27, 1869	May 14, 1940
Alexander Berkman	November 21, 1870	June 28, 1936
Harry Kelly	June 14, 1871	1953
Hippolyte Havel	1871	1950
Rudolf Rocker	March 25, 1873	September 19, 1953
GENERATION 3		
W. S. Van Valkenburgh	October 25, 1884	May 22, 1938
G. P. Maximoff	November 10, 1893	March 16, 1950
Marcus Graham	1893	1985
Ammon Hennacy	July 24, 1893	January 14, 1970
Rose Pesotta	November 20, 1896	December 6, 1965
Mollie Steimer	November 21, 1897	July 23, 1980
Sam Dolgoff	October 10, 1902	October 24, 1990
Abe Bluestein	November 1, 1909	December 3, 1997
GENERATION 4		
Dorothy Day	November 8, 1897	November 29, 1980
Kenneth Rexroth	December 22, 1905	June 6, 1982
Paul Goodman	September 9, 1911	August 2, 1972
David Dellinger	August 22, 1915	May 25, 2004
Holley Cantine	February 14, 1916	January 2, 1977
Audrey Goodfriend	1920	2012
David Thoreau Wieck	December 13, 1921	July 1, 1997
Diva Agostinelli	1921	2007
Judith Malina	June 4, 1926	April 10, 2015
GENERATION 5		
Murray Bookchin	January 1921	July 30, 2006
Fredy Perlman	August 20, 1934	July 25, 1985
Ben Morea	1941	–
Peter Werbe	1942	–
Penelope Rosemont	1942	–
Franklin Rosemont	October 2, 1943	April 12, 2009

"insurrections." Mass organizing (to win reforms while building capacity for revolution) took the form of syndicalism before the Second World War. After the war, organizing anarchists shifted focus from labor to antiwar and antiracist initiatives. Prefigurative strategies provide oases of freedom and solidarity in a world marked by oppression and personal competition; they attempt to win converts and delegitimize the establishment by modeling anarchist values in action.

It is useful to distinguish three kinds of prefiguration. Anarchists have often built prefigurative counterinstitutions. These range from the Stelton Colony's Modern School and the Walden School founded by Audrey Goodfriend and David Koven, to the Sunrise co-operative farming community and the nonprofit Solidarity Bookshop founded by the Rebel Worker Group. They model alternative, equitable ways to accomplish socially necessary tasks. A second form might be labeled "prefigurative lifestyle." Rather than a collective endeavor that seeks to accomplish specific tasks, lifestyle prefiguration revolves around making personal choices that deviate from social conventions and expectations. Emma Goldman's decision to have sex outside of marriage, Marcus Graham's refusal to eat meat or use large-scale machinery, and the San Francisco poets' decision to focus on writing and time outdoors rather than on earning a high salary are all examples. The hope has always been that the nonconformist acts of a few will inspire a critical mass of imitators.

The third form of prefiguration actually belongs to the mass-organizing anarchist strategy. It consists of the idea that a movement's organizations should function according to its principles, and in some cases, that these organizations will actually grow into the governing institutions of a post-revolutionary social order. This principle was most famously stated in the IWW's claim that it would "form the structure of the new society within the shell of the old." Anarchists wrestled with the implications of this principle continuously throughout the twentieth century. They judged whether groups—from the Congress of Industrial Organizations to the Student Nonviolent Coordinating Committee—were truly radical and whether their efforts would create "real change" based on matters such as their staffing structures and the autonomy of local chapters. After reading the pacifist philosophies of Mohandas Gandhi and Bart de Ligt, they argued whether adherence to the principle required them to disavow any use of violence. Prefigurative modes of organizing have, undoubtedly, become a defining characteristic of contemporary anarchism.

It is useful to recognize that the three strategies of change anarchists have pursued require different institutional features. Mass organizing efforts must coordinate the actions of large numbers of people spread across different locales. Insurrectionary groups need to emphasize secrecy and security owing to their focus on illegal activity. Prefigurative counterinstitutions put a premium on structures that place anarchist values and visions on display. These conflicting organizational requirements have routinely stymied anarchists' efforts.

Culture has always been vital to anarchism, both in the sense of daily practices with shared significance and in the production of representations and meaningful "texts" such as cartoons, poetry, songs, plays, and apparel.[1] Yet just as their goals and methods changed, the types of culture anarchists contributed to, and made use of, also shifted in relation to broader cultural developments. In the early twentieth century, non-English-speaking anarchists developed radical folk cultures in immigrant neighborhoods, wherein theater groups and singing societies crafted a group identity based on shared language and values. In the second decade of the twentieth century and again in the 1940s, anarchists made vital contributions to artistic and literary avant-garde movements that challenged the themes, styles, and assumptions of "high culture," ironically earning them places in the canon in the process. Anarchists tumbled into the nascent realm of mass commercial youth culture beginning in the late 1950s, when Beat culture began to trend in the mainstream, and again in the late 1960s, when the MC5 attempted to ride the major labor horse. The turn to DIY punk by many anarchists in the 1980s might be interpreted as a middle ground between the avant-garde and commodified youth culture in a period when few forms of meaning-making escaped marketization.

Although my primary goal has been to recover the history of twentieth-century U.S. anarchism rather than to discern strategic advice from it, a few interpretive comments seem in order. To my mind, the legacy of U.S. anarchism in this period is deeply ambivalent. Anarchists excelled at developing broad critiques of the social order. They were often ahead of the curve on identifying social problems (the oppression of gays and lesbians, environmental threats, the alienation of the affluent) and linking these issues to modes of domination. During the twentieth century they wove an array of new ideas into the body of anarchist thought, cultivating a rich set of tools for identifying and interrogating the many ways that power operates. The tradition is also replete with individuals who have modeled empathy, solidarity, perseverance, sacrifice, and bravery in their efforts to make the world a more humane place.

Yet significant limitations are also apparent. In the twentieth century, anarchists were either uninterested or unable to systematize their perspective, and they have not excelled at engaging ideological opponents in an effort to win the war of ideas. The tendency to criticize broadly, but to inconsistently refine and defend positions, is likely related to the scant resources and the institutional marginalization that most anarchists coped with throughout the period under study. Nevertheless, a number of consequences follow from it. Beginning in the 1940s, anarchists made important progress on updating the theory of power articulated by their nineteenth-century predecessors—exploring psychosexual aspects of domination and placing more emphasis on childhood socialization, for example. Yet from the perspective of the present, their lack of sustained attention to certain subjects is surprising.

Today, anarchism is often lauded for offering a broader analysis of power than Marxism—one that, like contemporary intersectional feminist theories, places as much weight on racial and gender oppression as on economic exploitation. The story offered in this book, however, suggests this is a more recent development. While U.S. anarchists directed significant energy toward combating forms of hetero/sexist domination during the first two decades of the twentieth century, they did not emphasize these matters again until the late 1960s, a full half century later. U.S. anarchists did not consistently theorize and confront racial oppression, at home or abroad, until the late 1940s. While they derived considerable inspiration from black freedom struggles during the 1950s and 1960s, anarchists did not develop a unique anarchist theory of racism, white supremacy, or imperialism during this period.

Broadly speaking, the anarchists studied here tended to theorize from their own experiences rather than investigating the ways in which groups of people occupying different subject positions experienced power. While they were more "internationalist" in outlook than many other U.S. citizens, this often boiled down to an attention to political dynamics in Europe (reflecting the early immigrant composition of the movement) rather than the world as a whole. This emphasis on Western ideological conflicts, rather than the dynamics of colonialism and anti-imperial struggle, for example, clearly shaped anarchist priorities.

As adherents to a political ideology often identified solely by its opposition to "the state," twentieth-century U.S. anarchists devoted surprisingly little time to developing a rigorous critical analysis of the nature and behaviors of different sorts of states. While anarchists were early and prescient critics of the regime established by the Bolsheviks in the Soviet Union, they were slow to sharpen their understanding of liberal democracies. The unique analytic contribution of anarchists from the 1920s to the 1950s was to show the similarities between fascist, communist, and liberal welfare states. Yet that lens also limited critics' abilities to see differences and to develop a clear-eyed analysis of the ways liberalism evolved after the Great Depression. This oversight, in turn, hindered anarchists' ability to organize new constituencies amid the changing circumstances of the mid-twentieth century.

Between the 1930s and the 1950s, anarchists overwhelmingly viewed the New Deal, and more generally the rise of the Keynesian welfare state, as a sophisticated form of co-optation that represented a severe setback for the labor movement and, hence, for social anarchism. This interpretation was essentially built into their bedrock belief that political states can do no good for ordinary people. Worries about the depoliticizing potential of state income supports were not unwarranted. Yet this perspective naturalized the outcomes of Keynesianism in two troubling respects. First, it discounted the pressure labor and radical movements had exerted on elites in order to win unemployment insurance, overtime pay, and other gains, reinforcing gloomy assessments of the midcentury labor movement. Thirty years later, however, the Diggers, Murray Bookchin, and others claimed that new utopian possibilities arose from the unprecedented growth of First World economies. They assumed this "postscarcity" condition would continue indefinitely, as it appeared to be an outgrowth of technological developments as capitalism ran its course, rather than (at least partly) a politically imposed division of wealth. For this reason, few anarchists saw the gains won by workers in the 1930s as vulnerable, or even as "their" gains to defend when the business class launched a concerted attack against them in the 1970s. Like many other progressive and radical forces, they were caught off guard by the onset of neoliberalism.

Anarchism is characterized by its simultaneous advocacy of social equality and personal freedom. But this study suggests these goals are taken up in different measures at different times. During the mid-twentieth century the threat of totalitarianism loomed large in the anarchist imagination. While most Americans feared and loathed fascism and Stalinism during these years, they saw the United States as a bulwark against the spread of these political forms. Anarchists, on the other hand, tended to view Cold War liberalism as another variant of state capitalism and a stealth totalitarianism. Given these concerns, and the fact that the 1940s through the 1960s was a period of rising living standards for many in the United States, anarchists tended to focus more on defending personal freedom and expression during these years than on fighting for equality.

In hindsight it appears many anarchists in this period dismissed the importance of economic-justice struggles too quickly and placed undue emphasis on the emotional toll caused by alienation and loss of particular kinds of human community. While this focus has continuously sparked interested in anarchism from certain groups, especially comfortably bored young people, it has not proven to be a problem so unbearable or irresolvable that it has inclined masses to seek revolution. The fact that some anarchists remained focused on expanding the scope of their own expression and pleasure proved divisive to late-twentieth-century anarchists as other groups issued new calls for gender, racial, economic, and global justice as neoliberalism exacerbated inequalities anew.

Twentieth-century anarchists have been consistent and ingenious inventors of new tactics, many of which have been put to great use by activists who do not share all their views. The self-imposed necessity of inventing nonelectoral means of struggle has, in this sense, certainly been the mother of invention. The movement's continuous marginality, however, suggests shortcomings in its broader strategic approaches. Anarchists lost sight of the importance of organizing people to join their movement or pursue goals aligned with anarchism during the doldrum decades. They did not build their own mass labor unions or establish the capacity to direct existing ones after the First World War, and they organized only sporadically after that. Anarchist pacifists attempted to organize against war and racism immediately after World War II, and anarchist-influenced students in SDS and the Resistance organized against the Vietnam War. But nagging questions about who constituted anarchists' "base" (workers? pacifists? rebel youth?), paired with the difficulties of winning recruits during this period, led to an emphasis on art, prefigurative practices, and small-group confrontations.

While certain prefigurative practices can be shown to produce personal and movement-building benefits, their touted "demonstration effects" have never proven sufficient as means of social transformation in themselves. The idea of immediately starting to build a new society has been enticing to successive generations, but it has also proven distracting from other necessary tasks. Similarly, many midcentury anarchists misspent energy on opposing organization and leadership *tout court*. They provided useful warnings about the potential for labor and movement leaders to become indifferent to the wishes of participants, to seek personal rather than group goals, and to be tempted to trade moderation for status. But their "misleaders" thesis could also blind anarchists to the tasks in front of them. Believing that workers would behave in a revolutionary fashion to forward their interests if only they were not misdirected by corrupted leaders assumes that such individuals naturally identify as workers and instinctively oppose capitalism. This belief precluded some anarchists from seeing the necessity of helping people interpret the world in a radical way. Perspectives that appeared inborn because they were so widespread in early-twentieth-century immigrant communities proved, by the 1950s, to be products of relentless political education and cultural production by organized movements.[2]

The misleader thesis also neglected to analyze the fact that informal leaders routinely emerged in purportedly leaderless formations, creating a different set of predictable organizational problems. In 1962, Sam Dolgoff shared some simple wisdom on this matter. "I think that all organization carries within itself the germ of bureaucratization," he told an interviewer. "To say that we need no organization at all is, of course, simply fantastic and idiotic in view of the interdependence of social life and the fact that man is by nature a social being who must combine with his fellow man in order to achieve common aims. So we must have organization, and the problem revolves around reducing to a minimum the apparent and real danger of concentration of power."[3] That said, anarchists have also often overlooked the opposite "danger"—the deconcentration of their own power to such an extent that they become incapable of widely promoting and defending their values.

During the interwar and postwar years, U.S. anarchists lost the ability to launch campaigns, move a crowd, and command national press coverage the way they had done quite effectively before World War I. In this light, the Mother Earth Group's multipronged strategy of building mass radical unions while boldly leading liberals on the issues of immigration, sexuality, and war remains, to my mind, a high-water mark of sophistication deserving greater study and replication. Yet this should not obscure, or prevent us from celebrating, the vital contributions anarchists made since that time in combating fascism, remaking adolescent education, developing cooperative enterprises, resisting militarism, confronting racial segregation, or inventing powerful new artistic and literary forms that have saved the lives and emotional wellbeing of countless misfits, nonconformists, and outraged souls.

While twentieth-century U.S. anarchism should not be idealized or overromanticized, nor should it be ignored or underappreciated as an intellectual tradition, way of life, and creative force of social transformation. Too often, scholars and radicals loyal to other traditions have imagined anarchism as a static and archaic ideology while recognizing the complex ways in which Marxism, feminism, and other liberatory schemas have evolved over time. Anarchists' own relative disinterest in documenting and studying their intellectual and organizational traditions has not helped matters. *Unruly Equality* demonstrates not only the dynamism of twentieth-century anarchism but also the ways in which anarchists' concerns have paralleled and even anticipated the developmental thrust of progressive and radical thought as authoritarian communism, social democracy, and racial liberalism have each proven themselves insufficient to the enormous task of human liberation. The sociologist Ben Aggers explains that critical social theory, as developed by leftist intellectuals since the 1930s, "distinguishes between the past and present, largely characterized by domination, exploitation, and oppression, and a possible future rid of these phenomena. . . . By focusing on the dialectical connection between everyday life and structure, critical social theory holds people responsible for their own liberation and admonishes them not to oppress others in the name of distant future liberation."[4] I am struck by the extent to which this description accords with anarchism as it has developed in the United States over the last century.

But more than a theory, anarchism remains a practice that today informs movements for justice and dignity throughout the world. After working on this book for more than a decade, I am not convinced that anarchism possesses all the tools necessary to achieve these far-reaching goals. However, I agree with organizer Chris Crass that "ideas, insights, and leadership from different Left traditions, such as anarchism, Marxism, feminism, revolutionary nationalism, queer liberation, and revolutionary non-violence are needed as we create a political movement that draws the best from the past and opens space for new visions, ideas, and strategies."[5] It is my underlying hope that, by recovering a nearly forgotten aspect of social-movement history, *Unruly Equality* takes us a step forward in that process.

Epilogue

The mass movements of the 1960s served as a prism through which the compact beam of 1950s anarchism was refracted into more than a dozen hues. Although the radical ferment of the period led thousands of people to investigate anarchist ideas, the inability of anarchists to agree on priorities, a common strategy, or an organizational structure at the Black River conference, or elsewhere, led to a diffusion of small anarchist and near-anarchist initiatives as the momentum of the New Left stalled after 1973. The history of anarchist ideas and activism in the four decades since that time is nearly as labyrinthine as that of the six decades chronicled in this book. No brief summary can do it justice. However, I endeavor to provide a cursory outline of major developments to indicate the continuing trajectory of a number of ideas and practices introduced in the book, and to further orient readers seeking to connect the dots from the 1970s to more recent initiatives.

In the early 1970s, as some campus radicals embedded themselves in blue-collar communities with the hopes of radicalizing labor unions, a few small groups attempted to revive a labor-oriented libertarian socialism or council communism. The Boston-based Root and Branch Group, for example, counted as members Paul Mattick Sr. and his son, Stanley Aronowitz, and Jeremy Brecher, author of a popular volume of radical labor history, *Strike!*.[1] Resurgence, based in Evanston, Illinois, issued a pamphlet by Sam Dolgoff and other material. Both formations focused on sharing ideas rather than on organizing. They dissolved by the early 1980s, leaving the project of promoting worker self-management to those intrepid individuals working, once again, to revive the fortunes of the Industrial Workers of the World. In 1986 Sam Dolgoff cofounded the *Libertarian Labor Review,* which changed its name to the *Anarcho-Syndicalist Review* in 1999. Beginning in the early

1970s, the organization Wages for Housework, and the journals *Zerowork* and *Midnight Notes,* developed the largely Italian tradition of "autonomist Marxism" through sophisticated analyses of high-tech capitalism, the importance of reproductive labor, and new forms of privatization, or "enclosure."[2]

Despite these varied initiatives, the majority of U.S. anarchists remained devoted in the 1970s and 1980s to exploring the foci and strategies proposed in the late 1960s—namely, eco-anarchist theory, the critique of spectacular culture, and belief that the counterculture held the greatest potential as the base of a revolutionary movement. However, groups in different parts of the country developed their own styles and emphases.

The *Fifth Estate* was likely the most widely distributed and consistently published anarchist periodical during the 1970s. After Fredy and Lorraine Perlman joined the project, Detroit anarchists hewed to a quasi-Situationist practice, seeing pranks and surrealist interventions as their best shot at shaking up a city settling into the despair of deindustrialization.[3] Contributors extolled a succession of European ultraleft thinkers, from Jacques Camatte to Jean Baudrillard, in the magazine's pages. Although the Situationist International had explicitly denounced and distinguished itself from anarchism before dissolving in 1972, microgroupings of "pro-situ" radicals, such as the Bay Area's Contradication, interacted with anarchists as part of a loose antiauthoritarian milieu.[4] The Social Revolutionary Anarchist Federation, a network that circulated a mimeographed newsletter, provided an additional communication vehicle.

In the 1970s, these groups focused a great deal of bitter analysis on the failings of the "traditional Left," as late-1960s dreams of world revolution dried up. Yet the natural world remained of interest, and Gary Snyder continued to exert considerable influence on these aging counterculturalists. His brilliant 1970s poetry and essays, including the Pulitzer Prize–winning *Turtle Island,* amplified themes voiced by techno-skeptics such as Jacques Ellul, leading the editors of *Fifth Estate* and individuals such as John Zerzan to begin questioning, by decade's end, whether "civilization" itself was good for people and the planet.[5]

Murray Bookchin's reputation grew within the burgeoning ecology and back-to-the-land movements upon publication of *Post-scarcity Anarchism,* a collection of his *Anarchos* essays, in 1971.[6] In 1974 he established the Institute for Social Ecology with a handful of scholars and activists in Plainfield, Vermont. The group offered courses at nearby Goddard College, and explored the practical sides of sustainable living, while developing the theory of Social

Ecology.[7] Bookchin's writings in the late 1970s and early 1980s suggested that the oppression of women by men, workers by owners, people of color by whites, and other antagonisms were all examples of social domination applied in the interest of maintaining hierarchies. These concepts were subsequently taken up widely in movement theory.

Informal anarcha-feminist groups emerged in the mid-1970s, often on or near college campuses. Anarcha-feminists contributed to a variety of anarchist journals, such as *Black Rose,* founded in Boston, and *Social Anarchism,* edited from Baltimore.[8] In 1976, black women, many of them lesbians, established the Combahee River Collective in Boston. Though it did not identify as an anarchist group in any way, Combahee declared its opposition to racism, sexism, classism, and homophobia, arguing convincingly that these forms of domination mutually reinforced one another, so struggle could not be reduced to combating one form of domination, such as class, alone. The group's "Black Feminist Statement" also noted that the group functioned as a leaderless collective and sought to reach consensus internally, because they believed movement organizations should model the forms of social life they seek.[9] The idea of the "intersectionality" of forms of oppression developed by feminists of color shared qualities with Bookchin's critique of social domination but focused more directly on the experiences of (often poor) women of color. It too has immeasurably shaped certain tendencies of contemporary anarchism.

Movement for a New Society, a nationwide radical pacifist organization formed in 1971, worked to bridge the emerging investments in ecology and feminism. While taking cues from Joan Baez's Institute for the Study of Nonviolence, the organization truly recalled the abortive Committee for a Nonviolent Revolution that Dave Dellinger and other World War II draft resisters sought to organize in 1946. Though not explicitly anarchist, the group functioned as a decentralized network, studied Bookchin and other anarchists, and sought to challenge multiple forms of oppression simultaneously. Tactically, it combined organizing campaigns, direct action, the creation of counterinstitutions, and the "personal growth" of members seeking to overcome internalized (sexist, racist, homophobic) conditioning.[10]

Beginning in 1976, a movement formed in opposition to the expansion of the nuclear power industry. Social ecologists, members of Movement for a New Society, and anarchists from Boston helped organize a mass nonviolent direct action to block construction of a plant in coastal New Hampshire. Their experimental use of affinity groups coordinated in a nonhierarchical "spokescouncil" proved so useful during the action and in jail afterward that the idea was adopted by antinuclear campaigners throughout the country. In California, anarcha-feminists from San Francisco and Palo Alto played important roles in the Abalone Alliance and subsequent direct action formations.[11] Antinuclear demonstrations and the need to feed thousands of demonstrators also led to the founding of Food Not Bombs, which grew into a network of groups providing free food in hundreds of cities and towns across the country. Food Not Bombs promoted decision making by consensus and has served as an important entry point to anarchist politics for many young people for more than twenty years.[12]

In 1980 two significant initiatives came into play. A group in the college town of Columbia, Missouri, launched *Anarchy: A Journal of Desire Armed.* The periodical reintroduced the ideas of "individualist anarchists" into the North American milieu. Though free market libertarians held up nineteenth-century American individualists, such as Benjamin Tucker, as precursors, this journal looked more to the tradition of Russian and European individualists, such as E. Armand, who sought to practice, in his own life, freedom from sexual and other social conventions.[13] The journal embraced Surrealism and served as a forum, alongside the *Fifth Estate,* in which Zerzan and others articulated a "primitivist" anarchism that claimed humanity had gone wrong as far back as when it adopted sedentary agriculture.[14]

The radical environmental organization Earth First! also emerged in 1980. Early Earth First! activists attempted to physically prevent resource extraction and development of natural areas through covert "monkey-wrenching," or destruction of construction equipment. Unsurprisingly, this new take on "propaganda of the deed" attracted many anarchists. Following cofounder Dave Foreman, many Earth First! activists came to embrace the philosophy of "deep ecology" as the decade wore on.[15] Deep ecology critiqued "anthropocentric" forms of environmentalism and suggested wilderness should be aggressively defended, regardless of human consequences. This led to a series of increasingly acrimonious debates among anarchist-oriented environmental radicals regarding which should be the guiding philosophy of the movement: social ecology, deep ecology, or anarcho-primitivism.[16] Simultaneously, a rift opened over what constituted legitimate forms of direct action. Earth First! militants practiced property destruction covertly, attempting to inflict damage without suffering legal consequences. Movement for a New Society and many antinuclear demonstrators upheld the tenets of nonviolent direct action, which prohibited most forms of property destruction and saw surrendering oneself for arrest as central to the strategic moral symbolism of the tactic.

Other approaches, too, proliferated in the 1980s. Beginning in the late 1970s, an explicitly anarchist pacifist wing developed in England's punk music scene. Bands such as Crass and Chumbawamba echoed the MC5 / White Panther project in that they functioned simultaneously as communes, performers, and political agitators who directly participated in labor strikes, antinuclear work, and other campaigns. They developed musical, graphic, and fashion aesthetics that proved attractive to angry young people around the world, spreading anarchist ideas in the process.[17] Anarchist punk bands, such as Crucifix, A.P.P.L.E., and Nausea, proliferated in the United States after 1983. By touring internationally and by distributing albums and photocopied fanzines with radical political content, punk bands connected North American anarchists to "autonomous" anticapitalist movements in Europe whose members squatted in abandoned buildings, fought neo-Nazis in the streets, and resisted militarism and the arms race. This influence was reflected in a vibrant anarchist squatting community on the Lower East Side of Manhattan, which battled the police in the Tompkins Square Park riot of 1988, and in the formation of the punk-anarchist magazine *Profane Existence* in Minneapolis the following year.[18]

A series of collectively operated nonprofit anarchist bookstores and infoshops helped distribute anarcho-punk music, literature, and apparel. Bound Together Bookstore in San Francisco, the Wooden Shoe in Philadelphia, the Lucy Parsons Center in Boston, and similar projects throughout the country first emerged in the in mid-1970s. They sold books and hosted speaking events for authors affiliated with other publishing ventures that contributed to the antiauthoritarian milieu. The Brooklyn-based Autonomedia/Semiotext(e) collective, for example, published an intellectually challenging journal and introduced French poststructuralist theory to American radicals and academics.[19]

In 1977, former Rosa Luxemburg SDS member Michael Albert and feminist playwright Lydia Sargent cofounded South End Press, which published Noam Chomsky's anarchist critiques of U.S. foreign policy as well as work by feminists of color such as bell hooks and Cherrie Moraga. South End Press developed a system of collective ownership and "balanced job complexes" that served as a working model for the theory of participatory economics (or Parecon) that Albert and Robin Hahnel developed in an influential series of books. Built on the economic-values section of the Port Huron Statement,

Parecon has been recognized as an economic vision compatible with anarchist values. In 1988, Albert and Sargent went on to launch *Z Magazine,* which continues to serve as a platform for writings by Chomsky and other libertarian socialists.[20]

As should be evident, anarchism was cacophonous in the 1980s. Representatives of the various factions came together, however, in a series of national gatherings, beginning with a conference held in Chicago to mark the hundred-year anniversary of the Haymarket Affair. Conferences in Toronto and San Francisco followed. The last of these, in 1989, prompted the formation of a new organization, the Love and Rage Revolutionary Anarchist Federation, which grew to include chapters in Mexico, Canada, and a dozen U.S. cities.

The approach taken by Love and Rage reflected significant shifts in the political and economic landscape. Social ecologists and post-Situationist anarchists had largely discounted workers as collective agents for change, under the assumption that they would remain comfortable in advanced industrial societies that had reached the postscarcity stage. The aggressive union-busting, welfare-cutting, and offshoring of factory work that defined Ronald Reagan's presidency exposed this view as shortsighted. Love and Rage refocused anarchism on economic justice issues and did so in a way mindful of analyses promoted by feminists of color and groups such as the Race Traitor collective, who exposed the ways "white skin privilege" structured class relations in the United States. Love and Rage members, along with other anarchists, physically defended access to abortion clinics when the organization Operation Rescue attempted to shut them down. Love and Rage was also attentive to the international dimensions of class struggle as globalization kicked into high gear. Like many other antiauthoritarians, they promoted the efforts of the indigenous Zapatista movement in southern Mexico, which emerged in 1994 in opposition to the North American Free Trade Agreement and the broader ideological shift toward neoliberalism.[21]

The early 1990s also saw the emergence of black anarchist organizations and publications for the first time in the United States. Black militants of the 1960s, including Kuwasi Balagoon, Lorenzo Kom'boa Ervin, and Ashanti Alston adopted anarchism in prison as they reflected on shortcomings of the Black Panther Party and other formations in which they had participated. Ervin's *Anarchism and the Black Revolution* and Alston's *Anarchist Panther* zine proposed nonstatist, collectivist strategies for poor black communities to combat racism and deindustrialization and, at the same time, critiqued the

North American anarchist movement for its white cultural assumptions and disconnection from the lives of those most affected by racial capitalism.[22]

In 1995 the Anarchist Black Cross Federation was established to coordinate anarchist efforts to send mail, money, books, and other resources to political prisoners. The group harkened back to the Anarchist Red Cross of the 1920s, which sent aid to Russian anarchists and social revolutionaries; but the new formation lent assistance to revolutionaries incarcerated in the United States for militant anti-imperialist and black liberationist activities, as well as to class-struggle prisoners around the world. Most visibly, anarchists contributed significantly to the campaign to free the incarcerated journalist and former Black Panther Mumia Abu-Jamal. They also helped develop a broader politics of prison abolition in conjunction with the national network Critical Resistance.[23] Owing to an upswing in organizing by neo-Nazi groups, anarchists also created the Anti-Racist Action network. Like the Italian American antifascist squads of the 1920s, Anti-Racist Action members attempted to physically disrupt Klan rallies and prevent far-right groups from marching.

The rise of queer politics and the movement to overcome the AIDS epidemic greatly increased anarchist involvement in the politics of sexuality and led to the formation of a variety of queer anarchist formations. Groups such as Queer Nation, the Lesbian Avengers, and ACT-UP made use of direct action, guerrilla theater, independent media, and other tactics central to the anarchist repertoire, operating as horizontal networks without staff or leadership positions.[24] The AIDS epidemic also inspired the Radical Faeries, communalist queers with a primitivist streak.[25] The rise of Riot Grrrl, a radical feminist offshoot of punk, made room for a new generation of queer and trans performers with loose affiliations to anarchism. It also prompted the formation of the Radical Cheerleaders, who added cheeky anarchist flair to marches and demonstrations.[26]

Tensions came to a head in the second half of the decade between the revived "organizing" tradition within anarchism and the counterculturalists and primitivists loosely grouped around *Fifth Estate, Anarchy: A Journal of Desire Armed,* and Autonomedia/Semiotext(e). Hakim Bey's widely read 1991 tract *T.A.Z.* suggested that, because the times were not propitious for a revolutionary transformation of society, anarchists should strive to create *temporary autonomous zones* in which self-selecting rebels could turn their backs on the world and experience a sense of festive freedom. Such zones would dissolve and reappear elsewhere before they could be quashed.[27]

Although during the 1960s Bookchin had argued that countercultural youth were a vital force for social change, he saw the holdouts in the 1990s as individualists practicing escapism. In 1996, he offered a scathing rebuke to Bey and his ilk in *Social Anarchism or Lifestyle Anarchism: An Unbridgeable Chasm*.[28] A polemical battle on the scale of the Galleani-Tresca hostilities extended into the next decade, during which Bookchin distanced himself from anarchism.[29]

The global justice movement of the late 1990s and early 2000s rejuvenated anarchist movements around the world. In 1999, a call for mass actions to shut down meetings of the World Trade Organization brought many strands of anarchism together in the streets of Seattle. Organizers taught a new generation the model of mass nonviolent direct action, coordinated by spokescouncils, that was developed by antinuclear activists in the 1970s. Some Earth First! activists deployed sophisticated blockading tactics they had honed in the forest, while others joined punks to vandalize property in anonymous black blocs, following a tradition established by European autonomists and antifascists.[30] In the new millennium, anarchists tried to apply the action model established in Seattle at a series of international financial summits and the conventions of the major political parties, but met with declining success.

Though the terrain shifted a bit, U.S. anarchism remained as fractured as ever. Love and Rage dissolved, but a distinctly class-struggle-oriented anarchism reemerged with the formation of the North Eastern Federation of Anarchist Communists. Less intersectional than Love and Rage, the federation looked back to "The Platform" proposed in 1927 by Petr Arshinov and others after the Russian anarchists were defeated by the Bolsheviks. It has been succeeded in the United States by groups such as the Black Rose / Rosa Negra Anarchist Federation.

An Anarchist People of Color Network (APOC) emerged in 2003 and helped shift the racial composition of the movement, particularly on the West Coast and in the Southwest. Although the network disbanded after a few years, an APOC analysis and strategic orientation remains influential.[31] In the same years, an anonymous collective of able propagandists, CrimethInc., issued a stream of attractive books and periodicals that promoted Situationist-esque lifestyle practices—and rioting—to a new generation discovering anarchism largely through the punk scene.[32] The traditions known variously as green anarchism, anarcho-primitivism, and anticivilization radicalism continued to promote withdrawal from consumer society and illegal action to stem environmental destruction.[33] A sharp rise in clandestine acts of arson claimed by the Earth Liberation Front caused millions of dollars in damage to ecology-damaging business operations before federal authorities clamped down in what came to be known as the Green Scare.[34]

After the 1999 Seattle demonstrations, another cluster of organizers who had been politicized in the anarchist milieu of the 1990s developed a synthetic approach to radical politics as expressed in groups such as No One Is Illegal and publications like *Upping the Anti.* Recently labeled the "antiauthoritarian current," this informal network attempts to combine the insights of anarchism with those of anti-racist feminists and community organizers. It opposes all forms of oppression and combines organizing campaigns, preferably driven by directly affected communities, with direct action and the creation of counterinstitutions that lessen dependency on capitalist and state institutions, while modeling alternative ways of life.[35] The Institute for Anarchist Studies, which has become loosely aligned with the antiauthoritarian current, was founded in the late 1990s by individuals previously involved with the Institute for Social Ecology.

In the mid-2000s, anarchists associated with *Anarchy: A Journal of Desire Armed* began to promote nihilism as a theoretical position. Inspired by recent contributions to radical theory in Europe, others began to explicitly identify as insurrectionary anarchists. Like their early-twentieth-century predecessors, they rejected all attempts to win reforms and argued that violent confrontations with authority figures would awaken revolutionary consciousness among large groups of people.[36] Individuals associated with this tendency organized a series of building occupations on college campuses in California and New York, issuing communiqués that linked student demands to larger economic trends.

In the summer of 2011 the anticonsumerist magazine *Adbusters,* which had promoted anarchist and Situationist ideas for a decade, called for a demonstration on Wall Street to challenge gaping economic inequality and the capture of the political system by the wealthy. Anarchist organizers who had cut their teeth in the global justice movement and the direct action campaigns of the 1980s worked with a younger cohort to plan an action. When thousands of people showed up, they turned to the mass democratic assembly form that had recently been adopted by radical groups from Argentina to Egypt. As the assembly turned into an encampment, prefigurative politics became a guiding touchstone for the phenomenon known as Occupy Wall Street.

The dissemination of images of police repression via social media led to occupations of various sizes in more than a hundred cities across the United States. The occupation in Oakland, California, captured the most attention save for the original in New York. The participation of insurrectionary anarchists, and simmering tensions over recent police killings of young black men, lent that gathering a different character. There, explicit attempts to promote widespread rioting and clashes with the police competed with strategies that foregrounded civil disobedience and prefigurative activities.[37] "Occupy" demonstrated both the strengths and the weaknesses of contemporary U.S. anarchism. It was creative and insouciant, strove to be inclusive, and boldly challenged aspects of modern life that many had accepted as inevitable. Yet its methods proved unwieldy, it was unable to develop a long-term strategy, it turned inward, and it was unable to survive a coordinated campaign of state repression.

After Occupy, commentators from other sectors of the Left felt compelled to acknowledge the ascendant influence of anarchism on the Left in the United States and around the world. Yet in seeking lessons from the experience, even some participants with antiauthoritarian sympathies have grown skeptical of anarchism's potential to reach beyond limited constituencies and to build movements that have the resources, longevity, and strategy needed to fundamentally alter social, economic, and political systems controlled by the wealthiest and most powerful people the world has ever known.[38] It remains to be seen what egalitarians will do with the wealth of experience and insight anarchists and their allies accumulated throughout the twentieth century and the years that have followed.

NOTES

INTRODUCTION

1. For a discussion of anarchists in the Battle of Seattle and the broader global justice movement, see David Graeber, "The New Anarchists," in *A Movement of Movements: Is Another World Really Possible?* ed. Tom Mertes (New York: Verso, 2004), 202–215; Eddie Yuen, George Katsiaficas, and Daniel Burton Rose, eds., *The Battle of Seattle: The New Challenge to Capitalist Globalization* (Brooklyn, NY: Soft Skull Press, 2001); David Solnit and Rebecca Solnit, *The Battle of the Story of the Battle of Seattle* (Oakland, CA: AK Press, 2009); Jeffrey S. Juris, *Networking Futures: The Movements against Corporate Globalization* (Durham, NC: Duke University Press, 2008). For anarchists and the Occupy movement, see Mark Bray, *Translating Anarchy: The Anarchism of Occupy Wall Street* (Winchester, U.K.: Zero Books, 2013); Nathan Schneider, *Thank You, Anarchy: Notes from the Occupy Apocalypse* (Berkeley: University of California Press, 2013); David Graeber, *The Democracy Project: A History, a Crisis, a Movement* (New York: Spiegel and Grau, 2013); Kate Khatib, Margaret Killjoy, and Mike McGuire, eds., *We Are Many: Reflections on Movement Strategy from Occupation to Liberation* (Oakland, CA: AK Press, 2012).

2. Giorel Curran, *21st Century Dissent: Anarchism, Anti-Globalization, and Environmentalism* (New York: Palgrave Macmillan, 2006); Will Potter, *Green Is the New Red: An Insider's Account of a Social Movement under Siege* (San Francisco: City Lights, 2011); C. B. Daring et al., eds., *Queering Anarchism: Addressing and Undressing Power and Desire* (Oakland, CA: AK Press 2012).

3. Chris Dixon, *Another Politics: Talking across Today's Transformative Movements* (Berkeley: University of California Press, 2014).

4. Notes from Nowhere Collective, eds., *We Are Everywhere: The Irresistible Rise of Global Anticapitalism* (New York: Verso, 2003); Derek Wall, *Babylon and Beyond: The Economics of Anti-Capitalist, Anti-Globalist and Radical Green Movements* (London: Pluto Press, 2005); Antonis Vradis and Dimitris Dalakoglou, *Revolt and Crisis in Greece: Between a Present Yet to Pass and a Future Still to Come* (London: Occupied London; Oakland, CA: AK Press, 2011); Marina Sitrin and Dario

Azzellini, *They Can't Represent Us! Reinventing Democracy from Greece to Occupy* (New York: Verso, 2014).

5. Marta Harnecker, *A World to Build: New Paths toward Twenty-First Century Socialism* (New York: Monthly Review, 2015); Benjamin Dangl, *Dancing with Dynamite: Social Movements and States in Latin America* (Oakland, CA: AK Press, 2010); Raul Zibechi, *Territories in Resistance: A Cartography of Latin American Social Movements* (Oakland, CA: AK Press, 2012); George Ciciarello-Maher, *We Created Chávez: A People's History of the Venezuelan Revolution* (Durham, NC: Duke University Press, 2013).

6. Elaine Yu, "The Anarchists of Occupy Central," *New Yorker,* December 10, 2014.

7. Goos Hofstee, "Anarchists in Egypt, Will the Real Black Bloc Please Stand Up?" Tahrir-ICN, November 3, 2013, https://tahriricn.wordpress.com/2013/11/03/egypt-anarchists-in-egypt-will-the-real-black-bloc-please-stand-up/#more-1356; Strangers in a Tangled Wilderness, eds., *A Small Key Can Open a Large Door: The Rojava Revolution* (Oakland, CA: AK Press, 2015).

8. See, for example, Randall Amster, *Anarchism Today* (Santa Barbara, CA: Praeger, 2012); Richard Day, *Gramsci Is Dead: Anarchist Currents in the Newest Social Movements* (London: Pluto Press; Toronto: Between the Lines, 2005); Cindy Milstein, *Anarchism and Its Aspirations* (Oakland, CA: Institute for Anarchist Studies and AK Press, 2010); David Graeber, *Direct Action: An Ethnography* (Oakland, CA: AK Press, 2009). For a comparison to the movement in the United Kingdom, see Benjamin Franks, *Rebel Alliances: The Means and Ends of Contemporary British Anarchism* (Oakland, CA: AK Press, 2006).

9. Michael Kazin, *American Dreamers: How the Left Changed a Nation* (New York: Alfred A. Knopf, 2011), 263–264. The revised edition of Paul Buhle's revered *Marxism in the United States: Remapping the History of the American Left* (New York: Verso, 2013) likewise gives short shrift to the new anarchism. Indeed, the latter title's implicit conflation of the American Left with Marxist ideas is typical of a generation of historians who came of age in the New Left. Paul Avrich and a few others did conduct foundational research on the history of American anarchism in these years, but that work tended to focus on the biographies of a few key figures—Emma Goldman, Sacco and Vanzetti—and typically extended only to the 1920s.

10. Lynd, and other writers, such as Noam Chomsky, use *libertarian socialism* as a near synonym of anarchism. I discuss this and other terminology later in the introduction.

11. Staughton Lynd and Andrej Grubacic, *Wobblies and Zapatistas: Conversations on Anarchism, Marxism, and Radical History* (Oakland, CA: PM Press, 2008), 19.

12. Uri Gordon, *Anarchy Alive! Anti-authoritarian Politics from Practice to Theory* (London: Pluto Press, 2008), 5.

13. Cindy Milstein, "Occupy Anarchism," in *We Are Many: Reflections on Movement Strategy from Occupation to Liberation,* ed. Kate Khatib, Margaret Killjoy, and Mike McGuire (Oakland, CA: AK Press, 2012), 293.

14. Joel Olson, "The Problem with Infoshops and Insurrection: U.S. Anarchism, Movement Building, and the Racial Order," in *Contemporary Anarchist Studies: An Introductory Anthology of Anarchy in the Academy,* ed. Randall Amster et al. (New York: Routledge, 2009), 36–37.

15. Ibid., 36.

16. Laura Portwood-Stacer, *Lifestyle Politics and Radical Activism* (New York: Bloomsbury Academic, 2013).

17. For example, Roderick Kedward claimed, "The great age of the anarchists in Europe and America lay between 1880 and 1914." James Joll ended his widely read account by discussing "the repeated failures of anarchism in action, culminating in the tragedy of the Spanish Civil War." Introducing a collection of Emma Goldman's writings released in 1972, however, Alix Kates Shulman explained, "Until somewhere toward the end of the 1960s, anarchism and feminism seemed irrelevant anachronisms to most Americans.... Now, as everyone knows, things have changed." In 1972 Paul Berman touted a "revival of anarchism" evident in the "contemporary youth movement" and in "anti-authoritarian action and agitation by yippie types and others with neo-Anarchist tendencies." A few years later, Terry Perlin wrote, "The anarchist challenge to authority and the anarchist promise of freedom and peace did not die with [Alexander] Berkman. It resurfaced, in America and Europe, during the 1960s and early 1970s." Roderick Kedward, *The Anarchists: The Men Who Shocked an Era* (New York: American Heritage Press, 1971), 5; James Joll, *The Anarchists* (New York: Grossett and Dunlap, 1964), 275; Alix Kates Shulman, ed., *Red Emma Speaks: Selected Writings and Speeches by Emma Goldman* (New York: Random House, 1972), 1; Paul Berman, introduction to *Quotations from the Anarchists,* ed. Paul Berman (New York: Praeger, 1972), 3, 23, 24; Terry Perlin, ed., *Contemporary Anarchism* (New Brunswick, NJ: Transaction Books, 1979), n.p.

18. Jonathan Purkis and James Bowen, introduction to *Changing Anarchism: Anarchist Theory and Practice in a Global Age,* ed. Purkis and Bowen (Manchester, U.K.: Manchester University Press, 2004), 5; Gordon, *Anarchy Alive!,* 6.

19. I distinguish social anarchism from other types in the section that follows.

20. This conceptualization is indebted to John Clark, who has usefully suggested that anarchist politics feature the following components: "1. a view of an ideal, noncoercive, nonauthoritarian society; 2. a criticism of existing society and its institutions, based on this antiauthoritarian ideal; 3. A view of human nature that justifies the hope for significant progress toward the ideal; 4. a strategy for change, involving institutions of noncoercive, nonauthoritarian, and decentralist alternatives." John Clark, "What Is Anarchism?" in *Anarchism: Nomos XIX,* ed. Roland J. Pennock and John W. Chaptman (New York: NYU Press, 1978), 13.

21. In an 1851 work, Proudhon wrote, "Experience, in fact, shows that everywhere and always the Government, however much it may have been for the people at its origin, has placed itself on the side of the richest and most educated class against the more numerous and poorer class; it has little by little become narrow and exclusive; and, instead of maintaining liberty and equality among all, it works persistently to destroy them, by virtue of its natural inclination toward privilege." "The

General Idea of the Revolution," in *Anarchism: A Documentary History of Libertarian Ideas,* ed. Robert Graham, vol. 1 (Montreal: Black Rose, 2005), 52. Proudhon's compatriot Anselme Bellegarrigue was even more direct: "Who says anarchy, says negation of government; Who says negation of government says affirmation of the people." Bellegarrigue, "Anarchy Is Order," in Graham, *Anarchism,* 59.

22. This police strategy goes some way to explaining why some radical organizations, such as the Weather Underground, have been mistakenly declared "anarchist" efforts despite their avowal of Marxism-Leninism or other doctrines. This is misleading because a single tactic becomes the sole defining characteristic of anarchism. Anarchist thought is not reducible to a tactical or strategic orientation, and the repertoire of anarchist tactics is not reducible to physical attacks on authority figures.

23. George Berger, *The Story of Crass* (Oakland, CA: PM Press, 2009); Mark Anderson, *All the Power: Revolution without Illusion* (Chicago: Punk Planet Books; New York: Akashic Books, 2004).

24. This is not to claim that the association between anarchism and punk (as well as other youth countercultures, to a lesser degree) is completely unfounded. Indeed, those associations determine which social groups contemporary anarchists have been able to recruit, the focus of their activism, and, within the movement, common understandings of the nature of politics. One of the goals of this project is to trace the prehistory of the anarchist punk connection in the ways earlier generations of anarchists made use of a variety of cultural forms.

25. The literature on neoliberalism is extensive and growing. Three useful places to start are David Harvey, *A Brief History of Neoliberalism* (Oxford: Oxford University Press, 2007); Lisa Duggan, *The Twilight of Equality? Neoliberalism, Cultural Politics, and the Attack on Democracy* (Boston: Beacon, 2004); and Wendy Brown, *Undoing the Demos: Neoliberalism's Stealth Revolution* (Brooklyn, NY: Zone Books, 2015).

26. See Ulrike Heider, *Anarchism: Left, Right, and Green* (San Francisco: City Lights, 1994), 92–150; Brian Doherty, *Radicals for Capitalism: A Freewheeling History of the Modern American Libertarian Movement* (New York: Public Affairs, 2009).

27. Theda Skocpol and Vanessa Williamson, *The Tea Party and the Remaking of Republican Conservatism* (Oxford: Oxford University Press, 2013).

28. Robert Paul Draper, "Major Threat: Rand Paul and the Libertarians Could Win Young Voters for the G.O.P—If the Party Doesn't Shut Them Down," *New York Times Magazine,* August 10, 2014.

29. Ramsey Cox, "Reid: 'Anarchists Have Taken Over' in Congress (Video)," *The Hill,* September 12, 2013, http://thehill.com/blogs/floor-action/senate/321835-reid-anarchist-have-taken-over-the-house-senate.

30. Nick Wing, "Harry Reid Defends Comparing Tea Party to Anarchists: They 'Throw Monkey Wrenches' into Government," *Huff Post Politics,* May 2, 2013, www.huffingtonpost.com/2013/05/02/harry-reid-tea-party_n_3200340.html.

31. Heather Gautney, "The Tea Party Is Giving Anarchism a Bad Name," *Washington Post,* October 11, 2013, www.washingtonpost.com/blogs/on-leadership/wp/2013/10/11/the-tea-party-is-giving-anarchism-a-bad-name/.

32. Chiara Bottici, "Black and Red: The Freedom of Equals," in *The Anarchist Turn,* ed. Jacob Blumenfeld, Chiara Bottici, and Simon Critchley (London: Pluto, 2013).

CHAPTER 1. ANARCHIST APOGEE, 1916

1. Estimating numbers of anarchists at a given time has been notoriously diffi- cult for historians. Subscription lists for anarchist periodicals offer important data, but they were frequently seized and destroyed by authorities. Kenyon Zimmer has compiled the most comprehensive list of the available circulation figures of anarchist periodicals to date. He shows that between the Haymarket Affair of 1886 and the suppression of anarchist periodicals during the First World War, combined circula- tion fluctuated between a low of 40,000 to a high of approximately 118,000. *Immi- grants against the State: Yiddish and Italian Anarchism in America* (Urbana: Uni- versity of Illinois Press, 2015). Historian Margaret Marsh estimates that between 1880 and 1920, "there were at least fifteen to twenty thousand committed anarchists in the United States, and perhaps an additional thirty to fifty thousand sympathiz- ers." *Anarchist Women: 1870–1920* (Philadelphia: Temple University Press, 1981), 10. By comparison, in 1886 the anarchist Mezeroff, who worked as a professor, estimated ten thousand anarchists lived in the United States, with half in Chicago, a quarter in New York City, and smaller numbers spread throughout the other industrial cities of the period. Tom Goyens, *Beer and Revolution: The German Anarchist Move- ment in New York City, 1880–1914* (Urbana: University of Illinois Press, 2007), 147.

2. Leonard Dinnerstein and David M. Reimers, *Ethnic Americans: A History of Immigration,* 5th ed. (New York: Columbia University Press, 2009). The figure of approximately 20 million is drawn from the chart on p. 24 of Dinnerstein and Reimers's book.

3. Mathew Frye Jacobson, *Barbarian Virtues: The United States Encounters Foreign Peoples at Home and Abroad, 1876–1917* (New York: Hill and Wang, 2000), 59–97.

4. Roy Rosenzweig et al., *Who Built America? Working People and the Nation's History,* 3rd ed. (Boston: Bedford/St. Martins, 2008), 2:27.

5. Lucy Fox Robins Lang, *Tomorrow Is Beautiful* (New York: Macmillan, 1948).

6. Steven J. Diner, *A Very Different Age: Americans of the Progressive Era* (New York: Hill and Wang, 1998), 155–199.

7. David von Drehle, *Triangle: The Fire That Changed America* (New York: Grove Press, 2004). On Mary Abrams, see chapter 2 of the present volume.

8. Alexander Keyssar, *The Right to Vote: The Contested History of Democracy in the United States* (New York: Basic Books, 2009).

9. James R. Grossman, "A Chance to Make Good, 1900–1929," in *To Make Our World Anew: A History of African Americans,* ed. Robin D. G. Kelley and Earl Lewis (New York: Oxford University Press, 2005), 2:67–130; William G. Jordan, *Black Newspapers and America's War for Democracy, 1914–1920* (Chapel Hill: University of North Carolina, 2001).

10. Keyssar, *The Right to Vote,* 202–217; Linda Gordon, *Woman's Body, Woman's Right: Birth Control in America,* 2nd ed. (New York: Penguin, 1990).

11. Melvyn Dubovfsky and Foster Rhea Dulles, *Labor in American History,* 6th ed. (Wheeling, IL: Harlan Davidson, 1999), 191.

12. The standard account of growth of the AFL in this period is David Montgomery, *The Fall of the House of Labor: The Workplace, the State, and American Labor Activism, 1865–1925* (Cambridge: Cambridge University Press, 1989). Critical perspectives are offered by Paul Buhle, *Taking Care of Business: Samuel Gompers, George Meany, Lane Kirkland, and the Tragedy of American Labor* (New York: Monthly Review, 1999); and Mike Davis, *Prisoners of the American Dream: Politics and Economy in the History of the American Working Class,* 2nd ed. (New York: Verso, 2000).

13. On the increasingly violent nature of labor struggles in the first decades of the twentieth century, see Sidney Lens, *The Labor Wars: From the Molly Maguires to the Sit Downs* (Chicago: Haymarket, 2008 [1973]). For an absorbing account of the Lawrence strike, see Bruce Watson, *Bread and Roses: Mills, Migrants, and the Struggle for the American Dream* (New York: Penguin, 2005). On the Ludlow conflict, see Thomas. G. Andrews, *Killing for Coal: America's Deadliest Labor War* (Cambridge, MA: Harvard University Press, 2010).

14. Michael Kazin, *American Dreamers: How the Left Changed a Nation* (New York: Alfred A. Knopf, 2011), 109–154.

15. Paul Avrich, *The Haymarket Tragedy* (Princeton, NJ: Princeton University Press, 1984), 39–98; Goyens, *Beer,* 86–109; Timothy Messer-Kruse, *The Haymarket Conspiracy: Transatlantic Anarchist Networks* (Urbana: University of Illinois Press, 2012), 27–99; Timothy Messer-Kruse, *The Trial of the Haymarket Anarchists: Terrorism and Justice in the Gilded Age* (New York: Palgrave Macmillan, 2011); James Green, *Death in the Haymarket: A Story of Chicago, the First Labor Movement and the Bombing That Divided Gilded Age America* (New York: Anchor Books, 2006); Franklin Rosemont and David Roediger, eds., *Haymarket Scrapbook,* 125th anniversary ed. (Oakland, CA: AK Press, 2012).

16. Scholars are just beginning to systematically map where anarchists lived in the United States. Kathy Ferguson provides a map based on Emma Goldman's speaking tours. *Emma Goldman: Political Thinking in the Streets* (Lanham, MD: Rowan and Littlefield, 2011), 94. Anarchists used the term *colony* to denote an intentional community, or settlement of people with a similar background, typically established in a rural area. On the Home Colony, see Justin Wadland, *Trying Home: The Rise and Fall of an Anarchist Utopia on Puget Sound* (Corvallis: Oregon State University Press, 2014). Colonies later became more significant to the movement, as indicated in the third and fourth chapters of the present volume.

17. See the oral history interviews collected in Paul Avrich, *Anarchist Voices: An Oral History of Anarchism in America* (Oakland: AK Press, 2005).

18. Jennifer Guglielmo, *Living the Revolution: Italian Women's Resistance and Radicalism in New York City, 1880–1945* (Chapel Hill: University of North Carolina Press, 2020), 151.

19. For example, twelve Philadelphia anarchists launched a "cooperative house" in 1906, but they ended the experiment after eight months. They tried again a few years later, again without much success. Chaim Leib Weinberg, *Forty Years in the Struggle: The Memoirs of a Jewish Anarchist,* ed. Robert P. Helms, trans. Naomi Cohen (Duluth, MN: Litwin Books, 2009), 63–69.

20. Zimmer, *Immigrants against the State;* Michael Miller Topp, *Those without a Country: The Political Culture of Italian American Syndicalists* (Minneapolis: University of Minnesota Press, 2001), 58–91.

21. Morris Greenshner interview in Avrich, *Anarchist Voices,* 377–378. In the second decade of the twentieth century, when forms of commercial entertainment, such as amusement parks, were just becoming affordable to working people, attending a lecture or a play staged by an anarchist drama club proved a popular way to spend free time on a Friday evening or Saturday afternoon. On working-class amusements, see Nan Enstad, *Ladies of Labor, Girls of Adventure: Working Women, Popular Culture, and Labor Politics at the Turn of the Twentieth Century* (New York: Columbia University Press, 1999).

22. Ferguson, *Emma Goldman,* 99–116.

23. Two useful collections of key anarchist writings are Robert Graham, ed., *Anarchism: A Documentary History of Libertarian Ideas, Volume One: From Anarchy to Anarchism (300 CE to 1939)* (Montreal: Black Rose Books, 2005); and Daniel Guerin, *No Gods, No Masters: An Anthology of Anarchism* (Oakland, CA: AK Press, 2005). For biographical information and consideration of the intellectual positions of these theorists, see Peter Marshall, *Demanding the Impossible: A History of Anarchism,* new ed. (Oakland, CA: PM Press, 2010).

24. On the influence of the French Revolution, see James Joll, *The Anarchists,* 2nd ed. (Cambridge, MA: Harvard University Press, 1980), 25–44; David Priestland, *The Red Flag: A History of Communism* (New York: Grove Books, 2009), 1–46. In *The Conquest of Bread,* Peter Kropotkin calls for a "revolution, intoxicated with the beautiful words Liberty, Equality, Solidarity" (Dialectics Annotated Edition [Augusta, MO: Dialectics, 2012], 112). In 1920, Malatesta wrote, "We want men united as brothers by a conscious and desired solidarity. . . . We want bread, freedom, love and science—for everybody." Quoted in Paul Berman, ed., *Quotations from the Anarchists* (New York: Praeger, 1972), 28.

25. Pierre-Joseph Proudhon, "What Is Property?" in Graham, *Anarchism,* 33–38.

26. "Comments," *The Blast,* January 15, 1916, in *The Blast: The Complete Collection* (Oakland, CA: AK Press 2005), 12. Anarchists reminded audiences that workers could not even be assured of steadily earning low wages, since capitalism, barely regulated at the time, alternated rapidly between periods of boom and bust, resulting in routine unemployment. While the productive capacity of the society as a whole soared, workers were not even guaranteed the means to provide for themselves at subsistence level, as they had been under feudalism. See, e.g., "The Pittsburgh Proclamation," in Graham, *Anarchism,* 190–191.

27. Michael Bakunin, *God and the State* (New York: Dover, 1970), 24.

28. "Comments: A Labor Issue," *The Blast,* January 29, 1916, in *The Blast: The Complete Collection,* 29.

29. Malatesta is most direct on this matter: "Throughout history, just as in our time, government is either the brutal, violent, arbitrary rule of the few over the many or it is an organized instrument to ensure that dominion and privilege will be in the hands of those who by force, by cunning, or by inheritance, have cornered all the means of life, first and foremost the land, which they make use of to keep the people in bondage and to make them work for their benefit. . . . The owning class . . . always ends by more or less openly subjecting the political power, which is the government, and making it into its own gendarme." *Anarchy* (London: Freedom Press, 1974 [1891]), 17–18, 19. On schools, newspapers, and political parties see, e.g., "The Pittsburgh Proclamation," 191–192.

30. Emma Goldman, "Woman Suffrage," in *Anarchism and Other Essays* (New York: Dover, 1969), 198.

31. Bakunin claimed, "It is the characteristic of privilege and of every privileged position to kill the mind and heart of men. . . . A scientific body to which had been confided the government of society would soon end by devoting itself no longer to science at all, but to quite another affair; and that affair, as in the case of all established powers, would be its own eternal perpetuation by rendering the society confided to its care ever more stupid and consequently more in need of its government and direction. But that which is true of scientific academies is also true of all constituent and legislative assemblies, even those chosen by universal suffrage." *God and the State,* 31–32. Kropotkin, likewise, notes, "We affirm that the best of men is made essentially bad by the exercise of authority." "Anarchism: Its Philosophy and Ideal," in *Kropotkin's Revolutionary Pamphlets,* ed. Roger Baldwin (New York: Dover, 1970), 135.

32. Goldman states this explicitly in her definition of anarchism: "The Philosophy of a new social order based on liberty unrestricted by man-made law; the theory that all forms of government rest on violence, and are therefore wrong and harmful, as well as unnecessary." Emma Goldman, "Anarchism: What It Really Stands For," in *Anarchism and Other Essays* (New York: Dover, 1969), 50.

33. Peter Kropotkin, *Mutual Aid: A Factor of Evolution* (St. Louis: Dialectics 2013 [1902]).

34. George Crowder, *Classical Anarchism: The Political Thought of Godwin, Proudhon, Bakunin, and Kropotkin* (New York: Oxford University Press, 1992), 7–38; Bakunin, *God and the State,* 28–29.

35. David Moreland, *Demanding the Impossible? Human Nature and Politics in Nineteenth-Century Anarchism* (London: Cassell, 1997). Scholars have debated the classical anarchists' understandings of human nature at length in recent years—a question spurred by considerations of the relationship between anarchist and poststructuralist thought. See the essays contained in Duane Rousselle and Süreyyya Evren, eds., *Post-Anarchism: A Reader* (London: Pluto Press, 2011).

36. In one of his later works, Kropotkin dedicates an entire chapter to organizations based upon "free agreement": *Conquest,* 113–125. For a contemporary reitera-

tion of the theme, see Cindy Milstein and Erik Ruin, *Paths toward Utopia* (Oakland, CA: PM Press, 2012).

37. Pierre-Joseph Proudhon, "The Principle of Federalism," in Graham, *Anarchism,* 72; Michael Bakunin, "The Organization of the International" and "The Sonvillier Circular," in Graham, *Anarchism,* 91–98.

38. Contemporary anarchists often refer to the idea that an organization's means of conducting itself should align with its social vision as "the principle of prefiguration," or prefigurative politics. See, for example, Cindy Milstein, *Anarchism and Its Aspirations* (Oakland, CA: AK Press and Institute for Anarchist Studies, 2010).

39. Max Baginski, "Without Government," in *Anarchy! An Anthology of Emma Goldman's* Mother Earth, ed. Peter Glassgold (Washington, DC: Counterpoint, 2001), 12.

40. Alex Prichard, "Deepening Anarchism: International Relations and the Anarchist Ideal," *Anarchist Studies* 18, no. 2 (2010): 29–57.

41. Kropotkin devotes a significant portion of *The Conquest of Bread* (45–67) to analyzing the wrong turns taken by revolutionaries involved in these and other upheavals before formulating specific plans for the next such occasion.

42. For personal ties between anarchists and Russian populists, see Alex Butterworth, *The World That Never Was: A True Story of Dreamers, Schemers, Anarchists, and Secret Agents* (New York: Vintage, 2011).

43. In the United States, this strategy was exemplified by Alexander Berkman's attack on the steel magnate Henry Clay Frick in 1892 and Leon Czolgosz's successful assassination of President William McKinley in 1901. Kathy Ferguson provides a fairly comprehensive list of acts of political violence committed by anarchists, in *Emma Goldman,* 41–43. See also Michael Schmidt and Lucien van der Walt, *Black Flame: The Revolutionary Class Politics of Anarchism and Syndicalism* (Oakland, CA: AK Press, 2009), 128–132; John Merriman, *The Dynamite Club: How a Bombing in Fin-de-Siècle Paris Ignited the Age of Modern Terror* (New York: Houghton Mifflin Harcourt, 2009).

44. Alexandre Skirda, *Facing the Enemy: A History of Anarchist Organization from Proudhon to May 1968*, trans. Paul Sharkey (Oakland, CA: AK Press, 2002), 42–59.

45. Melvyn Dubofsky, *We Shall Be All: A History of the Industrial Workers of the World,* abridged ed. (Urbana: University of Illinois Press, 2000); Fred W. Thompson and Jon Bekken, *The Industrial Workers of the World: Its First 100 Years, 1905–2005* (Cincinnati: IWW, 2006).

46. Joyce Kornbluh, ed., *Rebel Voices: An IWW Anthology,* 3rd ed. (Oakland, CA: PM Press, 2011), 12.

47. Salvatore Salerno, *Red November, Black November: Culture and Community in the Industrial Workers of the World* (Albany: SUNY Press, 1989), 90.

48. Salerno, *Red November,* 93–115; Saku Pinta, "Anarchism, Marxism, and the Ideological Composition of the Chicago Idea," *WorkingUSA: The Journal of Labor and Society* 12 (September 2009): 421–450; Schmidt and van der Walt, *Black Flame,* 149–160.

49. Max Baginski, "Aims and Tactics of the Trade-Union Movement," in *Anarchy! An Anthology of Emma Goldman's* Mother Earth, ed. Peter Glassgold (Washington, DC: Counterpoint, 2001), 300–301.

50. For a case study, see Peter Cole, *Wobblies on the Waterfront: Interracial Unionism in Progressive-Era Philadelphia* (Urbana: University of Illinois Press, 2007).

51. See Franklin Rosemont, *Joe Hill and the Making of a Revolutionary Working-Class Counterculture* (Chicago: Charles H. Kerr, 2003); Salerno, *Red November*, 119–140.

52. Archie Green et al., eds., *The Big Red Songbook* (Chicago: Charles H. Kerr, 2007); Kornbluh, *Rebel Voices*.

53. Wobblies descended en masse on towns and cities that arrested members for soapboxing, offering themselves up for collective incarceration until their numbers taxed the municipalities' legal systems to such an extent that officials were persuaded to rescind regulations prohibiting public speaking. Dubofsky, *We Shall Be All*, 173–197; Thompson and Bekken, *Industrial Workers of the World*, 40–42.

54. Beginning in the 1880s, German and Italian anarchists established singing societies, theater troupes, and other cultural organizations that regularly hosted pageants, concerts, parades, picnics, and plays. These cultural and recreational projects promoted an oppositional folk culture that might be considered a form of ambient organizing since it promoted an egalitarian worldview and resistance in daily life. See Goyens, *Beer*, 168–182; Bruce Nelson, *Beyond the Martyrs: A Social History of Chicago's Anarchists, 1870–1900* (New Brunswick, NJ: Rutgers University Press, 1988), 127–152; Marcella Bencivenni, *Italian Immigrant Radical Culture: The Idealism of the Sovversivi in the United States, 1890–1940* (New York: NYU Press, 2011).

55. Salvatore Salerno, "No God, No Master: Italian Anarchists and the Industrial Workers of the World," in *The Lost World of Italian American Radicalism: Politics, Labor, and Culture*, ed. Phillip V. Cannistraro and Gerald Meyer (Westport, CT: Praeger, 2003), 171–187; Nunzio Pernicone, *Carlo Tresca: Life of a Rebel* (New York: Palgrave Macmillan, 2005), 64–65.

56. Pernicone, *Carlo Tresca*, 78.

57. Nunzio Pernicone, "War among the Italian Anarchists: The Galleanisti's Campaign against Carlo Tresca," in Cannistraro and Meyer, *The Lost World of Italian American Radicalism*, 77–97.

58. Paul Avrich, *The Russian Anarchists* (Oakland, CA: AK Press, 2005), 79.

59. The Russian-speaking sector is the least studied of the foreign-language sectors of the U.S. anarchist movement. But see Kenyon Zimmer, "A Slice of Pittsburgh Anarchist History: The Union of Russian Workers," *Steel City Revolt*, Spring 2009. Paul Avrich claims *Golos Truda* became an "avowedly Anarcho-Syndicalist publication" only when Maksim Raevskii became editor "during World War I." *Russian Anarchists*, 115.

60. Steven Fischler and Joel Sucher, dir., *The Free Voice of Labor: The Jewish Anarchists* (Oakland, CA: AK Press Films, 2006), DVD.

61. Anarchists had led the United Brotherhood of Cloak Makers, which merged with the socialist Progressive Cloak Makers to form the International Ladies' Garment Workers' Union in 1901. See Zimmer, *Immigrants against the State;* Herman Frank, "Anarchism and the Jews," in *Struggle for Tomorrow: Modern Political Ideologies of the Jewish People,* ed. Basil J. Vlavianos and Feliks Gross (New York: Arts, Inc., n.d. [1953]), 281; Paul Avrich, "Jewish Anarchism in the United States," in *Anarchist Portraits* (Princeton, NJ: Princeton University Press, 1988), 176–199. For a personal account of the Jewish sector of the movement in Philadelphia, see Weinberg, *Forty Years in the Struggle.*

62. Avrich, *Anarchist Portraits,* 188.

63. Avrich, *Anarchist Voices,* 391–393; Salerno, "No God, No Master," 182; Guglielmo, *Living,* 158–159.

64. Claudio Lomintz-Adler, *The Return of Comrade Ricardo Flores Magón* (Brooklyn: Zone Books, 2014); Chaz Bufe and Mitchell Cowen Verter, eds., *Dreams of Freedom: A Ricardo Flores Magón Reader* (Oakland, CA: AK Press, 2005); Ward S. Albro, *Always a Rebel: Ricardo Flores Magón and the Mexican Revolution* (Fort Worth: Texas Christian University Press, 1992); Shelley Streeby, *Radical Sensations: World Movements, Violence, and Visual Culture* (Durham, NC: Duke University Press, 2013), 111–172; Colin M. MacLachlan, *Anarchism and the Mexican Revolution: The Political Trials of Ricardo Flores Magón in the United States* (Berkeley: University of California Press, 1991).

65. Rudolf Vecoli, "Luigi Galleani," in *Encyclopedia of the American Left,* ed. Paul Buhle, Mari Jo Buhle, Dan Georgakas (Oxford: Oxford University Press, 1998), 253.

66. Luigi Galleani, *The End of Anarchism?* (Orkney, U.K.: Cienfuegos Press, 1982), 13.

67. Ferrero quoted in Avrich, *Anarchist Voices,* 165.

68. Nunzio Pernicone has shown how the impact of specific moments in the early history of the anarchist movement in Italy shaped Galleani's beliefs about organization and strategy. *Italian Anarchism, 1864–1892* (Oakland, CA: AK Press, 2009), 165–200.

69. Nunzio Pernicone, "Luigi Galleani and Italian Anarchist Terrorism in the United States," *Studi Emigrazione/Etudes Migrations* 30, no. 111 (1993): 469–489.

70. This section is indebted to Michael Schmidt and Lucien van der Walt for their conceptual distinction between "mass anarchism" and "insurrectionist anarchism," articulated in *Black Flame: The Revolutionary Class Politics of Anarchism and Syndicalism* (Oakland, CA: AK Press, 2009), 123–147.

71. Pernicone, "War among the Italian Anarchists," 80–81.

72. Scholars of U.S. anarchism have devoted more attention to Goldman and Berkman than to any other figures. Among the many biographical works available, an accessible starting place is Paul Avrich and Karen Avrich, *Sasha and Emma: The Anarchist Odyssey of Alexander Berkman and Emma Goldman* (Cambridge, MA: Harvard University Press, 2012). Alice Wexler, *Emma Goldman in America*

(Boston: Beacon, 1984), masterfully situates Goldman's ideas, work, and personal life, up to 1919, in the broader political context.

73. Elizabeth Wilson helpfully defines the bohemian as a social position and character type—"the dissident artist-rebel" recognizable in Western culture as early as the mid-nineteenth century. She notes, "Bohemia is the name for the attempt by nineteenth- and twentieth-century artists, writers, intellectuals and radicals to create an alternative world within Western society (and possibly elsewhere). Despite the exaggerated individualism of its citizens, Bohemia was a collective enterprise; the bohemians created and participated in a social milieu created *against* the dominant culture, as the artist made a startling transformation from paid ideologue to violent critic of society in the unfamiliar world of 'modernity.'" *Bohemians: The Glamorous Outcasts* (New Brunswick, NJ: Rutgers University Press, 2000), 2–3.

74. Wexler, *Emma Goldman,* 121.

75. On the intellectual and artistic Left that was centered in New York's Greenwich Village, see John Patrick Diggins, *The Rise and Fall of the American Left* (New York: Norton, 1992), 93–143; Christine Stansell, *American Moderns: Bohemian New York and the Creation of a New Century* (Princeton, NJ: Princeton University Press, 2010). For an illuminating consideration of the function of early-twentieth-century "little magazines" and their relation to contemporary journals of radical criticism, see Michael Denning, "The Academic Left and the Rise of Cultural Studies," *Radical History Review* 54 (Fall 1992): 21–47.

76. Bill Lynskey, "'I Shall Speak in Philadelphia': Emma Goldman and the Free Speech League," *Pennsylvania Magazine of History and Biography* 133, no. 2 (April 2009): 167–202.

77. One of their strongest allies in this work was a young lawyer named Roger Baldwin, who would later found the American Civil Liberties Union, after the First World War. Christopher Finan, *From the Palmer Raids to the Patriot Act: A History of the Fight for Free Speech in America* (Boston: Beacon, 2008), 37.

78. Wexler, *Emma Goldman,* 176–185.

79. Sanger arranged to be trained in birth control methods in France by Goldman's anarchist friend Victor Dave. Bill Shatoff of the Union of Russian Workers and the IWW secretly printed Sanger's pamphlet *Family Limitation.* When Sanger was arrested for her work, Goldman disseminated birth-control information in her place, resulting in a short jail term and significant publicity for the cause. Wexler, *Emma Goldman,* 210–215. Sanger became more conservative after World War I. Breaking with the anarchist movement and playing down her earlier collaborations, she began advocating eugenic programs that called for the involuntary sterilization of poor women. Jean H. Baker, *Margaret Sanger: A Life of Passion* (New York: Hill and Wang, 2011).

80. Quoted in Terrence Kissack, *Free Comrades: Anarchism and Homosexuality in the United States, 1895–1917* (Oakland, CA: AK Press, 2008), 15.

81. Berkman wrote publicly about homosexual experiences he had while imprisoned, and Goldman's close associate Leonard Abbot was openly gay. Goldman also corresponded with lesbians seeking advice, support, and romance. Kissack, *Free*

Comrades; Candace Falk, *Love, Anarchy, and Emma Goldman* (New York: Holt, Reinhart, and Winston, 1984).

82. Goldman's essays on gender and sexuality are collected in Alix Kates Schulman, *Red Emma Speaks: An Emma Goldman Reader,* 2nd ed. (New York: Schocken, 1983). Also see Penny A. Weiss and Loretta Kensinger, *Feminist Interpretations of Emma Goldman* (University Park: Pennsylvania State University Press, 2007); Wexler, *Emma Goldman,* 188–208; Kissack, *Free Comrades,* 127–152. For her place in the anarcha-feminist pantheon, see Dark Star, ed., *Quiet Rumours: An Anarcha-Feminist Reader* (San Francisco: AK Press and Dark Star, 2002).

83. Quoted in Alix Kates Schulman, "Emma Goldman's Feminism: A Reappraisal," in *Red Emma Speaks: An Emma Goldman Reader,* 2nd ed. (New York: Schocken, 1983), 11.

84. See Timothy Campbell and Adam Sitze, eds., *Biopolitics: A Reader* (Durham, NC: Duke University Press, 2013).

85. Quoted in Ferguson, *Emma Goldman,* 256.

86. Ferguson, *Emma Goldman,* 78; Guglielmo, *Living,* 154.

87. On anarchist women, and on the forms of feminism they espoused and enacted, more generally, see Margaret S. Marsch, *Anarchist Women, 1870–1920* (Philadelphia: Temple University Press, 1981); and Sharon Presley and Crispin Sartwell, eds., *Exquisite Rebel: The Essays of Voltairine de Cleyre: Feminist, Anarchist, Genius* (Albany: State University of New York Press, 2005).

88. Guglielmo, *Living,* 139–175; Jennifer Guglielmo, "Donne Ribelli: Recovering the History of Italian Women's Radicalism in the United States," in Cannistraro and Meyer, *The Lost World of Italian American Radicalism,* 113–141.

89. Quoted in Guglielmo, "Donne Ribelli," 117.

90. A similar tension led to long-standing divisions between white women and women of color engaged in feminist activism in the 1960s and 1970s. See Paul J. Giddens, *Where and When I Enter: The Impact of Black Women on Race and Sex in America* (New York: William Morrow, 2007), 299–324; Wini Brienes, *The Trouble between Us: An Uneasy History of White and Black Women in the Feminist Movement* (New York: Oxford University Press, 2007).

91. Quoted in Guglielmo, *Living,* 164.

92. Goldman cited journalists, professors, teachers, writers, musicians, bookkeepers, actresses, and nurses as examples of intellectual proletarians. "Intellectual Proletarians," in Shulman, *Red Emma Speaks,* 222–231.

93. Peter Glassgold, "Introduction: The Life and Death of *Mother Earth,*" in *Anarchy! An Anthology of Emma Goldman's* Mother Earth, ed. Peter Glassgold (Washington, DC: Counterpoint, 2001), xxvi.

94. Ferguson, *Emma Goldman,* 218.

95. Ibid., 211–247.

96. Quoted in Salvatore Salerno, "*I Delitti Della Razza Bianca* (Crimes of the White Race): Italian Anarchists' Racial Discourse as Crime," in *Are Italians White? How Race Is Made in America,* ed. Jennifer Guglielmo and Salvatore Salerno (New York: Routledge, 2003), 121.

97. Ricardo Flores Magón, "The Repercussions of a Lynching," *Regeneración,* November 12, 1910, reprinted in Bufe and Verter, *Dreams of Freedom,* 198–201.

98. James R. Barrett and David Roediger, "Inbetween Peoples: Race, Nationality and the 'New Immigrant' Working Class," *Journal of American Ethnic History* 16, no. 3 (Spring 1997): 3–44.

99. Ibid., 3–34; David R. Roediger, *Working toward Whiteness: How America's Immigrants Became White* (Boston: Basic, 2005); Matthew Frye Jacobson, *Whiteness of a Different Color: European Immigrants and the Alchemy of Race* (Cambridge, MA: Harvard University Press, 1998).

100. The term *racialization* derives from the theory of Michael Omi and Howard Winant. In their highly influential formulation, these two authors argue that "race is a concept which signifies and symbolizes social conflicts and interests by referring to different types of human bodies." The meanings of race and the ways the concept functions, they argue, are "constantly being transformed by political struggle." This helps account for the fact that in certain times and places, individuals are recognized as members of one "race" and privileged or deprived accordingly, whereas in another period or location they are grouped differently. Omi and Winant urge us to view these ongoing transformations as the process of racial formation: "the sociohistorical process by which racial categories are created, inhabited, transformed, and destroyed." The authors argue that "race is a matter of both social structure and cultural representation." Political struggles involving race—which these authors call *racial projects*—link the symbolic realm of defining and attributing meaning to race with the realm of institutions, policies, and patterns of behavior that collectively constitute the structure of a society. "A racial project is simultaneously an interpretation, representation, or explanation of racial dynamics, and an effort to reorganize and redistribute resources along particular racial lines," Omi and Winant argue. *Racial Formation in the United States: From the 1960s to the 1990s,* 2nd ed. (New York: Routledge, 1994), 53–61.

101. Franklin Rosemont, "A Bomb-Toting, Long-Haired, Wild-Eyed Fiend: The Image of the Anarchist in Popular Culture," in *Haymarket Scrapbook,* ed. Dave Roediger and Franklin Rosemont (Chicago: Charles H. Kerr, 1986).

102. The cover of the September 1886 issue of *Puck* magazine, for instance, pictured anarchism as a rabid dog about to be drowned by a constable, while the *New York Daily Graphic* imagined the Haymarket defendants as black crows hanging from nooses. Images reproduced in Roediger and Rosemont, *Haymarket Scrapbook,* 112, 93.

103. The image of anarchists as long-haired and bearded was based in large measure on Johann Most, the aging, bearded editor of *Freiheit,* who was never known to have committed an act of violence himself, but who explicitly promoted violent attacks on politicians and the wealthy in his newspaper and his pamphlet *The Science of Revolutionary Warfare.* Most grew his beard long to partially cover his heavily scarred face, the result of a botched operation when he was a child, which served as an enduring embarrassment to him. That the image of anarchists as unkempt, mentally ill, and foreign grew in part from this bodily condition is of interest from the

perspective of disability studies, which examines the relationships between the discriminatory treatment of people with nonnormative bodies and that of queer and racialized peoples. See Robert McCruer, *Crip Theory: Cultural Signs of Queerness and Disability* (New York: NYU Press, 2006).

104. Rosemont, "Bomb-Toting," 203.

105. Image reproduced in Roediger and Rosemont, eds., *Haymarket Scrapbook,* 128. On Thomas Nast, see Morton Keller, *The Art and Politics of Thomas Nast* (New York: Oxford University Press, 1968).

106. Kenyon Zimmer, "Positively Stateless: Marcus Graham, the Ferrero-Sallitto Case, and Anarchist Challenges to Race and Deportation," in *The Rising Tide of Color: Race, State Violence, and Radical Movements across the Pacific,* ed. Moon-Ho Jung (Seattle: University of Washington Press, 2014), 132.

107. Czolgosz was born in Detroit to Polish parents but was frequently depicted as foreign and unsound.

108. Eric Rauchway, *Murdering McKinley: The Making of Theodore Roosevelt's America* (New York: Hill and Wang, 2003), 110.

109. William J. Preston Jr., *Aliens and Dissenters: Federal Suppression of Radicals, 1903–1933,* 2nd ed. (Champaign: University of Illinois Press, 1994), 4.

110. John Higham, *Strangers in the Land: Patterns of American Nativism, 1860–1925* (New York: Atheneum, 1970 [1955]), 78.

111. Mathew Frye Jacobson has described this intermediate social position as "probationary whiteness." Jacobson demonstrates that, beginning in the 1860s, native-born U.S. Americans argued for the exclusion of, or the refusal to naturalize, many immigrants on the basis of the principles of republican self-government. If immigrants could not demonstrate the virtues of self-control—independence from the influence of others or the dictates of their own passions—they were unfit for citizenship. Such logic appears ironic when used as a justification for excluding anarchists, since anarchist political activism was based on the notion that humans had the natural capacity to rule themselves according to the principles of natural law, and that capitalism and political states served as the primary impediments to this practice of egalitarian self-governance. *Whiteness of a Different Color,* 22–31.

112. Paul Avrich, *The Modern School Movement: Anarchism and Education in the United States* (Oakland, CA: AK Press, 2006).

113. These approaches sometimes came into conflict, as I describe in chapter 3. For a historical and comparative consideration of Ferrer's pedagogy, see Geoffrey C. Fidler, "The Escuela Moderna Movement of Francisco Ferrer: 'Por la Verdad y la Justicia,'" *History of Education Society* 25, no. 1–2 (Spring–Summer 1985): 103–132.

114. Avrich, *Modern School,* 121–122.

115. Harry Kelly, "Roll Back the Years," n.d., chap. 20, pp. 1–2, unpublished manuscript, John Nicholas Beffel Papers, Tamiment Library, New York University.

116. Avrich, *Modern School,* 43, 100; Kissack, *Free Comrades,* 14.

117. Richard Sonn, *Anarchism and Cultural Politics in Fin de Siècle France* (Lincoln: University of Nebraska Press, 1989); Patricia Leighten, "Reveil Anarchiste:

Salon Painting, Political Satire, Modernist Art," in *Realizing the Impossible: Art against Authority,* ed. Josh MacPhee and Erik Reuland (Oakland, CA: AK Press, 2007), 26–41; Patricia Leighton, *Re-ordering the Universe: Picasso and Anarchism, 1897–1914* (Princeton, NJ: Princeton University Press, 1989).

118. Whereas the academies emphasized realistic representation and scenes that celebrated traditional Western values, the new artists sought to depict a wider range of subjects, including the lives of common people, and saw style and form as expressions of the artist's perspective or identity. Challenging the academies required artists to develop new spaces for creating and displaying art, since the schools monopolized gallery space and chose works to exhibit on narrowly defined criteria. On the interrelations of the anarchist movement and avant-garde art before World War I, see Allan Antliff, *Anarchist Modernism: Art, Politics, and the First American Avant-Garde* (Chicago: University of Chicago Press, 2001); Allan Antliff, *Art and Anarchy: From the Paris Commune to the Fall of the Berlin Wall* (Vancouver: Arsenal Pulp, 2007); Avrich, *Modern School,* 121–182; Lawrence Veysey, *The Communal Experience: Anarchist and Mystical Communities in Twentieth Century America* (Chicago: University of Chicago Press, 1978).

119. *Le Père Peinard* presented an attitude and visual style similar to that of the British anarchist tabloid *Class War,* produced a century later. Both displayed an utter contempt for the ruling class and regularly featured images and writing that encouraged individual acts of retribution by workers against their bosses and the rich in general. On *Le Père Peinard,* see Antliff, *Anarchist Modernism,* 17–21. On *Class War,* see Class War Federation, *Unfinished Business: The Politics of Class War* (San Francisco: AK Press, 2001); and Ian Bone, *Bash the Rich: True Confessions of an Anarchist in the U.K.* (Bristol, U.K.: Tangent, 2007).

120. Quoted in Francis M. Naumann, *Conversion to Modernism: The Early Work of Man Ray* (New Brunswick, NJ: Rutgers University Press, 2003), 25. George Bellows, a founding figure of the "Ashcan school," assisted Henri during these lessons. Ferrer Center students included individuals who would make names for themselves after the war, including Rockwell Kent, Robert Minor, and Man Ray. Robert Minor contributed striking covers to *The Blast,* as Man Ray did to *Mother Earth.*

121. Antliff, *Anarchist Modernism,* 41–43.

122. The area of Chicago near the headquarters of the IWW had developed a reputation as a hotbed of free speech and bohemianism as early as the 1890s. Beginning in the 1890s a small city park in the neighborhood became a popular site for soapbox oration and open-air debates. The Radical Bookstore, on nearby Clark Street, carried literature hard to find elsewhere and hosted evening discussions on art and politics. In 1914 the Chicago-based lesbian feminist literary critic Margaret Anderson established a lasting friendship with Goldman and Berkman, publishing Goldman's essays alongside those of leading figures of literary modernism—James Joyce, Ezra Pound, and Ernest Hemmingway among them. In turn, the anarchists sold issues of Anderson's *Little Review* through the mail-order services offered by *Mother Earth* and *The Blast.* In 1917 the IWW organizer Jack Jones launched the

Dil Pickle Club, with promotional assistance from Goldman's former lover and manager, Ben Reitman. The surreally decorated Dil Pickle served as an experimental venue for nearly two decades, hosting readings by emerging writers such as Carl Sandberg one evening, touring anarchist speakers the next, and a play or jazz band later in the week. Frank O. Beck, *Hobohemia: Emma Goldman, Lucy Parsons, Ben Reitman, and other Agitators/Outsiders in 1920s/30s Chicago* (Chicago: Charles H. Kerr, 2000).

123. Hippolyte Havel, an Austrian anarchist who had lived in the United States since 1900, also helped to cement relations with artists. While serving as an editor of *Mother Earth* and publishing his own journal, *Revolt,* Havel helped operate Polly's Restaurant, a bohemian café on Greenwich Village's MacDougal Street, with his love interest, Polly Halliday. After striking up a friendship with Eugene O'Neill, Havel participated in productions at the nearby Provincetown Playhouse, later serving as inspiration for the character Hugo Kalmer in *The Iceman Cometh.* Another member of the Provincetown Players, the British actor Teddy Ballantine, married Goldman's niece and secretary, Stella Cominsky. On the basis of such relationships, artists invited anarchists to vacation with them in a variety of "artists' colonies" in idyllic locales such as Woodstock, New York, and Provincetown on Cape Cod. Havel and Halliday maintained a second restaurant in Provincetown for a time. Avrich, *Modern School,* 131–134; Rose Pesotta, "Hippolyte Havel," p. 8, unpublished manuscript, 1932, Miscellaneous Manuscripts—Pesotta, Rose, Labadie Collection, Harlan Hatcher Graduate Library, University of Michigan.

124. The most detailed account of the bomb incident is Thai Jones, *More Powerful Than Dynamite: Radicals, Plutocrats, Progressives, and New York's Year of Anarchy* (New York: Walker, 2012). Also see Avrich, *Modern School,* 203–239.

125. Avrich, *Modern School,* 231–233.

126. Harry Kelly, "Anarchism: A Plea for the Impersonal," *Mother Earth,* February 1908, quoted in Wexler, *Emma Goldman,* 205.

127. Quoted in Avrich, *Anarchist Voices,* 74.

128. "Comments—Electing the Boss's Wife," *The Blast,* February 5, 1916, in *The Blast: The Complete Collection,* 38.

129. Michel Foucault, *Discipline and Punish: The Birth of the Prison* (New York: Viking, 1995); Michel Foucault, *The History of Sexuality,* vol. 1 (New York: Viking, 1990); Michel Foucault, *Abnormal: Lectures at the Collége de France, 1974–1975* (New York: Picador, 2004). For a powerful recent application of this mode of analysis, see Dean Spade, *Normal Life: Administrative Violence, Critical Trans Politics and the Limits of Law* (Boston: South End Press, 2011).

130. Antliff, *Anarchist Modernism,* 49–50.

131. Titì and Di Sciullo quoted in Guglielmo, *Living,* 166–167.

132. My analysis here draws on the concepts of subject position, floating signifiers, and chains of equivalency developed by Ernesto Laclau and Chantal Mouffe in *Hegemony and Socialist Strategy: Towards a Radical Democratic Politics* (New York: Verso, 1985).

1. On Mollie Steimer, see Abe Bluestein, ed., *Fighters for Anarchism: Mollie Steimer and Senya Fleshin* (Minneapolis: Libertarian Publications Group, 1983); Richard Polenberg, *Fighting Faiths: The Abrams Case, the Supreme Court, and Free Speech* (Ithaca, NY: Cornell University Press, 1987). For Ella Antolini, see Paul Avrich, *Sacco and Vanzetti: The Anarchist Background* (Princeton, NJ: Princeton University Press, 1991), 104–121; Paul Avrich, *Anarchist Voices: An Oral History of Anarchism in America* (Oakland, CA: AK Press, 2005), 134–136, 138, 180.

2. Avrich, *Sacco and Vanzetti,* 108.

3. Melech Epstein, *Jewish Labor in U.S.A., 1882–1914* (Jersey City, NJ: KATV Publishing House, 1950), 1:130.

4. Polenberg, *Fighting Faiths,* 18. Peter Kropotkin, *The Conquest of Bread* (St. Louis: Dialectics, 2012 [1906]).

5. Chaz Bufe and Mitchell Cowen Verter, eds., *Dreams of Freedom: A Ricardo Flores Magón Reader* (Oakland, CA: AK Press, 2006), 365.

6. Avrich, *Sacco and Vanzetti,* 94.

7. William Preston Jr., *Aliens and Dissenters: Federal Suppression of Radicals, 1903–1933* (New York: Harper and Row, 1963); Robert K. Murray, *Red Scare: A Study in National Hysteria, 1919–1920* (New York: McGraw Hill, 1964); Edwin Palmer Hoyt, *The Palmer Raids, 1919–1920: An Attempt to Suppress Dissent* (New York: Seabury Press, 1969); Roberta Reuerlicht, *America's Reign of Terror: World War I, the Red Scare, and the Palmer Raids* (New York: Random House, 1971); Beverly Gage, *The Day Wall Street Exploded: A Story of America in Its First Age of Terror* (Oxford: Oxford University Press, 2009).

8. The idea of class decomposition was developed by Italian Marxists of the *operaismo* tradition as a means of evaluating relations of power at a given moment. For them, class composition is a measure of the extent to which workers are able to control the process of production and its rewards and to resist the direction of owners and managers. Class decomposition occurs when the capitalist class is able to weaken or destroy working-class cooperation and power. The opposite, class recomposition, occurs as workers find new ways to unite and increase their power. Theorists have distinguished between the "technical" composition of workers, which refers to their production skills vis-à-vis labor-saving technology, and the "political" composition of workers, which refers to their ability to effectively organize unions, political parties, and other collective means of struggle. I suggest that in racially divided societies, the "social" composition of the workforce is an additional aspect of struggle. See Harry Cleaver, "The Inversion of Class Perspective in Marxian Theory: From Valorization to Self-Valorization," in *Open Marxism,* vol. 2: *Theory and Practice,* ed. Werner Bonefeld, Richard Gunn, and Kosmas Psychopedis (London: Pluto Press, 1992), 106–144; Nick Dyer-Witheford, *Cyber-Marx: Cycles and Circuits of Struggle in High-Technology Capitalism* (Urbana: University of Illinois, 1999), 66–67.

9. "International Anarchist Manifesto on the War," *Mother Earth,* May 1915, reproduced in *Anarchy! An Anthology of Emma Goldman's* Mother Earth, ed. Peter Glassgold (Washington, DC: Counterpoint, 2001), 383–388.

10. Reb Rainy, "The Meaning of Margaret Sanger's Stand," *The Blast,* February 12, 1916, reproduced in *The Blast: Complete Collection of the Incendiary San Francisco Bi-Monthly Anarchist Newspaper* (Oakland, CA: AK Press, 2005), 42; *The Blast,* July 15, 1916, reproduced in *The Blast: Complete Collection,* 131.

11. Ricardo Flores Magón, "The World War," *Regeneración,* November 14, 1914, reproduced in Bufe and Verter, *Dreams of Freedom,* 295–296; Ricardo Flores Magón, "The Bourgeois Country and the Universal Country," speech, September 19, 1915, reproduced in Bufe and Verter, *Dreams of Freedom,* 301; Luigi Galleani quoted in Avrich, *Sacco and Vanzetti,* 58.

12. George Woodcock, *Anarchism: A History of Libertarian Ideas and Movements,* 2nd. ed. (Peterborough, ON: Broadview Encore Editions, 2004), 180–181; Peter Marshall, *Demanding the Impossible: A History of Anarchism* (London: HarperCollins, 1992), 331–332; Peter Kropotkin, "Kropotkin on the Present War," *Mother Earth,* November 1914, reproduced in Glassgold, *Anarchy!* 374–379.

13. Paul Avrich, *Anarchist Portraits* (Princeton, NJ: Princeton University Press, 1988), 194.

14. Scott Bennett, *Radical Pacifism in America: The War Resisters League and Gandhian Nonviolence in America, 1915–1963* (Syracuse, NY: Syracuse University Press, 2003), 1–22.

15. Daniel Kanstroom, *Deportation Nation: Outsiders in American History* (Cambridge, MA: Harvard University Press, 2007), 140.

16. Christopher Capozzola, "The Only Badge Needed Is Your Patriotic Fervor: Vigilance, Coercion, and the Law in World War I America," *Journal of American History* 88, no. 4 (March 2002): 1354–1382; Kim E. Nielsen, *Un-American Womanhood: Antiradicalism, Antifeminism, and the First Red Scare* (Columbus: Ohio State University Press, 2001).

17. William H. Thomas, *Unsafe for Democracy: World War I and the U.S. Justice Department's Covert Campaign to Suppress Dissent* (Madison: University of Wisconsin Press, 2008), 20.

18. Avrich, *Sacco and Vanzetti,* 58.

19. Alice Wexler, *Emma Goldman in America* (Boston: Beacon, 1984), 227–231; Kanstroom, *Deportation Nation,* 138.

20. "Espionage Act, June 15, 1917," First World War.com: A Multimedia History of World War I, "Primary Documents—U.S. Espionage Act, 15 June 1917," www .firstworldwar.com/source/espionageact.htm.

21. Avrich, *Sacco and Vanzetti,* 93.

22. Ohio Criminal Syndicalist Law of 1919, quoted in Murray, *Red Scare,* 231–233. See also Eldridge F. Dowell, *A History of Criminal Syndicalism Legislation in the United States* (New York: Da Capo, 1969).

23. Polenberg, *Fighting Faiths,* 29–35; Kanstroom, *Deportation Nation,* 140.

24. Kenneth D. Ackerman, *The Young J. Edgar: Hoover, the Red Scare, and the Assault on Civil Liberties* (New York: Carroll and Graf, 2007).

25. Todd J. Pfannestiel, *Rethinking the Red Scare: The Lusk Committee and New York's Crusade against Radicalism, 1919–1923* (New York: Routledge, 2003); Frank Donner, *Protectors of Privilege: Red Squads and Police Repression in Urban America* (Berkeley: University of California Press, 1990).

26. Though their indictment was timed conspicuously with the ratification of the Espionage Act, Goldman and Berkman were actually indicted under the Draft Act of May 18, 1917, for interfering with conscription. Richard Drinnon, *Rebel in Paradise: A Biography of Emma Goldman* (Chicago: University of Chicago Press, 1961), 188.

27. Ibid., 196.

28. Avrich, *Sacco and Vanzetti,* 94–95.

29. James A. Sandos, *Rebellion in the Borderland: Anarchism and the Plan of San Diego, 1904–1923* (Norman: University of Oklahoma, 1992), 166–168; Chaz Bufe, "Biographical Sketch," in Bufe and Verter, *Dreams of Freedom,* 94–99.

30. Nunzio Pernicone, *Carlo Tresca: Portrait of a Rebel* (New York: Palgrave Macmillan, 2005), 103–104.

31. Paul Avrich, *The Russian Anarchists* (Oakland, CA: AK Press, 2005 [1967]), 137–139.

32. Melvyn Dubovksy, *We Shall Be All: A History of the Industrial Workers of the World* (New York: Quadrangle, 1969), 406–408; Preston, *Aliens and Dissenters,* 118–122.

33. Ted Morgan, *Reds: McCarthyism in 20th Century America* (New York: Random House, 2003), 56.

34. Murray, *Red Scare,* 11; Preston, *Aliens and Dissenters,* 88–117; Fred W. Thompson and Jon Bekken, *The Industrial Workers of the World: Its First 100 Years, 1905–2005* (Cincinnati: IWW, 2006), 105–120.

35. Avrich, *Sacco and Vanzetti,* 94; Roy Rosenzwieg et al., *Who Built America? Working People and the Nation's History* (Boston: St. Martin's, 2008), 1:310.

36. Roger Daniels, *Guarding the Golden Door: American Immigration Policy and Immigrants since 1882* (New York: Hill and Wang, 2004), 46–47; Polenberg, *Fighting Faiths,* 158–159; Kanstroom, *Deportation Nation,* 136–141.

37. Preston, *Aliens and Dissenters,* 99.

38. Daniels, *Guarding,* 33–34.

39. Ibid., 45–46.

40. Capozzola, "Only Badge"; Murray, *Red Scare,* 84–94.

41. Joan Jensen, *The Price of Vigilance* (Chicago: Rand McNally, 1969).

42. Capozzola, "Only Badge," 1364–1369.

43. Murray, *Red Scare,* 181.

44. Avrich, *Russian Anarchists,* 152–170.

45. Ibid., 127–129.

46. Quoted in Polenberg, *Fighting Faiths,* 36.

47. Avrich, *Anarchist Portraits,* 214–215.

48. Ibid., 215–216; Polenberg, *Fighting Faiths,* 43–69.

49. Trial transcript quoted in Polenberg, *Fighting Faiths,* 62.

50. Avrich, *Anarchist Portraits,* 218–219.

51. Polenberg, *Fighting Faiths,* 179–189.

52. Marcus Graham's given name was Shmuel Marcus. His life is not well documented. This account is drawn from the autobiographical note in Marcus Graham, *Man! An Anthology of Anarchist Ideas Essays, Poetry, and Commentary* (London: Cienfuegos Press, 1974), viii–xxi. Also see Kenyon Zimmer, "Positively Stateless: Marcus Graham, the Ferrero-Sallitto Case, and Anarchist Challenges to Race and Deportation," in *The Rising Tide of Color: Race, State Violence, and Radical Movements across the Pacific,* ed. Moon-Ho Jung (Seattle: University of Washington Press, 2014).

53. "To the Workers, Farmers, Soldiers, and Sailors," *Anarchist Soviet Bulletin,* April 1919, 1.

54. The editors of the *Bulletin* clearly saw the councils of workers that the Bolsheviks called soviets as political cognates—in an urban setting—of the self-managing communes of workers extolled by Kropotkin and other anarchist theorists.

55. Murray, *Red Scare,* 58–64.

56. Ibid., 111–112.

57. Melvyn Dubofsky and Foster Rhea Dulles, *Labor in America: A History,* 6th ed. (Wheeling, IL: Harlan Davidson, 1999), 217–224.

58. Cameron McWhirter, *Red Summer: The Summer of 1919 and the Awakening of Black America* (New York: Henry Holt, 2011); William M. Tuttle, *Race Riot: Chicago in the Red Summer of 1919* (Urbana: University of Illinois Press, 1996).

59. Quoted in Salvatore Salerno, "*I Delitti Della Razza Bianca* (Crimes of the White Race): Italian Anarchists' Racial Discourse as Crime," in *Are Italians White? How Race Is Made in America,* eds. Jennifer Guglielmo and Salvatore Salerno (New York: Routledge, 2003), 118.

60. "Would Arm Home Guards for Reds," *Detroit Free Press,* October 23, 1919.

61. Dubofsky and Dulles, *Labor in America,* 220; Barbara Foley, *Spectres of 1919: Class and Nation in the Making of the New Negro* (Urbana: University of Illinois, 2003), 13. Foley provides a detailed consideration of the complex relationships between African Americans and the socialist and communist Left, as well as of the convergence of racist and antiradical rhetoric and violence in the immediate postwar period.

62. Marcus Graham Freedom of the Press Committee, *Freedom of Thought Arraigned: Four Year Persecution of MAN!, 19 Year Persecution of Marcus Graham* (Los Angeles: MGFPC, 1939), 8. Vertical File: Anarchism—Marcus, Shmuel—Arrest and Trial—Marcus Graham Freedom of the Press Committee, Labadie Collection, University of Michigan.

63. Avrich, *Anarchist Portraits,* 219–221; Polenberg, *Fighting Faiths,* 247, 285.

64. Michael A Gordon, "'To Make a Clean Sweep': Milwaukee Confronts an Anarchist Scare in 1917," *Wisconsin Magazine of History* 93, no. 2 (Winter 2009–2010): 16–27; Avrich, *Sacco and Vanzetti,* 104–107.

65. Avrich, *Sacco and Vanzetti,* 109–114.

66. Quoted in ibid., 137, emphasis in original.

67. On the bombing campaign, see Nunzio Pernicone, "Luigi Galleani and Italian Anarchist Terrorism in the United States," *Studi Emigrazione/Etudes Migrationes* 30, no. 111 (1993); Avrich, *Sacco and Vanzetti;* Gage, *Day Wall Street Exploded.*

68. Avrich, *Sacco and Vanzetti,* 135.

69. Pernicone, *Carlo Tresca,* 114.

70. Avrich, *Russian Anarchists.*

71. Christopher M. Finan, *From the Palmer Raids to the PATRIOT Act: A History of the Fight for Free Speech in America* (Boston: Beacon), 1–2; Murray, *Red Scare,* 196–197.

72. A. Mitchell Palmer, "The Case against the 'Reds,'" *Forum,* February 1920, quoted in Avrich, *Sacco and Vanzetti,* 174, my emphasis.

73. Murray, *Red Scare,* 206.

74. Polenberg, *Fighting Faiths,* 175.

75. *Ellis Island Anarchist Weekly,* May 10, 1919, Miscellaneous Manuscripts, Labadie Collection, University of Michigan. A single, two-sided, copy of the *Ellis Island Anarchist Weekly* survives today. It is unclear if other copies or editions were ever created. It is uncertain who created the *Weekly,* but clues point strongly to Marcus Graham. The *Weekly* bears the date May 10, 1919. Graham was detained on Ellis Island for two weeks in May 1919, after he was caught with copies of the *Anarchist Soviet Bulletin* in Paterson, New Jersey. The masthead of *Free Society,* which Graham is known to have edited, reproduces almost exactly the masthead of the *Ellis Island Anarchist Weekly.* Whoever was in possession of the paper had to have eventually gotten off the island, which Graham did, and been in correspondence with the Labadie Collection at the University of Michigan, which Graham was. On Graham's detention on Ellis Island, see Polenberg, *Fighting Faiths,* 183–184; Marcus Graham, "A Statement of Facts," *Man!* August–September 1936, 4; Marcus Graham Freedom of the Press Committee, *Freedom of Thought Arraigned,* 8.

76. Drinnon, *Rebel in Paradise,* 215–223.

77. "Second Lot of Reds Sails Soon," *Los Angeles Times,* December 23, 1919; "U.S. to Ship Reds' Wives on Next 'Ark,'" *New York Tribune,* December 23, 1919.

78. "Relatives of Reds Mob Barge Office," *New York Times,* December 23, 1919.

79. "Second Lot of Reds Sails Soon," *Los Angeles Times,* December 23, 1919.

80. "Relatives of Reds Mob Barge Office," *New York Times,* December 23, 1919.

81. Daniels, *Guarding,* 274, note 52.

82. Polenberg, *Fighting Faiths,* 323–345.

83. Gage, *Day Wall Street Exploded,* 214.

84. The literature on the Sacco and Vanzetti case is extensive. See Avrich, *Sacco and Vanzetti;* Bruce Watson, *Sacco and Vanzetti: The Men, the Murders, and the Judgment of Mankind* (New York: Viking, 2007); *Sacco and Vanzetti: Developments and Reconsiderations—1979, Conference Proceedings* (Boston: Boston Public Library, 1982); Peter Miller, dir., *Sacco and Vanzetti* (New York: First Run Features, 2007), DVD.

85. For a description of the bombing and the investigation that followed, see Gage, *Day Wall Street Exploded*. For Buda as the culprit, see Avrich, *Sacco and Vanzetti*, 204–207; Pernicone, *Carlo Tresca*, 118; and Charles H. McCormick, *Hopeless Cases: The Hunt for the Red Scare Terrorist Bombers* (Lanham, MD: University Press of America, 2005). Mike Davis uses this evidence to name Mario Buda as the inventor of the car bomb. *Buda's Wagon: A Brief History of the Car Bomb* (London: Verso, 2007).

86. Pernicone, *Carlo Tresca*, 119. The first Sacco-Vanzetti Defense Committee was formed on May 9, four days after their arrest. Gage, *Day Wall Street Exploded*, 222. Throughout the decade a host of additional defense committees would be formed and would implement a wide variety of tactics and discursive strategies to free the pair. See Rebecca Hill, *Men, Mobs, and Law: Anti-lynching and Labor Defense in U.S. Radical History* (Durham: Duke University Press, 2008), 162–208.

87. *Free Society,* September 1921, 2.

88. Mae Ngai, *Impossible Subjects: Illegal Aliens and the Making of Modern America* (Princeton, NJ: Princeton University Press, 2004), 21–55; Matthew Frye Jacobson, *Whiteness of a Different Color: European Immigrants and the Alchemy of Race* (Cambridge, MA: Harvard University Press, 1998), 78–90; David Roediger, *Working toward Whiteness: How America's Immigrants Became White: The Strange Journey from Ellis Island to the Suburbs* (New York: Basic Books, 2005), 139–145.

89. Daniels, *Guarding,* 56–57.

90. Ibid., 50.

91. Roediger, *Working toward Whiteness,* 150.

92. Ngai, *Impossible Subjects,* 4.

CHAPTER 3. A MOVEMENT OF DEFENSE, OF EMERGENCY, 1920–1929

1. *Road to Freedom,* December 1924, 5.

2. Patrick Renshaw, *The Wobblies: The Story of Syndicalism in the United States* (New York: Doubleday, 1967), 159–184.

3. John S. Gambs, *The Decline of the I.W.W.* (New York: Columbia University Press, 1932); Melvyn Dubofsky, *We Shall Be All: A History of the Industrial Workers of the World* (New York: Quadrangle, 1969), 445–468; Fred Thompson and Jon Bekken, *The Industrial Workers of the World: Its First One Hundred Years* (Philadelphia: IWW, 2006), 133–148; Renshaw, *The Wobblies,* 245–271.

4. Melech Epstein, *Jewish Labor in U.S.A., 1882–1914* (n.p.: KATV Publishing House, 1950), 1:38.

5. See Kenyon Zimmer, *Immigrants against the State: Yiddish and Italian Anarchism in America* (Urbana: University of Illinois, 2015); Paul Avrich, *Anarchist Portraits* (Princeton, NJ: Princeton University Press, 1988), 176–199; Tony Michels, *Jewish Radicals: A Documentary History* (New York: NYU Press, 2012); Epstein, *Jewish Labor,* 192–219.

6. Quoted in "The Jewish Anarchist Movement," *Free Society,* December 1921, 4.

7. Audrey Goodfriend, interview by author, Berkeley, CA, November 10, 2008.

8. On the housing cooperatives, see *At Home in Utopia,* produced by Michal Goldman with Ellen Brodsky (Harriman, NY: New Day Films, 2008), DVD.

9. Elaine Leeder, *The Gentle General: Rose Pesotta, Anarchist and Labor Organizer* (Albany: SUNY Press, 1993), 7–9. Pesotta's adolescent life is also documented in her second memoir, *The Days of Our Lives* (Boston: Excelsior, 1958).

10. See Daniel Katz, *All Together Different: Yiddish Socialists, Garment Workers, and the Roots of Multiculturalism* (New York: NYU Press, 2011).

11. Leeder, *Gentle General,* 22–26.

12. Epstein, *Jewish Labor,* 129, 367.

13. Benjamin Stolberg, *Taylor's Progress: The Story of a Famous Union and the Men Who Made It* (Garden City, NY: Doubleday, Doran, 1944), 110.

14. From 1917 through the early 1920s, council forms of Marxism were central to the worker's movement throughout Europe. Before information to the contrary was widely available, it appeared that the Bolshevik movement would truly rely on the power of workers' councils (soviets). Movements in Italy and Germany relied on councils, and the theoretical writings of Anton Panekoek, Rosa Luxembourg, and other councilists were taken more seriously. The councilist moment, sharing much in common with anarcho-syndicalism, provided a short period of hope for collaboration among anarchists and soon-to-be communists. See Darrow Schecter, *The History of the Left: From Marx to the Present* (New York: Continuum, 2007), 117–120.

15. Epstein, *Jewish Labor,* 131.

16. Leeder, *Gentle General,* 33.

17. On anarchists in the Russian Revolution, see Paul Avrich, *The Russian Anarchists* (Oakland, CA: AK Press, 2005 [1967]); Voline, *Nineteen-Seventeen: The Russian Revolution Betrayed* (New York: Libertarian Book Club, 1954); James Joll, *The Anarchists* (New York: Grosset and Dunlap, 1964), 181–193; Peter Marshall, *Demanding the Impossible: A History of Anarchism* (Oakland, CA: PM Press, 2010), 467–478.

18. Emma Goldman, *My Disillusionment in Russia* (Mineola, NY: Dover, 2003 [1923]); Emma Goldman, *My Further Disillusionment in Russia* (Garden City, NY: Doubleday and Page, 1924); Alexander Berkman, *The Bolshevik Myth: Diary 1920–1922* (New York: Boni and Liverwright, 1925).

19. Leeder, *Gentle General,* 30–31.

20. Avrich, *Russian Anarchists,* 113; Boris Yelensky, *In the Struggle for Equality: The Story of the Anarchist Red Cross* (Chicago: Anarchist Red Cross, 1958). In 1974 the Russian-born anarchist Morris Ganberg told Paul Avrich, "The Anarchist Red Cross was founded in 1911, and I was active from the start. The center was in New York, with branches in Detroit, Chicago, Philadelphia, and other cities. . . . The New York branch had about sixty or seventy members and met every week on East Broadway." Avrich, *Anarchist Voices: An Oral History of Anarchism in America* (Oakland, CA: AK Press,

2005 [1995]), 373–374. It may be that branches in London and other European cities were organized in 1907 and the New York Branch did not form until 1911.

21. Kenyon Zimmer, "Premature Anti-Communists?: American Anarchism, the Russian Revolution, and Left-Wing Libertarian Anti-Communism, 1917–1939," *Labor: Studies in Working Class History of the Americas* 6, no. 2 (2009): 45–71.

22. *Report and Proceedings of the International Ladies' Garment Workers' Union, 16th Convention, Cleveland,* 1922, 120–121, 188, American Labor Unions' Constitutions, Proceedings, Officers' Reports and Supplementary Documents, Microfilm, Reel 45, Tamiment Library and Robert F. Wagner Labor Archives, New York University. I thank Daniel Katz for suggesting I investigate the published reports of ILGWU conventions.

23. Ibid., 150–151.

24. Ibid., 180.

25. Epstein, *Jewish Labor,* 132. It is not clear how many members belonged to this new formation or what locals they were drawn from. However, participants likely numbered in the hundreds and belonged to the predominantly Jewish radical locals of New York City—namely, Locals 1, 9, 22, and 25.

26. Stanley Nadel, "Reds versus Pinks: A Civil War in the International Ladies Garment Workers Union," *New York History* 66, no. 1 (1985): 59.

27. Epstein, *Jewish Labor,* 140.

28. Nadel, "Reds versus Pinks," 65–72.

29. A. Blecher, "Problems of Theory and Practice, Part II," *Road to Freedom,* August 1926, 7–8.

30. Sam Dolgoff, *Fragments: A Memoir* (Cambridge, U.K.: Refract, 1986), 26.

31. Literature on the Italian anarchist movement has grown quickly in recent years. See Jennifer Guglielmo, *Living the Revolution: Italian Women's Resistance and Radicalism in New York City, 1880–1945* (Chapel Hill: University of North Carolina Press, 2010); Michael Miller Topp, *Those without a Country: The Political Culture of Italian American Syndicalism* (Minneapolis: University of Minnesota Press, 2001); Nunzio Pernicone, *Carlo Tresca: Portrait of a Rebel* (New York: Palgrave Macmillan, 2005); Nunzio Pernicone, "Luigi Galleani and Italian Anarchist Terrorism in the United States," *Studi Emigrazione/Etudes Migrations* 30, no. 111 (1993): 469–488; Philip Cannistraro and Gerald Meyer, eds., *The Lost World of Italian American Radicalism: Politics, Labor, and Culture* (Westport, CT: Praeger, 2003); Rudolf Vecoli, ed., *Italian American Radicalism: Old World Origins and New World Developments* (New York: Italian American Historical Association, 1973); Rebecca N. Hill, *Men, Mobs, and Law: Anti-lynching and Labor Defense in U.S. Radical History* (Durham, NC: Duke University Press, 2008), 162–208; Beverly Gage, *The Day Wall Street Exploded: A Story of America in Its First Age of Terror* (Oxford: Oxford University Press, 2009).

32. Salvatore Salerno, "*I Delitti della Razza Bianca* (Crimes of the White Race): Italian Anarchists' Racial Discourse as Crime," in *Are Italians White? How Race Is Made in America,* ed. Jennifer Guglielmo and Salvatore Salerno (New York: Routledge, 2003), 111–123.

33. Nunzio Pernicone, "War among the Italian Anarchists: The Galleanisti's Campaign against Carlo Tresca," in Cannistraro and Meyer, *The Lost World of Italian American Radicalism,* 84.

34. These include *Il Domani* and *L'Ordine,* published by Roberto Elia and Andrea Salsedo, soon to be implicated in the May 1 and June 2, 1919, bomb campaigns. Pernicone, *Carlo Tresca,* 115.

35. Hill, *Men, Mobs, and Law,* 176.

36. Quoted in ibid., 183.

37. Valerio Isca quoted in Avrich, *Anarchist Voices,* 147.

38. The conflict between Carlo Tresca and the Luigi Galleani is traceable to the aftermath of the historic Lawrence textile strike of 1912, in which both men and their followers were involved. Tresca was chosen over Galleani by the IWW to lead agitation to free Ettor and Giavannitti, two syndicalist organizers framed for murder during the conflict. In the fall of 1912, the IWW called for a general strike in the garment industry to free the pair. Galleani and his insurrectionist collaborators devoted themselves to constant militant propaganda in order to build support for the strike (and perhaps even more militant tactics). When the IWW leadership called off the strike, fearing it would fail and that more blood would be shed, the Galleanisti focused their derision on Tresca, accusing him of having "eviscerated the enthusiasm of the proletariat." Throughout the Lawrence strike, Tresca had identified as a revolutionary syndicalist, but in 1913 he declared himself an anarcho-syndicalist. Galleani, however, did not concur; citing Tresca's disagreements with his group's tactics, he declared, "We will no longer travel on the same path: no longer can you be an anarchist." Pernicone, "War among the Italian Anarchists," 80, 82.

39. See Carl Levy, *Gramsci and the Anarchists* (Oxford: Berg, 1999).

40. Pernicone, *Carlo Tresca,* 133; Topp, *Those without a Country,* 247–248; Philip V. Cannistraro, *Blackshirts in Little Italy: Italian Americans and Fascism, 1921–1929* (West Lafayette, IN: Bordighera Press, 1999).

41. Pernicone, *Carlo Tresca,* 105.

42. Ibid., 136–137.

43. Ibid., 139.

44. Ibid., 165. Regular routings such as these emboldened the fascists to retaliate. In 1925, at the behest of the Italian embassy, Tresca was sentenced to four months in prison for printing a two-line advertisement for birth control information. Later, a fascist group attempted to bomb a rally organized by Tresca but only killed themselves in the process (147–161, 172). Topp, *Those Without,* 251.

45. Avrich, *Anarchist Voices,* 175–188.

46. Quoted in ibid., 181.

47. Quoted in ibid., 183.

48. Joseph Cohen and Alexis C. Ferm, *The Modern School of Stelton: A Sketch* (New York: Factory School, 2006 [1925]), 53. Anarchists used the terms *colony* and *colonization* without apparent concern for the imperialist implications of the terms. In the late nineteenth and early twentieth centuries the term *colony* was commonly

used to describe any settlement of a particular group of people, such as an immigrant community, in a locale in which they were not previously concentrated.

49. Paul Avrich, *The Modern School Movement: Anarchism and Education in the United States* (Oakland, CA: AK Press, 2006), 241–244.

50. Harry Kelly, "Roll Back the Years," n.d., chap. 26, p. 8, unpublished manuscript, John Nicholas Beffel Papers, Tamiment Library, New York University.

51. Laurence Veysey, *The Communal Experience: Anarchist and Mystical Counter-Cultures in America* (New York: Harper & Row, 1973), 122.

52. Avrich, *Modern School,* 266, 303

53. Kelly, "Roll Back the Years," chap. 25, pp. 5–6.

54. Avrich, *Modern School,* 250.

55. Peter Kropotkin, *Fields, Factories, and Workshops; or, Industry Combined with Agriculture and Brain Work with Mental Work* (New York: Greenwood Press, 1968 [1901]).

56. Veysey, *Communal Experience,* 149. The Ferms explain their pedagogical practice in Cohen and Ferm, *Modern School;* and Elizabeth Byrne Ferm, *Freedom in Education* (New York: Factory School, 2005 [1949]).

57. Veysey, *Communal Experience,* 152–153.

58. Kelly, "Roll Back the Years," chap. 27, pp. 1–2.

59. Ibid., chap. 37, p. 2.

60. Avrich, *Modern School,* 317–318.

61. Ibid., 335–336.

62. Joseph Spivak, "A Coast to Coast Observation," *Road to Freedom,* September 1927, 7.

63. Ibid., 8.

64. Boris Yelensky, "25 Years of 'Free Society' Activity in Chicago," in *The World Scene from the Libertarian Point of View* (Chicago: Free Society Group, 1951), 90. Chicago had hosted a group under the same name before the war, organized around publication of the journal *Free Society,* founded by Mary and Abraham Isaak. See Alice Wexler, *Emma Goldman in America* (Boston: Beacon, 1986), 100–102.

65. Yelensky, "25 Years," 90.

66. Gregory Petrovich Maximoff, *The Guillotine at Work,* vol. 1: *The Leninist Counter-Revolution* (Somerville, MA: Black Thorne Books, 1979 [1940]). The book includes a biographical sketch of the author penned by Sam Dolgoff.

67. Upon being subsumed in the International Working Men's Association, the committee adopted the burdensome name the Relief Fund of the International Working Men's Association for Anarchists and Anarcho-Syndicalists Imprisoned or Exiled in Russia.

68. *Bulletin of the Joint Committee for the Defense of the Revolutionists Imprisoned in Russia,* March–April 1925, reprinted in Alexander Berkman Social Club, ed., *The Tragic Procession: Alexander Berkman and Russian Prisoner Aid* (Berkeley, CA: Alexander Berkman Social Club and Kate Sharpley Library, 2010).

69. Alexander Berkman Social Club, *The Tragic Procession,* 8–9.

70. The March–April 1925 issue, for example, records a $75 donation from "Los Angeles Aid Society Polit. Pris., per J. Spivak," and $45 from "Chicago Group, per Yelensky." New York anarchists also did their part. The December 1926 issue of the *Bulletin* lists a $250 donation from "An. Aid Com., N.Y. (former Red Cross)" and a personal donation of $25 from Anna S[osnovsky]." Despite their focus on securing funds for the Sacco and Vanzetti defense, Italian anarchists in the United States also pitched in regularly. The November 1927 *Bulletin,* for instance, records donations "Per L'Adunata" from the Group Libertario of Rochester, New York, and from the "Group Germinal, Chicago, per Armando Tiberi." Alexander Berkman Social Club, *Tragic Procession,* 13, 27, 33.

71. *Road to Freedom,* January 1925, 8.

72. Avrich, *The Russian Anarchists,* 215.

73. An anarchist who began writing for the paper toward the end of its run noted, "I will always gratefully remember that it was Van who encouraged us youngsters to write in the *Road to Freedom*." Dolgoff, *Fragments,* 9. Like his coeditor Havel, however, Van was known for drinking too much. Sarah Taback, a member of the Road to Freedom Group, recalls, "One day while walking to a meeting I saw him lying in the gutter on Fourteenth Street, drunk and dirty and mumbling to himself." Avrich, *Anarchist Voices,* 430. On Van Valkenburgh's life, see "Finding Aid," Van Valkenburgh Papers, Labadie Collection, University of Michigan.

74. [Hippolyte Havel], "Anarchist Communism," *Road to Freedom,* November 1924, 5–6.

75. "To Our Readers," *Road to Freedom,* November 1924, 5.

76. For a rare exception, see "Woman and the Fundamentalists," *Road to Freedom,* July 1925. Women contributed content to the newspaper sporadically, but their articles tended to be reports on group activities or project finances rather than news items, opinion pieces, and forays into political analysis, which men typically contributed.

77. The black labor leader Thomas Dabney contributed a single article to the *Road to Freedom,* in which he bemoaned the small numbers of African Americans participating in radical movements. "The Negro and the Radical Movements," *Road to Freedom,* April 1926.

78. *Road to Freedom,* October 1925, 8.

79. Anna Sosnovsky, "The Anarchist Conference," *Road to Freedom,* August 1925, 5–7; "The Anarchist Conference: Discussion on Propaganda and Press, " *Road to Freedom,* September 1925, 3, 7–8; "The Anarchist Conference: Discussion on Propaganda and Press," *Road to Freedom,* October 1925, 7–8.

80. Marcus Graham, "From New York to Detroit," *Road to Freedom,* September 1927, 6–7.

81. D. Isakovitz, "Anarchism and Revolution," *Road to Freedom,* June 1925, 2–4.

82. Theo L. Miles, "Revisionism in the Anarchist Movement," *Road to Freedom,* September 1925, 1; "Comments," *Road to Freedom,* July 1925, 4.

83. Joseph Spivak, "What's Wrong with Our Movement?" *Road to Freedom,* April 1928, 3.

84. Ibid., 2–3.

85. For a discussion of the debates surrounding "The Platform," see Alexandre Skirda, *Facing the Enemy: A History of Anarchist Organization from Proudhon to May 1968* (Oakland, CA: AK Press, 2002), 121–143; and Michael Schmidt and Lucien van der Walt, *Black Flame: The Revolutionary Class Politics of Anarchism and Syndicalism* (Oakland, CA: AK Press, 2009), 253–261.

86. Quoted in Veysey, *Communal Experience,* 167.

87. W. S. Van Valkenburgh, "What Is Wrong with Our Movement?" *Road to Freedom,* May 1928, 3.

88. *Road to Freedom,* May 1927, 1.

89. Yelensky, "25 Years," 91.

90. "Freedom: A Weekly Journal Devoted to Anarchist Thought," circular, Vertical File: Anarchist—Freedom Group—New York, Labadie Collection, University of Michigan.

91. Nunzio Pernicone, "Luigi Galleani," 488.

92. Avrich, *Anarchist Voices,* 166.

CHAPTER 4. THE UNPOPULAR FRONT, 1930–1939

1. The synoptic account of the Great Depression provided in this chapter draws on David Kennedy, *Freedom from Fear: The American People in Depression and War, 1929–1945* (Oxford: Oxford University Press, 1999); Ira Katznelson, *Fear Itself: The New Deal and the Origins of Our Times* (New York: Liveright, 2013); and Steve Fraser and Gary Gerstle, *The Rise and Fall of the New Deal Order* (Princeton, NJ: Princeton University Press, 1989).

2. Paul Avrich, *Anarchist Voices: An Oral History of Anarchism in America* (Oakland, CA: AK Press, 2005), 352.

3. Marcus Graham, "Biographical Note," in *"Man!": An Anthology of Anarchist Ideas, Essays, Poetry, and Commentary,* ed. Marcus Graham (London: Cienfuegos Press, 1974), ix; Avrich, *Anarchist Voices,* 266, 423.

4. Avrich, *Anarchist Voices,* 165.

5. Sam Dolgoff quoted in ibid., 421.

6. Graham to Inglis, February 14, 1934, Box 9, Agnes Inglis Papers, Labadie Collection, University of Michigan (hereafter, LC).

7. Graham, "Biographical Note," xvii.

8. For more on the International Group, see Kenyon Zimmer, "Positively Stateless: Marcus Graham, the Ferrero-Sallitto Case, and Anarchist Challenges to Race and Deportation," in *The Rising Tide of Color: Race, State Violence, and Radical Movements across the Pacific,* ed. Moon-Ho Jung (Seattle: University of Washington Press, 2014), 128–158.

9. Marcus Graham, "In Retrospect," *Man!* January 1933, 1.

10. Marcus Graham, "Defending Anarchy," *Man!* January 1933, 6.

11. Marcus Graham, "Anarchists and the Labor Movement," *Man!* January 1934, 4–5.

12. *Man!* received "protest resolutions" from the Free Society Group of Chicago, the Spanish Anarchist Groups of the United States, and the Spanish CNT regarding this position. See "Can Organization Be Anti-authoritarian?" *Man!* June–July 1934.

13. Marcus Graham, "The Evils of Organization," *Man!* November–December 1934, 4; Edwin Cunningham, "Whom Does Organized Labor Benefit?" *Man!* November–December 1935, 3.

14. Marcus Graham, "Anarchists and the Labor Movement," *Man!* January 1934, 4–5.

15. Marcus Graham, "Labor's Enemies," *Man!* January 1933, 1. See also Candido, "Miners," *Man!* April 1933, 5. On the mine wars, see William C. Blizzard, *When Miners March* (Oakland, CA: PM Press, 2010).

16. S. Menico, "To Seekers of 'Conferences' and 'Congresses,'" *Man!* February 1933, 4.

17. C. H. Mitchell, "Is Anarchism Dead?" *Man!* February 1933, 4.

18. Marcus Graham, "About Planless Anarchy," *Man!* May–June 1935, 5.

19. Marcus Graham, "Liberation," *Man!* January 1933, 1. This vision of largely independent artisans shared much in common with the vision that nineteenth-century American individualist anarchists, such as Josiah Warren, had articulated a century before, as the country's industrial revolution was commencing.

20. As Maia Ramnath astutely explains, "If by asking 'Is anarchism modern or antimodern?' we mean 'Is anarchism really part of the rationalist or Romanticist tradition?' . . . then we fail to grasp that the cultural profile of modernity itself is not wholly identifiable with either side. . . . What's unique about the anarchist tradition among Western political discourses is its continuous struggle for a synthesis between the two polarities, rejecting neither." *Decolonizing Anarchism* (Oakland, CA: Institute for Anarchist Studies and AK Press, 2011), 35. On the "scientism" in nineteenth-century anarchist thought, see George Crowder, *Classical Anarchism: The Political Thought of Godwin, Proudhon, Bakunin, and Kropotkin* (Oxford: Oxford University Press, 1991). On anarchism and romanticism, see Max Blechman, ed., *Revolutionary Romanticism: A Drunken Boat Anthology* (San Francisco: City Lights, 2001).

21. Marcus Graham, "What Ought to Be the Anarchist Attitude towards the Machine?" *Man!* March 1934, 3.

22. Graham, "Defending Anarchy," 6.

23. "Machine Age Doom of Man, Poet Asserts—Marcus Graham Finds Civilization of Today Sterile—Speaks in Albany Tonight at Workmen's Circle Institute," *Albany News,* December 18, 1931, newspaper clipping, Vertical File: Anarchism—Marcus, Shmuel-Lectures, LC.

24. Anarcho-primitivism, green anarchism, and anticivilization radicalism refer to closely related intellectual tendencies promoted by authors such as Fredy Perlman, John Zerzan, David Watson, John Moore, and Derrick Jensen (though Jensen has distanced himself from anarchism). Although these tendencies have not been

adequately studied, see Ruth Kinna, *Anarchism: A Beginner's Guide* (Oxford: One World, 2005); Randall Amster, *Anarchism Today* (Santa Barbara, CA: Praeger, 2012), 64–86; Steve Millet, "Technology Is Capital: Fifth Estate's Critique of the Megamachine," in *Changing Anarchism: Anarchist Theory and Practice in a Global Age,* ed. James Bowen and Jonathan Purkis (Manchester, U.K.: Manchester University Press, 2004), 72–98; and Uri Gordon, *Anarchy Alive! Anti-authoritarian Politics from Practice to Theory* (London: Pluto Press, 2007), 109–138.

25. "Machine Age Doom of Man, Poet Asserts."

26. "The Movement around *Man!*" *Man!* May–June 1933, 5.

27. Marcus Graham, "A Statement of Facts," *Man!* August–September 1936, 4; Marcus Graham Freedom of the Press Committee, *Freedom of Thought Arraigned: Four Year Persecution of MAN!, 19 Year Persecution of Marcus Graham* (Los Angeles: MGFPC), 1939, 3. In Vertical File: Anarchism—Marcus, Shmuel—Arrest and Trial—Marcus Graham Freedom of the Press Committee, LC; Zimmer, "Positively Stateless."

28. Avrich, *Anarchist Voices,* 148.

29. Ibid., 163.

30. Abe Bluestein, oral history, H-30 to H-31, Abe and Selma Bluestein Papers, LC. Like Rose Pesotta, Bluestein became a general organizer for the union in the 1930s.

31. Avrich, *Anarchist Voices,* 380.

32. Bluestein, oral history, H-1.

33. See Robert Cohen, *When the Old Left Was Young: Student Radicals and America's First Mass Student Movement, 1929–1941* (New York: Oxford University Press, 1993); Alan Wald, *The New York Intellectuals: The Rise and Decline of the Anti-Stalinist Left from the 1930s to the 1980s* (Chapel Hill: University of North Carolina, 1987).

34. Bluestein, oral history, B-12 to B-15.

35. Avrich, *Anarchist Voices,* 422.

36. Dolgoff, *Fragments,* 47.

37. Ibid., 10.

38. Sidney Soloman, quoted in Avrich, *Anarchist Voices,* 450. Solomon later married Freedman, so his recollections may be biased. Nonetheless his comments indicate that although men did the preponderance of speaking and writing in the Vanguard Group, the unsung efforts of women were fundamental to keeping the group's projects operating smoothly.

39. Avrich, *Anarchist Voices,* 423–424, 450–451; George Creighton, "Self-Determination for Black Belt," *Vanguard,* April–May 1936, 12–14.

40. Avrich, *Anarchist Voices,* 424, 444.

41. Dolgoff, *Fragments,* 23.

42. Avrich, *Anarchist Voices,* 444.

43. Ibid., 448.

44. "A Declaration of Policy," *Vanguard,* April 1932, 2–3.

45. Interview of Sam and Esther Dolgoff, 1975, compact disc, LC.

46. Sam Weiner [Dolgoff], "Anarchist Communism," *Vanguard,* July 1932, 6–8; Sam Weiner [Dolgoff], "Anarchist Communism," *Vanguard,* August–September 1932, 6–9; Sam Weiner [Dolgoff], "Anarchist Communism," *Vanguard,* November 1932, 11–13; G. Maximoff, "The Economics of the Transition Program," *Vanguard,* April 1933, 4–8.

47. "Why This Magazine?" *Vanguard,* March 1935, 1; Dolgoff, *Fragments,* 31.

48. Avrich, *Anarchist Voices,* 450.

49. Sam and Esther Dolgoff, interview.

50. This stood in contrast to the broadening cultural engagements of socialists and communists during the same years. See Michael Denning, *The Cultural Front: The Laboring of American Culture in the Twentieth Century* (New York: Verso, 1998).

51. "A Declaration of Policy," *Vanguard,* April 1932, 3.

52. Avrich, *Anarchist Voices,* 438.

53. S. Morrison, "The I.L.G.W.U Calls upon Youth," *Vanguard,* February 1933, 8–11.

54. *Vanguard Group Internal Bulletin,* no. 1, Vertical File: Anarchism—Vanguard, LC.

55. Avrich, *Anarchist Voices,* 451.

56. Ibid., 457–458.

57. Audrey Goodfriend, interview by author, Berkeley, CA, November 10, 2008.

58. Marcus Graham, "The New Deal," *Man!* April 1933, 4; Marcus Graham, "The New Savior for Capitalism—Fascism!" *Man!* August–September 1933, 4.

59. Melvyn Dubofsky, *The State and Labor in Modern America* (Chapel Hill: University of North Carolina Press, 1994), 111–113.

60. Senex [Mark Schmidt], "The 'New Deal,'" *Vanguard,* May–June 1933, 1–2; Melchior Seele, "A New Deal?" *Man!* January 1934, 1–2.

61. Dubofsky, *State and Labor,* 113–115; Irving Bernstein, *The Turbulent Years: A History of the American Worker, 1933–1940,* new ed. (Chicago: Haymarket Books, 2010).

62. Staughton Lynd, ed., *"We Are All Leaders": The Alternative Unionism of the Early 1930s* (Urbana: University of Illinois Press, 1996); Alice Lynd and Staughton Lynd, eds., *Rank and File: Personal Histories by Working-Class Organizers,* 2nd ed. (Chicago: Haymarket Books, 2012).

63. Marcus Graham, "Was There a General Strike?" *Man!* August 1934, 1, 4.

64. Dubofsky, *State and Labor,* 119–135; Nelson Lichtenstein, *State of the Union: A Century of American Labor* (Princeton, NJ: Princeton University Press, 2003), 20–39.

65. Theorists in the operaismo, or autonomist Marxist, tradition emphasize that procapitalist governments legitimized unions as part of a larger scheme of Keynesian demand management, which explicitly sought to undermine radical alternatives that business and political leaders deemed threatening. See Antonio Negri, "Keynes and the Capitalist Theory of the State," in *Labor of Dionysus: A Critique of the State Form,* ed. Michael Hardt (Minneapolis: University of Minnesota Press, 1994), 23–52.

66. For a visceral sense of employer resistance to unionization in the automobile industry, see "Ford's Brass Knuckles: Harry Bennett, the Cult of Muscularity, and Anti-Labor Terror, 1920–1945," in *Strikebreaking and Intimidation: Mercenaries and Masculinity in Twentieth Century America,* by Stephen H. Norwood (Chapel Hill: University of North Carolina, 2002), 171–193.

67. Melvyn Dubofsky and Foster Rhea Dulles, *Labor in America: A History,* 6th ed. (Wheeling, IL: Harlan Davidson, 1999), 282. On the rise of the CIO, see Robert H. Zieger, *The CIO, 1935–1955* (Chapel Hill: University of North Carolina, 1995).

68. "Anarchist Position on C.I.O.," *Vanguard,* October–November 1936, 6–7.

69. Mike Davis notes, "The original CIO was an alliance of dissident trade-union bureaucrats, with important financial resources and friends in high places, created for the purpose of capturing an already existent mass movement of industrial shop committees and rebel locals—a movement with dangerous proclivities toward an anti-Gompersian model of 'class struggle unionism.'" *Prisoners of the American Dream: Politics and Economy in the History of the American Working Class* (New York: Verso, 1986), 56–57. For case studies, see Lynd, ed., *We Are All Leaders.*

70. Joseph Zack, "The Rise of the CIO," *Vanguard,* June 1937, 11–13; Joseph Zack, "Gentlemen, Be Seated!" *Vanguard,* February–March 1937, 11–12.

71. Among other issues, Mills criticized the means by which CIO union leaders provided stability to corporate managers by exercising discipline over their own members and settling disputes through bureaucratic procedures rather than direct action on the shop floor. C. Wright Mills, *The New Men of Power: America's Labor Leaders,* new ed. (Urbana: University of Illinois Press, 2001 [1948]). Worker intellectuals involved with the Johnson-Forest Tendency, a dissident caucus within the U.S. Trotskyist movement, made similar points about unionism while also developing a theory of state capitalism that they applied to both the United States and the Soviet Union. See Martin Glaberman, *Punching Out and Other Writings,* ed. and introduced by Staughton Lynd (Chicago: Charles H. Kerr, 2002); C. L. R. James, Raya Dunayevskaya, and Grace Lee Boggs, *State Capitalism and World Revolution* (Oakland, CA: PM Press; Chicago: Charles H. Kerr, 2013 [1950]). The Johnson-Forest Tendency's ideas on these matters significantly influenced the development of autonomist Marxism. See Harry Cleaver, *Reading Capital Politically* (Leeds, U.K.: AntiTheses; San Francisco: AK Press, 2001), 58–77; Nick Dyer-Witheford, *Cyber-Marx: Cycles and Circuits of Struggle in High-Technology Capitalism* (Urbana: University of Illinois, 1999). I address the influence of autonomist Marxist ideas on a later phase of U.S. anarchism in chapter 8.

72. Gerald Mayer, *Union Membership Trends in the United States* (Washington, DC: Congressional Research Service, 2004), appendix A; Judith Stephan-Norris and Maurice Zeitlin, *Left Out: Reds and America's Industrial Unions* (Cambridge: Cambridge University Press, 2002); Zieger, *CIO,* 253–293.

73. S. Weiner, "The United Front," *Vanguard* 2, no. 5 (October–November 1935): 10–11.

74. Ibid., 11.

75. Abe Bluestein, *Forgotten Men, What Now?* (New York: Libertarian Publishers, n.d. [1935]), n.p.

76. Marcus Graham, "The Industrial Age and Social Plans," *Man!* November–December 1934, 4. "Speaker Urges Idle Men Take Up Farming," *Austin Statesman,* March 18, 1932; "Poet Will Lecture on Mooney Defense," *Memphis Commercial Appeal,* February 24, 1932, newspaper clippings, Vertical File: Anarchism—Marcus, Shmuel-Lectures, LC.

77. Joseph Cohen, "Project for a Collectivist Co-operative Colony," reprinted in *In Quest of Heaven: The Story of the Sunrise Co-operative Farm Community,* by Joseph Cohen (New York: Factory School, 2008 [1957]).

78. Michael Betzold, "Sunrise: Michigan's Failed Utopia Lives on in the Hearts of Its Elderly Children," *Detroit Free Press Magazine,* December 26, 1993, 9.

79. Cohen, *In Quest,* 100; Philip Slomovitz, "Sunrise in Michigan: Jewish Colony Faces Acid Test in Great Farmer-Labor Experiment," *B'nai B'rith Magazine,* March 1935, 188.

80. Betzold, "Sunrise," 12; Avrich, *Anarchist Voices,* 435.

81. Slomovitz, "Sunrise in Michigan," 206–208.

82. Cohen, *In Quest,* 99, 109–110, 120, 196; Betzold, "Sunrise," 13.

83. See James Horrox, *A Living Revolution: Anarchism in the Kibbutz Movement* (Oakland, CA: AK Press, 2009); Gordon, *Anarchy Alive!* 139–162.

84. On the Catholic Worker Movement, see Mel Piehl, *Breaking Bread: The Catholic Worker and the Origins of Catholic Radicalism in America* (Philadelphia: Temple University Press, 1982); Michele Teresa Aronica, *Beyond Charismatic Leadership: The New York Catholic Worker Movement* (New Brunswick, NJ: Transaction Books, 1987).

85. Dorothy Day, *The Long Loneliness: An Autobiography* (New York: Harper and Row, 1952); Dorothy Day, *Loaves and Fishes* (Maryknoll, NY: Orbis Books, 1997 [1963]); William D. Miller, *A Harsh and Dreadful Love: Dorothy Day and the Catholic Worker Movement* (New York: Liveright, 1973); Nancy L. Roberts, *Dorothy Day and the Catholic Worker* (Albany: State University of New York Press, 1984); Arthur Sheehan, *Peter Maurin, the Gay Believer* (Garden City, NY: Hanover House, 1959).

86. Roberts, *Dorothy Day,* 179.

87. Thomas Cornell and James Forest, eds., *A Penny a Copy: Readings from the Catholic Worker* (New York: Macmillan, 1968), 9. Maurin's easy essays are collected in Peter Maurin, *Easy Essays* (London: Sheed and Ward, 1938).

88. From the prospectus of the personalist journal *L'Esprit,* edited by Emmanuel Mounier, quoted in James J. Farrell, *The Spirit of the Sixties: The Making of Postwar Radicalism* (New York: Routledge, 1997), 262n10. Farrell defines personalism, explains its links to anarchism, and demonstrates its broad, largely unrecognized impact on postwar radicalism. I have drawn extensively on his pathbreaking work. I thank Chris Crass for introducing me to it.

89. Mark and Louis Zwick, "Emmanuel Mounier, Personalism, and the Catholic Worker Movement," *Houston Catholic Worker,* July–August 1999; Peter G. Coy,

"Beyond the Ballot Box: The Catholic Worker Movement and Nonviolent Direct Action," in *Dorothy Day and the Catholic Worker Movement: Centenary Essays,* ed. William Thorn, Philip Runkel, and Susan Mountin (Milwaukee, WI: Marquette University Press, 2001), 169–183.

90. Roberts, *Dorothy Day,* 7; Coy, "Beyond," 175; Mark and Louise Zwick, "Roots of the Catholic Worker Movement: Saints and Philosophers Who Influenced Dorothy Day and Peter Maurin," in Thorn, Runkel, and Mountin, *Dorothy Day,* 74.

91. Fred Boehrer, "Diversity, Plurality, and Ambiguity: Anarchism in the Catholic Worker Movement," in Thorn, Runkel, and Mountin, *Dorothy Day,* 95–127; Frederick Boehrer, "Christian Anarchism and the Catholic Worker Movement: Roman Catholic Authority and Identity in the United States" (PhD diss., Syracuse University, 2001).

92. Roberts, *Dorothy Day,* 180; Jeffrey D. Marlett, "Down on the Farm, Up to Heaven: Communes and the Spiritual Virtues of Farming," in Thorn, Runkel, and Mountin, *Dorothy Day,* 408.

93. Hundreds of books have been written on the Spanish Civil War. Standard works include Hugh Thomas, *The Spanish Civil War,* rev. ed. (New York: Modern Library, 2001); and Paul Preston, *The Spanish Civil War: Reaction, Revolution, and Revenge* (New York: Norton, 2007). For an incisive overview, see Helen Graham, *The Spanish Civil War: A Very Short Introduction* (Oxford: Oxford University Press, 2005).

94. On Spanish anarchism before the war, see Chris Ealham, *Anarchism and the City: Revolution and Counter-revolution in Barcelona, 1898–1937* (Oakland, CA: AK Press, 2010); Jerome Mintz, *The Anarchists of Casas Viejas* (Bloomington: Indiana University Press, 2004). For the concept of "militant minority," see Michael Schmidt and Lucien van der Walt, *Black Flame: The Revolutionary Class Politics of Anarchism and Syndicalism* (Oakland, CA: AK Press, 2009), 239–267. The estimate of 30,000 members of the FAI: Marshall, *Demanding the Impossible,* 458; Murray Bookchin, citing participant Diego Abad de Santillan, approximates 39,000 FAI members in 1936. Bookchin claims the CNT reported 550,000 members at its May 1936 national convention. *The Spanish Anarchists: The Heroic Years, 1868–1936* (New York: Harper Colophon, 1977), 215, 291.

95. Ealham, *Anarchism and the City;* Martha Ackelsberg, *The Free Women of Spain: Anarchism and the Struggle for the Emancipation of Women* (Oakland, CA: AK Press, 2004); Frank Mintz, *Anarchism and Workers' Self-Management in Revolutionary Spain* (Oakland, CA: AK Press, 2013). A classic firsthand account is George Orwell, *Homage to Catalonia* (New York: Harcourt Brace Jovanovich, 1980).

96. Fund-raising total provided by Eric R. Smith, *American Relief Aid and the Spanish Civil War* (Columbia: University of Missouri Press, 2013), 131. See also Peter N. Carroll and James D. Fernandez, eds., *Facing Fascism: New York and the Spanish Civil War* (New York: NYU Press, 2007); Peter Carroll, *The Odyssey of the Abraham Lincoln Brigade: Americans in the Spanish Civil War* (Stanford, CA: Stanford University Press, 1994).

97. Bluestein, oral history, C-10 to C-38; Avrich, *Anarchist Voices,* 439.

98. *Vanguard Group Internal Bulletin,* no. 1, 4.

99. "Financial Report of International Libertarian Committee Against Fascism in Spain," Vertical File: Spain—Civil War—International Libertarian Committee Against Fascism in Spain, LC.

100. Boris Yelensky, "25 Years of 'Free Society' Activity in Chicago," in *The World Scene from the Libertarian Point of View,* ed. Free Society Group (Chicago: Free Society Group, 1951), 93.

101. Form letter, August 19, 1937, Vertical File: Anarchism—United Libertarian Organizations, LC.

102. Van Valkenburgh to Maximillian Olay, September 15, 1937, Spanish Revolution Correspondence, outgoing, Box 2, Warren Star Van Valkenburgh (1884–1938) Papers, LC.

103. "Why the 'Spanish Revolution,'" *Spanish Revolution,* December 23, 1936.

104. Dolgoff, *Fragments,* 21.

105. Ibid., 23–24; Avrich, *Anarchist Voices,* 453.

106. Avrich, *Anarchist Voices,* 458; Dolgoff, *Fragments,* 24.

107. Marcus Graham, "Government's Foul Conspiracy to Destroy *Man!" Man!* May 1934, 1.

108. Inglis to Graham, May 9, 1938, Agnes Inglis Papers, Box 9, LC.

109. Marcus Graham Freedom of the Press Committee, *Freedom of Thought Arraigned.*

110. Avrich, *Anarchist Voices,* 439.

111. Bluestein, oral history, H-15 to H-18.

112. Harry Kelly to Ammon Hennacy, April 21, 1942, Ammon Hennacy Papers, LC.

113. Avrich, *Anarchist Voices,* 459.

114. Marcus Graham, "Our Position toward War," *Man!* November–December 1935, 1.

115. Veysey, *Communal Experience,* 171–172; Avrich, *Modern School,* 349.

116. Rocker's *Nationalism and Culture* addressed theories of race and nation via a critique of Nazi and communist ideology but was not read by U.S. anarchists until the 1940s.

CHAPTER 5. ANARCHISM AND
REVOLUTIONARY NONVIOLENCE, 1940–1948

1. For the concept of "prefigurative politics," see Wini Breines, *Community and Organization in the New Left, 1962–1968: The Great Refusal* (New Brunswick, NJ: Rutgers University Press, 1989); Francesca Polletta, *Freedom Is an Endless Meeting: Democracy in American Social Movements* (Chicago: University of Chicago, 2002).

2. David Kennedy, *Freedom from Fear: The American People in Depression and War, 1929–1945* (New York: Oxford University Press, 1999), 746–797; Alice Kessler-Harris, *Out to Work: A History of Wage-Earning Women in America,* twentieth-anniversary ed. (New York: Oxford University Press, 1993), 273–299; Nelson Lichtenstein, *Labor's War at Home: The CIO in World War II* (Philadelphia: Temple University Press, 1993).

3. Franz Fleigler quoted in Paul Avrich, *Anarchist Voices: An Oral History of Anarchism in America* (Oakland, CA: AK Press, 2005), 455–456.

4. Bill Young, "The Great Surrender," *Why?* April 1942, 2–3.

5. Mina Graur, *An Anarchist "Rabbi": The Life and Teachings of Rudolf Rocker* (Jerusalem: Magnes Press; New York: St. Martin's Press, 1997), 224–228.

6. Guy Liberti quoted in Avrich, *Anarchist Voices,* 158.

7. Avrich, *Anarchist Voices,* 456, 462.

8. Audrey Goodfriend, interview by author, Berkeley, CA, November 10, 2008.

9. Diva Agostinelli, "A 79 Year Old Woman Who Bowls: An Interview with Diva Agostinelli, Anarchist," *Perspectives on Anarchist Theory* 5, no. 1 (Spring 2001). Available at http://flag.blackened.net/ias/9diva.htm.

10. Sam Dolgoff writes of "the L'Adunata group" and "their Cook Street Center," in *Fragments: A Memoir* (London: Refract, 1986), 33.

11. Although they had changed the name of their publication numerous times in the past decade, the editorial group of *War Commentary* traced a lineage back to the newspaper *Freedom,* founded by Peter Kropotkin when he settled in England in 1886. George Woodcock, *Anarchism: A History of Libertarian Ideas and Movements* (Peterborough, ON: Broadview Encore Editions, 2004 [1986]), 376, 383.

12. "Our Policy in Brief," *Why?* November–December 1942, 7. In April 1945 all but one of the editors of *War Commentary* were imprisoned for nine months on charges of inciting "disaffection" among soldiers. Woodcock, *Anarchism,* 385.

13. *War or Revolution? An Anarchist Statement* (New York: Why? Publications Committee, 1944), 46, 66.

14. Peter van den Dungen, "Introduction to the 1989 Edition," in *The Conquest of Violence: An Essay on War and Revolution,* by Bart de Ligt (London: Pluto Press, 1989 [1937]), xiii.

15. De Ligt, *Conquest of Violence,* 58, 64.

16. Ibid., 162.

17. Ibid., 196.

18. van den Dungen, "Introduction," xvii; Woodcock, *Anarchism,* 369.

19. Goodfriend, interview.

20. On the origins of the CPS system, see Lawrence Wittner, *Rebels against War: The American Peace Movement, 1941–1960* (New York: Columbia University Press, 1969), 70–75; Scott H. Bennett, *Radical Pacifism: The War Resisters League and Gandhian Nonviolence in America, 1915–1963* (Syracuse, NY: Syracuse University Press, 2003), 79–94; James Tracy, *Direct Action: Radical Pacifism from the Union Eight to the Chicago Seven* (Chicago: University of Chicago Press, 1996), 14–16.

21. Goodfriend interview; David Koven, "Live an Anarchist Life!" *Social Anarchism* 42 (2008–2009): 72–77.

22. Agostinelli, "A 79 Year Old Woman."

23. Goodfriend, interview; untitled reminiscence about Edward Wieck, n.d., Box 1, David Wieck Papers, Tamiment Library, New York University (hereafter DTW, TL).

24. David Wieck, *Woman from Spillertown: A Memoir of Agnes Burns Wieck* (Carbondale: Southern Illinois University Press, 1991), 199; David Wieck to Paul Avrich, March 2, 1992, Box 1, DTW, TL.

25. In the early 1940s, the argument that the United States was sliding toward totalitarianism by its attempts to combat the same was also developed by Trotskyists in their publications and by Dwight MacDonald in the pages of *Partisan Review* and *politics,* for example. See Alan Wald, *The New York Intellectuals: The Rise and Fall of the Anti-Stalinist Left from 1930 to 1980* (Chapel Hill: University of North Carolina Press, 1987), 198, 200, 207.

26. Wieck, *Woman,* 202–203.

27. Alf Evers, *Woodstock: History of an American Town* (Woodstock, NY: Overlook Press, 1987), 616.

28. On Cantine's life, see Dachine Rainer, "Holley Cantine, February 14, 1916-January 2, 1977," in *Drunken Boat: Art, Rebellion, Anarchy,* ed. Max Blechman (Brooklyn, NY: Autonomedia; Seattle: Left Bank Books, 1994); Allan Antliff, *Anarchy and Art: From the Paris Commune to the Fall of the Berlin Wall* (Vancouver: Arsenal Pulp Press, 2007), 115–117; David Wieck, letter to the editor, *The Match!* 82, November 11, 1987.

29. Toni Weidenbacher, Cantine's daughter, interview by author, Woodstock, NY, July 2, 2014.

30. Holley Cantine, editorial statement, *Retort,* Winter 1942, 3.

31. Ibid., 4.

32. Ibid., 5.

33. Holley Cantine, "Egoism and Revolution," *Retort,* Winter 1942, 22–29.

34. Holley Cantine, "The Mechanics of Class Development," *Retort,* June 1942, 7.

35. Among these forms, he included the sexual oppression of women by men, providing a glimpse of the theoretical affinities feminists would find with anarchism in the 1970s. See *Quiet Rumours: An Anarcha-Feminist Reader,* ed. Dark Star (Edinburgh: Dark Star; Oakland, CA: AK Press, 2002).

36. I am borrowing from Stuart Hall's conception of a "Marxism without guarantees." See "The Problem of Ideology: Marxism without Guarantees," in *Stuart Hall: Critical Dialogues in Cultural Studies,* ed. David Morley and Kuan-Hsing Chen (New York: Routledge, 2005), 24–45.

37. Cantine, editorial statement, 6. In a famous passage in his prison notebooks, Gramsci argues, "In the case of the most advanced States … "civil society" has become a very complex structure and one which is resistant to the catastrophic 'incursions' of the immediate economic element (crises, depressions, etc.). The super-

structures of civil society are like the trench-systems of modern warfare. In war it would sometimes happen that a fierce artillery attack seemed to have destroyed the enemy's entire defensive system, whereas in fact it had only destroyed the outer perimeter; and at the moment of their advance and attack the assailants would find themselves confronted by a line of defence which was still effective. The same thing happens in politics, during the great economic crises." Quintin Hoare and Geoffrey Nowell Smith, eds., *Selections from the Prison Notebooks of Antonio Gramsci* (New York: International Publishers, 1971), 235. Gramsci famously went on to argue that the complexities of the social order in the advanced capitalist democracies of his day required a struggle for cultural hegemony rather than a direct revolutionary insurgency.

38. Cantine, "Mechanics of Class Development," 12.

39. Holley Cantine, "Editorials," *Retort,* Winter 1945, 6.

40. Cantine, "Mechanics," 13.

41. Holley Cantine, "Editorials," 8.

42. Leo Tolstoy, "Cathargo Delenda Est," *Retort,* Spring 1943, 5–11.

43. Toni Weidenbacher, interview.

44. On George Woodcock and *NOW*, see David Goodway, *Anarchist Seeds beneath the Snow: Left-Libertarian Thought and British Writers from William Morris to Colin Ward,* reprint ed. (Oakland, CA: PM Press, 2011), 208–211.

45. Nunzio Pernicone, *Carlo Tresca: Portrait of a Rebel* (New York: Palgrave Macmillan, 2005), 265–296.

46. Michael Wreszin, *A Rebel in Defense of Tradition: The Life and Politics of Dwight MacDonald* (New York: Basic Books, 1994); Gregory Sumner, *Dwight MacDonald and the Politics Circle: The Challenge of Cosmopolitan Democracy* (Ithaca, NY: Cornell University Press, 1996); Wald, *New York Intellectuals.*

47. Goodfriend, interview.

48. "Dachine Rainer," *Daily Telegraph,* September 8, 2000, 31. See also Toni Weidenbacher, "Making Her Own Electricity, *Woodstock Times,* August 31, 2000, 16; John Rety, "Death and the Imagination," *Freedom,* September 9, 2000, 5. Her chosen name, Dachine Rainer, combined a Hindi word with the first name of the poet Rainer Maria Rilke.

49. Taylor Stoehr, introduction to *Drawing the Line: The Political Essays of Paul Goodman,* ed. Taylor Stoehr (New York: E. P. Dutton, 1979), xvii.

50. Louis Cabri, "'Rebus Effort Remove Government': Jackson Mac Low, Why?/Resistance, Anarcho-Pacifism," *Crayon* 1 (1997): 44–68; Ekbert Faas, *Young Robert Duncan: Portrait of the Poet as a Homosexual in Society* (Santa Barbara, CA: Black Sparrow Press, 1983), 190–191; Franklin Rosemont, "Surrealist, Anarchist, Afrocentrist: Philip Lamantia before and after the 'Beat Generation,'" in *Are Italians White? How Race is Made in America,* ed. Jennifer Guglielmo and Salvatore Salerno (New York: Routledge, 2003), 124–143.

51. On Goodman's life, see Taylor Stoehr, preface to *Drawing the Line Once Again: Paul Goodman's Anarchist Writings,* by Paul Goodman (Oakland, CA: PM Press, 2010).

52. Paul Goodman, "Reflections on Drawing the Line," in *Drawing the Line: The Political Essays of Paul Goodman,* ed. Taylor Stoehr (New York: E. P. Dutton, 1979), 2–3. Goodman's perspective has much in common with what Todd May has termed the "poststructuralist anarchism" of Jacques Rancière. See *The Political Thought of Jacques Rancière: Creating Equality* (Edinburgh: Edinburgh University Press, 2008).

53. Avrich, *Anarchist Voices,* 462.

54. David Wieck to Agnes Wieck, August 25, 1943, David Wieck Papers, Swarthmore College Peace Collection (hereafter DW, SCPC).

55. Tracy, *Direct Action,* 16.

56. Bennett, *Radical Pacifism.*

57. Leilah Danielson, *American Gandhi: A. J. Muste and the History of Radicalism in the Twentieth Century* (Philadelphia: University of Pennsylvania Press, 2014); Jo Ann Robinson*, Abraham Went Out: A Biography of A. J. Muste* (Philadelphia: Temple University Press, 1981).

58. Richard B. Gregg, *The Power of Nonviolence* (Philadelphia: J. B. Lippincott, 1934); Joseph Kosek, *Acts of Conscience: Christian Nonviolence and Modern American Democracy* (New York: Columbia University Press, 2009). For Gandhi's influence on the African American community, see Sudarshan Kapur, *Raising Up a Prophet: The African-American Encounter with Gandhi* (Boston: Beacon Press, 1992).

59. David Dellinger, *From Yale to Jail: The Life Story of a Moral Dissenter* (New York: Pantheon, 1993), 81–97.

60. David Wieck to Agnes Wieck, October 18, 1943, DW, SCPC.

61. Wieck, *Woman,* 203–205.

62. On the CO and draft resister protests, see Tracy, *Direct Action,* 35–39; Bennett, *Radical Pacifism,* 98–133; Wittner, *Rebels against War,* 75–93. On Bill Sutherland's life, see Bill Sutherland and Matt Meyer, *Guns and Gandhi in Africa: Pan African Insights on Nonviolence, Armed Struggle and Liberation in Africa* (Trenton, NJ: Africa World Press, 2000). On Bayard Rustin, see John D'Emilio, *Lost Prophet: The Life and Times of Bayard Rustin* (Chicago: University of Chicago Press, 2003).

63. Bennett, *Radical Pacifism,* 88.

64. G. A. [Audrey Goodfriend], "C.P.S. and the State," *Why?,* May 1945, 9.

65. Paul Lieber Adams to Holley Cantine, October 24, 1945, Box 11, Dachine Rainer Papers, Beinecke Library, Yale University (hereafter DR, BL).

66. David Thoreau Wieck, "Peace-Related Activities, Post World War II," DW, SCPC.

67. DiGia was an editor of the self-declared "libertarian" periodical *Alternative,* described later in the chapter. When asked shortly before his death to discuss his political commitments during the 1940s, Sutherland noted, "The thing I remember most was the anarchist movement." Interview by author, Brooklyn, NY, June 27, 2008. To my knowledge, Peck never identified explicitly as an anarchist. A 1966 magazine profile asserts, "Jim Peck is nonpolitical (he did, ironically, vote for Johnson). His closest philosophical affinity to any social organization, he says, is for the

old International [*sic*] Workers of the World, which declined long before he reached his teens." Sylvia Alberts, "The Man Who Stood Up," *Fact Magazine,* July–August 1966, 53. In his memoir, Peck critiqued state communism while endorsing the struggle against economic and political inequality. He explained, "Under Communism, whether Soviet or Chinese, a new class of upperdogs, consisting of top government bureaucrats, dominates. As I expressed it in [a] pamphlet: 'In various revolutions, underdogs have succeeded in overthrowing an entire group of upperdogs. But no sooner did the underdog leaders become upperdogs, than they turned against the underdogs, using fresh slogans to carry on the same old exploitation. THROUGH THE CENTURIES, HOWEVER, UNDERDOGS GRADUALLY HAVE IMPROVED THEIR LOT.'" *Underdogs vs. Upperdogs* (New York: AMP&R, 1980), 13. Moreover, Peck sided with Roy Finch and the Libertarian League in their criticisms of *Liberation* magazine's position on Cuba, discussed in chapter 7 of the present volume.

68. Goodfriend, interview.

69. See Ammon Hennacy, *The Autobiography of a Catholic Anarchist* (New York: Catholic Worker Books, 1954); Joan Thomas, *Years of Grief and Laughter: A "Biography" of Ammon Hennacy* (Salt Lake City, UT: Hennacy Press, 1974).

70. Hennacy to Cantine and Rainer, June 15, 1948, Box 8, DR, BL.

71. Ammon Hennacy, *The One-Man Revolution in America* (Salt Lake City, UT: Hennacy Publications, 1970). For example, he noted in a letter to Holley Cantine: "Had a letter from Dave Dellinger today. I understand his wife is something special, in that unlike most wives she did not try to tame him." Hennacy to Cantine and Rainer, June 15, 1948, Box 8, DR, BL. A failure to question traditional gender roles and sexist patterns of thought was, in fact, widespread in the postwar radical pacifist milieu. Contra Hennacy, David Dellinger's political commitments did lead to considerable conflict in his marriage with Elizabeth Peterson. Her sacrifices and commitment to the cause, Dellinger later admitted, were continuously undervalued by the movement and by Dellinger himself. *From Yale to Jail,* 170–175. Also see Marian Mollin, *Radical Pacifism in Modern America: Egalitarianism and Protest* (Philadelphia: University of Pennsylvania Press, 2006).

72. "Is Thinking a Crime? Men and Women of Danbury!" leaflet, Subject Vertical File, Folder: Anarchism—Resistance, LC.

73. Dorothy Rogers to Agnes Inglis, May 14, 1946, Box 22, Agnes Inglis Collection, LC; Goodfriend, interview.

74. Goodfriend, interview; "Millions Are Starving! Cut the Red Tape . . . Open the Mails!" leaflet, Subject Vertical File, Folder: Anarchism—Resistance, LC.

75. Dellinger to Cantine, October 13, 1944, Box 8, DR, BL.

76. Dellinger to Roy Finch, February 21, 1945, Roy Finch Papers, DG 195, ACC 98A-001, Box 1, "David Dellinger" Folder, SCPC.

77. Dellinger to Cantine, April 20, 1944, Box 8, DR, BL.

78. Ibid.

79. Ibid., March 28, 1945, Box 8, DR, BL.

80. Ibid., April 20, 1944, Box 8, DR, BL.

81. Ibid., February 4, 1945, Box 8, DR, BL.

82. Andrew E. Hunt, *David Dellinger: The Life and Times of a Nonviolent Revolutionary* (New York: New York University Press, 2006), 86.

83. Ibid., 82.

84. Dellinger, *From Yale to Jail*, 138.

85. David Dellinger, "Declaration of War," *Direct Action*, Autumn 1945, reprinted in Dellinger, *From Yale to Jail*, 139–142, emphasis in the original.

86. This remark implicitly raises questions about whether property destruction should be considered an act of violence. That debate has recurred among anarchists for more than half a century. See, for example, Uri Gordon, *Anarchy Alive! Anti-authoritarian Politics from Practice to Theory* (London: Pluto Press, 2008), 78–108.

87. Dwight MacDonald, untitled, *politics*, August 1945.

88. Quoted in Tracy, *Direct Action*, 50.

89. Rexroth to Cantine and Rainer, n.d., Box 11, DR, BL.

90. For anarchism and antinuclear protest in the United States, see Barbara Epstein, *Political Protest and Cultural Revolution: Nonviolent Direct Action in the 1970s and 1980s* (Berkeley: University of California Press, 1991). Many people were introduced to anarchism in the British Campaign for Nuclear Disarmament and in the international peace punk movement of the 1970s and 1980s, for example. On the Campaign for Nuclear Disarmament, see Dennis Dworkin, *Cultural Marxism in Postwar Britain: History, the New Left, and the Origins of Cultural Studies* (Durham, NC: Duke University Press, 1997); David Goodway, *Anarchist Seeds beneath the Snow: Left-Libertarian Thought and British Writers from William Morris to Colin Ward* (Liverpool, U.K.: Liverpool University Press, 2006). On the peace punk movement, see George Berger, *The Story of Crass* (Oakland, CA: PM Press, 2009).

91. Robert Cooney and Helen Michalowski, eds., *The Power of the People: Active Nonviolence in the United States* (Philadelphia: New Society Publishers, 1987), 115.

92. "The February Conference on Non-Violent Revolutionary Socialism: Comments on the Call to a Conference," pp. 4, 8, Committee for Nonviolent Revolution (New York Group) Manuscript Collection, SCPC.

93. "Decentralized Democratic Socialism," p. 1, Committee for Nonviolent Revolution (New York Group) Manuscript Collection, SCPC.

94. Ibid., 2–3.

95. Ibid., 4, 5, 7.

96. CNVR leaflet reproduced in Cooney and Michalowski, *Power of the People*, 109; Postcard to Roy Finch, Roy Finch Collection (DG 195), Box 1 of 3, "Alternative Letters" Folder, SCPC.

97. Kenneth Ives to CNVR Coordinator, June 6, 1946, Committee for Nonviolent Revolution (New York Group), SCPC.

98. Robert C. Ludlow, "Meeting at Newburgh: Plans Made for Non-Violent Revolt," *Catholic Worker*, September 1947, 1, 7.

99. Dellinger, *From Yale to Jail*, 137–157; Hunt, *David Dellinger*, 84–107.

100. *Alternative* 1, no. 1 (April 1948): 2.

101. John D'Emilio, *Lost Prophet: The Life and Times of Bayard Rustin* (Chicago: University of Chicago Press, 2003), 133–140.

102. Tracy, *Direct Action*, 57.

103. Houser had worked with Dellinger in the Harlem Ashram before the war, and he contributed to *Direct Action* afterward. He identified as a socialist, however. Peck had become close friends with David Wieck at Danbury Federal Penitentiary, where the two participated in the anti-Jim-Crow strike together. When Peck was released, Wieck's parents, Edward and Agnes, befriended him and provided emotional support while he got back on his feet. Later in life Peck wrote to Wieck, "I'm grateful to you for having sent me to Ed and Agnes when I got out. As I said in that letter, they and Mat Kauten were my only friends at that time. I got to love them like the parents I never had." Peck to Wieck, September 28, 1979. See also Peck to Wieck, October 26, 1966, DTW, TL.

104. See, for example, Wieck's address to a 1952 WRL conference, "Problems of Anti-war Activity," published in the London anarchist periodical *Freedom,* August 2, 1952, Box 5, Folder 4, DTW, TL.

105. Lizabeth Cohen, *A Consumer's Republic: The Politics of Mass Consumption in Postwar America* (New York: Knopf, 2003); Rosalyn Baxandall and Elizabeth Ewen, *Picture Windows: How the Suburbs Happened* (New York: Basic Books, 2000).

106. Stephen J. Whitfield, *The Culture of the Cold War* (Baltimore: Johns Hopkins University Press, 1996).

107. On Peacemakers, see Cooney and Michalowksi, *Power of the People,* 118; Marian Mollin, *Radical Pacifism in Modern America: Egalitarianism and Protest* (Philadelphia: University of Pennsylvania Press, 2006), 44–72.

108. Leaflet, DW, SCPC. The leaflet is undated, but since the advertised event is endorsed by both the CNVR and Peacemakers, it was likely distributed in early 1948.

CHAPTER 6. ANARCHISM AND
THE AVANT-GARDE, 1942–1956

1. Kenneth Rexroth, "Again at Waldheim," *Retort,* Winter 1942, 8.

2. Linda Hamalian, *A Life of Kenneth Rexroth* (New York: Norton, 1991), 16. Also see, Franklin Rosemont, "Rexroth's Chicago, Chicago's Rexroth: Wobblies, Dil Picklers, and Windy City Dada," *Chicago Review* 52, no. 2–4 (Autumn 2006): 151–163.

3. Kenneth Rexroth, *In What Hour?* (New York: Macmillan, 1940).

4. Rexroth to Cantine, n.d., Box 11, DR, BL. George Fox was one of the originators of the Quaker faith. Quakers were one of the "historic peace churches" that helped establish the conscientious objector system after the First World War.

5. Ibid. Rexroth astutely continued: "Why don't you try to find Mss. in the Japanese camps? The fact that the intellectuals who all got a good feel out of

Sacco-Vanzetti ignored the existence of 250,000 Sacco-Vanzetti kind of tired me out with the intellectuals."

6. Steve McQuiddy, *Here on the Edge: How a Small Group of World War II Conscientious Objectors Took Art and Peace from the Margins to the Mainstream* (Corvallis: Oregon State University Press, 2013), 212.

7. Quoted in Glenn Wallach, "The C.O. Link: Conscientious Objection to World War II and the San Francisco Renaissance" (BA thesis, Yale University, 1984). Wallach's thesis is available in the Roy Kepler Papers, Swarthmore College Peace Collection.

8. See André Breton, "The Lighthouse," in *Drunken Boat: Art Rebellion Anarchy,* ed. Max Blechman (New York: Autonomedia; Seattle: Left Bank Books, 1994), 159–161. On anarchism and Surrealism, see Michael Löwy, *Morning Star: Surrealism, Marxism, Anarchism, Situationism, Utopia* (Austin: University of Texas Press, 2010); Richard Sonn, *Sex, Violence, and the Avant-Garde: Anarchism in Interwar France* (University Park: Pennsylvania State University Press, 2005), 72–87.

9. Franklin Rosemont, "Surrealist, Anarchist, Afrocentrist: Philip Lamantia before and after the 'Beat Generation,'" in *Are Italians White? How Race Is Made in America,* ed. Jennifer Guglielmo and Salvatore Salerno (New York: Routledge, 2003), 124–143; Steven Frattali, *Hypodermic Light: The Poetry of Philip Lamantia and the Question of Surrealism* (New York: Peter Lang, 2005).

10. Robert J. Bertholf, "Decision at the Apogee: Robert Duncan's Anarchist Critique of Denise Levertov," in *Robert Duncan and Denise Levertov: The Poetry of Politics, the Politics of Poetry,* ed. Albert Gelpi and Robert J. Bertholf (Stanford: Stanford University Press, 2006), 7; Ekbert Faas, *Young Robert Duncan: Portrait of the Poet as Homosexual in Society* (Santa Rosa, CA: Black Sparrow Press, 1984), 63–64.

11. Robert Duncan, "Notes on Some Painters and Poets," *Retort,* Winter 1945, 31–34.

12. Bertholf, "Decision," 8.

13. Faas, *Young Robert Duncan,* 190–191.

14. Antonia Weidenbacher, interview by author, Woodstock, NY, July 1, 2014. Weidenbacher is the daughter of Holley Cantine Jr. and Dorothy Paul.

15. Robert Duncan, "The Homosexual in Society," *politics,* August 1944. Reprinted in Faas, *Young Robert Duncan.*

16. *Prison Etiquette* eventually became "a classic of criminological literature." Erving Goffman drew on it heavily while writing his landmark work *Asylums,* and it was excerpted in a recent prison abolitionist anthology *Warfare in the American Homeland. Asylums: Essays on the Social Situation of Mental Patients and other Inmates* (Garden City, NY: Anchor Books, 1961); Joy James et al., eds., *Warfare in the American Homeland: Policing and Prison in a Penal Democracy* (Durham, NC: Duke University Press, 2007).

17. Dachine Rainer, interview by Julie Herrada, cassette, LC.

18. See Jackson Mac Low, "John Cage: A Celebration," and Max Blechman, "Last Words on Anarchy: An Interview with John Cage," in Blechman, *Drunken Boat,* 216–225.

19. Hamalian, *Kenneth Rexroth,* 149–150.

20. Kenneth Rexroth, *An Autobiographical Novel,* expanded ed. (New York: New Directions, 1991), 518.

21. Rexroth to Rainer, n.d., Box 11, DR, BL.

22. Wieck to Taylor Stoehr, July 1, 1983, David Wieck Papers, Tamiment Library, New York University (hereafter DTW, TL); Diva Agostinelli, "A 79 Year Old Woman Who Bowls: An Interview with Diva Agostinelli, Anarchist," *Perspectives on Anarchist Theory* 5, no. 1 (Spring 2001).

23. Kenneth Rexroth, *The Phoenix and the Tortoise* (New York: New Directions, 1944), 30.

24. My analysis draws on Morgan Gibson, *Kenneth Rexroth* (New York: Twain, 1972), 31–34, 60.

25. Alice Wexler, *Emma Goldman in America* (Boston: Beacon Press, 1984), 205.

26. Henry Miller, *The Air-Conditioned Nightmare* (New York: New Directions, 1970 [1945]). On Miller's ties to Surrealism and anarchism while in Europe, see James Gifford, "The Personal Landscape and New Apocalypse Networks: Philhellenic, Anarchist, and Surrealist Late Modernisms," *Global Review* 1, no. 1 (2013): 77–114.

27. Kenneth Rexroth, introduction to *The Selected Poems of D. H. Lawrence,* quoted in Gibson, *Kenneth Rexroth,* 68.

28. On Reich's life and ideas, see Chris Turner, *Adventures in the Orgasmatron: How the Sexual Revolution Came to America* (New York: Farrar, Straus and Giroux, 2011). For a brief summary of his attempted synthesis of psychoanalysis and Marxism, see Eugene Victor Wolfenstein, *Psychoanalytic-Marxism: Groundwork* (New York: Guilford Press, 1993), 53–63.

29. Wilhelm Reich, *The Sexual Revolution: Toward a Self-Governing Character Structure* (New York: Farrar, Straus and Giroux, 1963 [1936]); Wilhelm Reich, *The Mass Psychology of Fascism* (New York: Farrar, Straus and Giroux, 1980 [1933]).

30. Martin Buber, *I and Thou* (New York: Touchstone, 1971). For a sophisticated treatment of Rexroth's use of Buber, see Ken Knabb, "The Relevance of Rexroth," in *Public Secrets: Collected Skirmishes of Ken Knabb, 1970–1997* (Berkeley, CA: Bureau of Public Secrets, 1997), 323–336.

31. James Brown, "The Zen of Anarchy: Japanese Exceptionalism and the Anarchist Roots of the San Francisco Poetry Renaissance," *Religion and American Culture: A Journal of Interpretation* 19, no. 2 (2009): 211.

32. Kenneth Rexroth, "Climbing Milestone Mountain, August 22, 1937," in *Swords That Shall Not Strike: Poems of Protest and Rebellion,* ed. Geoffrey Gardner (Enfield, NH: Glad Day Books, 1999), 24–25.

33. Gregory Knapp, "The State Is the Great Forgetter: Rexroth and Goodman as Antecedents of Cultural Ecology, Political Ecology, and the New Cultural Geography" (paper presented at the ninety-third Annual Meeting of the Association of American Geographers, Fort Worth, TX, April 2, 1997), at http://theanarchistlibrary .org/library/gregory-knapp-the-state-is-the-great-forgetter. See Peter Kropotkin, *Mutual Aid: A Factor in Evolution* (Boston: Porter Sargent, 1976 [1902]); John Clark

and Camille Martin, eds., *Anarchy, Geography, Modernity: Selected Writings of Elisée Reclus* (Oakland, CA: PM Press, 2013).

34. Paul Messersmith-Glavin, "Between Social Ecology and Deep Ecology: Gary Snyder's Ecological Philosophy," in *The Philosophy of the Beats,* ed. Sharin N. Elkholy (Lexington: University of Kentucky Press, 2012), 246.

35. Gary Snyder, *Myths and Texts* (New York: New Directions, 1978 [1962]), 5.

36. Quoted in Messersmith-Glavin, "Between," 245. The passage is drawn from Gary Snyder, *Turtle Island* (New York: New Directions, 1974), 75.

37. See Kenneth Rexroth, "Smoky the Bear Bodhisattva," in *With Eye and Ear* (New York: Herder and Herder, 1970), 212.

38. Editorial, *The Ark,* Spring 1947, 3.

39. Audrey Goodfriend, interview by author, Berkeley, CA, November 10, 2008.

40. Rexroth to Macdonald, November 22, 1946, Dwight Macdonald Papers, quoted in Wallach, "C.O. Link," 55.

41. Adrian Wilson, *Printing for Theater* (San Francisco: self-published, 1957), 12, quoted in Wallach, "C.O. Link," 52–53.

42. Mildred Edie Brady, "The New Cult of Sex and Anarchy," *Harper's Magazine,* April 1947, 312–322.

43. Ibid., 319.

44. Ibid., 313.

45. Hamalian, *Kenneth Rexroth,* 181–182.

46. Goodfriend, interview.

47. Brady, "New Cult," 320.

48. Diva Agostinelli to Edward and Agnes Wieck, October 24, 1947, and November 2, 1947, DTW, TL.

49. David Wieck to "Dear Folks," December 23, 1947, DTW, TL; Goodfriend, interview.

50. Wieck and other draft resisters had invented the term *beardy,* meaning "religious," while debating matters of faith during their incarceration. It referred to the popular imagination of the Christian God as sporting a long, white beard.

51. Wieck to "Dear Folks."

52. Ibid.

53. Rexroth to Cantine and Rainer, n.d., Box 11, DR, BL.

54. William Everson, "Of Robert Duncan," *Credences* 8–9 (1980): 150. Also quoted in Wallach, "C.O. Link."

55. Gibson, *Kenneth Rexroth,* 20.

56. Untitled notes, Box 4, Folder 3, DTW, TL.

57. David Wieck to Edward and Agnes Wieck, March 29, 1948, DTW, TL.

58. Stephen J. Whitfield, *The Culture of the Cold War,* 2nd ed. (Baltimore: Johns Hopkins University Press, 1996); Ellen Schrecker, *Many Are the Crimes: McCarthyism in America* (Princeton, NJ: Princeton University Press, 1999); David K. Johnson, *The Lavender Scare: The Cold War Persecution of Gays and Lesbians in the Federal Government* (Chicago: University of Chicago Press, 2004).

59. G. P. Maximoff, "State of the World," in *The World Scene from the Libertarian Point of View,* ed. Free Society Group (Chicago: Free Society Group, 1951), 5–6.

60. David Wieck, "Anarchism, Anarchy, Anarchists," in Free Society Group, *The World Scene from the Libertarian Point of View,* 51.

61. Mildred Loomis, "Decentralized Human Well-Being," *Green Revolution* 35, no. 5 (June 1978): 12.

62. Goodfriend, interview.

63. Percival and Paul Goodman, *Communitas: Means of Livelihood and Ways of Life* (Chicago: University of Chicago Press, 1947).

64. Martin Buber, *Paths in Utopia* (New York: Syracuse University Press, 1996 [1950]).

65. Landauer quoted in Buber, *Paths in Utopia,* 46. Buber suggested that the best contemporary example of such a process was the experiment with developing kibbutzim in the new state of Israel. See James Horrox, *A Living Revolution: Anarchism in the Kibbutz Movement* (Oakland, CA: AK Press, 2009). *Resistance,* however, indicted left-wing Zionists for practicing a form of colonialism as they displaced Arab residents of Palestine.

66. David Wieck, "Anarchism," *Resistance,* November–December 1948, 4.

67. Ibid., 5.

68. Ibid., 14.

69. Ibid., 15.

70. Ibid., 5.

71. Wieck to Taylor Stoehr; "Outline History of Anarchism in the United States," DTW Papers, TL.

72. Judith Malina, *The Diaries of Judith Malina, 1947–1957* (New York: Grove Press, 1984), 131–132.

73. Ibid., 42–43, 82.

74. Charles L. Mee Jr., "The Becks' Living Theatre," *Tulane Drama Review* 7, no. 2 (Winter 1962): 194–205.

75. Roszak quoted in Lawrence Wittner, *Rebels against War: The American Peace Movement, 1941–1960* (New York: Columbia University Press, 1969), 160. On the founding of Pacifica, see James Tracy, *Direct Action: Radical Pacifism from the Union Eight to the Chicago Seven* (Chicago: University of Chicago Press, 1996), 52, 59–60; John Whiting, "The Lengthening Shadow: Lewis Hill and the Origins of Listener-Sponsored Broadcasting in America," www.whitings-writings.com/lengthening_shadow.htm, accessed February 21, 2010.

76. Peter Martin's mother was Sabina Flynn, the younger sister the famous organizer Elizabeth Gurley Flynn, to whom Tresca was at one time married. Peter was born as the result of an affair Tresca and Sabina Flynn carried on while Sabina shared an apartment with Elizabeth and Tresca in 1922. Martin's surname was that of James J. Martin, Sabina's estranged husband at the time of the affair. Tresca visited with Martin regularly during his childhood until Sabina remarried and the family relocated to Arizona. Nunzio Pernicone, *Carlo Tresca: Portrait of a Rebel* (New York: Palgrave Macmillan, 2005), 244–245.

77. Steven Watson, *The Birth of the Beat Generation: Visionaries, Rebels, and Hipsters, 1944–1960* (New York: Pantheon, 1995), 208.

78. Patrick Frank, "San Francisco 1952: Painters, Poets, Anarchism," *Drunken Boat,* no. 2 (1994): 148.

79. Malina, *Diaries,* 231–241.

80. Frank, "San Francisco 1952," 150. On Kees and *Why?,* see Hamalian, *Kenneth Rexroth,* 184.

81. David Koven, "Live an Anarchist Life!" *Social Anarchism* 42 (2008–2009): 72–77; Goodfriend, interview.

82. David Koven, "The Needle," *The Needle,* April 1956, 1.

83. Quoted in Lawrence Lipton, *The Holy Barbarians* (New York: Julian Messner, 1959), 58–59.

84. Judith Malina, *Diaries,* 110; Stuart Perkoff, "If Everything Returns . . .," in *Seeds of Liberation,* ed. Paul Goodman (New York: George Braziller, 1964), 528–529; Stuart Z. Perkoff, "O, Para / O, Dox," *The Needle,* November 1956.

CHAPTER 7. ANARCHISM AND
THE BLACK FREEDOM MOVEMENT, 1955–1964

1. "The South's Negroes Are in Motion," *Views and Comments,* no. 11 (February 1956): 11.

2. Dellinger to Cantine, March 28, 1945, Dachine Rainer Papers, Beinecke Library, Yale University.

3. James Farrell, *Spirit of the Sixties: The Making of Postwar Radicalism* (New York: Routledge, 1997), 112–124.

4. Andrew Hunt, *David Dellinger: The Life and Times of a Nonviolent Revolutionary* (New York: NYU Press, 2006), 114.

5. "Tract for the Times," *Liberation,* March 1956, 3–6.

6. Ibid.

7. Dellinger and his wife, Elizabeth, dedicated long hours to producing the magazine, often making personal sacrifices to do so when the magazine lacked funds to pay them in a timely fashion. Hunt, *David Dellinger,* 114.

8. Dolgoff, *Fragments: A Memoir* (Cambridge, U.K.: Refract, 1986), 74–75; Paul Avrich, *Anarchist Voices: An Oral History of Anarchism in America* (Oakland, CA: AK Press, 2005), 417, 431. The book club's first publishing project reflected the longstanding interests of the older anarchists, but it also brought them into contact with the younger generation of the 1940s. The Libertarian Book Club financed the publication of *Nineteen-Seventeen,* a volume of Voline's history of the Russian Revolution, which Holley Cantine had translated from French. Interest in anarchist literature was so low and anti-Russian sentiment so high, however, that the club had a difficult time convincing stores to stock the title, and ended up losing money on the

venture. Afterward, a lack of funds made it impossible for the club to issue new books. The members settled on republishing three out-of-print titles on anarchist topics. Their choices, including Paul Eltzbacher's *Anarchism,* Max Stirner's *The Ego and Its Own,* and James Martin's *Men against the State,* a history of nineteenth-century individualist anarchists in the United States, attest to the influence of individualist anarchists in the club. The Libertarian Book Club maintained a presence in New York City into the first years of the twenty-first century, providing a means for generations of young radicals to connect with anarchists who had come of age in the 1920s and 1930s.

9. Dolgoff, *Fragments,* 74–75; Jack Frager quoted in Avrich, *Anarchist Voices,* 434; Robert Calese quoted in Avrich, *Anarchist Voices,* 471; David Sachs, interview by author, Oakland, CA, June 28, 2013.

10. "What We Stand For," *Views and Comments,* no. 8 (October 1955). This statement appeared in each issue of *Views and Comments,* the Libertarian League's journal.

11. Dolgoff, *Fragments,* 75; Dolgoff quoted in Avrich, *Anarchist Voices,* 426.

12. Ronald D. Cohen, *Rainbow Quest: The Folk Music Revival and American Society, 1940–1970* (Amherst: University of Massachusetts Press, 2002).

13. Dave Van Ronk with Elijah Wald, *The Mayor of MacDougal Street: A Memoir* (Cambridge, MA: Da Capo, 2005), 34.

14. Robert Calese quoted in Avrich, *Anarchist Voices,* 472.

15. Van Ronk, *Mayor,* 34. This attitude apparently extended to performance as well. Van Ronk recalled that one May Day, "Holly Cantine, 'the Hermit of Woodstock,' showed up with a trombone and asked if he could lead the assembled masses in 'The International.' He proceeded to produce a series of farts and howls that almost emptied the hall" (158).

16. Dolgoff quoted in Avrich, *Anarchist Voices,* 426.

17. Dolgoff, *Fragments,* 89.

18. Members of the league organized the Committee to Defend Franco's Labor Victims, which secured publicity in the mainstream media, organized rallies, and collected petition signatures to pressure the U.S. State Department to intervene on behalf of the anarchist unionists. Dolgoff believed the committee's work helped save the lives of at least five Spanish anarchists. Dolgoff, *Fragments,* 85–86; Avrich, *Anarchist Voices,* 426.

19. "Civil Liberties and Civil Defense," *Views and Comments,* no. 5 (July 1955): 1–2, 12. The Libertarian League also established friendly relations with other elements of the anticommunist Left during the 1950s. In 1956 the group issued a statement calling for an investigation of the disappearance of a professor critical of the Trujillo regime in the Dominican Republic that was cosigned by the IWW, Catholic Worker, the War Resisters League, Solidaridad Internacional Antifascista, and two socialist organizations. Dolgoff, *Fragments,* 92.

20. Toni Weidenbacher, interview by author, Woodstock, NY, June 2, 2014.

21. "Some New Voices Speak," *Views and Comments,* no. 13 (May 1956).

22. "My Country 'Tis of Thee," *Views and Comments,* no. 8 (October 1955). On the Till case, see Kenneth A. Beauchamp, dir., *The Untold Story of Emmett Till* (New York: Velocity/Thinkfilm, 2006), DVD.

23. Melvyn Dubofsky, *The State and Labor in Modern America* (Chapel Hill: University of North Carolina Press, 1994), 197–217; Nelson Lichtenstein, *The State of the Union: A Century of American Labor,* rev. ed. (Princeton, NJ: Princeton University Press, 2013), 98–177; Philip Dray, *There Is Power in a Union: The Epic Story of Labor in America* (New York: Anchor Books, 2011), 410–484.

24. Sam Weiner [Dolgoff], *Ethics and American Unionism—and the Path Ahead for the Working Class* (New York: Libertarian League, 1958), self-published pamphlet, Roy Finch Papers, 1940–1969, DG 195, Box 2 [Acc. 98A-001], "Cuba—Libertarians" Folder, Swarthmore College Peace Collection.

25. Kathy Ferguson, *Emma Goldman: Political Thinking in the Streets* (Lanham, MD: Rowman and Littlefield, 2012), 211–247.

26. Following recent scholarly convention, I use the capitalized term *Black Freedom Movement* to refer to the complex array of political and cultural initiatives that fundamentally transformed race relations (though did not eradicate racism) in the United States during the years 1955 to 1975. The term serves as an umbrella for what earlier scholars characterized as two phases of struggle—the civil rights movement and the Black Power movement—suggesting that these efforts were not distinct and sequential but are better understood as congruous tendencies expressed with different emphasis in different times and places throughout the period. The Black Freedom Movement can also be seen as a temporally demarcated moment in the longer black freedom struggle, which has been and will remain a feature of American life so long as antiblack racism exists. Literature on the Black Freedom Movement is extensive. I have drawn on the following overview accounts, as well as the more focused studies referenced in additional notes. Clayborne Carson et al., eds., *The Eyes on the Prize Civil Rights Reader: Documents, Speeches, and Firsthand Accounts from the Black Freedom Struggle* (New York: Penguin Books, 1991); Peniel Joseph, *The Black Power Movement: Rethinking the Civil Rights–Black Power Era* (New York: Routledge, 2006); Peniel Joseph, *Waiting for the Midnight Hour: A Narrative History of Black Power in America* (New York: Holt, 2007); Robin D. G. Kelley, *Freedom Dreams: The Black Radical Imagination* (Boston: Beacon Press, 2003); Bettye Collier-Thomas and V. P. Franklin, eds., *Sisters in the Struggle: African American Women in the Civil Rights–Black Power Movement* (New York: NYU Press, 2001); Jeanne Theoharis, Komozi Woodard, and Charles Payne, eds., *Groundwork: Local Black Freedom Movements in America* (New York: NYU Press, 2005).

27. See Stewart Burns, ed., *Daybreak of Freedom: The Montgomery Bus Boycott* (Chapel Hill: University of North Carolina Press, 1997); Danielle McGuire, *At the Dark End of the Street: Black Women, Rape, and Resistance—A New History of the Civil Rights Movement from Rosa Parks to the Rise of Black Power* (New York: Vintage, 2011).

28. "The South's Negroes Are in Motion," *Views and Comments,* no. 11 (February 1956): 12.

29. Farrell, *The Spirit of the Sixties,* 81–95. Sudarshan Kapur notes that it is wrong to assume that African Americans embraced Gandhian strategies solely based on King's urgings. Rather, African Americans had been broadly attentive to the Gandhian movement since the era of the First World War. *Raising Up a Prophet: The African-American Encounter with Gandhi* (Boston: Beacon, 1991).

30. Farrell, *Spirit of the Sixties,* 90.

31. John D'Emilio, *Lost Prophet: The Life and Times of Bayard Rustin* (Chicago: University of Chicago Press, 2004), 184–205. Organizations were under additional pressure to distance themselves from homosexuals in the early 1950s as anticommunist crusaders claimed gay men and lesbians posed a national security risk, since their sexual practices made them especially vulnerable to blackmail or recruitment by communist agents. See David K. Johnson, *The Lavender Scare: The Cold War Persecution of Gays and Lesbians in the Federal Government* (Chicago: University of Chicago Press, 2004).

32. For anarchists, see chapter 6. For the WRL and the radical pacifist milieu more broadly, see Martin Duberman, *A Saving Remnant: The Radical Lives of Barbara Deming and David McReynolds* (New York: New Press, 2011).

33. Hunt, *David Dellinger,* 90–91, 105.

34. D'Emilio, *Lost Prophet,* 206–219; Hunt, *David Dellinger,* 104–105.

35. Martin Luther King, "Our Struggle," *Liberation,* April 1956, 3–6.

36. Bayard Rustin, "Montgomery Diary," *Liberation,* April 1956, 7–10; D'Emilio, *Lost Prophet,* 239.

37. On communist influences on the Southern Christian Leadership Conference, see Jack O'Dell and Nikhil Pal Singh, *Climbin' Jacob's Ladder: The Black Freedom Movement Writings of Jack O'Dell* (Berkeley: University of California Press, 2010).

38. On antiracist struggles in New York City between the 1940s and 1970s, see Martha Biondi, *To Stand and Fight: The Struggle for Civil Rights in Postwar New York* (Cambridge, MA: Harvard, 2003); Thomas Sugrue, *Sweet Land of Liberty: The Forgotten Struggle for Civil Rights in the North* (New York: Random House, 2008).

39. "Little Rock," *Views and Comments,* no. 25 (December 1957): 6–7.

40. Ibid.

41. For valuable critiques of economism from an antiracist, socialist perspective, see Stuart Hall, "Gramsci's Relevance for the Study of Race and Ethnicity," *Journal of Communication Inquiry* 10, no. 5 (1986): 5–27; Anna Marie Smith, *Laclau and Mouffe: The Radical Democratic Imaginary* (New York: Routledge, 1998), 42–83.

42. "Little Rock," 6–7.

43. Ibid.

44. Communist countries did routinely publicize accounts of American racism to challenge the country's claims to be a democracy. Scholars have since shown that a desire to minimize such propaganda was a significant factor shaping executive and congressional policy regarding the civil rights movements. See Mary Dudziak, *Cold War Civil Rights: Race and the Image of American Democracy* (Princeton, NJ: Princeton University Press, 2000).

45. David Wieck, "The Invention of Responsibility," *Liberation,* November 1957.

46. David Thoreau Wieck, "Report from Little Rock," *Liberation,* October 1958, 4–9.

47. For example, a league correspondent described the hostile political terrain of North Carolina in D. R., "Letter from the Bible Belt," *Views and Comments,* no. 29 (July 1958).

48. See, for example, "Negro Struggle Sharpens," *Views and Comments,* no. 34 (April 1959): 1; Sean Mitchell, "Direct Action," *Views and Comments,* no. 42 (December 1961).

49. "Negro Struggle Sharpens," 1.

50. Timothy Tyson, *Radio Free Dixie: Robert F. Williams and the Roots of Black Power* (Chapel Hill: University of North Carolina, 1999); Robert F. Williams, *Negroes with Guns* (New York: Marzani and Munsell, 1962).

51. "Dixie," *Views and Comments,* no. 37 (February 1960): 13–14.

52. Scholars continue to debate the extent to which Fanon's considerations of violence were influenced by writings within the anarchist and syndicalist traditions, particularly those of George Sorel. See, for example, George Ciciarello-Maher, "To Lose Oneself in the Absolute: Revolutionary Subjectivity in Sorel and Fanon," *Human Architecture: Journal of the Sociology of Self-Knowledge* 5 (Summer 2007): 101–112.

53. Robert F. Williams, "Can Negroes Afford to Be Pacifists?" *Liberation,* September 1959. In debates among global justice activists during demonstrations modeled on the 1999 "Battle of Seattle," anarchist advocates of the tactic of street trashing regularly insisted that other demonstrators respect a "diversity of tactics"— language highly reminiscent of Williams's phrase "acceptance of diverse tactics." See Francis Dupuis-Déri, "The Black Blocs Ten Years after Seattle: Anarchism, Direct Action, and Deliberative Practices," *Journal for the Study of Radicalism* 4, no. 2 (2010): 45–82.

54. David Dellinger, "Are Pacifists Willing to Be Negroes?" *Liberation,* September 1959, 3. See also Dorothy Day, "Crusader in Exile: A Visit with Robert Williams," *Liberation,* December 1962.

55. Clayborne Carson, *In Struggle: SNCC and the Black Awakening of the 1960s* (Cambridge, MA: Harvard University Press, 1981), 11. Additional important works on SNCC include Wesley C. Hogan, *Many Minds, One Heart: SNCC's Dream for a New America* (Chapel Hill: University of North Carolina, 2009); Charles Payne, *I've Got the Light of Freedom: The Organizing Tradition and the Mississippi Freedom Struggle,* 2nd ed. (Berkeley: University of California Press, 2007); Faith Holsaert et al., eds., *Hands on the Freedom Plow: Personal Accounts by Women in SNCC* (Urbana: University of Illinois Press, 2012); Hasan Kwame Jeffries, *Bloody Lowndes: Civil Rights and Black Power in Alabama's Black Belt* (New York: NYU Press, 2010).

56. E. W., "The 'Civil Rights' Struggle," *Views and Comments,* no. 38 (May 1960).

57. Baker crafted her political vision during years of collaboration with radicals of many stripes: socialists, communists, Garveyites, Pan-Africanists, feminists, and

anarchists among them. During the 1930s, for example, her "closest political ally," according to biographer Barbara Ransby, was George Schuyler, an African American newspaper columnist who had once written for the socialist *Messenger*. In 1930, Baker and Schuyler launched the Young Negroes Cooperative League, a national association of co-ops and buying clubs that intended to serve as an alternative economy for the black community during the Great Depression, and to begin building a social order where workers owned the means of production. Schuyler argued, "Whereas the Socialists hope to usher in such a Utopia society by the ballot and the Communists hope to turn the trick with the bullet, the cooperator (who is really an Anarchist since the triumph of his society will do away with the state in its present form—and I am an Anarchist) is slowly and methodically doing so through legal, intelligent economic cooperation or mutual aid." Barbara Ransby, *Ella Baker and the Black Freedom Movement: A Radical Democratic Vision* (Chapel Hill: University of North Carolina Press, 2005), 87. While Baker remained active in radical causes until her death, Schuyler became politically conservative in the 1950s, denouncing Martin Luther King Jr. and contributing essays to the publication of the John Birch Society. I thank Nikhil Pal Singh for bringing this to my attention.

58. Ibid., 188–190.

59. Farrell, *Spirit of the Sixties*, 98; Carson, *In Struggle*, 30.

60. After a stint in federal prison as one of the few men to refuse the draft during the Korean War, Lawson had traveled to India to study Gandhian nonviolence. As a seminary student in Nashville, and the first southern field secretary of FOR, he served as an inspiring political mentor to students such as Diane Nash and John Lewis, who would play key roles in the movement in the years to come. Part of that training consisted of using the consensus process to make decisions, which the Nashville-area students used as they organized sit-ins in their area. Farrell, *Spirit of the Sixties*, 96; Kapur, *Raising Up a Prophet*, 155–156.

61. Francesca Polletta, *Freedom Is an Endless Meeting: Democracy in American Social Movements* (Chicago: University of Chicago, 2002), 55–87.

62. Quoted in Ransby, *Ella Baker*, 188.

63. Dellinger to Cantine, February 4, 1945, Box 8, Dachine Rainer Papers, Beinecke Library, Yale University.

64. Eric Burner, *And Gently He Shall Lead Them: Robert Parris Moses and Civil Rights in Mississippi* (New York: NYU Press, 1994).

65. Moses quoted in Polletta, *Freedom*, 56. The term *participatory democracy* was not used by SNCC members at the time but was popularized by members of Students for a Democratic Society who were heavily influenced by SNCC. See chapter 8.

66. "Leaders and Led in the Negro Revolt," *Views and Comments*, no. 45 (Fall 1963): 1–3.

67. "Labor Comments: Bigots," *Views and Comments*, no. 47 (Summer 1964): 18–19.

68. In the United States, Luigi Galleani and Marcus Graham exemplified this perspective. See chapters 1 and 4, as well as Michael Schmidt and Lucien van der

Walt, *Black Flame: The Revolutionary Class Politics of Anarchism and Syndicalism* (Oakland, CA: AK Press, 2009), 129–130; Paul Avrich, *Sacco and Vanzetti: The Anarchist Background* (Princeton, NJ: Princeton University Press, 1991), 52–53. I describe this position as economistic because it was based on an essentialist logic that assumed that class position ensured a principled radical subjectivity, thereby privileging the working class as revolutionary subject. See Hall, "Gramsci's Relevance" and Smith, *Laclau and Mouffe.*

69. "Labor Comments: Bigots," *Views and Comments,* no. 47 (Summer 1964): 18–19.

70. Francesca Polletta astutely concludes, "As black staffers struggled to find a way to give voice to new feelings of racial identity, they grew frustrated with a deliberative style on which whites seemed to be insisting as a way to hang onto their positions in the organization. Participatory democracy came to be seen *as* white, and, in contrast, a centralized and top-down organizational structure came to symbolize not only programmatic certainty but also a black orientation." *Freedom,* 90. Polletta's work provides insights into the development of anarchism, its racial character, and the relationships between anarchists and other sectors of the U.S. Left after 1965. Conflicts have repeatedly resurfaced between radicals that map anarchism and nonhierarchical organization as white, philosophical, and impractical, in contrast to (working-class) people-of-color-led organizations that are results driven and, therefore, accept the need for strong, central leadership. Anarchists have exacerbated such conceptions through their confusion about the ways participatory democracy contributed to SNCC's successes. In the Committee for Nonviolent Revolution and Peacemakers, anarchists promoted consensus and nonhierarchical forms as prefigurative practices among a committed group that could sustain the group and provide a persuasive example of an alternate social system to others. SNCC participants drew on these concepts but developed them in new directions and for different ends. They found consensus decision-making and local, grassroots leadership development to be beneficial in raising a mass movement to confront and transform unjust political institutions. Conflations of the exemplary and the developmental benefits of these organizational forms have complicated debates about when and how to use them. See Andrew Cornell, "Occupy Wall Street and Consensus Decision Making: Historicizing the Preoccupation with Process," *Social Text: Periscope* (Fall 2013), http://what-democracy-looks-like.com /occupy-wall-street-and-consensus-decision-making-historicizing-the-preoccupation-with-process.

71. Benedict Anderson, *Under Three Flags: Anarchism and the Anti-colonial Imagination* (New York: Verso, 2005), 2.

72. "Tract for the Times," *Liberation,* March 1956, 5–6.

73. Vinoba Bhave, "What I Believe," *Liberation,* March 1956, 7–10. For more on Bhave's relationship to anarchism, see Maia Ramnath, *Decolonizing Anarchism* (Oakland, CA: AK Press and Institute for Anarchist Studies, 2011), 188–191; Geoffrey Ostergaard and Melville Currell, *The Gentle Anarchists* (Oxford: Oxford University Press, 1971). *Liberation* also published essays by other high-profile African

leaders. For example, Julius K. Nyerere, "An African View: Communitarian Social-ism," *Liberation,* July–August 1962, 13–15.

74. "Position of the Libertarian League on Imperialism and Colonialism," *Views and Comments,* no. 24 (October 1957): 14–15.

75. "National Independence Is Not Enough," *Views and Comments,* no. 30 (August 1958); "Liberated Tunisia," *Views and Comments,* no. 31 (October 1958). See also "Nationalism vs. Freedom," *Views and Comments,* no. 35 (May 1959); "Congo: Greenbacks and Black Blood," *Views and Comments,* no. 49 (Spring 1965).

76. See, for example, Vijay Prashad, *The Darker Nations: A People's History of the Third World* (New York: New Press, 2007); Mahmoud Mamdani, *When Victims Become Killers: Colonialism, Nativism, and the Genocide in Rwanda* (Princeton, NJ: Princeton University Press, 2001); Martin Meredith, *The Fate of Africa from the Hopes of Freedom to the Heart of Despair: A History of 50 Years of Independence* (New York: Public Affairs, 2005).

77. David Dellinger, "Cuba: America's Lost Plantation, Part 1," *Liberation,* December 1960; David Dellinger, "Cuba: America's Lost Plantation, Part 2," *Liberation,* January 1961.

78. Roy Finch, "Interview with Cuban Libertarians," *Liberation,* March 1961.

79. Dave Dellinger, "The Campaign against Castro," *Liberation,* April 1961.

80. Roy Finch, "Cuba and Liberation . . . an Editor Resigns," *Liberation,* May 1961.

81. Dolgoff, *Fragments,* 87.

82. Dellinger to Wieck, October 30, 1964, David Wieck Papers, Tamiment Library, New York University (hereafter DTW, TL).

83. DTW to Dellinger, November 2, 1964, DTW, TL.

84. David T. Wieck, "Cuba: An Effort at Interpretation," *Liberation,* May 1965.

85. DTW to Roy Finch, May 20, 1965, DTW, TL.

86. Late in life, Dellinger returned to openly declaring himself an anarchist, as did some of his close associates, such as Bill Sutherland. See the documentary *A Peace of the Anarchy.* Marcus Patrick Blaise Page, dir., *A Peace of the Anarchy: Ammon Hennacy and other Angelic Troublemakers in the USA* (Avery, CA: Lovarchy-Shalom, 2004), DVD.

87. See D'Emilio, *Lost Prophet,* 393–416.

88. Wieck to Dellinger, October 19, 1965, DTW, TL.

89. Quoted in Farrell, *Spirit of the Sixties,* 99.

CHAPTER 8. NEW LEFT AND
COUNTERCULTURAL ANARCHISM, 1960–1972

1. Marshall S. Shatz, ed., *The Essential Works of Anarchism* (New York: Bantam Books, 1971); Paul Berman, *Quotations from the Anarchists* (New York: Pall Mall Press, 1972).

2. On the "long 1960s," see Blake Slonecker, *A New Dawn for the New Left: Liberation News Service, Montague Farm, and the Long Sixties* (New York: Palgrave Macmillan, 2012). This framing builds on the concept of the "long civil rights movement" articulated in Jacquelyn Dowd Hall, "The Long Civil Rights Movement and the Political Uses of the Past," *Journal of American History* 91, no. 4 (March 2005): 1233–1263.

3. Important texts on the period that ignore or downplay anarchism include James Miller, *Democracy Is in the Streets: From Port Huron to the Siege of Chicago* (Cambridge, MA: Harvard University Press, 1994); Maurice Isserman and Michael Kazin, *America Divided: The Civil War of the 1960s* (Oxford: Oxford University Press, 2004); Terry H. Anderson, *The Movement and the Sixties: Protest in America from Greensboro to Wounded Knee* (Oxford: Oxford University Press, 1995). Exceptions to this tendency that I have drawn on include Gregory NeVala Calvert, *Democracy from the Heart: Spiritual Values, Decentralism, and Democratic Idealism in the Movement of the 1960s* (Eugene, OR: Communitas Press, 1991); and James J. Farrell, *The Spirit of the Sixties: The Making of Postwar Radicalism* (New York: Routledge, 1997).

4. Jack Newfield, *A Prophetic Minority* (New York: New American Library, 1966), 30; Arthur Lothstein, ed., *"All We Are Saying . . .": The Philosophy of the New Left* (New York: Capricorn Books, 1970); Gil Green, *The New Radicalism: Anarchist or Marxist?* (New York: International Publishers, 1971).

5. Van Gosse uses the term *movement of movements* to describe the totality of progressive and radical social movements active between the mid-1950s and mid-1970s. "A Movement of Movements: The Definition and Periodization of the New Left," in *A Companion to Post-1945 America,* ed. Roy Rosenzweig and Jean-Christophe Agnew (London: Blackwell, 2002), 277–302; Van Gosse, *Rethinking the New Left: An Interpretative History* (New York: Palgrave Macmillan, 2005), 4–6. For application of the concept to a later cycle of struggles, see Tom Mertes, ed., *A Movement of Movements: Is Another World Really Possible?* (New York: Verso, 2004).

6. Standard accounts of SDS include Kirkpatrick Sale, *SDS* (New York: Vintage, 1974); Todd Gitlin, *The Sixties: Years of Hope, Days of Rage,* rev. ed. (New York: Bantam, 1993); Miller, *Democracy Is in the Streets.* Recent reconsiderations include Dan Berger, *Outlaws of America: The Weather Underground and the Politics of Solidarity* (Oakland, CA: AK Press, 2006); and John McMillian and Paul Buhle, eds., *The New Left Revisited* (Philadelphia: Temple University Press, 2003). The interpretation presented here relies most heavily on Francesca Polletta, *Freedom Is an Endless Meeting: Democracy in American Social Movements* (Chicago: Chicago University Press, 2002); Calvert, *Democracy from the Heart.*

7. Calvert, *Democracy from the Heart,* 88–114; Miller, *Democracy Is in the Streets,* 106–127.

8. The Port Huron Statement is reprinted in full as an appendix to Miller, *Democracy Is in the Streets,* 329–374. The following three citations are to that edition.

9. "Port Huron Statement," 332.

10. Ibid.

11. Ibid., 333.

12. Quoted in Miller, *Democracy Is in the Streets,* 144.

13. Calvert, *Democracy from the Heart,* 68.

14. Wini Breines, *Community and Organization in the New Left, 1962–1968* (New Brunswick, NJ: Rutgers University Press, 1989), 143.

15. Breines's study of SDS helped to popularize the term *prefigurative politics* to describe this approach to change. Anarchists used the term *prefigure* at least as early as 1969, as I demonstrate later in this chapter. By the late 1990s, U.S. anarchists used the term *prefigurative politics* regularly to describe a distinguishing characteristic of their approach to politics. I use the term throughout this book to describe an aspect of anarchist strategy dating back to the nineteenth century, even though the term was not used until later.

16. Kenneth Rexroth, "Disengagement: The Art of the Beat Generation," *World outside the Window: The Selected Essays of Kenneth Rexroth,* ed. Bradford Morrow (New York: New Directions, 1987), 43.

17. Jack Kerouac, *The Dharma Bums* (New York: Penguin, 2005 [1958]), 10.

18. Gary Snyder, "Buddhist Anarchism," *Journal for the Protection of All Beings* 1 (1961). Available at Bureau of Public Secrets, www.bopsecrets.org/CF/garysnyder .htm.

19. Franklin Rosemont, "To Be Revolutionary in Everything: The *Rebel Worker* Story, 1964–1968," in *Dancin' in the Streets! Anarchists, IWWs, Surrealists, Situationists and Provos in the 1960s as Recorded in the Pages of* The Rebel Worker *and* Heatwave, ed. Franklin Rosemont and Charles Radcliffe (Chicago: Charles H. Kerr, 2005), 5–6.

20. Ibid., 45. On the connection between jazz and an expansive notion of freedom, see Scott Saul, *Freedom Is, Freedom Ain't: Jazz and the Making of the Sixties* (Cambridge, MA: Harvard University Press, 2003).

21. Penelope Rosemont, *Dreams and Everyday Life: André Breton, Surrealism, Rebel Worker, SDS & the Seven Cities of Cibola* (Chicago: Charles H. Kerr, 2008), 10–13.

22. Stewart, born in 1925, is mentioned in Allen Ginsberg's "Howl" and in Lawrence Lipton's early account of the Beat generation, *The Holy Barbarians* (New York: Julian Messner, 1959).

23. P. Rosemont, *Dreams,* 18–19.

24. Ibid., 24–25.

25. Facing Reality was an organizational offshoot of the Johnson-Forest Tendency, a dissident caucus within the U.S. Trotskyist movement during the 1940s grouped around the Trinidadian Marxist C. L. R. James, the Russian American theorist Raya Dunayevskaya, and the Chinese American philosopher Grace Lee (later Grace Lee Boggs). Johnson-Forest exchanged ideas with the French group Socialisme ou Barbarie, which had also taken leave from Trotskyism in the 1940s. In the aftermath of the Hungarian uprising of 1956, James, Lee, and one of Socialisme ou Barbarie's leading intellects, Cornelius Castoriadis, coauthored a treatise on anti-Stalinist

Marxism called *Facing Reality,* from which the American group took its name. In the 1960s, Castoriadis served as the strongest influence on the political positions of the British group Solidarity. This radical network, and its influence on the Rebel Worker Group is significant because it also proved important to the formation of Italian operaismo and autonomist Marxism—currents of thought that became important to U.S. anarchism in the early twenty-first century. Frank Rosengarten, *Urbane Revolutionary: C. L. R. James and the Struggle for a New Society* (Jackson: University of Mississippi Press, 2008); Grace Lee Boggs, *Living for Change: An Autobiography* (Minneapolis: University of Minnesota Press, 1998); Arnold Hirsch, *The French Left: A History and Overview* (Montreal: Black Rose Books, 1982), 108–135; Harry Cleaver, *Reading Capital Politically* (Leeds, U.K.: AntiTheses; San Francisco: AK Press, 2001), 59–64; C. L. R. James, Grace C. Lee, and Cornelius Castoriadis, *Facing Reality: The New Society, Where to Look for It and How to Bring It Closer* (Chicago: Charles H. Kerr, 2006 [1958]); David Goodway, ed., *For Workers' Power: The Selected Writings of Maurice Brinton* (Oakland, CA: AK Press, 2004).

26. Martin Glaberman, *Punching Out and Other Writings,* ed. Staughton Lynd (Chicago: Charles H. Kerr, 2002); George Rawick, *Listening to Revolt: Selected Writings,* ed. David Roediger and Martin Smith (Chicago: Charles H. Kerr, 2010).

27. Franklin Rosemont, "Mods, Rockers and the Revolution," *Rebel Worker* 3 (1965), reprinted in Rosemont and Radcliffe, *Dancing in the Streets,* 127–131. The Rebel Worker Group subsequently released the article as a pamphlet. This article, and others like it, predicted many of the themes academic cultural studies would take up a decade later. See, for example, Tony Jefferson and Stuart Hall, *Resistance through Rituals: Youth Subcultures in Postwar Britain,* 2nd ed. (New York: Routledge, 2006).

28. Polletta, *Freedom,* 88–119; Clayborne Carson, *In Struggle: SNCC and the Black Awakening of the 1960s* (Cambridge, MA: Harvard University Press, 1995 [1981]), 133–211; Peniel Joseph, *Waiting 'til the Midnight Hour: A Narrative History of Black Power in America* (New York: Henry Holt, 2006).

29. James Foreman, *The Making of Black Revolutionaries* (Seattle: University of Washington Press, 1997 [1972]); Stokely Carmichael with Michael Thelwell, *Ready for Revolution: The Life and Struggles of Stokely Carmichael (Kwame Toure)* (New York: Scribner, 2003); Jalil Al-Amin [H. Rap Brown], *Die, Nigger, Die! A Political Autobiography* (New York: Dial Press, 1969).

30. On the ways Third World Marxism departed from orthodox Marxism, and other variants, see Robert Young, *Postcolonialism: An Historical Introduction* (Oxford, U.K.: Blackwell, 2001). On Third World Marxism in the United States, see Laura Pulido, *Black, Brown, Yellow, and Left: Radical Activism in Los Angeles* (Berkeley: University of California Press, 2006); and Max Elbaum, *Revolution in the Air: Sixties Radicals Turn to Lenin, Mao, and Che* (New York: Verso, 2002).

31. F. Rosemont, "To Be Revolutionary," 45.

32. P. Rosemont, *Dreams,* 52–105; F. Rosemont, "To Be Revolutionary," 55–57.

33. See Guy Debord, *The Society of the Spectacle,* trans. Donald Nicholson-Smith (New York: Zone Books, 1995 [1967]); Ken Knabb, ed. and trans., *The Situationist*

International Anthology, rev. and expanded ed. (Berkeley, CA: Bureau of Public Secrets, 2007); Sadie Plant, *The Most Radical Gesture: The Situationist International in a Postmodern Age* (London: Routledge, 1992); McKenzie Wark, *The Beach beneath the Street: The Everyday Life and Glorious Times of the Situationist International* (New York: Verso, 2011).

34. P. Rosemont, *Dreams,* 105–109; F. Rosemont, "To Be Revolutionary," 59–64.

35. See Sara M. Evans and Harry C. Boyte, *Free Spaces: The Sources of Democratic Change in America,* repr. ed. (Chicago: University of Chicago Press, 1992).

36. Stewart Burns, interview by author, Williamstown, MA, June 17, 2013.

37. Michael Doyle, *Radical Chapters: Pacifist Bookseller Roy Kepler and the Paperback Revolution* (Syracuse, NY: Syracuse University Press, 2012), 176–205; Tom Wolfe, *The Electric Kool-Aid Acid Test* (New York: Picador, 2008).

38. Mime Troupe director R. G. Davis had come to adopt more radical views under the influence of Robert Scheer, a City Lights clerk, and Saul Landau and Nina Serrano, who had helped found the influential journal *Studies on the Left* at the University of Wisconsin before moving west. Michael William Doyle, "Staging the Revolution: Guerilla Theater as a Countercultural Practice, 1965–68," in *Imagine Nation: The American Counterculture of the 1960s and '70s,* ed. Peter Braunstein and Michael William Doyle (New York: Routledge, 2002), 73.

39. Roel van Duijn, "Netherlands: The Second Liberation," in *1968—Memories and Legacies of a Global Revolt,* ed. Philipp Gassert and Martin Klimke (Washington, DC: German Historical Institute, 2009), 226.

40. Richard Kempton, *Provo: Amsterdam's Anarchist Revolt* (Brooklyn: Autonomedia, 2007), 41–50.

41. On the Diggers, see Timothy Hodgdon, *Manhood in the Age of Aquarius: Masculinity in Two Countercultural Communities* (New York: Columbia University Press, 2008); Julie Stephens, *Anti-disciplinary Protest: Sixties Radicalism and Postmodernism* (Cambridge: Cambridge University Press, 1998); Peter Coyote, *Sleeping Where I Fall: A Chronicle* (Berkeley, CA: Counterpoint, 1998); Emmett Grogan, *Ringolevio: A Life Played for Keeps* (New York: New York Review of Books, 1970).

42. Hodgdon, *Manhood,* 14.

43. Doyle, "Staging," 80.

44. Coyote, *Sleeping,* 69–70.

45. Billy Murcott, "Mutants Commune," *Barb* 5, no. 7, quoted in Doyle, "Staging," 80.

46. Doyle, "Staging," 81.

47. Coyote, *Sleeping,* 86–87.

48. Literature on the Black Panther Party is large and growing. Recent standouts include Joshua Bloom and Waldo E. Martin, *Black against Empire: The History and Politics of the Black Panther Party* (Berkeley: University of California Press, 2014); Alondra Nelson, *Body and Soul: The Black Panther Party and the Fight against Medical Discrimination* (Minneapolis: University of Minnesota Press, 2013); Kathleen Cleaver and George Katsiaficas, eds., *Liberation, Imagination, and the Black Panther Party: A New Look at the Panthers and Their Legacy* (New York: Routledge, 2001).

49. Hodgdon, *Manhood,* 25.

50. Coyote, *Sleeping,* 89.

51. For consideration of the Diggers' perspectives on race and masculinity, see Hodgdon, *Manhood,* 38–61. On the broader counterculture, see Sherry L. Smith, *Hippies, Indians, and the Fight for Red Power* (Oxford: Oxford University Press, 2014); and Philip Deloria, "Counterculture Indians and the New Age," in Braunstein and Doyle, *Imagine Nation,* 159–188.

52. Hodgdon, *Manhood,* 7.

53. Lytle Shaw, "Everyday Archaic: Fieldworkers in New Left Poetry," *The Sixties: A Journal of History, Politics and Culture* 3, no. 1 (June 2010): 63; Hodgdon, *Manhood,* 45.

54. Hodgdon, *Manhood,* 27–28; Coyote, *Sleeping,* 130–241.

55. Timothy Miller, *The Sixties Communes: Hippies and Beyond* (Syracuse, NY: Syracuse University Press, 2000).

56. Doyle, "Staging," 85–91; David Farber, *Chicago '68* (Chicago: University of Chicago Press, 1994), 3–54; Stephens, *Anti-disciplinary Protest.*

57. The *Fraye Arbeter Shtime* and *L'Adunata dei Refrattari* were published by and circulated to a declining number of aged Yiddish- and Italian-speaking anarchists until the 1970s.

58. David Sachs, interview by author, Oakland, CA, June 28, 2013.

59. Dolgoff quoted in Paul Avrich, *Anarchist Voices: An Oral History of Anarchism in America* (Oakland, CA: AK Press, 2005), 427; Sam Dolgoff, *Fragments: A Memoir* (Cambridge, U.K.: Refract, 1986), 89–91.

60. *Resurgence* 1, September–October 1964, 2, Labadie Collection, University of Michigan (hereafter LC).

61. On Bookchin's life, see Murray Bookchin, *Anarchism, Marxism, and the Future of the Left: Interviews and Essays, 1993–1998* (San Francisco: AK Press, 1999); Damian F. White, *Bookchin: A Critical Appraisal* (London: Pluto Press, 2008), 12–28. A biography by Bookchin's life partner, Janet Biehl, is forthcoming from Oxford University Press.

62. Marcel van der Linden, "The Prehistory of Post-scarcity Anarchism: Josef Weber and the Movement for a Democracy of Content (1947–1964)," *Anarchist Studies* 9, no. 2 (2001): 127–145.

63. Lewis Herber [Murray Bookchin], *Our Synthetic Environment* (New York: Knopf, 1962).

64. Bookchin, *Anarchism, Marxism,* 64–65, 73; White, *Bookchin,* 19–20.

65. Murray Bookchin, "Ecology and Revolutionary Theory," in *Post-scarcity Anarchism,* Working Classics Series ed. (Oakland, CA: AK, 2004), 20–40.

66. White, *Bookchin,* 23–25; Theodor Adorno and Max Horkheimer, *The Dialectic of Enlightenment* (Stanford, CA: Stanford University Press, 2007 [1947]); Herbert Marcuse, *One-Dimensional Man: Studies in the Ideology of Advanced Industrial Society* (Boston: Beacon, 1991 [1964]).

67. Murray Bookchin, "Introduction to First Edition," in Bookchin, *Post-scarcity Anarchism,* xix.

68. Bookchin, *Anarchism, Marxism,* 74.

69. Ben Morea, interview by author, New York, March 29, 2009.

70. Ibid.

71. Ibid.

72. Ibid.; Ben Morea and Ron Hahne, *Black Mask and Up Against the Wall Motherfucker: The Incomplete Works of Ron Hahne, Ben Morea, and the Black Mask Group* (Oakland, CA: PM Press, 2011).

73. Morea, interview.

74. Hahne and Morea, *Black Mask and Up Against the Wall Motherfucker,* 4–5.

75. Morea, interview.

76. Morea, interview. On the Provos, see Kempton, *Provo.* On the Zengakuren, see Stuart Dowsey, ed., *Zengakuren* (Berkeley, CA: Ishi Press, 1970).

77. As recounted in the pages of *Internationale Situationniste,* Situationist theorist Raoul Vaneigem visited New York in 1967 to make contact with potential recruits. Vaneigem had "been obliged to break off a conversation with a certain [Allan] Hoffman, who was eulogistically expounding to him a mystical interpretation of his text 'Basic Banalities' and who was at that time the main collaborator in Morea's publications: the enormity of this fact naturally led Vaneigem no longer even to want to discuss our other more general divergences with Morea." The British section of the SI was subsequently excluded because they continued to communicate with Morea after the French members had forbade them to do so. "The Latest Exclusions," *Internationale Situationniste* 12 (1969), reprinted in Ken Knabb, trans. and ed., *Situationist International Anthology* (Berkeley, CA: Bureau of Public Secrets, 1981), 293–294.

78. For a history and analysis of the black bloc tactics, see Francis Dupuis-Déri, *Who's Afraid of the Black Blocs? Anarchy in Action around the World* (Oakland, CA: PM Press, 2014).

79. Leaflet signed "A Communal Freakout," dated October 21, 1967, Ben Morea and Aldo Tambellini Papers, Box 1, Folder 35 Tamiment Library, New York University (hereafter TL).

80. On the Pentagon demonstration, see Miller, *Democracy Is in the Streets,* 282; Norman Mailer, *Armies of the Night: History as a Novel, the Novel as History,* reprint ed. (New York: Plume, 1995).

81. Leaflet signed "Black Mask and Totalists," dated October 21, 1967, Ben Morea and Aldo Tambellini Papers, Box 1, Folder 35, TL.

82. Osha Neumann, *Up Against the Wall Motherf**ker: A Memoir of the '60s, with Notes for Next Time* (New York: Seven Stories, 2008), 53–67. LeRoi Jones later changed his name to Amiri Baraka. On Baraka and the Newark uprising, see Komozi Woodard, *A Nation within a Nation: Amiri Baraka (LeRoi Jones) and Black Power Politics* (Chapel Hill: University of North Carolina Press, 1999).

83. Jones had declared, "You can't steal nothin from a white man, he's already stole it he owes you anything you want, even his life. All the stores will open if you will say the magic words. The magic words are: Up against the wall mother fucker this is a stick up." Morea's group apparently saw no irony in appropriating Jones's

words for their own usage. LeRoi Jones/Amiri Baraka, "Black People!" in *The LeRoi Jones/Amiri Baraka Reader,* ed. W. J. Harris (New York: Thunder's Mouth Press, 1991), 224.

84. The Situationists and anarchists played significant roles in the French "events." See Daniel Singer, *Prelude to Revolution: France in May 1968*, 2nd ed. (Chicago: Haymarket Books, 2013); René Viénet, *Enragés and Situationists in the Occupation Movement, France, May '68* (Brooklyn: Autonomedia/London: Rebel Press, 1992); Daniel Cohn-Bendit, *Obsolete Communism: The Left Wing Alternative* (Oakland, CA: AK Press, 2001); Kristin Ross, *May '68 and Its Afterlives* (Chicago: University of Chicago Press, 2002).

85. Morea quoted in the *Boston Free Press,* reproduced in Hahne and Morea, *Black Mask and Up Against the Wall Motherfucker,* 89.

86. Morea, interview.

87. Ibid.

88. Neumann, *Up Against the Wall,* 66.

89. See Farber, *Chicago '68*; Doyle, "Staging," 85–91; Stephens, *Anti-disciplinary Protest,* 73–95;

90. Neumann, *Up Against the Wall,* 96; Coyote, *Sleeping,* 71.

91. Neumann, *Up Against the Wall,* 75–90; Morea, interview; Dan Berger, *Outlaws of America: The Weather Underground and the Politics of Solidarity* (Oakland, CA: AK Press, 2005); Mark Rudd, *Underground: My Life with SDS and the Weathermen* (New York: William Morrow, 2009).

92. Neumann, *Up Against the Wall, 113–142*; "Ben Morea: Interview," in Hahne and Morea, *Black Mask and Up Against the Wall Motherfucker,* 165.

93. Greil Marcus, *Lipstick Traces: A Secret History of the Twentieth Century* (Cambridge, MA: Harvard University Press, 1990); George Robertson, "The Situationist International: Its Penetration into British Culture," in *What Is Situationism? A Reader,* ed. Stewart Home (San Francisco: AK Press, 2006), 107–133; David Wise and Stuart Wise, *King Mob: A Critical Hidden History* (London: Bread and Circuses Publishing, 2014); Robert Garnett, "Too Low to Be Low: Art Pop and the Sex Pistols," in *Punk Rock: So What?* ed. Roger Sabin (New York: Routledge, 1999), 17–30; Gordon Carr, *The Angry Brigade: A History of Britain's First Urban Guerrilla Group* (Oakland, CA: PM Press, 2010).

94. On Sinclair's relationship to free jazz, see Saul, *Freedom Is,* 292–301.

95. On the *Fifth Estate,* see Peter Werbe, "The History of the *Fifth Estate,*" *Fifth Estate,* no. 368–369 (Spring–Summer 2005): 8–19; Bob Hippler, "Fast Times in the Motor City," in *Voices from the Underground,* vol. 1: *Insider Histories of the Vietnam Era Underground Press,* ed. Ken Wachsberger et al. (Tempe, AZ: Mica Press, 1993).

96. Pun Plamondon quoted in Steve Gebhardt, dir., *20 to Life: The Life and Times of John Sinclair* (Pottstown, PA: MVDVisual, 2007), DVD. For an extended account of this period, see Pun Plamondon, *Lost from the Ottawa: The Story of the Journey Back* (Victoria, BC: Trafford Publishing, 2004).

97. Peter Werbe, interview by author, Royal Oak, MI, April 25, 2008.

98. Wayne Kramer quoted in Gebhardt, *20 to Life.*

99. On the Black Freedom Movement in Detroit, see Heather Thompson, *Whose Detroit? Politics, Labor, and Race in a Modern American City* (Ithaca, NY: Cornell University Press, 2001); Dan Georgakas and Marvin Surkin, *Detroit: I Do Mind Dying* (Cambridge, MA: South End Press, 1998); Muhammad Ahmad, *We Will Return in the Whirlwind: Black Radical Organizations, 1960–1975* (Chicago: Charles H. Kerr, 2007); Angela Dillard, *Faith in the City: Preaching Radical Social Change in Detroit* (Ann Arbor: University of Michigan Press, 2007).

100. Jeff Hale, "The White Panthers' 'Total Assault on the Culture,'" in Braunstein and Doyle, *Imagine Nation*, 125–156.

101. [John Sinclair], "The White Panther State/Meant," in *Guitar Army: Rock and Revolution with the MC5 and the White Panther Party,* by John Sinclair, reprint ed. (Port Townsend, WA: Process, 2007), 89–91.

102. Ibid., 90.

103. Knabb's letter went on to extol the relevance of Snyder's and Rexroth's writings to anarchism and the counterculture. Soon, Knabb would become a major proponent and translator of the writings of the Situationist International. Ken Knabb, "Brother and Sister Anarchists," n.d., photocopy of the original, in the author's possession.

104. Plamondon, *Lost,* 118.

105. New England Region White Panther Party, *Survival Manual-1,* n.d., n.p., Subject Vertical File: Youth & Student Protest—Michigan—White Panthers, LC.

106. "White Panther Statement," Leaflet, 1969, Subject Vertical File: Youth & Student Protest—Michigan—White Panthers, LC.

107. Sinclair, *Guitar Army,* 91.

108. Hale, "White Panthers," 145–151; Plamondon, *Lost,* 143–241.

109. George Berger, *The Story of Crass,* reprint ed. (Oakland, CA: PM Press, 2009); Boff Whalley, *Footnote* (Keighley, U.K.: Pomona, 2003); Stacey Thompson, *Punk Productions: Unfinished Business* (Albany: State University of New York, 2004).

110. Werbe, interview.

111. Lorraine Perlman, *Having Little, Being Much: A Chronicle of Fredy Perlman's Fifty Years* (Detroit, MI: Black and Red, 1989), 48.

112. Fredy Perlman, "The Reproduction of Daily Life," 24, quoted in ibid., 51.

113. "To Nonsubscribers of Radical America," wall poster composed by Situationist International, from Ken Knabb's personal collection, photocopy in author's possession; "To Readers of Black and Red," open letter from Roger Grégoire and Linda Lanphear, January 1971, from Ken Knabb's personal collection, photocopy in author's possession.

114. Werbe, interview.

115. Ibid.

116. Ibid.

117. Perlman, *Having Little,* 83.

118. David Watson, "Notes toward a History of the *Fifth Estate*," *Fifth Estate,* no. 368–369 (Spring–Summer 2005): 26–37; Steve Millett, "Technology Is Capital:

Fifth Estate's Critique of the Megamachine," in *Changing Anarchism: Anarchist Theory and Practice in a Global Age,* ed. Jonathan Purkis and James Bowen (Manchester: Manchester University Press, 2004).

119. Doyle, *Radical Chapters,* 158–175.

120. Ibid., 218–238.

121. Burns, interview.

122. Michael Ferber and Staughton Lynd, *The Resistance* (Boston: Beacon, 1971), 78–91.

123. Burns, interview.

124. Ernest Larsen, "The Treasury Will Go Up in Smoke in Half an Hour," in *If I Can't Dance to It, It's Not My Revolution,* ed. Natalie Musteata (Haverford, PA: Cantor Fitzgerald Gallery, 2014).

125. David Harris, *Goliath* (New York: Richard W. Baron, 1970), 124–132.

126. Paul Goodman, *Growing Up Absurd: Problems of Youth in an Organized Society* (New York: Vintage, 1960).

127. Goodman's *May Pamphlet,* which first appeared as essays in the pages of *politics, Retort,* and *Why?* was republished as Paul Goodman, *Drawing the Line: A Pamphlet* (New York: Random House, 1962). On Goodman's influence, see Richard King, *The Party of Eros: Radical Social Thought and the Realm of Freedom* (Chapel Hill: University of North Carolina Press, 1972); Michael C. Fisher, introduction to *New Reformation: Notes of a Neolithic Conservative,* by Paul Goodman, 2nd ed. (Oakland, CA: PM Press, 2010).

128. David Dellinger, *Revolutionary Nonviolence* (New York: Anchor Books, 1971). The book contains Dellinger's "Statement upon Entering Prison," which had first been published by *Retort,* as well as his "Declaration of War," which he self-published in the journal *Direct Action* in 1946.

129. Ferber and Lynd, *The Resistance,* 11.

130. Matt Meyer and Paul Magno, "Hard to Find: Building for Nonviolent Revolution and the Pacifist Underground," in *The Hidden 1970s: Histories of Radicalism,* ed. Dan Berger (New Brunswick, NJ: Rutgers University Press, 2010): 250–266; Murray Polner and Jim O'Grady, *Disarmed and Dangerous: The Radical Lives of Daniel and Philip Berrigan* (New York: Basic Books, 1997); David Hartsough, *Waging Peace: Global Adventures of a Lifelong Activist* (Oakland, CA: PM Press, 2014), 78–98.

131. Andrew Cornell, *Oppose and Propose! Lessons from Movement for a New Society* (Oakland, CA: AK Press and Institute for Anarchist Studies, 2011).

132. Todd Gitlin, quoted in Doug Rossinow, *The Politics of Authenticity: Liberalism, Christianity, and the New Left in America* (New York: Columbia University Press, 1998), 160.

133. Doug Rossinow, "'The Revolution Is about Our Lives': The New Left's Counterculture," in Braunstein and Doyle, *Imagine Nation,* 108.

134. Paul Avrich, *The Haymarket Tragedy* (Princeton, NJ: Princeton University Press, 1984), 175, 282, 375–378.

135. P. Rosemont, *Dreams,* 190–191.

136. Robert Barsky, *Noam Chomsky: A Life of Dissent* (Cambridge, MA: MIT Press, 1998), 16.

137. Robert Barsky, *The Chomsky Effect: A Radical Works beyond the Ivory Tower* (Cambridge, MA: MIT Press, 2007), 136–143.

138. Noam Chomsky, *American Power and the New Mandarins* (New York: New Press, 2002 [1969]). For Chomsky's anarchism, see his *On Anarchism* (New York: New Press, 2013); and Barry Pateman, ed., *Chomsky on Anarchism* (Oakland, CA: AK Press, 2005).

139. See Howard Zinn, "A Fresh Look at Anarchism," in *A Living Spirit of Revolt: The Infrapolitics of Anarchism,* by Žiga Vodovnik (Oakland, CA: PM Press, 2013).

140. Michael Albert, *Remembering Tomorrow: From SDS to Life after Capitalism: A Memoir* (New York: Seven Stories, 2006), 222.

141. Ibid., 110.

142. Bookchin later admitted, "We were not students, nor official members of SDS, but by 1969 SDS was so loose organizationally that anyone could attend its conventions if he or she was a known radical." Bookchin, *Anarchism, Marxism,* 99.

143. Ibid., 74.

144. The title played on a popular tract in favor of the Cuban Revolution by C. Wright Mills, "Listen, Yankee!"

145. "Radical Decentralist Project, Resolution No. 2, On Organization," Box 2, Folder 2, Sam Dolgoff Papers, TL.

146. Ibid.

147. Bookchin, *Anarchism, Marxism,* 101. Gitlin, *The Sixties,* 387. One member of the caucus was James Miller, who later authored a widely read book on SDS. Miller, *Democracy Is in the Streets,* 17.

148. Dan Berger, *Outlaws of America,* 75–93; Mark Rudd, *Underground: My Life with SDS and the Weathermen* (New York: HarperCollins, 2009), 141–153; Elbaum, *Revolution in the Air.*

149. "About the Black River," leaflet, n.d., Subject Vertical File: Anarchism—Black River Movement, LC.

150. Louise Crowley, "Black River," *Black River* 1, September 24, 1969, Subject Vertical File: Anarchism—Black River Movement, LC.

151. Bookchin, *Anarchism, Marxism,* 103–105.

152. "A Draft Statement," *Black River* 1, September 24, 1969, Subject Vertical File: Anarchism—Black River Movement, LC. The usage of the term *prefigures* is significant in that it indicates not only the concept but also that the language of "prefigurative politics" predated Wini Breines's usage of it in *Community and Organization in the New Left.*

153. Michael Brownstein, *Black River* 1, p. 3.

154. Hahne and Morea, *Black Mask and Up Against the Wall Motherfucker,* 118.

155. See, for example, Benita Roth, *Separate Roads to Feminism: Black, Chicana, and White Feminist Movements in America's Second Wave* (Cambridge: Cambridge

University Press, 2003); Wini Breines, *The Trouble between Us: An Uneasy History of White and Black Women in the Feminist Movement* (Oxford: Oxford University Press, 2007).

156. Alix Kates Shulman, "Emma Goldman's Feminism: A Reappraisal," in *Red Emma Speaks: An Emma Goldman Reader,* ed. Shulman (New York: Schocken Books, 1971), 4.

157. Ruth Rosen, *The World Split Open: How the Modern Women's Movement Changed America,* rev. ed. (New York: Penguin, 2006), 204.

158. Su Negrin, *Begin at Start: Some Thoughts on Personal Liberation and World Change* (Washington, NJ: Times Change Press, 1972). I thank Matt Dineen for introducing me to Negrin's book.

159. I thank Julia Tanenbaum for introducing me to this journal.

160. Terence Kissack, "Freaking Fag Revolutionaries: New York's Gay Liberation Front, 1969–1971," *Radical History Review* 62 (1995): 104–134.

161. Tommi Avicolli Mecca, introduction to *Smash the Church, Smash the State! The Early Years of Gay Liberation,* ed. Mecca (San Francisco: City Lights, 2009), xi.

162. Kissack, "Freaking," 116.

163. Jo Freeman, "The Tyranny of Structurelessness," reprinted with responses and commentary on the debate, appears in Dark Star Collective, eds., *Quiet Rumours: An Anarcha-Feminist Reader,* 3rd ed. (Oakland, CA: AK Press, 2012). Also see Alice Echols, *Daring to Be Bad: Radical Feminist in America, 1967–1975* (Minneapolis: University of Minnesota Press, 1989).

164. Farber, *Chicago '68,* 212.

165. See Myles Horton, with Judith Kohl and Herbert Kohl, *The Long Haul: An Autobiography* (New York: Teachers College Press, 1998).

166. Calvert, *Democracy from the Heart,* 10.

CONCLUSION

1. See Jesse Cohn, *Underground Passages: Anarchist Resistance Culture, 1848–2011* (Oakland, CA: AK Press, 2015). Cohn's book was published too recently to inform my research, but I have benefited from conversations with the author.

2. This analysis draws on "postanarchist" theory, which has helped to shape the interpretive framework of this project as a whole. See Todd May, *The Political Philosophy of Poststructuralist Anarchism* (University Park: Penn State University Press, 1994); Saul Newman, *From Bakunin to Lacan: Anti-authoritarianism and the Dislocation of Power* (Lanham, MD: Lexington Books, 2001); Duane Rousselle and Süreyyya Evren, eds., *Post-anarchism: A Reader* (London: Pluto Press, 2011).

3. Sam Weiner Interview, WKCR-FM, New York, December 1962, compact disc, Labadie Collection, University of Michigan.

4. Ben Aggers, *Critical Social Theories: An Introduction,* 3rd ed. (Oxford: Oxford University Press, 2013), 5–6.

5. Chris Crass, *Towards Collective Liberation: Anti-racist Organizing, Feminist Praxis, and Movement Building Strategy* (Oakland, CA: PM Press, 2013).

EPILOGUE

1. Jeremy Brecher, *Strike!* expanded, revised, and updated ed. (Oakland, CA: PM Press, 2014).

2. Craig Hughes and Team Colors, eds., *Towards the Last Jubilee! Thirty Years of Midnight Notes* (Brooklyn, NY: Autonomedia and Perry Editions, 2010); Harry Cleaver, *Reading Capital Politically* (Oakland, CA: AntiThesis and AK Press, 2001); Midnight Notes, *Midnight Oil: Work, Energy, War, 1973–1992* (Brooklyn, NY: Autonomedia, 1992); Silvia Federici, *Revolution at Point Zero: Housework, Reproduction, and Feminist Struggle* (Oakland, CA: PM Press, 2012).

3. See the articles on the magazine's history in *Fifth Estate,* no. 368–369, Spring–Summer 2005, available at *Fifth Estate,* www.fifthestate.org/archive/368–369-spring-summer-2005/. Also, Lorraine Perlman, *Having Little, Being Much: A Chronicle of Fredy Perlman's Fifty Years* (Detroit, MI: Black and Red, 2002), 86–90.

4. See Ken Knabb, "Confessions of a Mild-Mannered Enemy of the State," in *Public Secrets: The Collective Skirmishes of Ken Knabb* (Berkeley, CA: Bureau of Public Secrets, 1997), 111–115.

5. Gary Snyder, *Turtle Island* (New York: New Directions, 1974).

6. Murray Bookchin, *Post-scarcity Anarchism* (Oakland, CA: AK Press, 2004 [1971]).

7. Murray Bookchin, *Social Ecology and Communalism* (Oakland, CA: AK Press, 2007).

8. See contributions from Lynne Farrow, Peggy Kornegger, Marian Leighton, and Carol Ehrlich in Dark Star Collective, eds., *Quiet Rumours: An Anarcha-Feminist Reader,* 3rd ed. (Oakland, CA: AK Press, 2012).

9. See Kimberly Springer, *Living for the Revolution: Black Feminist Organizations, 1968–1980* (Durham, NC: Duke University Press, 2005); and Wini Breines, *The Trouble between Us: An Uneasy History of White and Black Women in the Feminist Movement* (Oxford: Oxford University Press, 2007), 117–151.

10. Andrew Cornell, *Oppose and Propose! Lessons from Movement for a New Society* (Oakland, CA: AK Press and the Institute for Anarchist Studies, 2011).

11. Barbara Epstein, *Political Protest and Cultural Revolution: Direct Action Movements in the 1970s and 1980s* (Berkeley: University of California Press, 1991).

12. C. T. Butler and Keith McHenry, *Food Not Bombs,* rev ed. (Tucson, AZ: See Sharp Press, 2000). Also see Chris Crass, "Food Not Bombs and the Building of a Grassroots Anarchist Left in the 1990s," in *Towards Collective Liberation: Anti-racist Organizing, Feminist Praxis, and Movement Building Strategy* (Oakland, CA: PM Press, 2013).

13. See Jason McQuinn, "The Life and Times of Anarchy: A Journal of Desire Armed: 25 Years of Critical Anarchist Publishing," available at http://theanarchistlibrary.org/library/jason-mcquinn-the-life-and-times-of-anarchy-a-journal-of-desire-armed-25-years-of-critical-anar.

14. See John Zerzan, *Future Primitive and Other Essays* (Brooklyn, NY: Autonomedia, 1994); "A Dialog [*sic*] on Primitivism," available at http://theanarchistlibrary.org/library/various-authors-a-dialog-on-primitivism.

15. Christopher Manes, *Radical Environmentalism and the Unmaking of Civilization* (Boston: Back Bay Books, 1991); Dave Forman and Bill Haywood, eds., *Ecodefense: A Field Guide to Monkeywrenching* (Tucson, AZ: Ned Ludd Books, 1987).

16. See Steve Chase, ed., *Defending the Earth: A Dialogue between Murray Bookchin and Dave Foreman* (Montreal: Black Rose Books, 1991).

17. George Berger, *The Story of Crass,* repr. ed. (Oakland, CA: PM Press, 2009); Ian Glasper, *The Day the Country Died: A History of Anarcho Punk, 1980–1984* (Oakland, CA: PM Press, 2014).

18. On European autonomous movements, see George Katsiaficas, *The Subversion of Politics: European Autonomous Social Movements and the Decolonization of Everyday Life* (Oakland, CA: AK Press, 2006). On *Profane Existence,* see Dan Troll, ed., *Profane Existence: Making Punk a Threat Again; The Best Cuts, 1989–1993* (Minneapolis, MN: Profane Existence, 1993). On the Tompkins Square Riots, see Neil Smith, *The New Urban Frontier: Gentrification and the Revanchist City* (New York: Routledge, 1996).

19. François Cusset, *French Theory: How Foucault, Derrida, Deleuze, and Co. Transformed the Intellectual Life of the United States* (Minneapolis: University of Minnesota Press, 2008), 71–75.

20. On South End Press and Z Magazine, see Michael Albert, *Remembering Tomorrow: From SDS to Life after Capitalism: A Memoir* (New York: Seven Stories, 2007). On participatory economics, see Michael Albert and Robin Hahnel, *Looking Forward: Participatory Economics for the 21st Century* (Boston: South End Press, 1991); Michael Albert, *Parecon: Life after Capitalism* (New York: Verso, 2003); Chris Spannos, ed., *Real Utopia: Participatory Society for the 21st Century* (Oakland, CA: AK Press, 2008).

21. Roy San Filippo, ed., *A New World in Our Hearts: Eight Years of Writings from the Love and Rage Revolutionary Anarchist Federation* (Oakland, CA: AK Press, 2003).

22. Lorenzo Kom'boa Ervin, *Anarchism and the Black Revolution* (Philadelphia: Monkeywrench Press, 1994). Some of Alston's writings are available at Anarchist Panther, www.anarchistpanther.net.

23. See the group's website, Critical Resistance, www.criticalresistance.org.

24. Deborah B. Gould, *Moving Politics: Emotion and ACT-UP's Fight against AIDS* (Chicago: University of Chicago Press, 2009); Benjamin Shepard and Ronald Hayduk, eds., *From ACT-UP to the WTO: Urban Protest and Community Building in the Era of Globalization* (New York: Verso, 2002).

25. Scott Lauria Morgensen, "Arrival at Home: Radical Faerie Configurations of Sexuality and Place," *GLQ: A Journal of Lesbian and Gay Studies* 15, no. 1 (2009): 67–96. I thank Jaclyn Pryor for bringing this article to my attention.

26. See Sara Marcus, *Girls to the Front: The True Story of the Riot Grrrl Revolution* (New York: Harper Perennial, 2010); Judith Halberstam, "What's That Smell? Queer Temporalities and Subcultural Lives," in *A Queer Time and Place: Transgender Bodies, Subcultural Lives* (New York: NYU Press, 2005); Neal Ritchie, "The Anarchist Influence on Queer Youth Cultures," in *Queer Youth Cultures,* ed. Susan Driver (Albany: State University of New York Press, 2008), 261–278.

27. Hakim Bey, *T.A.Z.: The Temporary Autonomous Zone, Ontological Anarchy, Poetic Terrorism* (Brooklyn, NY: Autonomedia, 1991).

28. Murray Bookchin, *Social Anarchism or Lifestyle Anarchism: An Unbridgeable Chasm* (San Francisco: AK Press, 1995).

29. See Murray Bookchin, *The Next Revolution: Popular Assemblies and the Promise of Direct Democracy,* ed. Debbie Bookchin and Blair Taylor (New York: Verso, 2015).

30. George Katsiaficas, Eddie Yuen, and Daniel Burton-Rose, eds., *The Battle of Seattle: The New Challenge to Capitalist Globalization* (Brooklyn, NY: Soft Skull Press, 2002).

31. See "Interview with Ernesto Aguilar of the Anarchist People of Color (APOC)," Colours of Resistance Archive, www.coloursofresistance.org/596/interview-with-ernesto-aguilar-of-the-anarchist-people-of-color-apoc/.

32. See the group's website, CrimethInc. Ex-Workers' Collective, www.crimethinc.com.

33. See Green Anarchy Collective, *Uncivilized: The Best of Green Anarchy* (Eugene, OR: Green Anarchy Press, 2012); Wolfi Landstreicher, *Willful Disobedience* (San Francisco: Ardent Press, 2009).

34. Will Potter, *Green Is the New Red: An Insider's Account of a Social Movement under Siege* (San Francisco: City Lights, 2011).

35. Chris Dixon, *Another Politics: Talking across Today's Transformative Movements* (Berkeley: University of California Press, 2014); Crass, *Towards Collective Liberation.* The journals *Left Turn* and *Upping the Anti* were important forums for this tendency.

36. Important texts include the Invisible Committee, *The Coming Insurrection* (Los Angeles: Semiotext(e), 2009) and the essays collected in Benjamin Noyes, ed., *Communization and Its Discontents: Contestation, Critique, and Contemporary Struggles* (Brooklyn, NY: Minor Compositions/Autonomedia, 2011).

37. See page 301, note 1.

38. Blair Taylor, "From Alterglobalization to Occupy Wall Street: Neoanarchism and the New Spirit of the Left," *City: Analysis of Urban Trends, Culture, Theory, Policy, Action* 17, no. 6 (2013): 729–747; Jonathan Smucker, "Can Prefigurative Politics Replace Political Strategy?" *Berkeley Journal of Sociology* 58 (2014), available at http://berkeleyjournal.org/2014/10/can-prefigurative-politics-replace-political-strategy/.

INDEX

Abalone Alliance, 293–94

Abbott, Leonard, 46, 312

abolition movement (slavery), 214

Abraham Lincoln Brigade, 138, 141. *See also* Communist Party of the United States of America; Spanish Civil War

Abrams, Jacob, 65–66, 74–75

Abrams, Mary, 23, 65, 75

Abu-Jamal, Mumia, 297

ACLU (American Civil Liberties Union), 64, 312n77

ACT-UP, 297

Adams, Paul Lieber, 168

Adbusters, 299

Adorno, Theodor, 257

affinity groups, 4–5, 180, 268, 293

AFL-CIO, 219, 224 *See also* American Federation of Labor

African American anarchists. *See* Alston, Ashanti; Balagoon, Kuwasi; Carrington, Glenn; DeWeiss, Dan; Ervin, Lorenzo Kom'boa; Stewart, Joffre; Sutherland, Bill

African Blood Brotherhood, 103–4

Agent Orange, 271

Aggers, Ben, 290

Agostinelli, Diva, 155–56, 188, 209, 235; biographical details of, 151, 178, 202, 283*fig.*; connecting Italian- and English-speaking anarchists, 151, 195–96; outside of New York, 195–96, 198

AIDS, 297

Albert, Michael, 271, 295–96

Alston, Ashanti, 296

alterglobalization movement, 17

Alternative, 178, 205. See also *Direct Action*

Amalgamated Co-ops, 85, 118

Amalgamated Garment Workers, 85

American Civil Liberties Union, 64, 312n77

American Defense Society, 64

American Federation of Labor, 24, 33–35, 64, 68, 82–83, 87, 103, 126–27, 219. *See also* AFL-CIO

Americanization of anarchism, 14, 61, 78–79, 99, 100–1, 104–5, 109–10, 148–49, 209. *See also* English-language, move towards

American Protective League, 64

Am-Shol Group, 85

anarcha-feminism, 31*fig.*; classical anarchism and, 40–42; 50, 51, 103, 276; contemporary anarchism and, 274–76, 280, 293–94, 338n35. *See also* de Cleyre, Voltairine; Goldman, Emma; gruppi femminili di propaganda; Roda, Maria

anarchism, definition of, 6–10, 119, 167–68, 303n20, 308n32

Anarchist Aid Society for Political Prisoners, 104

anarchist as figure of threat, 9, 21, 22, 38, 45–46, 199, 261

Anarchist Black Cross Federation, 297

anarchist capitalists, 11–12

resistance; modernist art; poetry and literature

203; and cooperative living, 134–36, 254; and mutual aid, 14–15, 112, 133–36; and nonviolent protest, 133–36, 169–71, 218, 256, 269, 278, 349n19

Catholicism, 42, 134, 136–37, 139, 169, 207, 269

Caughey, Walter, 255

Central Labor Council, 67

Chasse, Robert, 259

Chicago, 195; anarcha-feminism in, 275; Anarchist Red Cross in, 316n122; and Spanish Civil War, 139; and the Haymarket Affair, 25, 296; and artists, 48, 184, 316n122; estimated numbers of anarchists in, 305n1; Free Society Group in, 100–1, 108, 119, 199; fundraisers in, 117, 328n70; individual anarchists in, 23; Jewish Anarchist Federation in, 83; Louis Lingg Memorial Chapter of Students for Democratic Society in, 270; militant unionism and IWW in, 25, 33, 82–83, 184, 246, 254, 316n122; post-1972, 296; publishing in, 142; radical pacifism in, 175–76, 180; Rebel Worker Group in, 246–51;

Chicano movement, 269–70

Chomsky, Noam, 10, 271, 278, 295, 296

Christian anarchism, 160, 169

Christianity: and African Americans, 44, 222, 228, 230, 237; and education, 97–98; and normativity, 41–43, 46, 189; and pacifism, 153–55, 162, 164, 165, 168; and personalism, 133–36, 221, 222, 237. *See also* Catholicism; Christian anarchism; peace churches; Quakers; Social Gospel Protestantism; religion

Chumbawamba, 10, 266, 295

CIO. *See* Congress of Industrial Organizations

City College, 118–20

City Lights, 15, 203, 205, 246, 251, 254–55, 359n38

Civil Defense demonstrations, 218

Civilian Conservation Corps, 124

Civilian Public Service camps, 155; detainees' activities after, 175, 178–79, 188, 205; influence and politicization of,

148, 167–68, 185, 190, 213; protests in, 148, 167–68

civil rights movement, 12, 148, 172–73, 212, 220–31, 236–38, 244, 249, 256, 277, 350n26, 351n44. *See also* Black Freedom Movement

Clark, John, 303n20

class decomposition, 14, 58, 78–79, 281, 318n8. *See also* immigration reforms

class exploitation and oppression, 23, 32, 143, 158; and art, 47, and imperialism, 211, 233; and pacifists, 164–65, 168, 173–74, 209, 214, 341n67; and postwar economy, 195; and the New Left, 238–39, 241, 247, 248, 270, 287; and the state, 9–10, 12–13, 27–28, 175; and World War I, 54, 56; contemporary, 5, 295–99; David Dellinger on, 174; Holley Cantine, Jr. on, 158; in early twentieth century, 24, 27, 38, 42, 49, 115, 117; Industrial Workers of the World on, 33; Libertarian League on, 216, 223, 225, 231, 238, 286; moving beyond sole focus on, 15, 48, 50, 148, 212, 288; Resistance Group on, 201; Vanguard Group on, 121; Wilhelm Reich on, 189. *See also* class reductionism; power, theories of

classical anarchism, 4–5, 7, 12–15, 21–144, 153, 174, 188–89, 201, 207, 215, 238, 246–47, 271, 277, 281

class privilege, 8*fig.,* 216; and role of state, capitalism, and the church, 28, 37, 56, 303n21, 308nn29,31; of some radicals and anarchists, 2, 43, 17

class reductionism, 4, 8*fig.,* 121, 267, 354n68; and gender, 42, 49–51; and race, 223–25, 231, 238

Class War, 316n119

Cleveland, OH, anarchism in, 73, 88–89, 105, 119, 217–18

CNT. *See* Confederación Nacional de Trabajadores

CNVR (Committee for Nonviolent Revolution). *See* Committee for Nonviolent Revolution

CO. *See* conscientious objector status

Coda, Emilio, 92

Cody, Fred, 205
Cody, Pat, 205
Cody's Books, 205, 251
Cohen, Joseph, 67, 83, 96, 129–31
Cold War, 180; anarchists' reactions to, 198–203, 216, 237, 256, 287; anti-imperialist struggles during, 212, 234–35; and Civil Defense protests, 203, 218; and culture, 15, 148
collective bargaining, 126
college education of anarchists, 15, 161, 209, 216–17; at Anticoch College, 255; at Brooklyn College, 163; at Hunter College; 150, 162; at New School for Social Research, 202; at Roosevelt University, 246; at Swarthmore College, 156; at Temple University, 151; at University of Chicago, 163; at Yale University, 166. *See also* City College; Columbia University; University of California
colonies. *See* communes; Home Colony; intentional communities; Mohegan Colony; Stelton Colony; Sunrise Co-operative Farm Community
Columbia, MO, anarchism in, 294
Columbia University, 155–56, 158, 202, 262, 274
Combahee River Collective, 293
Comfort, Alex, 185
Committee for Nonviolent Revolution, 31*fig.*, 293; and David Wieck, 195, 198; and organizational forms, 176–77, 354n70; and Peacemakers, 180; and War Resisters League leadership, 179; establishment of, 176; members of, 205, 213, 251; on the state, 177; struggles against the draft by, 177–78, 181*fig.*, 182
Committee on Racial Equality, 167. *See also* Congress of Racial Equality; Fellowship of Reconciliation
Committee to Defend Franco's Labor Victims, 349n18
Communication Company, 253
communism, non-party affiliated, 120, 287
Communist International, 90–91
communism internationally, 77, 80, 87–88, 98, 137–39, 234–36, 249, 341n67. *See also*

Cuban Revolution; national liberation; Russian Revolution
Communist Party of the United States of America: and Black Freedom Movement, 222; and fascism, 94, 128; and the New Left, 243–44, 267, 276–77; and Sacco and Vanzetti, 93; and Spanish Civil War, 137–41; and World War II, 147; anarchist battles with, 108–9, 122, 281; emergence of, 88; in unions, 33, 81–83, 87, 89–91, 94, 95, 111, 122, 126, 128, 197, 219; leaders of, 68, 82, 105; members of, 89, 94, 96, 99, 105, 130, 167–68, 184, 216, 217, 247, 256; publications of, 103, 240; repression of, 74, 180, 199, 219, 351n31; youth groups of, 122, 155
Comstock laws, 40, 312n79
Comte de Lautréamont, 249
communes: before the New Left and counterculture, 25, 36, 112, 129–33, 134, 136, 180, 188, 321n34; New Left and counterculture, 254, 262, 263, 265, 267, 274, 282, 295. *See also* intentional communities; kibbutzim; School of Living
Confederación Nacional de Trabajadores, 115, 137–39, 154, 216, 218, 330n12, 335n94. *See also* Spanish Civil War
Conflict, 10
Congress of Industrial Organizations, 112, 126–28, 149–50, 219, 284, 333nn69,71. *See also* AFL-CIO
Congress of Racial Equality, 167, 212–13, 255–56; desegregation campaigns of, 177–79, 225, 227, 229
conscientious objector status, 154–55, 167, 343n4. *See also* Civilian Public Service camps; draft resistance. *See also under* imprisonment and arrest
consciousness, 15, 30, 32, 46, 65, 98, 114, 189, 258, 272, 276, 282
conscription. *See* conscientious objector status; draft resistance. *See under* imprisonment and arrest
consensus decision-making: adoption of, 180, 182, 229, 248, 275, 293–94, 353n60, 354n70; origin of, 180; purpose and

deep ecology, 294

de Ligt, Bart, 31*fig.*, 152–54, 165, 172, 174, 222, 284; *Peace as Deed: Principles, History, and Methods of Direct Action,* 153; *The Conquest of Violence: An Essay on War and Revolution,* 152–54

Dellinger David, *283fig.*, 355n86; and Committee for Nonviolent Revolution, 177–78, 205, 293; and Fellowship of Reconciliation, 166, 172; and Harlem Ashram, 166, 186, 343n103; and Libertarian Press, 187, 192; and nonviolence, 171–74, 202, 238; and Peacemakers, 180; and periodicals, 171, 178, 205, 213–14, 348n7; and Bayard Rustin, 221, 236–37; and War Resisters League, 179, 221; "Are Pacifists Willing to be Negroes?," 227; "Declaration of War," 173–74; draft resistance by, 166–68, 173, 181*fig.*, 182, 209, 229; on Cuba, 234–36; personal relationships of, 221, 341n71; *Revolutionary Nonviolence,* 269

Deming, Barbara, 268

democratic and collective decision-making, non-consensus, 29, 82, 126–27, 242–43, 278, 354n70. *See also* consensus decision-making; organizational forms; soviets

Democratic National Convention, 272

Demographic base of anarchism: bohemians as, 183; changes of, 5, 52, 208; counterculture as, 252, 292; humanity as, 175; immigrants as, 22, 281, 286; immigration restrictions and, 63–64; possibilities of, *8*, 121, 288; race of, 298; working-class as, 105, 136, 197

demonstrations. *See* marches, rallies, pickets, and demonstrations

Department of Justice, 60, 62–64, 71–72, 76, 88

deportation, 14, 55, 62–63, 69–76, 80–81, 92, 118, 142, 147, 281

Der Shturm, 65. See also *Frayhayt*

Der Yunyon Arbeiter, 90

de Silver, Margaret, 161

Detroit: anarchists from, 95, 130, 218, 315n107; classical anarchism in, 72, 95, 105, 117, 118, 139, 195, 324n20;

contemporary anarchism in, 218, 259, 262–67, 292

De Vrije, 252

DeWeiss, Dan, 163, 192, 194

Dewey, John, 97

Dielo Truda, 101, 117

Diggers, 16, 31*fig.*, 251–54, 259, 261, 263, 265, 287

DiGia, Ralph, 166–68, 173, 178, 221, 340n67

Dil Pickle Club, 184, 235, 316n122

Direct Action, 173–75, 178, 182, 187, 205, 343n103. See also *Alternative*

direct action, concept of: and anarchist contributions to Black Freedom Movement, 15, 212–13, 222, 226, 237; and contemporary anarchism, 269, 276, 293–94, 297–99; and Diggers, 252; and gender, 208–9; and Sacco and Vanzetti, 93, 108; importance of, 180, 201, 208, 219; instead of electoral strategies, 33, 129, 220; nonviolent, development of, 148, 153, 168, 174, 203, 208, 237

direct action, kinds of. *See* boycotts; expropriation; physical confrontations; property destruction; marches, rallies, pickets, and demonstrations; nonviolent civil disobedience; sabotage; sit-ins; strikes

Di Sciullo, Camillo, 51

diversity of tactics, 227, 352n53

Dixon, Chris, 1

Dolgoff, Esther (née Miller), 119, 150–51, 215–16, 219, 255

Dolgoff, Sam, 91, 119, 128, 161, 249, 283*fig.*, 289; and Libertarian Book Club, 215; and Libertarian League, 215–17, 219, 231, 235, 255; and Vanguard Group, 119–21, 141; and Why? Group, 150–51; support for World War II by, 152

Dow Chemical, 271

Doyle, Michael William, 252

Draft Act of May 18, 1917, 320n26

draft resistance: analysis of, 56, 153–54, 163–64, 173–74; and Vietnam War, 264, 268–69; and World War I, 54, 59–60, 85, 169, 320n26; and World War II, 154–55, 160, 166–67, 169, 178–79,

181*fig.*, 182; influence of pacifism on, 15–16, 148, 168, 209. *See also* conscientious objector status; No Conscription League; Resistance, The. *See also under* imprisonment and arrest

drama. *See* theater and performance

drugs: and the Beat Generation, 192, 206; as distraction from anarchism or detriment to anarchists, 255, 258, 262, 265; for consciousness-raising, 246, 255, 282; LSD and psychedelics, 251, 253, 255, 261–63; marijuana, 192, 264, 266, 270

Dubinsky, David, 122

Du Bois, W.E.B., 24

Dunayevskaya, Raya, 357n25

Duncan, Robert: and art as revolution, 197; and education, 186, 192, 198, 209; and homosexuality, 187, 221; and King Ubu Gallery, 206; and the Libertarian Circle, 187–88; and the Libertarian League, 218; in New York, 186–87

Dylan, Bob, 268

Earth First!, 294, 298

Earth Liberation Front, 299

East Side Anarchists, 256–58, 272

ecology, 4, 16, 182, 239; and environmentalism, 191, 299; and Murray Bookchin, 257, 272, 292; and Su Negrin, 275. *See also* deep ecology; social ecology

Economic Research and Action Projects, 243–44

economism. *See* class reductionism

education, 14–15, 81, 85, 281–82, 289; theories about, 46, 88–89, 97–98, 109–10, 202. *See also* Modern Schools

Ehrlich, Carol, 276

Eikhenbaum, V.M. (Voline), 62, 80, 87, 102, 348n8; *Nineteen-Seventeen,* 348n8

Eisenhower, Dwight D., 223–24

Elektra Records, 263

Elia, Roberto, 76, 93

Ellington, Patricia, 216, 256

Ellington, Richard, 216, 256

Elliot, T.S., 203

Ellis Island, 69, 72–74, 73*fig.*, 76, 80, 322n75

Ellis Island Anarchist Weekly, 72–73, 73*fig.*, 117, 322n75

Ellul, Jacques, 292

Eltzbacher, Paul, 349n8

Elwell, Bruce, 259

Engels, Friedrich, 172

English-language, move towards, 38–39, 46, 49, 81, 100–2, 104, 106, 109, 112–14, 121, 142, 144, 149, 188, 255

environmentalism, 1, 17, 244–45, 257, 282, 285, 292; and the arts, 47, 190–91; radical activism for, 5, 292, 294, 298–99. *See also* anarcho-primitivism; ecology

Epstein, Melech, 53, 87

Eramo, Giovanni, 60

ERAP (Economic Research and Action Projects), 243–44

Ervin, Lorenzo Kom'boa, 296

Espionage Act, 59–62, 65, 77, 134, 320n26. *See also* Red Scare

Esteve, Pedro, 26, 35–36

Evanston, IL, anarchism in, 291

Everson, William, 185, 188, 192, 197

expropriation, 37, 84, 106, 117, 129, 174, 253; outside of U.S., 87, 137

Fabbri, Luigi, 119

Facing Reality, 357n25

Facing Reality (group), 247, 259, 357n25

Faegre, Tor, 248*fig.*

FAI (Federación Anarquista Ibérica), 137–39

Fanon, Frantz, 226, 231, 249, 258, 264, 352n52

Farber, David, 276

Farber, Simon, 88, 90, 91, 99

Farmer, James, 167, 186

family. *See* marriage, relationships, and family structures

Farrell, James, 221, 228

FAS (*Fraye Arbeter Shtime*), See *Fraye Arbeter Shtime*

Fascism, 14–15, 92, 135, 212, 281; and united front, 128, 141; concern U.S. government was turning to, 112, 124–25, 223, 287; Italian anarchist opposition to, 81, 94–96, 121, 151, 2289, 297, 326n44; outside of the U.S., 1, 112, 123, 137–43, 150, 154–55, 298; theories of, 152, 189

Faubus, Orval, 223, 225

FBI. *See* Federal Bureau of Investigation

Federación Anarquista Ibérica, 137–39

Federal Bureau of Investigation, 229, 254. *See also* Bureau of Investigation

federal intervention in civil rights movement, 12, 212, 223–27

Fellowship of Reconciliation, 162, 164–65, 171–72, 185, 213, 353n60; and A.J. Muste, 165, 178, 218, 221; and Bayard Rustin, 178, 218, 221. *See also* Congress of Racial Equality

feminism: and early pacifism, 57, 153, 164; and the New Left, 240–21, 258, 274–76, 278, 282; contemporary, 1–2, 4–5, 16–17, 103, 286, 290, 293–97; in early twentieth century, 14, 39–43, 58, 281, 316n122; in mid-twentieth century, 189–90, 208–9. *See also* anarcha-feminism; suffrage movement; women of color feminism; women's liberation group

Ferdinand, Franz, 55

Ferguson, Kathy, 41, 43, 219

Ferlinghetti, Lawrence, 205, 264

Ferm, Alexis, 97–98

Ferm, Elizabeth, 97–98

Ferrer, Francisco, 46, 97

Ferrer Center. *See* Francisco Ferrer Center

Ferrer Modern School: at Ferrer Center, 46, 48, 96; at Stelton Colony, 49, 88–89, 96–99, 109–10, 118, 284

Ferrero, Vincenzo, 37, 113–14, 118, 142

Fifth Estate, 31*fig.,* 262–63, 266–67, 292, 294, 297

Figner, Vera, 85

Finch, Roy, 171, 175, 178–79, 221, 234–36, 269, 341n67

First International, 29, 33, 102, 160, 327n67

First World War. *See* World War I

Fleigler, Bessie, 150–51

Fleigler, Franz, 150–51

Fleshin, Senya, 75*fig.,* 102, 123

Flynn, Elizabeth Gurley, 92–93, 347n76

Flynn, Sabina, 347n76

folk culture, 25, 52, 208, 245, 285, 310n54

Food Not Bombs, 294

FOR (Fellowship of Reconciliation). *See* Fellowship of Reconciliation

Foreman, Dave, 294

Forman, James, 232

Foster, William Z., 68, 82

Foucault, Michel, 41, 50

Fox, George, 185, 343n4

Francisco Ferrer Association, 96

Francisco Ferrer Center, 31*fig.,* 65, 83, 280; and art, 46–47, 316n120; and educating children, 46–49, 96–98; as event and meeting space, 46–47, 54, 84, 85, 97; explosion near, 48

Franco, Francisco, 137, 139, 141, 154, 349n18. *See also* Spanish Civil War

Fraye Arbeter Shtime, 31*fig.,* 35, 100, 107; and Joseph Cohen, 130; and Spanish Civil War, 138–39; and trade unions, 89, 91; and World War I, 57, 61, 65, 83; as influence on other anarchists, 67, 84, 123, 271. *See also* Jewish Anarchist Federation

Frayhayt, 65–66

Frayhayt Group, 65–66, 69, 74–75

Free, the (concept), 252–53, 261, 263

Freedman, Clara, 120, 124, 150, 331n38

Freedom (London), 337n11. See also *War Commentary*

Freedom (U.S). See *Road to Freedom*

Freedom Group, 152, 198, 161, 208, 337n11

Freedom Rides, 179, 229

Freedom Summer, 231, 244

free love. *See* sex radicalism

Freeman, Alden, 47

Freeman, Jo, 275–76

Free Society, 77–78, 102, 113, 322n75. See also *Anarchist Soviet Bulletin*

Free Society Group, 100–3, 101*fig.,* 108, 119, 139, 199, 330n11

Free Society Forums, 101, 108

free speech: and Communist Party, 199; and Industrial Workers of the World, 34, 40; and University of California, 244, 246; support by middle- and upper-class liberals for, 14, 40, 47, 66, 281

Free Speech League, 40, 66, 142

Free Speech Movement, 244, 246

Free Workers Forum, 100

Freiheit, 314n103

French Revolution, 27, 30, 207n24

Freud, Sigmund, 158, 189
Frick, Henry Clay, 38, 309n43
Friends of Durruti, 216
fundraising: for anarchist comrades abroad, 94, 138–39 171; for anarchist institutions and activities, 89, 119, 222, 253; for anarchist periodicals, 101, 103–4, 117, 194; social function of, 26, 84, 101, 104, 117, 119, 120, 139, 151–52, 194; for prisoner defense, 40, 75, 92, 93, 100, 101, 118, 264

Galleani, Luigi, 113–14, 280, 283*fig.*, 353n68; and *Cronaca Sovversiva,* 37, 53, 60, 105; and feud with Carlo Tresca, 38, 92, 326n38; and propaganda of the deed, 37, 69–71; as unofficial leader, 26, 36–38, 136; in exile, 71, 80; on war, 57, 60, 143, 152; opposition to formal organization by, 37–38, 116
Galleanisti: and propaganda of the deed, 69–71, 76–77; and Sacco and Vanzetti, 76–77; 92–95; on organizations, 37–38, 93, 107, 169; origin of term, 37–38. *See also* Alberto Antolini; Andrea Salsedo; Attilio Bortolotti; August "Gugu" Segata; Bartolomeo Vanzetti; Carlo Valdinoci; Ella Antolini; Emilio Coda; Giovanni Eramo; Mario Buda; Nicola Sacco; Raffaele Schiavina; Ricardo Orcianni; Roberto Elia; Vincenzo Ferrero
Galleanisti groups. *See* Grupo Autonomo; Grupo Bresci; Gruppo I Liberi; Gruppo I Refrattari
Galleanisti periodicals. See *Cronaca Sovversiva; L'Adunata dei Refratarri; L'Emancipazione; Man!*
Gallery Bugs Bunny, 250
Gandhi, Mohandas, 31*fig.,* 203, 224, 233, 351n29; and ashrams, 186; and Bart de Ligt, 153; and prefiguration, 160, 176; and violence, 227; nonviolence of and inspired by, 148, 165–66, 172, 174, 179, 213–14, 221–22, 232–33, 268, 278, 284, 353n60
Ganberg, Morris, 324n20
Gautney, Heather, 11–12

Gay Liberation Front, 275. *See also* homosexuality; queer
General Recruiting Union, 128. *See also* Industrial Workers of the World
General Strike for Peace, 255
Genn, Sally, 84, 124
Georgakas, Dan, 258
German American anarchists, 25, 29, 34, 99, 121, 123, 150, 310n54
German-speaking American anarchists, 25, 29, 34, 99, 121, 123, 150, 310n54, 316n123
gestalt therapy, 203
Gibson, Morgan, 197
Ginsberg, Allen, 206, 245, 259
Gitlin, Todd, 270
Glassgold, Peter, 43
Glen Gardner World Citizens Community, 177–78
Goddard College, 292
Goldman, Emma, 240, 283*fig.;* and anarcha-feminism, 28, 43, 49–50, 302n9; and birth control, 40–41, 49, 312n79; and English language, 38–39, 43, 81; and free speech, 40; and racism, 43–44; and Russian Revolution, 87–90, 144; and sexuality, 41–42, 45, 49, 196, 284; and Spanish Civil War, 138; and struggle against war and conscription, 56–57, 59, 85; and the arts, 39, 196, 316n122; and Vanguard Group, 121; as bogeyman, 21; as inspiration to other anarchists, 80, 124, 155, 184, 188–89, 275–76, 282; benefectors of, 39, 40, 47, 142; definition of anarchism by, 308n32; extended social network of, 150, 312n81, 316n122, 217n123; *My Disillusionment in Russia,* 88, 144; state repression of, 40, 60, 70, 72, 74, 320n26
Goliath, 268–69
Golos Truda, 31*fig.,* 35, 62, 310n59
Goodfriend, Audrey, 283*fig.;* and KPFA-Pacifica Radio, 205; and printing press, 162; and The School of Living, 200; and Vanguard Juniors, 124; and the Walden School, 202, 284; childhood of, 84–85; education of, 209; move to California by, 178, 192–95; struggle against draft by, 170, 181*fig.,* 182

Goodman, Paul, 173, 197, 201, 283*fig.;* and
    Colin Ward,198; and *Liberation,* 214,
    224; and Living Theatre, 203; and
    poststructuralist anarchism, 340n52;
    and prefiguration, 208; and sexuality,
    163, 188, 221; and *The Ark,* 192; and
    Why? Group, 163–64; *Communitas,*
    200; during the 1960s, 268–69;
    education of, 209; *Growing Up Absurd,*
    163, 269; *Faustina,* 203; novels of, 178,
    187, 202; *The Breakup of Our Camp,*
    202; *The May Pamphlet,* 163, 200
Goodman, Percival, 200
Good Soup, 257
Gordon, Uri, 4
Graeber, David, 278
Graham, Marcus, 283*fig.,* 321n52; and
    Man!, 113–18, 124–26, 128–29, 142;
    criticisms of technology by, 113, 116–17,
    129, 161, 284; during Red Scare, 66–67,
    69, 77–78, 102, 322n75; lectures by, 105,
    113, 117, 129; *The Anthology of
    Revolutionary Poetry,* 113
Gramsci, Antonio, 159, 338n37
Grateful Dead, 251, 253
Grave, Jean, 57
Great Depression, 165, 353n57; anarchist
    response to, 14, 108, 111–13, 117, 124–25,
    127–29, 133, 287
green anarchism. *See* anarcho-primitivism
Green Scare, 299
Greenshner, Becky, 26
Greenshner, Morris, 26, 118
Greenwich Village, 39, 47, 182, 203, 217,
    317n123
Greggs, Richard, 165
Grieg, Michael, 156, 163, 192, 194
Grieg, Sally, 156, 163, 192, 194
Group Center Space, 258
Grupo Autonomo, 76, 92
Grupo Bresci, 92
gruppi femminilli di propaganda, 42,
    50, 103
Gruppo I Liberi, 53
Gruppo I Refrattari, 95
Gruppo Libertario, 194, 196–97, 328n70
guerrilla theater, 251–54, 259–60, 276, 297
Guevara, Che, 249

Guglielmo, Jennifer, 25
Guillaume, James, 57

Hahne, Ron, 258
Hahnel, Robin, 271, 295
Halliday, Polly, 317n123
Hapgood, Hutchins, 48
Harding, Warren, 78, 82
Harlem Ashram, 165–67, 186, 343n103
Harper's Magazine, 193–95
Harrington, Michael, 214
Harris, David, 268–69
Harrison, Byron, 68
Hartford, CT, anarchism in, 73
Havel, Hippolyte, 67, 102–6, 156, 283*fig.,*
    317n123, 343n103
Hayden, Tom, 239
Haymarket Affair, 25, 32–33, 45, 240, 247,
    270, 282, 296, 314n102
Haywood, Big Bill, 197
Hennacy, Ammon, 143, 169–71, 170*fig.,*
    170, 192, 218, 283*fig.,* 341n71
Hennacy, Sharon, 169
Henri, Robert, 47, 104, 316n120
Herzen, Alexander, 85
hierarchy, 4, 8*fig.,* 27, 120, 159, 209, 228–9,
    231, 265, 275, 293. *See also* organizational
    forms; participatory democracy; social
    domination
Higham, John, 46
high culture, 52, 247, 258, 285
Hill, Lewis, 175, 205
Hilliard, David, 253
Hinduism, 165
hippies, 245, 251–54, 260–61, 263, 268, 282.
    See also counterculture
Hitler, Adolph, 123, 124, 137, 141–42. *See
    also* Nazism
Ho Chi Minh, 271
Hodgdon, Timothy, 254
Hoffman, Abbie, 254
Hoffman, Allan, 257–59, 361n77
Home Colony, 25
homosexuality, 209; and Alexander
    Berkman, 312n81; and anarchist
    supporters from middle- and upper-
    classes, 47, 280; and bohemian
    anarchism, 39, 41; and Combahee River

Collective, 293; and David Dellinger, 221; and Emma Goldman, 39, 41, 312n81; and gay liberation, 16, 241, 275; and Glenn Carrington, 120; and homophobia, 51, 163, 177, 221–22, 285, 293, 351n31; and Paul Goodman, 163; and Robert Duncan, 186–87; and the Beat Generation, 186–87, 189, 206. *See also* queer; sex radicalism

hooks, bell, 295

Hoover, J. Edgar, 60

Horkheimer, Max, 257

Horton, Myles, 277

House Painters Union, 215

Houser, George, 166–67, 173, 175, 179–80, 186, 343n103

House Un-American Activities Committee. *See* McCarthyism

Human Be-In, 253

human nature, 6–7, 8*fig.*, 289, 308n31; and pacifism, 185; and poststructuralist anarchism, 303n21; as naturally altruistic, 9, 12, 28–29, 116; midcentury anarchists' complications of, 158, 207; Resistance Group on, 202

Humphrey, William, 186

Hunt, Andrew, 173, 221

ILGWU (International Ladies' Garment Workers Union), 83–85, 88–91, 94, 115–16, 118, 122–23, 311n61, 331n30

Illiterati, The, 185

Il Martello, 9, 31*fig.*, 61, 94, 121, 124, 161

Il Martello Group, 95, 138

immigrant groups, of American anarchists. *See* Chinese American anarchists; German American anarchists; Italian American anarchists; Jewish American anarchists; Mexican American anarchists; Russian American anarchists; Spanish American anarchists

Immigration Act of 1917, 62–64, 71–72

immigration reforms: from Red Scare, 16, 55, 62–64, 78–79, 109, 118. *See also* deportation; nativism; No One Is Illegal

imprisonment and arrest, 24, 36, 38, 262, 270, 294; and Civil Defense

demonstrations, 203, 218; and Comstock laws, 312n79, 326n44; and drugs, 258, 265; and free speech, 38, 40, 310n53; and Red Scare, 55, 59–63, 65–66, 69–78, 81–82, 89, 92–93, 104, 113, 118, 142, 144, 247, 281, 320n26; for homosexuality, 187, 221; moral symbolism of, 262, 294–95; of anarchists in Russia, 26, 81, 87–90, 101–2, 195; of Korean War draft resisters, 353n60; of people struggling for racial justice, 179, 220, 296–97; of Second World War draft resisters, 155–56, 164–69, 171, 173, 175, 177–79, 187, 213, 229, 344n16, of Vietnam War draft resisters, 268

inbetween people, 45, 78–79, 315n111

individualism, 37, 41, 113, 119, 135, 170–71, 242, 298, 312n73

individualist anarchism, 12–13, 41, 294, 330n19, 349n8

individual expression, 39–41, 49, 50, 99, 148, 206, 209, 260, 261, 277, 287, 288

individual transformation. *See* personal transformation

Industrial Worker, 31*fig.*, 171. *See also* Industrial Workers of the World

Industrial Workers of the World, 31*fig.*, and Catholic Workers, 133; and communism, 82–83; and connected institutions, 34–35, 71, 122, 138, 170, 349n19; and culture, 34, 245, 248*fig.*; and free speech fights, 34, 40, 310n53; and insurrectionary anarchism, 38, 326n38; and revolutionary unionism, 5, 32–34, 126–27, 160, 196, 219, 284, 291; and war, 57, 147; during Red Scare, 60, 62, 64, 68, 81–82, 87, 92–93, 100, 147, 239; importance to anarchism of, 14, 33–34, 51, 82–83, 105, 281; inspiration of, 126, 168, 184, 208, 217, 245, 340n67; institutional spaces of, 121, 246–47, 254, 272, 316n122; members of, 90, 92, 101, 119, 150, 186, 191, 215, 246, 312n79, 316n122; strikes by, 24, 34–35, 38, 64, 67, 326n38. See also *Industrial Worker*

infoshops, 5, 246, 295

Inglis, Agnes, 142

Locatelli, Antonio, 95
Lombroso, Cesare, 45
Los Angeles, anarchism in, 36, 100, 103, 106, 117. *See also* Libertarians (Los Angeles group); Regeneración
Love and Rage Revolutionary Anarchist Federation, 4, 296, 298
Lowndes County Freedom Organization, 258
Lucy Parsons Center, 295
Ludlow Massacre, 48, 55–56
Lukács, Georg, 250
L'Umanitá Nova, 205
Lusk Committee, 60, 72
Luxembourg, Rosa, 185, 271, 342n14
Lynd, Staughton, 3–4, 125

MacDonald, Dwight, 161–63, 171, 174–75, 177–80, 187, 192, 221, 268, 338n25
MacDonald, Nancy, 161–62
Mac Low, Jackson, 163, 183, 186–87
Magón, Enrique Flores, 36, 44
Magón, Ricardo Flores, 25, 36, 44, 54, 57, 60, 80
Mahkno, Nestor, 87, 107
mail, restriction of, 40, 59–61, 72. *See also* Comstock laws; Espionage Act
Mailer, Norman, 184
Malatesta, Errico, 26, 103, 188, 240, 307n24, 308n29
Malina, Judith, 203, 204*fig.*, 218, 256, 258, 283*fig.*
Man!, 31*fig.*, 113–18, 114*fig.*, 120–21, 124–26, 129, 134, 142, 149, 330n12
Mandarin-speaking American anarchists, 114, 119
Mandela, Nelson, 215
Man Ray, 47, 316n120
Mao, Zedong, 240, 264
marches, rallies, pickets, and demonstrations: after 1972, 1–2, 5, 293–300, 352n53; against Civil Defense campaign, 218; against conscription, 59, 85, 177–79, 181*fig.*, 182; against fascism, 44, 69, 95; and Catholic Workers, 133–34, 136, 218, 256; and Haymarket Affair, 25, 45; and Students for a Democratic Society, 243–44; and

symbolism, 69, 218; and the Spanish Civil War, 138, 140*fig.*, 348n18; antinuclear, 252, 256, 268, 293–96; antiwar, 244, 257, 259*fig.*, 259–60, 262, 271; for racial justice, 220, 225, 230–31, 256; inattention or rejection of, 15, 117, 164, 236; on May Day, 26; 90, 134; others in the early twentieth century, 48, 94, 99; others in the mid-twentieth century, 170*fig.*, 254, 262, 266; picketing, 57, 169, 171, 177, 180, 235
Marcuse, Herbert, 257, 260
Maritain, Jacques, 136
marriage, relationships, and family structures: in anarchists' lives, 25, 41–42, 109; breaking norms in, 163, 209, 221, 284; criticisms of breaking norms in, 50, 72, 189, 201; jealousy because of, 142, 193–94, 209; prefiguration and, 51, 130, 202, 208. *See also* homosexuality; sexism; sex radicalism
Marsh, Margaret, 305n1
Martin, James, 349n8
Martin, Peter, 205, 247n76
Marx, Karl: and Bakunin, 29, 160; criticism by anarchists, 65, 160, 188, 196; influence on anarchists, 27, 53, 172
Marxism: and artists and intellectuals, 163, 189, 277; and attempts to convert to anarchism, 122–23; and economism, 111, 158–59; and Industrial Workers of the World, 33; and New Left, 230, 237, 247, 267, 250, 270, 272, 275, 278, 357n25; criticisms of, 165, 201, 217, 267, 272, 286; today, 290
Marxism, Third World, 241, 249
Marxist-Leninism, 251, 272, 304n22
masculinity, 57, 253–54, 261–62, 274, 276
Masses, The, 39, 134
mass organizing, 2, 8*fig.*, 50, 84, 112, 143, 160, 182, 277, 282, 284–5, 291; after 1972, 293, 298–99; and Black Freedom Movement, 212, 220, 237, 239, 354n70; for prisoner defense, 81, 93, 108; for unions, 62, 71, 83, 121, 122, 137, 148, 158, 239, 288, 289, 311n70, 333n69; in the long 1960s, 203, 239, 244, 260, 279, 282
Mattick, Paul, 162, 203, 291

National Recovery Administration, 127
National Security League, 64
Native Americans, 254, 269–70
nativism, 16, 45–46, 54, 56, 58, 63, 93, 315n111. *See also* immigration reforms
Nausea, 295
Nazism, 123, 142, 166, 186. *See also* Hitler, Adolph
Needle, The, 206
Negrin, Su, 275
Neill, A.S., 202
Nelson, Chris, 207
Nelson, Juanita, 180
Nelson, Wally, 180
neoliberalism, 10–13, 279, 287–88, 296
Neumann, Osha, 260–61
Newark Ashram, 166–67
New Deal, 14, 111–12, 124–29, 132, 148, 190, 287
Newfield, Jack, 240
Hew Haven, CT, anarchism in, 95, 105
New Jersey, anarchism in. *See* Ferrer Modern School; L'Era Nuova Group; Newark Ashram; Paterson, NJ, anarchism in; Stelton Colony
New Left Review, 234
new society within the shell of the old, 33, 135, 160, 208, 284. *See also* Industrial Workers of the World; prefigurative organizing
Newton, Huey, 263
New Left, 16–17, 148, 211–79, 291, 293, 302n9, 356n5, 365n147
New York Diggers, 254, 275. *See also* Yippie!
New York Times, 11, 74
Ngai, Mae, 78
Nieuwenhuis, Ferdinand Domela, 252
nihilism, 30, 299
Nin, Anaïs, 186
Nkrumah, Kwame, 214–15
NIRA (National Industrial Recovery Act), 125–26
No Conscription League, 59, 280
Noir et Rouge Group, 198
nonhierarchical organizations and relationships. *See* hierarchy; organizational forms

nonviolence, 6; and national liberation, 233; and pacifist draft resisters, 15, 148, 153–54, 165–68, 171–72, 174–82, 209, 213–14, 218, 353n60; and the Beat Generation, 239, 251; and the Black Freedom Movement, 221–22, 226–28, 231, 237, 249; and the Catholic Workers, 133–36, 177, 278; and the New Left, 203, 268–69, 276, 278–79; contemporary, 290, 293–94, 298; in early twentieth century, 35, 105–6. *See also under* direct action
nonviolent civil disobedience, 174, 195, 300. *See also* sit-ins
No One Is Illegal, 299
North American Free Trade Agreement, 296
North Eastern Federation of Anarchist Communists, 298
NOW, 161, 192
N.R.A. (National Recovery Administration), 127
nuclear weapons: and bombing of Hiroshima and Nagasaki, 173–74, 177, 190; worries about, 175, 199, 208, 216. *See also* antinuclear movement
Nyerere, Julius, 214

Occupy movement, 1–2, 280, 299–300
October Revolution. *See* Russian Revolution
O'Hare, Kate Richards, 70
Olson, Joel, 4–5
Omi, Michael, 314n100
O'Neill, Eugene, 317n123
operaismo, 1, 318n8, 332n65, 333n71, 358n25
Operation Rescue, 296
Orcianni, Ricardo, 76
organizational forms, 8*fig.;* affinity groups, 4–5, 180, 268, 293–94; authoritarian, 29, 159; centralized, 82, 159, 231, 247, 249, 265; conspiratorial, 37–38, 285; council, 4, 85–86, 247, 293–94; decentralized, 82, 150, 180, 182, 228–29, 231, 237, 270, 272–73, 275–76, 285, 297, 299–300; formal vs. informal, 21, 37–38, 93, 106, 114, 119, 136, 169–70, 176, 265, 275–76, 288, 289, 293, 297; necessity of,

protest. *See* marches, rallies, pickets, and demonstrations

Provo, 251–52, 254, 259, 266

Puck, 45, 314n102

punk: anarchism's association with, 10, 11, 266, 285, 295, 298, 304n24; as lifestyle anarchism, 51; comparison of mid-twentieth century avant-garde to, 17, 193, 262, 266

pure means. *See* means of change

Put'k Svobode, 102

Quakers, 57, 154–55, 165, 167, 180, 207, 269, 343n4

queer liberation, 1, 4, 17, 275, 290, 297; and gay liberation, 16, 241, 275. *See also* homosexuality; sex radicalism

Queer Nation, 297

race and the labor movement: and interracial organizing, 34, 44, 126–27; and racism, 68, 230–31. *See also* class reductionism

Race Traitor collective, 296

racialization of anarchists, 16, 45–46, 68, 76, 78–79, 314n100. *See also* inbetween people

racial segregation:, 177–80, 195, 211–13, 215, 220, 223–29, 231, 237, 249, 289; of federal prisons and Civilian Public Service camps, 148; 166–68, 173, 177–78, 197, 213, 237

racial violence, 14, 43, 44, 68, 78, 218–19, 226–27

racism. *See* African American anarchists; antiracism; Black Freedom Movement; Black Power movement; class reductionism; Congress of Racial Equality; Fellowship of Reconciliation; NAACP; race and the labor movement; racialization of anarchism; racial segregation; racial violence; Red Summer; Student Nonviolent Coordinating Committee

Radical America, 250, 266–67

Radical Bookstore, The, 316n122

Radical Cheerleaders, 297

Radical Decentralist Project, 272–73

Radical Faeries, 297

Radical Library, 83

Rainer, Dachine (née Sylvia Newman), 162, 169–70, 186–88, 197, 202, 235, 339n48

Rainey, Reb, 56

Rall, Jeff, 186

rallies. *See* marches, rallies, pickets, and demonstrations

Ramnath, Maia, 330n20

Rancière, Jacques, 340n52

Rand, Ayn, 11

Ransby, Barbara, 353n57

Reagan, Ronald, 11, 296

Rebel Worker, 247–51, 259, 265

Rebel Worker Group, 31*fig.,* 247–51, 259, 261, 284, 358nn25,27

Rebel Youth, 123–24, 144, 149–50 155–56

Reclus, Élisée, 26, 191

Red International of Labor Unions, 82–83

Red Scare, 5, 54–79, 80–81, 85, 104, 199, 281; and immigration, 45, 55, 59, 77–81, 62–63, 72–75; and Red Summer, 14, 68–69, 71, 78; impact on anarchist periodicals by, 59–62, 65, 66, 70, 72, 83, 100, 102; impact on specific anarchist individuals and groups, 60–77, 80, 83, 92–93, 118; prisoner defense for, 66, 73–77, 89, 93

Red Summer, 14, 68, 71, 78

Reeves, George, 188

reforms: and the Great Depression, 14, 112, 128–29; and weak unions, 33, 87, 112, 144; in the Progressive Era, 21, 40; opposition from anarchists to, 14, 37, 106, 143–44, 299; support from anarchists for, 106, 201–2, 242, 284; within unions, 87, 90

Regneración, 31*fig.,* 36, 57, 60

Reich, Wilhelm, 31*fig.,* 163, 188–90, 193, 202–3, 209; *The Mass Psychology of Fascism,* 189; *The Sexual Revolution,* 189

Reid, Harry, 11

religion: anarchism seen as threat to, 69, 72, 137; and hierarchy, 27, 228, 230; as authoritarian and source of power, 8*fig.,* 25, 27, 46, 58, 158, 172, 174, 189, 275; opposition to, 4, 27, 166, 174, 346n50. *See also* Catholicism; Christianity;

Rose, Bill, 216
Rosemont, Franklin, 246, 248–50, 258, 283*fig.;* "Mods, Rockers, and the Revolution," 248, 248*fig.,* 358n27
Rosemont, Penelope (née Bartik), 246–47, 249–50, 270, 274, 283*fig.*
Rossinow, Doug, 270
Roszak, Theodore, 205
Rothbard, Murray, 10–11
Rubin, Jerry, 254, 264
Russian American anarchists: and intentional communities, 96, 98; and immigration restrictions, 109; and race, 45; returning to Russia, 62, 71–74, 80, 83; working in English, 38, 100
Russian American anarchist groups and institutions. *See* Russian People's House; Union of Russian Workers
Russian American anarchist individuals. *See* Abe Brooks; Alexander Berkman; Clara Brooks; Emma Goldman; G.P. Maximoff; Joseph Spivak; Lucy Robins Lang; Mark Mratchney; Mollie Steimer; Morris Greenshner; Murray Bookchin; Olga Maximoff; Rose Pesotta; Esther Doloff; Sam Dolgoff; Voline
Russian-language anarchist periodicals, 142. *See also* Dielo Truda; Golos Truda
Russian People's House, 35, 72
Russian Revolution, 14, 30, 58, 324n14, 348n8; American reaction to, 62, 65–66, 67–68, 71–74, 77–78; anarchist criticism of Bolshevik regime in, 87, 89–90, 94, 144, 150, 152, 287, 321n54; as inspiration, 54, 59–60, 66, 85, 98, 120, 147; disagreement over, 87–90, 98; lessons of, 107, 153, 159; October Revolution of, 64–65, 87; repression of anarchists in, 26, 81–82, 87–90, 93, 100–2, 105, 107, 297
Russian-speaking anarchists, 14, 22, 162
Russian Toilers. *See* Union of Russian Workers
Rustin, Bayard: and Bob Moses, 229; and Civil Defense Protest, 218; and Congress of Racial Equality, 167, 178–80; and *Liberation,* 213; and

Montgomery Bus Boycott, 220–22; and move "from protest to politics," 236–37; and struggle against conscription, 178, 181*fig.,* 182; homosexuality of, 221–22

sabotage, 5, 33, 34, 174, 278
Sacco, Nicola, 76–77, 107–8; as inspiration for later anarchists, 162, 191, 271. *See also* Sacco and Vanzetti defense campaign
Sacco and Vanzetti defense campaign, 323n86, 343n5; by Galleanisti, 77, 81, 92–95, 328n70; by Road to Freedom Group, 104, 107–8; by Rose Pesotta, 88, 103
Sachs, David, 230, 255
Salerno, Salvatore, 33
Sallitto, Domenico, 109, 114, 116, 118, 142
Salsedo, Andrea, 76, 93, 326n34
Sandberg, Carl, 317n122
Sandperl, Ira, 251, 268
San Francisco Bay Area, 15, 39, 83, 117, 126, 178; after 1972, 292, 294–96, 299–300; and Italian insurrectionists, 109, 113–14; and the New Left, 251–54, 259, 264. *See also* San Francisco Renaissance
San Francisco Mime Troupe, 251, 359n38
San Francisco Renaissance, 148, 162, 182, 185–98, 200, 205–7, 245–46, 277, 284. *See also* Beat Generation
Sanger, Margaret, 24, 40, 49, 56, 312n79
Sargent, Lydia, 295–96
Scarceriaux, Jules, 100
Scheer, Robert, 359n38
Schiavina, Raffaele, 71, 113, 152
Schmidt, Mark, 120, 123, 125, 141. *See also* Senex
School of Living, 200, 254
Schwartz, Jacob, 66
Schuyler, George, 353n57
SDS (Students for a Democratic Society). *See* Students for a Democratic Society
Second World War. *See* World War II
Sedition Act, 59–63, 66, 69, 78
segregation. *See* racial segregation
Seguta, August "Gugu," 53
Selective Service Act, 60, 72
self-expression. *See* individual expression
self-governance: as intrinsic to human

nature, 28, 215n111; as political goal, 4, 13, 239, 243, 265, 282

self-management in the workplace, 2, 29, 32, 59, 67, 133, 176, 247, 291, 321n54

Sellers, Cleveland, 231–32

Semiotext(e), 295, 297

Senex, 120, 123, 125, 141. *See also* Schmidt, Mark

Serrano, Nina, 359n38

sexism, 4, 42, 177, 208–9, 266, 274, 276, 293, 331n8, 341n71

Sex Pistols, 10, 262

sex radicalism: and bohemian anarchism, 39–42, 47–48, 50, 52, 196–97, 289; and Ferrer Center community, 98, 280; and free love, 15, 25, 163, 194, 196, 203, 245, 255–56, 274, 282, 284, 294; and racialization, 45–46, 72; and Wilhelm Reich, 163, 188–90, 208–9, 276. *See also* homosexuality; marriage, relationships, and family structures; queer

Shalom Aleichem Houses, 84, 155

Shatoff, Vladimir "Bill," 35, 56, 62, 80, 312n79

Shop Delegate League, 85–90

shop delegate movement, 85–90

Shulman, Alix Kates, 275, 303n17

SI. *See* Situationist International

Sigman, Morris, 90–91

Sinclair, John, 262–65

Siren: A Journal of Anarcho-Feminism, 275

sit-ins, 225, 227–29, 241, 353n60

Situationism, 249–50; 279, 296; and Detroit anarchists, 266–67; and interventions in daily life, 252, 292; and Students for a Democratic Society, 273–74; influence in Britain of, 262; in the U.S. after 1972, 292, 298–99

Situationist International, 249–50, 259, 266, 292, 363n103

Six Gallery, 15, 206

Slater, Louis, 120

Smith Act, 199

Smith, Lillian, 224

SNCC (Student Nonviolent Coordinating Committee). *See* Student Nonviolent Coordinating Committee

Snyder, Gary, 183, 198, 206, 264, 363n103;

and environmentalism, 191, 254, 292; and Zen Buddhism, 190, 245; "Buddhist Anarchism," 245; *Turtle Island,* 292

Social Anarchism, 293

social domination, 4, 8*fig.,* 27, 50–51, 158, 207–8, 238, 257, 285–6, 290, 293. *See also* class reductionism; hierarchy; power, theories of

social ecology, 273, 279, 292–93, 294, 296. *See also* ecology

Social Gospel Protestantism, 166, 173, 214, 221

socialism, 2, 17, 20, 165, 167, 216; anarchism as extension of, 121; anarchist rejection of strategy of, 119, 128, 171, 228; and pacifism, 176, 213, 214, 343n103; and the New Left, 240–42, 253, 272, 276; as prior political identification of anarchists, 25, 34, 119, 166, 167, 169, 173, 255; in Cuba, 234–37; in intentional communities, 99; in Russia, 89, 159; in Spanish Civil War, 137; in the nineteenth century, 9; strategy of, 24, 91, 106; utopian, 30, 153, 172, 353n57

Socialisme ou Barbarie, 357n25

Socialist Party: and communists, 74, 88, 91, 122; and the Great Depression, 111; and the Industrial Workers of the World, 33; and the Spanish Civil War, 137; and Students for a Democratic Society, 242; electoral strategy of, 33, 175, 247; newspapers by, 103; organizing by, 24, 85, 87, 111, 128; responses to war by, 57, 62, 77, 147, 164

Socialist Workers Party, 152, 256

Social Revolutionary Anarchist Federation, 292

social sciences, 15, 158, 163, 189, 202, 207, 209, 224–25

Solanas, Valerie, 258

Solidaridad Internacional Antifascista, 139, 162, 178, 202, 203, 217, 349n19

Solidarity, 247, 358n25

Solidarity Bookshop, 246–47, 250, 270, 284

solitary confinement, 166, 169

Soloman, Sidney, 120, 123, 331n38

Solovetsky Monastery, 102, 108

Sorel, George, 352n52

Sosnovsky, Anna, 91, 115–16, 328n70
South End Press, 295
soviets, 59, 64, 67, 85, 87, 321n54, 324n14
Spain and the World, 139
Spanish American anarchists, 35–36, 96,
    139, 207, 217, 255, 267. *See also*
    Solidaridad Internacional Antifascista
Spanish Civil War, 14, 136–39, 141; as
    inspiration for later anarchists, 266, 271;
    disagreements over, 153–54;
    disappointment over, 188, 191; exiles in
    the United States from, 217, 255, 267;
    solidarity from U.S. anarchists during,
    112, 138–41, 140*fig.,* 143, 161–62, 166,
    216, 218, 349n18
Spanish-language anarchist periodicals. See
    Cultura Obrera; Regeneración
Spanish Refugee Aid Committee, 161–62
Spanish Revolution, 138–41
Spanish-speaking American anarchists, 14,
    22, 35–36, 44, 38, 100, 104, 162. See also
    Cultura Observa; Regeneración
Spanish Youth Group, 138
spectacle, 249–50, 267, 292
Spies, August, 25
Spivak, Joseph, 100, 106–7, 328n70
spokescouncil, 4, 293–94, 298
squatting, 295
Stalinism, 135, 189, 207; opposition to, 123,
    141, 184, 234, 287, 357n25
state, the: and changes from the New Deal,
    111–12, 124–25, 287; and decolonization,
    232–34; and defending privilege, 9, 13,
    27–29, 175, 303n21, 308n29; and
    everyday relations, 159–60, 200–1; and
    violence, 176, 227; and war, 168, 174–75;
    as unnecessary, 28, 159, 212, 214;
    beneficial functions of, 12–13, 286
state capitalism, 128, 135, 150, 287, 333n71
Steele, Melchior, 125
Steffens, Lincoln, 47
Steimer, Mollie, 53–55, 75*fig.,* 85, 283*fig.;*
    after deportation, 87, 102, 123; and
    Anarchist Soviet Bulletin, 66–67; and
    Frayhayt Group, 65–67, 74–75; and
    state repression, 66, 69, 70, 74–75
Stein, Gertrude, 203
Stelton Colony, 49, 96–100, 284; events at,

84, 85, 104, 108, 165; inhabitants of, 83,
    91, 102, 110, 113, 118, 119, 130, 143
Sterling, Irving, 123–24, 143
Stewart, Joffre, 246, 357n22
Stirner, Max, 349n8
Stolberg, Benjamin, 85
strikes: decline of, 77, 149; importance of,
    32–34, 66, 85, 108, 125, 154, 160, 174, 198;
    instances of, 24, 34–35, 36, 38, 58, 64,
    67–68, 85, 116, 125–26, 137, 166–68,
    326n38, 343n103; repression of, 24, 38,
    48, 58, 64, 68, 70–71; sit-down, 127–28;
    support of, 135, 196, 295
Student League for Industrial Democracy.
    See Students for a Democratic Society
Student Nonviolent Coordinating
    Committee, 15, 31*fig.;* influence on other
    groups, 241–43, 258; organizational and
    leadership philosophies, 173, 228–32,
    238–39, 248–49, 265, 284, 353n65, 354n70
student movements. *See* Free Speech
    Movement; Paris, May 1968; Student
    Nonviolent Coordinating Committee;
    Students for a Democratic Society;
    Students for a Democractic Society;
    Zengakuren
Students for a Democratic Society, 16,
    31*fig.,* 241–42, 365n142,147; and
    Vietnam, 244, 269, 288; chapters of,
    270–73; chapter of, Columbia
    University, 262; chapter of, Louis Lingg
    Memorial, 270; chapter of, Rosa
    Luxembourg, 271, 295; chapter of,
    University of Texas, Austin, 270;
    chapter of, Up Against the Wall/
    Motherfuckers, 262; national
    conventions of, 270, 272–73;
    organizational structure and leadership
    of, 239, 242–44, 265, 277–78, 282,
    353n65, 357n25
Studies on the Left, 359n38
subculture, 5, 184, 258. *See also* Beat
    Generation; counterculture; punk;
    youth culture
suffrage movement, 23–24, 28, 41, 42, 49,
    58, 80. *See also* voting
Sunrise Co-operative Farm Community,
    129–33, 131*fig.,* 132*fig.,* 143, 284

Supreme Court, 66, 69, 126, 179, 211
Surrealism, 115, 185–86, 206, 246, 249–51, 255, 258, 294
Sutherland, Bill, 167–68, 179, 181*fig.*, 182, 205, 340n67, 355n86
symbolic protest, 69, 169–70, 178–79, 218, 260, 262, 275, 277, 294–5. *See also* marches, rallies, pickets, and demonstrations

Taback, Sarah, 328n73
Taft-Hartley Act, 219
Tambellini, Aldo, 258
tax refusal, 136, 160, 169–70, 180
Tea Party movement, 11
technology, criticisms of: and environmentalism, 256, 292; and nuclear weapons, 175; by Situationists, 249–50; in classical anarchism, 116–17, 129, 161, 284. *See also* anarcho-primitivism
temporary autonomous zones, 4, 254, 297
Thatcher, Margaret, 10
theater and performance, 16–17, 26, 317n123; in early twentieth century, 34, 39–40, 43, 47–48, 49, 53, 84, 97, 139, 208, 285, 307n21, 310n54; in mid-twentieth century, 191–92, 203, *204fig.*, 206, 246, 251–52, 256. *See also* guerrilla theater; Living Theatre; symbolic protest
third camp politics, 212, 234–35, 237
Thompson, Fred, 170, 247
Thoreau, Henry David, 65, 148, 155, 156, 160, 165
Till, Emmett, 218–19
Times Change Press, 275
Titì, 51
Tolstoy, Leo, 134, 148, 160–61, 162, 165, 169, 222; *Cathargo Delenda Est,* 160
Tompkins Square Park riot, 295
Tone, Yat, 120
Torch, 257
Tracy, James, 164
Trade Union Education League, 90
Trading with the Enemy Act, 59
Trans-Love Energies, 263. *See also* Artist's Workshop; White Panther Party

Tresca, Carlo, 25, 34–35, 161, 205, 347n76; and fascists, 94–95, 121, 326n44; and feud with Galleanisti, 38, 92–93, 298, 326n38; and Lawrence textile strike, 34, 38, 165, 326n38; and newspapers, 35, 61, 94, 121; and United Libertarian Organizations, 138, 140*fig.*, 141
Trip Without a Ticket, 252
Trotsky, Leon, 172, 216
Trotskyism, 111, 152, 161, 338n25; dissidents of, 247, 333n71, 357n25; past adherents to, 186, 216, 256
Truman, Harry S., 180, 199
Tucker, Benjamin

UAW/MF. *See* Up Against the Wall/Motherfuckers
Uhrie, Al, 225
ULO (United Libertarian Organizations), 138–39
ultraleftism, 16, 31*fig.*, 245, 247, 249, 256, 278–79, 292
undercover agents and infiltrators, 32, 37, 72, 76, 106, 265
underground, going, 92, 118, 142, 156, 265
Union 8, 166
unions, rejection of, 37, 114–16, 169–70. *See also* bureaucracy; reform struggles
Union of Russian Workers, 26, 31*fig.*, 35, 54, 62, 66, 71–75, 138
Union Theological Seminary, 166
United Brotherhood of Cloak Makers, 311n61
united front, 94–95, 128, 141
United Libertarian Organizations, 138–39
United Mine Workers, 125
United Nations, 177
Universal Negro Improvement Association, 103
University of California, 186, 192, 193, 298, 244, 246
Untide Press, 185, 205
Up Against the Wall/Motherfuckers, 260–62, 266, 267, 274–75, 278, 282, 361n83
Upping the Anti, 299
URW. *See* Union of Russian Workers
Utica, NY, anarchism in, 95

Valdinoci, Carlo, 60, 70–71

van den Dungen, Peter, 153–54

van Duijn, Roel, 252

Vaneigem, Raoul, 259, 361n77

Vanguard: A Libertarian Communist Journal, 31*fig.*, 113, 120–29, 134, 142, 149–50, 215

Vanguard Group, 113, 118–24; and Great Depression, 126–27; and Spanish Civil War, 138, 141; and Vanguard Juniors, 149–50, 123–24; and World War II, 143; women in, 331n38

Vanguard Juniors, 123–24, 144, 149–50 155–56

Van Ronk, Dave, 217, 349n15

Van Valkenburgh, Warren Starr, 103, 105, 107, 138–41, 283*fig.*, 328n41

Vanzetti, Bartolomeo, 76–77, 107–8; as inspiration for later anarchists, 162, 191, 271. *See also* Sacco and Vanzetti defense campaign

veganism, 113, 284

Verlaan, Tony, 259

Vermont, anarchism in, 37, 292–93

Veysey, Laurence, 98

Vidali, Vittorio, 95

Vietnam War, 1, 236, 244, 258, 260, 263, 269, 271, 288

View, 186

Views and Comments, 216–18, 244, 255; on Black Freedom Movement and decolonization, 211, 218–20, 222, 226, 233, 237

Village Voice, 240

Voline (E.M. Eikhenbaum), 62, 80, 87, 102, 348n8; *Nineteen-Seventeen*, 348n8

Volontà, 198–99

voting: and African Americans, 24, 229, 231, 236–37; and women, 28, 41, 80; immigrants' relation to, 23–24; rejection of, 23–24, 27–28, 136, 159, 170. *See also* suffrage movement

VVV, 186

Wages for Housework, 292

Walden School, 202, 284

Waldport, OR, Civilian Public Service camp in, 185, 191–92, 205

Wall Street, 3, 77, 259–60, 262, 175, 299–300

war, support by anarchists for, 57, 83, 142–43, 150–51

War Commentary, 152, 337n11, 337n12

War Resisters League, 164, 277, 349n19; anarchist staffing of, 178–79, 212–13, 237; and Bayard Rustin, 218, 220–22; and Danbury Federal Penitentiary, 171; and Jim Peck, 225; and Roy Kepler, 205; and Why? Group, 169, 171

Ward, Colin, 198

Warren, Josiah, 330n19

War Resisters International, 153

Washington, DC, anarchism in, 68, 105, 225, 244, 260

Watts, Alan, 190, 205

Watts uprising, 249, 258

wealthy benefactors of anarchism: and Emma Goldman, 39–40, 47, 49, 142, 281; and the New Left, 253, 268

Weather Underground, 262, 273, 304n22

Weber, Max, 47

Weinberger, Harry, 73

Weinrebe, Roman, 120–21

Wells, Ida B., 24

Werbe, Peter, 262–63, 264*fig.*, 266–67, 283*fig.*

Whalen, Philip, 206

whiteness: and anarchism, 5; and inbetween people, 45, 78–79, 315n111; and pacifism, 164–66; and participatory democracy, 354n70; consciousness of, 224–25, 227, 254, 258, 260, 263, 296

white supremacy. *See* racism

White Panther Party, 16, 31*fig.*, 263–67, 274–75, 295

Why?, 31*fig.*, 161–63, 198, 203; and Ammon Hennacy, 169; and Kenneth Rexroth, 162–63, 184–84; and Paul Goodman, 163; and World War II, 149–52, 154–56, 167–68; name change of, 187. *See also Resistance*

Why? Group: and Catholic Workers, 168–69, 171; and literature, 186–87, 206; and Paul Goodman, 163–64, 188; and World War II, 150–52, 154–56, 162, 215;

name change of, 178. *See also* Resistance
Group
Wieck, David Thoreau, 194*fig.*, 214, 283*fig.*;
"Anarchism," 200–2; and draft
resistance after World War II, 179,
181*fig.*, 182; and Resistance Group, 178,
198–203; education of, 209;
imprisonment during World War II,
155–56, 164–66, 168, 171, 178, 343n103;
in San Francisco, 195–98; on Black
Freedom Movement, 224–26; on
Cuban Revolution, 235–37; on
organizational forms, 249, 270
Williams, Robert F., 220, 226–27, 352n53;
"Can Negroes Afford to be Pacifists?,"
226–27
Williams, William Carlos, 192
Wilson, Adrian, 188, 192
Wilson, Elizabeth, 312n73
Wilson, Woodrow, 56, 58, 59, 64, 78
Winant, Howard, 314n100
WITCH (Women's International Terrorist
Conspiracy from Hell), 275
wobblies. *See* Industrial Workers of the
World
Woodcock, George, 161, 192, 214
Wooden Shoe, 295
Wolfson, Kate, 49
women of color feminism, 1, 4, 17, 293,
295–96
Women's International Terrorist
Conspiracy from Hell, 275
women's liberation movement, 16, 31*fig.*,
210, 239, 274–76, 281, 293
Wong, Eddie, 120
Woodstock, NY, anarchism in, 156, 162,
173, 186, 261, 317n123, 349n15
Worcester, MA, anarchism in, 105
Workers' Centre, 105
Worker's Party. *See* Communist Party of
the United States of America
Workers' Party of Marxist Unification, 216
working class, anarchism's distancing from,
99, 148, 160, 195–97, 208–9, 288. *See
also* Americanization of anarchism;
middle class supporters of anarchism
Workmen's Circle, 26, 84, 100, 117, 130,
188, 215

Workmen's Loyalty League, 64
Works Progress Administration, 128, 184
World Trade Organization, 298
World War I, 5, 14, 22, 54–61, 107, 152.
World War II, 4, 13–14, 142–44, 147–52,
156, 168–69, 188, 281.
WPP (White Panther Party). *See* White
Panther Party
WRL (War Resisters League). *See* War
Resisters League

X, Malcolm, 226, 231

Yanovsky, Saul, 25, 35, 83, 91
Yelensky, Boris, 100–101, 139
Yellow Springs, OH, anarchism in, 255
Yiddish-language anarchist periodicals. See
*Der Shturm, Der Yunyun Arbeiter,
Fraye Arbeter Shtime; Frayhayt*
Yiddish-speaking American anarchists, 14,
22, 38, 43, 65–66, 67, 91; and intentional
communities, 104, 131; and newspapers,
35, 57, 65, 83, 90, 138–39, 142; and war,
57, 83; groups of, 35, 100, 114
Yippie!, 254, 261, 263, 265, 275, 276, 303n17
Young Communist League, 155
Young Negroes Cooperative League, 353n57
Young People's Socialist League, 122–23
Youngstown, OH, anarchism in, 105,
217–18
youth culture, 5, 248, 252–53, 257, 277, 298,
304n24; and commodification, 10, 285
Youth International Party. *See* Yippie!
YPSL (Young People's Socialist League),
122–23

Zack, Joseph, 127
Zapatistas, 1, 296
Zen Buddhism and meditation, 15, 190, 197,
205–6, 245–46, 282
Zengakuren, 259–60
Zerowork, 292
Zerzan, John, 292, 294
Zimmer, Kenyon, 45, 305n1
zines, 295–96
Zinn, Howard, 271
Zionism, 131, 133, 167, 271, 347n65
Z Magazine, 296